This book is dedicated to my husband, Colonel Richard Slack USMC (Ret), who cheerfully led the year-long assault in tasting countless fondues and hot pots, and to my son, Captain Todd Slack USMC, my most discriminating and valuable critic. You have both been an invaluable source of encouragement, love and laughter.

In memory of Polly Clingerman,
Great food writer and treasured friend

CONTENTS

Fondues and Hot Pots is the collective effort of many behind-the-scenes individuals. I am especially grateful for the skill and enthusiasm of editing wizard, Jeanette Egan, my editor. My appreciation extends to publisher John Duff and the talented people at Penguin Putnam for their expertise in turning my manuscript into a solid cookbook graced with a beautiful cover.

Special thanks to many others who took a turn at stirring the pot: To Dorothy Gerard and Le Creuset of America, Inc.; to Bryon Stanger at Trudeau and to Nisha Kara at Swissmar Imports. The recipes in this cookbook were tested with a variety of fondue pots and cooking equipment from these fine companies. To Paul Schilt, vice president, and Rosemari Schilt of Switzerland Cheese Marketing, Inc. for graciously helping me research the extraordinary cheeses of Switzerland.

Special thanks to Shelburne Farms in Vermont for introducing me to their quality cheddar cheeses and to Jeanette Hanberry for introducing me to the memorable blue cheese made on campus at Clemson University in South Carolina.

A bow to Mrs. Yuri Kita for her invaluable input on Japanese nabémono. Thanks to my monthly cooking class of charming young Japanese wives who shared memories and notes of favorite nabémono dishes that they often serve when at home in Japan. Also to Mrs. Setsuko Manabe and Mrs. Michiko Takezawa for assistance and Miss Sayaka Takezawa for translations.

To Ms. Tane Chan of San Francisco for information on Asian hot pots and Dee Bradney of Ridgecrest, California, for invaluable fondue tips and memories from Italy and Switzerland. To Nancy Tringale, director of the National Chicken Council, Lotus Foods and Hollowick, Inc.

To good friends Captain Ernest Castle USN (Ret) and Dr. Jeannie Castle for their support and for sharing nephew and publisher Peter W. Wagner's insight on mixing fondue with politics. To the busy executive chefs, friends, family, neighbors and the Chapin Stinking Creek Yacht Club for sharing recipes and being enthusiastic tasters.

To all my sisters in PEO for their loving support, especially during this project.

Introduction

SWISS FONDUE

*The discovery of a new dish does more for human
happiness than the discovery of a new star.*
—Jean Anthelme Brillat-Savarin

Fondue is Switzerland's national dish. It has become an international friendship dish and symbol of goodwill. A popular Swiss aphorism proclaims, ". . . fondue tastes delicious and brings good cheer." The Swiss will rally around a fondue pot at the drop of a hat, whether at home, in a restaurant or in an out-of-the-way location when people feel the need to converge.

The word *fondue* ("melted") comes from the French verb *fondre*, which means "to melt." Fondue has an enigmatic past shrouded in legend. There are several theories about its origin; each may contain a seed of truth. Many Swiss say it began as a dish of necessity during the winter when cowherds and shepherds were isolated in the snow-covered Alps. As provisions dwindled, leftover pieces of cheese were melted in wine or milk. The creamy cheese sauce was scooped up with crusts of homemade bread. This provident cooking method turned stale ingredients into an appealing, nourishing dish.

Another popular legend places the origin of cheese fondue near Zurich, Switzerland, in the sixteenth century. Zurich was the former seat of the Swiss Reformation and experienced some of its greatest battles. During the war between the Protestants and Catholics, food supplies were severely limited. In spite of the religious upheaval, the Swiss spirit prevailed. In nothing less than a miracle, each side agreed to pool dairy and bread reserves. To stretch the food, cheese and milk were melted into a sauce and eaten with the bread.

Fondue au fromage developed in the French-Swiss Alps and became a treasured dish in Switzerland and France. Mid-twentieth century, the French-speaking Swiss expanded the concept of fondue to create Fondue Bourguignonne, the classic hot oil fondue. Tender steak cubes are skewered onto fondue forks and cooked, to taste, in boiling-hot oil then dunked into a variety of zesty sauces. Broth-based fondue, an offshoot of the Asian hot pot, is a tasty low-fat version; foods are briefly cooked in a simmering broth instead of hot oil. Chocolate fondue, an international favorite, was created in New York in the 1960s.

Fondue is also a French cooking term for finely chopped vegetables slowly cooked to a pulp. The flavorful mixture is used as a seasoning component in many dishes or as a garnish for fish and meats. The word *fondue* is applied to various foods with a cooked sauce or soft, thick filling. Another form of French fondue is an unusual liquefied cheese called cancoillotte or *fromagère*. A specialty of the Franche-Comté, this unique cheese has been glorified in song and legend. Its long history reaches back to the days of the Gaul-Romans. Warmed cancoillotte is served as a sauce or fondue dip but it is also eaten cold.

With a mountain of cheese at their disposal, the Swiss have put it to good use in the renowned dish, râclette. The name comes from the French word *racler*, which means, "to scrape off." Râclette (page 37) is the quintessential fireside cuisine, made by melting a half-wheel of rich cheese by the heat of a fragrant wood fire. The molten cheese is scraped off with a knife and served on warm plates with boiled potatoes and bread. Râclette is standard restaurant fare; one enthusiastic Swiss connoisseur compared the râclette experience to an evening of "barbarian fun!" The dish does have a primal quality, making it an excellent choice for spontaneous, laid-back home entertaining.

FONDUE IN AMERICA

Fondue landed on American shores in the late eighteenth century and made its debut at an elegant French restaurant on Congress Street in Boston. It was presented by Jean Anthelme Brillat-Savarin (1755–1826), Paris lawyer and distinguished epicure, who fled the French Revolution in 1792. In his eminent work, *The Physiology of Taste: Or, Meditations on Transcendental Gastronomy* (1825), Brillat-Savarin recounts a visit when he "taught the restaurant keeper Julien to make a fondue." He recorded the recipe, noting public enthusiasm for the dish. His "ancient" recipe,

Fondue au Fromage Brillat-Savarin, came from Monsieur Trollet of Bern, Switzerland. Made with eggs, Gruyère cheese, butter and black pepper, the dish may have resembled scrambled eggs more than a present-day fondue.

In 1939 and 1940, fondue and sausages were served at the Swiss pavilion at the World's Fair in Flushing Meadows, New York. The same year, *House and Garden* magazine wrote about the exhibit. The article provided a blueprint for fondue and reflected on the use of exotic, imported cheeses. In retrospect, the general consensus was that fondue wasn't a practical dish for entertaining. The current mood of the country was in a slump. The fair was wedged between years of economic failure caused by the Depression and the growing tension in Europe, which would result in World War II and food rationing. Due to the anxiety over existing food supplies, the timing wasn't right for people to embrace an indulgence like fondue. Although years would pass before fondue gained widespread, national acceptance, it was a typical dish in the diet of Swiss immigrants. Mostly of German descent, the immigrants had formed colonies in several states including Minnesota, Tennessee, Georgia, Kentucky, Indiana and Northern California. Two of the earliest were established in Ohio in 1809 and Illinois in 1836. The Swiss-American Connection (page 4) provides an overview of one of America's largest Swiss colonies.

Welsh Rabbit had been quite popular since the early Colonial days. Made with domestic cheese, it was a nourishing, inexpensive meal spooned over crackers or toast. In 1918, Fanny Merritt Farmer included several versions in *The Boston Cooking School Cookbook* using ingredients like oysters and stewed tomatoes. A single fondue recipe resembled similar fondues of the era.

A sauce of stale bread crumbs and American cheese were lightened with beaten egg whites then baked into a puffed cheese dish. In 1928, the Kraft Phenix Company published a charming cookbook, *Cheese—and Ways to Serve It*. They introduced a "delightful new cheese food" called Nukraft. It was a "product of science, combined with the cheesemaker's art." The "superior food" was used in three cheese rabbit recipes and one puffed cheese–type fondue. In the postwar era of the late 1940s and early 1950s, suburban home-makers embraced a plethora of new convenience foods, "doctored up" with personal touches. In *The American Hostess* (Dunne Press, 1948), a prominent Hollywood homemaker shared her recipe for Quick Tomato Rabbit, suggesting it as a light repast for an impromptu company din-ner. Her recipe calls for one can of condensed tomato soup, one pound of American cheese, minced onion and a dash of Worcestershire sauce.

In 1950, Mrs. Mildred O. Knopf wrote, *The Per-fect Hostess Cookbook* (Alfred A Knopf, Inc.). She presented "a series of authentic and distinguished cheese recipes of Switzerland." She had discov-ered the recipes at the New York World's Fair in 1940 and received permission from the Switzer-land Cheese Council to include them in her book. An entire chapter was filled with sophisticated fondues, roulades, pastries and soufflés made with imported Swiss cheese. Also included were recipes for bologna éclairs, an Old French Fondue reminiscent of Brillat-Savarin's dish and a Gay Nineties Rarebit.

America's fascination with fondue blossomed in the psychedelic '60s. Women's magazines and cookbooks began touting fondue as an informal party dish. Newlywed baby boomers served fon-due at baby showers and "supper parties," an innovation from the 1950s. One author in the '60s called the Swiss "happy folk who loved to dunk their food so much they developed a number of dishes and meals bubbling with *Gemütlichkeit* or friendly congeniality." She went on to explain that fondue was "never to be served to cranks or bores or people who don't like something just a little different." Fondue had become smashing fun! Even Austin Powers, super spy and international man of mystery, would have enjoyed an occasional dip into the fondue pot, finding it groovy.

For most of the 1970s, fondue was a hot food fashion with about thirty-five cookbooks pub-lished on the subject by the end of the decade. During the following fat-free decades, cheese fon-due bubbled quietly on a backburner, eventually to reemerge as a chic and indulgent retro-trend of the www.com 90s. In the twenty-first century, fon-due has matured into an eclectic melting pot by virtue of the multiplicity of cultures that make up our vast land. Like a chameleon that changes col-ors to reflect its surroundings, the taste of a con-temporary fondue can be transposed to reflect our multi-ethnic food traditions, creating a sense of culinary adventure. Fondue cooks have gained savoir-fare thanks to the availability of more than two-hundred fine domestic and imported arti-sanal cheeses, imported chocolates, new ingredi-ents for dipping and a bold palate of updated dipping sauces.

THE ASIAN INFLUENCE

The genius of a chef, as with any artist, is not in the selection of his materials but in knowing how to combine them.

—Lin Yu Tang

The resourceful Western kitchen has wisely embraced a mélange of Asian cooking styles that are the Eastern counterpart of Swiss fondue. Asian Americans are one of the most diverse and fastest growing minority groups in America. The Chinese believe that kitchen harmony through feng shui, the ancient Chinese art of placement, comes with a proper balance of nutritious foods, the energy of good company and the correct table setting. This harmony is apparent in Asian hot pot meals. Every day we learn more about the Asian philosophy that considers food a natural medicine, rich with compounds that prevent disease and contribute to our body wellness. Dishes like Japanese Shabu Shabu (page 95), Thai Seafood Hot Pot (page 77), Chrysanthemum Pot (page 83) and Korean Steak Pot with Sesame Noodles (page 78) are thoughtfully composed with delicious ingredients that are nutritious and light. The ingredients and dipping sauces offer a medley of crisp natural textures, exciting flavors and visual appeal. Much of the preparation for these dishes can be done in advance. You don't have to become an "iron chef" to prepare the Asian tabletop dishes in this cookbook. The cooking techniques are not laborious and can be shared equally by the guests. For a detailed description of Asian tabletop cooking equipment, refer to the chapters on Japanese Nabémono (page 89) and Chinese Hot Pots (page 71).

A TASTE OF TRADITION

Tabletop dishes such as fondue and hot pot are ideal for people with time-crunched lifestyles. Trend forecasters predict an increase in dining as home entertainment in the twenty-first century. Many people prefer relaxed, spontaneous gatherings to more formal affairs. Inviting friends to help with some of the preparation makes entertaining easier and much more fun. Tabletop cooking fits comfortably into this niche. In our frenetic world of e-mail, faxes, voice mail and the Internet, people come in contact less frequently. Mealtime is often reduced to "portafoods" and "dashboard dining." Tabletop cooking, a conversational piece in itself, is designed for good fellowship and fun. Dining becomes an interactive form of entertainment as people take an active role in cooking and plating their food.

When we gather around the table to take part in one of these social meals, the occasion becomes a celebration of the traditions of a culture encoded within a cooking pot. It creates an opportunity for us to respectfully examine and experience many of these traditions. We can feed our sense of wonder as we experience the vivid flavors, bright colors and seductive smells of an unfamiliar ethnic cuisine. The unique presentation and cultural diversity of the foods can be educational and stimulate lively discussions. The use of chopsticks or fondue forks for one-pot dining is beneficial. Besides lending an air of authenticity and fun, these dining implements tend to slow down the eating process so we can appreciate the flavor of each bite. Many culinary traditions are being abandoned in this harried, fast-paced world. Switzerland's fondues and Asia's one-pot dishes continue to be a source of sociability and leisurely pastime that underscore the well-being and tranquility of the societies that developed them.

THE SWISS-AMERICAN CONNECTION

In Wisconsin, Americans have an inherent appreciation for Switzerland's hospitality, culture and cheesemaking traditions. In 1845, the Emigration Society of the Canton of Glarus arranged for the purchase of twelve hundred acres in Green County, Wisconsin, to establish a large Swiss settlement. Around 120 Swiss immigrants sailed from Glarus to settle in the idyllic Wisconsin countryside. Most became dairy farmers and began producing Swiss-style cheeses. Within twenty-five years, more than seven thousand Swiss immigrants of German descent lived in the settlement, now called New Glarus. In the early 1920s, there were more than two-thousand cheese factories in Wisconsin. Their direct descendants still live in New Glarus and nearby Monroe, called the "Swiss Cheese Capitol of the United States" by Swiss visitors. The area boasts prime pasturage; fine, brown Swiss cows can be seen roaming the hillsides. Although there are fewer cheese factories today, the area produces some of the finest cheese in the world.

Wisconsin's Swiss-Americans say *"Willkommen!"* There are numerous festivals that focus on this unique heritage and traditions such as the alpenhorn, yodeling, Swiss turning, Swiss woodcarving, Swiss-style embroidery and Swiss folk painting. If you visit the area, listen for the German-Swiss dialect and take note of the Swiss names, the chalet-style architecture and museums like the Swiss Historical Village that celebrate the local history.

Fine restaurants offer delicious examples of Swiss cuisine, râclette and fondue. Fondue has been a fundamental part of the culture since the Swiss immigrants arrived in the nineteenth century. Wisconsin friends I spoke with were nostalgic relating childhood stories from the 1920s and 1930s. Their most vivid memories center on the times their families gathered around the supper table for friendly conversation and a pot of cheese fondue. Quality Switzerland-style cheese can be mail-ordered from Wisconsin, Ohio and New York State. Authentic Swiss râclette cheese is made in Indiana. (See the Mail-Order Resources, page 225.)

Part of the secret of success in life is to eat what you want and let the food fight it out inside.
—Mark Twain

PLEASE EAT THE CENTERPIECE!

- Tabletop cooking allows the flexibility to be creative. You can vary the ingredients and seasonings in a fondue or hot pot to suit your taste. But the measure of the meal will be judged by the high quality and freshness of the ingredients, which should never be varied.
- Diners should be encouraged to "jump in" and lend a hand with the cooking chores. Fondue for two can stimulate a romantic tête-à-tête. Fondue for four is an ideal assemblage, but six diners will have even more fun! More than six becomes a crowd, diminishing the enjoyment of the diners as they contend for a dipping spot in the pot. For more than six diners, set up another table with a second pot. Everyone should be able to reach it comfortably. One pot can serve many more people at a cocktail party or buffet.
- Provide two sets of forks for each diner: a fondue fork for dipping and a regular fork for eating. Some people provide two fondue forks for each person, but the pot can quickly become crowded, lowering the oil temperature.
- As each diner dips a fondue fork of food into the mellifluous cheese mixture, instruct him

to swirl it in a figure eight motion, reaching to the bottom of the pot. This motion keeps the cheese moving and prevents burning. Twirl the fork gently over the pot to prevent excess dripping. If the fondue becomes too hot, turn down the heat, or briefly remove the pot from the burner and place it on a hot pad while making the necessary adjustment.

• An essential rule of etiquette when eating cheese fondue is never double dip! Don't take a bite from a piece of dipped food then place it back into the pot.

• A side salad or tray of raw vegetables, cornichons (gherkins) and cocktail onions will cut the richness of a cheese fondue. Some Swiss grind black pepper onto their plates to season each forkful of dipped cheese. As a final flavor boost, many epicures conduct an additional small ritual. Just before dipping a bread cube into the fondue, they immerse it quickly into a small glass of fine cherry or plum *eau de vie*.

• The Swiss recommend that cold liquids not be drunk with cheese fondue or there will be a "revolution" in your stomach, as one Frenchman put it. The Swiss believe fondue cheese will solidify into a ball, causing major digestive upsets. They suggest sipping on a glass of the same wine used in the fondue, at room temperature. Small shot glasses of kirsch, or another brandy, are often served half way through the meal. Many Swiss enjoy a cup of hot peppermint or black tea to cleanse the palate and aid digestion. Still, many Americans do enjoy a glass of lightly chilled white wine or beer with cheese fondue. Hard cider, a favorite drink in Appenzell, or sparkling apple cider would be delightful choices, as well.

• As the fondue is eaten, a crusty brown layer of cheese forms on the bottom of the pot. It is called *la religieuse* or *la croûte*. In Switzerland, it is a considered a tasty treat, much like the layer of rice skin that forms on the bottom of the Asian rice pot. Remove the flavorful cheese snack and share it with the diners. Some diners scramble an egg in the bottom of the pot to help loosen the cheese layer.

• Dried cheese can be difficult to remove from some fondue pots. Fill the pot with soapy water and soak several hours or overnight. Some pots have nonstick interiors, avoiding this problem. In Switzerland, the French-speaking Swiss salute each other with *"bon appetit,"* before breaking bread and sharing a pot of fondue. The German-speaking Swiss say, *"en guete"* and the Italian-speaking Swiss say, *"buon appetito!"* The languages are different but the good wishes and feelings of hospitality are the same

---

FONDUE EQUIPMENT

During the 1970s, most people owned one fondue pot and used it for making every type of fondue. Usually made from metal, it worked well for oil and broth fondues but scorched chocolate and cheese. To consistently achieve good results, use a fondue set designed specifically for each type of fondue. Fondue pots come with a stand/burner designed to hold either alcohol fuel or a gelled fuel canister. Better fondue sets have convertible burners that can use both.

A sleek lineup of fondue pots can be found in department stores, kitchenware stores, specialty food markets, mail-order catalogs and from the Internet. Fondue specialty shops may sell the pots and burners separately so you can mix and match the components to create your own set. Today's fondue pots are crafted from functional materials in a variety of high-voltage colors and stylish new designs. They come in a wide range of price points to please every budget; today's consumer is tempted to own more than one. A quality fondue pot, whether starter set or state of the art, will maximize your fondue enjoyment and last a lifetime.

Cheese Fondue Pots

In Switzerland, the traditional cheese fondue pot is called a *caquelon*. Made from glazed earthenware or pottery, the broad, shallow pot has a thick, sturdy handle attached to one side. Heated on a *réchaud*, or spirit burner, it diffuses heat slowly and evenly, protecting the cheese against curdling.

Swiss fondue pots are an ideal table accessory, efficient yet balanced with charm. They come in a variety of classic fashion colors; some are decorated with Alpine designs. The traditional pot is unglazed on the outside bottom to allow moisture to escape during the firing process. It requires care similar to the Japanese *donabé*, discussed on page 91.

A *caquelon* can be found in almost every Swiss home. If you decide to purchase one, don't soak water in it for a long period; store it upside down after washing to allow thorough drying. Occasionally, the pot will crackle or develop fine lines with use. Some cooks fill a new pot with equal amounts of milk and water then simmer it on low heat for about twenty minutes. Similarly, a Japanese cook will season an earthenware casserole or *donabé* by simmering rice gruel. Used prudently, fondue can be made directly in a quality Swiss fondue pot placed over a low or medium-low

burner. A heat-diffusing pad underneath offers protection from excessive heat. A *donabé* is also useful for making cheese and western-style broth fondues. These pots are quite durable if handled properly, but will shatter if dropped.

Cheese fondue pots in North America are often made from fireproof ceramic or stoneware and shaped like a casserole without a handle. Heat spreads efficiently through the bottom of the pot and up the sides. Do not use this type of ceramic pot to make cheese fondue on the kitchen stove; it can easily crack. It is safer and more efficient to prepare fondue in a heavy-bottomed saucepan on the stove then pour it into the fondue pot. Never use a ceramic, stoneware or earthenware fondue pot for hot oil or broth fondues. The high temperature of heated oil or broth can cause the pot to crack, dangerously spilling the contents.

Hot Oil and Broth Fondue Pots

Metal fondue pots are designed for hot oil and broth fondues. The containers are narrow and deep with heatproof safety handles for lifting. They come in stainless steel, brushed steel, enamel on steel or cast iron, anodized aluminum and lined copper. These sturdy materials can withstand the high temperatures needed for heating oil or broth. Quality stainless steel pots are attractive and easy to clean. Bar Keeper's Friend is a mildly abrasive product from the supermarket that will remove heat discoloration, keeping your pot shiny.

Some metal pots are not suitable for all fondues. Thin-gauge metal pots can heat unevenly and develop hot spots, causing cheese and chocolate to scorch. Ceramic pots work best, but if you prefer a metal pot, look for one that is heavy gauge. A handsome copper or stainless steel fondue pot with a removable porcelain insert is ideal for cheese and chocolate. An anodized aluminum fondue pot with a durable stick-resistant coating is another good choice. When heating cheese fondue in a metal pot, use gelled fondue fuel, which burns less hot; adjust the heat to a low setting.

If you lack storage space for more than one pot, consider an enamel cast-iron fondue pot, excellent for oil, broth and cheese fondues. The heavy iron core excels at even heat conduction; the enamel coating reduces maintenance chores. Cast-iron fondue pots are versatile and can be used directly on the stovetop or in the oven. They make handy deep fryers for small amounts of food. Some pots can be conveniently stored upside down over their metal burners. Enameled cast-iron fondue pots are available in a variety of colors and designs.

New combination sets that include both a metal pot and a ceramic pot have recently come on the market. Electric fondue pots lack the romance of the flame, but elimination of the fuel might be a safer option for some people. Electric fondues are attractive and come with efficient adjustable controls that regulate the cooking temperature just as successfully for a chocolate fondue as a hot oil fondue. Electric pots can double as a deep-fryer. Nonstick cooking surfaces make cleanup easy.

Chocolate Fondue Pots

A metal pot is not a good choice for chocolate fondue. Chocolate and other delicate dessert fondues scorch easily and must be warmed gently in a ceramic or stoneware pot. Chocolate pots are smaller than cheese fondue pots and reasonably priced. They are designed to hold a tea light or slightly larger votive candle and provide just enough heat to keep the chocolate warm and fluid. A ceramic cheese pot may burn too hot for chocolate fondue; tame the heat by substituting a votive candle for the fondue fuel. Small ceramic pots for warming butter or sauce are perfect for a romantic dessert fondue for two. Or consider a metal fondue pot with porcelain insert. Susan Duncan, proprietor of the South Carolina cookware store Vista Cucina explains how to improvise a similar setup. "Pour a little warm water in your metal fondue pot and set it over a lit burner. Place a heatproof, ceramic bowl filled with chocolate fondue into the pot. In essence, you will be creating a protective *bain marie* or water bath to temper the heat, keeping the chocolate warm." For added protection, you can place a clean, thin, folded dishcloth under the bowl.

Râclette Cookers

Râclette, a staple food of the Swiss shepherds, is becoming quite popular in America. With a râclette cooker, your guests can enjoy the rustic conviviality of heating portions of cheese in small metal pans while grilling sausages, meats and vegetables on a nonstick grill. Several models are available to accommodate four to eight people. Each cooker has variable heat controls and comes with wooden spatulas.

Fondue Accessories

Accessories can add to the efficiency of a fondue pot. A splatter guard will shield against sputtering hot oil. It may have a magnetic rim attached or notches for holding the fondue forks in place. Fondue sets include six to eight long fondue forks that protect the hands from the heat. Stay-cool handles are essential for hot oil and broth fondues. Forks are usually color-coded so the diners can keep track of their food. Fondue paraphernalia includes attractive trays that can be placed under a fondue set, condiment sets with a rotating carousel (lazy Susan), bowls and spoons and trendy fondue plates with sections for holding the foods and sauces.

Fondue Fuels

Alcohol and gelled fuel are used to heat fondue pots. Alcohol is recommended for oil and broth fondues because of its maximum heat output and long-burning flame. It is used in fondue pots fitted with an alcohol burner, a round, metal fuel cup with an alcohol pad and a metal grid cover. An adjustable heat diffuser fits on top; the handle controls the flame. For the highest flame, slide the handle to completely open the holes. A filled fuel cup will burn for at least one hour over a high flame, about one and one-half hours over a medium flame and at least two hours over a low flame. A burn snuffer is included to safely extinguish the fire when you finish cooking.

Alcohol fuels for fondue pots can contain methyl alcohol or ethyl alcohol. They are formulated to be smokeless, odorless and clean burning. Normally colorless, the fuel may be tinted with blue or red-pink coloring. Methyl alcohol is labeled POISON; the fuel bottles are marked with a skull and crossbones. The container tops are child-resistant. Alcohol can be used for cheese fondues, but keep a closer eye on the heat, making adjustments, as necessary. Check in cookware stores for products such as blue-tinted Fondue Fuel or Blue Flame Fondue Fuel. Sterno fondue fuel (tinted red-pink) can be found in restaurant and catering supply houses or hardware stores. Some people use denatured alcohol from the hardware store or pharmacy.

Fondue pot manufacturers recommend gelled fuel for cheese fondue, which needs a low to medium flame. Thickened gelled fuels such as ethanol (ethyl alcohol) or methanol (methyl alcohol) are made from converted alcohol. In gel form, there is no risk of spill, no flare-up when lighting and no uneven burning. Two popular Swiss brands are Swiss Fire Gel and Firestar gel canisters. Swiss Fire Gel comes in 1.1 quart bottles for alcohol burners and in 2.8-ounce canisters for chafing fuel-style burners. To use a container, tear off the cover then place it into the fuel cup. Close the gridlike burner cover and ignite the fuel with a match. Adjust the flame, as necessary.

Gelled fuels are considered a safer heat formulation. Purchase in stores that sell fondue pots or through mail order. Ethanol-based fuel is made from organic materials such as corn, grains and potatoes. The starch is converted to simple sugars, fermented and distilled. Ethyl alcohol is used in alcoholic beverages but denatured (made unfit for human consumption) for use as fuel. Gelled fuel in a bottle can be used for lighting charcoal briquettes for Asian hot pots.

Small canisters of Sterno brand Canned Heat® cooking fuel are used in chafing dishes and camp stoves. The manufacturer, Candle Corporation of America, does not recommend their use in fondue pots. Canned, liquid chafing fuel with an adjustable wick is formulated from diethylene glycol. It is produced for food service chafing dishes. The fuel is efficient, burns clean and is nonflammable. Small sizes for room service and coffee service fit into home chafing dishes. Obtain this product in restaurant and catering supply houses. See the Mail-Order resources (page 225).

SAFETY POINTS FOR FONDUE POTS

- Always read and follow the manufacturer's instructions packaged with your fondue pot. Read all the directions and warnings on the fuel containers.
- Never heat hot oil in an earthenware, ceramic or stoneware fondue pot.
- To prevent cracking, do not heat a ceramic, stoneware or earthenware fondue pot when empty. Warm foods over low to medium-low heat for a brief period; a heat diffuser can add extra protection.
- Make sure the handles are securely attached before you pick up a filled fondue pot.
- At the table, place the fondue base on a heat-proof surface like a thick wooden cutting board or colorful ceramic tiles.
- Fill the fuel cup with fondue fuel. If alcohol fuel splashes, wipe it up; wash and dry your hands. Fit the fuel cup into the fondue stand. Close the liquid alcohol bottle and remove from the lighting area. Light the fuel with a long match. Once lit, do not move or tip the burner.
- Never add fuel to a hot fuel cup, with or without a flame. Some fondue pots come with an extra fuel cup, which you can safely fill and replace if the fuel runs out. Fuel cups are inexpensive; keep a second one on hand.
- Never try to extinguish a burner by blowing out the flame. It can spread over the table. Use the flame snuffer included with your fondue set.
- Tie or tape the electric fondue pot cord to a table leg to prevent unintentionally pulling over the pot. Unplug it immediately after use.
- Do not pour cold water into a hot fondue pot, no matter what material it is made of. Avoid rapid temperature changes.
- Remind the diners, especially children, that a fondue fork dipped into boiling hot oil or stock can cause burns if placed in the mouth.
- Never leave a hot fondue pot unattended in the presence of children.

SKINNY DIPPING

In the 1960s and 1970s, cheese fondue was all the rage. The '80s ushered in the age of nutritional enlightenment and fat control. Before you could say Jack Sprat, fondue was out the door, replaced by a trinity of yogurt, skim milk and "no-fat, no-flavor" cheese. Admittedly, fondues made with cheese, chocolate and hot oil are not a form of skinny-dipping. Eaten in large amounts, they can shipwreck a decent diet. But excess is the real culprit; the harm coming more from the dose than from the substance.

Fat must be consumed in moderation yet the body requires a small amount for good health. It is the body's transport for the fat-soluble vitamins A, D, E and K. Fat is essential for cell development, regulates metabolism and provides energy. It adds flavor to the foods we eat and helps keep our appetites satisfied. Fat becomes a problem when we overindulge or at the other end of the spectrum, we don't get enough.

Cheese is an excellent source of protein and calcium. It contains phosphorus and other minerals and vitamins. In Europe, a cheese course is often served before dessert, as an aid to digestion. The *British Dental Journal* published a report in

1999 suggesting meals that contain cheese can help fight tooth decay. It seems cheese can significantly increase the amount of plaque calcium that coats the teeth. This promotes hardening of the tooth surface and protects against cavities. Even a small cube of cheese seems to be beneficial and can increase the plaque-calcium concentration by up to 112 percent.

Chocolate may not be as unhealthy as previously believed, according to new studies. Researchers at the University of Scranton, Pennsylvania, have determined that dark chocolate contains antioxidants. And one ounce of chocolate is said to contain as much phenolic acid (a phytochemical) as a five-ounce glass of red wine. Scientists suggest that phenolic substances act like antioxidants and may offer protection from cancers and heart disease. Japanese studies show that compounds in cocoa extract can inhibit cholesterol oxidation leading to plaque buildup in the arteries when fed to rabbits.

We all know the bad news; dietary fat is the main offender in raising blood cholesterol levels, a risk factor for heart disease. The good news is that a regular diet of healthy eating has room for balance, so when the craving hits, we can pull out the fondue pot and splurge without doing ourselves any harm.

THE TAO OF FONDUE

The Swiss share a passion for the pleasures of the table and are avid devotees of fondue. They have a sense of knowing how to incorporate it into their diets and maintain good health. The Chinese would call this a yin-yang balance, designed to keep one on a "middle road." Supported by the philosophies of Taoism and Buddhism, the Chinese believe that foods are a natural medicine with compounds able to prevent disease and contribute to body wellness. Good health and long life through the proper combination of foods is the Tao of eating and the foundation of the universal balance that rules every Chinese kitchen.

The manner in which you eat is as important as your choice of foods. Fondues, like the hot pots of Asia, are meant to be savored slowly in moderation and shared with friends. Japanese nutritionists are urging parents to improve their children's academic performance by shifting westernized diets back to traditional fare eaten with chopsticks. They have discovered the brain's blood circulation can increase 20 percent when small bites are thoroughly chewed and eaten at a leisurely pace. Foods eaten without chopsticks are often wolfed down, putting stress on digestion. These are convincing reasons for picking up those chopsticks or a fondue fork!

When I interviewed Julia Child for a military lifestyle magazine, she shared some healthy advice that could be applied to tabletop dining. She suggested that if we avoid processed foods, buy a great deal of fresh, seasonal foods and eat them in moderation, we should have no problems with our health. The main thing is to enjoy your food and have fun with it. Julia's advice on dieting, "I would rather have one spoonful of chocolate mousse than three bowls of Jell-O." Or perhaps, one dip of a luscious, rich chocolate fondue?

MISE EN PLACE

To get the best results from the fondue recipes in this book, follow the French system of organization called *mise en place*. The phrase, meaning, "put in place," is the professional chef's method of preparing and organizing all the ingredients up to the point of cooking. To put this system to work, plan the party ahead. Read the recipe completely through. This will tell you which ingredients to gather and the type of prepping you may need to do. It will also tell you if special techniques are required within a recipe and allow you to gather pieces of cooking equipment, part of the *mise en place*. Read through the fondue recipe to decide if there are elements that can be prepared ahead, such as preparing the dipping sauces and the foods for dipping or grating the cheese. Fondue parties can be simple to prepare for since much of the work can be done in advance: Set the table, make the croutons and cookies for dipping, shred the cheese or prepare elements of the salad like washing the greens and making the dressing. When buying key ingredients such as cheese, buy a little extra in case you need to thicken a fondue or stretch the recipe for an extra guest. Gather the ingredients in advance (keep dairy products, seafood and meats refrigerated); measure and arrange them on a tray. Certain steps are taken for granted in a recipe. Cheese should be cold for

shredding. Onions, fresh ginger and garlic should always be peeled; carrots scrubbed, bell peppers seeded, lettuce, herbs and flowers carefully rinsed and well dried. *Mise en place* is especially important when entertaining. It simplifies last-minute preparations and allows you to give your undivided attention to making the fondue without repeatedly stopping to search for ingredients.

Recent trend surveys indicate many people are beginning to appreciate the value of spontaneity. They prefer relaxed, last-minute gatherings in which friends can come over and help with some of the preparations. The work is reduced for the party givers and the evening is much more fun. An Asian hot-pot party works well within these parameters. Pick up the basic ingredients at the market and organize them in the kitchen. Gather your tabletop cooking equipment and dishes. Guests can help slice the meat, prepare the sauces, cut the vegetables and arrange the platters of food. Not much else is needed; perhaps cooked rice, beer, hot tea and fresh fruit with sorbet for dessert. This will guarantee to get you out of the kitchen fast so you can join your guests at the table.

Cheese
Fondues

There is something homey and completely irresistible about dishes that include melted cheese. Some even rank as the defining dishes of several of the world's great cuisines. A classic example is Switzerland's Fondue Neuchâtel.

Have you ever heard the popular phrase, "Switzerland was born to make cheese"? Cheese making has been conducted in the pastoral setting of the Swiss Alps for at least one thousand years. Systematic dairy production, controlled by the strictest set of standards in the world, keeps the quality of cheese consistently high. Master cheese makers, respected as skilled artisans, earn federal accreditation only after graduating from state-run dairy colleges, years of training, dairy apprenticeships and examinations. Besides skilled cheese makers, the criterion for Switzerland's quality cheese production includes superior cattle, pure air, sunshine, clear glacial waters and lush Alpine pasturage with aromatic grasses and fragrant sweet flowers. A taste of these mountain cheeses will give you a taste of the true flavor of Switzerland.

In the spring, pampered cattle are festooned with ribbons, flowers and melodious bells as they begin their pilgrimage to high grazing pastures. The lead cow, or *Herrkuh*, proudly carries the largest and loudest bell attached to her neck with a beautiful handcrafted leather strap. Swiss farmers offer visitors a "taste of Switzerland" through their summer "adopt-a-cow" program. During summer trips, my sister Dee remembers falling in love with more than one pair of big, brown Swiss eyes.

Râclette refers to a group of superb melting cheeses as well as the dish that may have originated long ago with Swiss shepherds who melted their meal of cheese by the fire. At its most basic, râclette is a dish of unctuous, creamy, melted cheese served with boiled potatoes and crusty bread. It is popular in the Swiss Canton of Valais where it originated and the eastern part of France. Valais is wine country; it is said râclette cheese tastes best melted over a fire of dry branches from the vineyards. Treat your family and friends to the congenial experience of a râclette party following the directions on page 37. Select a fine cheese with good melting qualities and feels creamy in the mouth.

Fonduta, a signature dish of Northern Italy, is an aristocratic relative of Swiss and French fondue. The name comes from the Italian word *fondere*, meaning, "to melt." The dish calls for Fontina Val d'Aosta, a creamy cheese named for Mount Fontin in the Valle d'Aosta near the Swiss and French borders. Fontina is one of Italy's great cheeses. It is a superb melter, especially in this fondue-style dish. Spoon creamy Fonduta over new potatoes, risotto, gnocchi or pasta. It is heavenly over poached chicken, cooked eggs or vegetables. My version is served in warm bowls with elegant Asparagus Toasts (page 34) and crisp vegetables on the side for dipping. Not for forks only, Fonduta can be served as a luxurious appetizer fondue with an assortment of dippers.

Wales, a land of rolling green hills and storybook castles, is known for rich dairy dishes, which provide fortitude in the often chilly, damp Welsh air. Dating from the fourteenth century, Welsh rabbit may have first appeared on the tables of hapless hunters who failed to bag a live rabbit for dinner. The dish reflects a great fondness for "toasted cheese" throughout the British Isles. Queen Victoria was known to whip up a chafing dish of cheese rabbit, now and then, using Scottish Dunlop cheese and champagne. In the Victorian days, small portions were served as a savory course, just before dessert.

Controversy has existed over the name since the eighteenth century. The Welsh prefer rabbit, but "rarebit" has become popularized. The Welsh word for soft is "rare." The word rarebit might be a description of the dish's texture or its delicious taste. According to Mrs. N.K.M. Lee, American author of, *The Cook's Own Book*, (Boston, 1832), ". . . properly prepared, toasted cheese well deserves its ancient appellation of a rare-bit." Mrs. Lee advised her readers to ". . . trim away rotten parts on the cheese and serve up Welsh rabbit in individual portions." She further instructed that it was ". . . imperatively indispensable that it be introduced to the mouth as soon as it appears on the table." Sensible advice even for today! Enjoy a taste of this Welsh classic and try my recipe on

page 26. It is perfect for a quick lunch or cozy late-night supper.

THE FUNDAMENTALS OF CHEESE FONDUE

Melting cheese in hot liquid for fondue is a simple technique but can be a recipe for disaster. Cheese is high in protein; when overheated, it is susceptible to curdling. When fondue curdles, protein molecules and fat in the cheese separate, turning into a lumpy, stringy, oily mess. You can avoid this pitfall and produce a creamy-smooth fondue by adding three fundamental ingredients and using the right techniques.

The addition of wine, lemon juice and starch are helpful in preventing curdled fondue. Wine adds flavor, but it also provides acidity. Tartaric acid is a natural crystalline compound that is the principal acid in wine. Food scientists believe it helps prevent protein molecules from bonding too much and becoming stringy in cheeses like domestic Swiss cheese, Emmentaler and mozzarella. They contain calcium phosphate, a compound that promotes a slight lumpiness and stringiness. The ample amount of wine added to a Swiss-cheese fondue helps keep it smooth. I have found these undesirable qualities can be diminished if the cheese is melted with a smooth-melting cheese such as Gruyère. Choose a crisp, dry wine or an off-dry wine with just a faint perception of sweetness. For more information on wine, read, The "Spirit" of Fondue (page 19).

Lemon juice contains citric acid that combines even more favorably with the cheese proteins to prevent curdling. A small amount of lemon juice added at the beginning of a fondue recipe provides a measure of prevention. Vinegar and sour cream can be beneficial, when appropriate to the recipe. These ingredients are especially helpful if the cheese fondue isn't made with an acidic liquid.

The Swiss depend on potato starch to swell and bind the proteins in cheese fondue, keeping the consistency smooth. Wheat flour and cornstarch are good substitutes. Cake flour produces a smoother consistency than all-purpose flour. Cornstarch has almost twice the thickening power of flour; keep a fresh supply on hand stored in an airtight container. Cornstarch that is over a year old may lose some of its ability to thicken. Add the cornstarch in a slurry, blended with a room temperature liquid. Cook the fondue enough for the starch to gelatinize, but watch carefully to prevent overheating.

It is essential to melt cheese at a low temperature with a short cooking time to prevent fat separation, stringing and toughening. If heated properly, cheese melts to a creamy smoothness without curdling. Heat the wine in a heavy-bottomed pan. When the cheese mixture begins to bubble around the edge of the pot, simmer gently for 1 to 2 minutes. Do not allow the fondue near a boil. As it simmers, stir the cheese steadily with a whisk or a wooden spoon. Swiss cooks often stir with a figure-eight motion. Domestic Swiss cheese and Emmentaler may become slightly lumpy in the initial stage of melting. Keep stirring; the fondue will smooth out as the mixture bubbles and the starch begins to thickens.

Shredded cheese at room temperature melts quickly, reducing the heating time. To protect the cheese from the excess heat of my professional home range, I find it helpful to place a heat diffuser under the pan. This trick also works well with electric stoves. Once a fondue breaks and the cheese separates, no amount of culinary first aid can repair the damage. Basic cheese fondues made with wine and cheese seems to be the most vulnerable to curdling.

The ratio of liquid to cheese is balanced in the recipes; stay close to the recommended amount. If you add too much wine and the fondue seems thin, stir in more shredded cheese, about 1/2 cup at a time. If you run out of cheese, dissolve another teaspoon of cornstarch in a little wine, kirsch or lemon juice and whisk it in. Stir over medium-low heat until the fondue bubbles gently around the edge and thickens. Try to avoid additional starch; to my taste the texture becomes slightly grainy. Cheese fondue will thicken naturally as it heats over the fondue burner. If your fondue becomes too thick, slowly whisk in some tepid wine or other liquid until you reach the desired consistency. Never use water.

Doubling or tripling a cheese fondue recipe can be tricky. A double amount of liquid has less surface area in the pot for evaporation and the fondue can end up the consistency of soup. If you increase the simmering time to reduce the liquid, the cheese will toughen, becoming stringy. For a double batch of fondue, reduce the total amount of liquid by at least one-third. Or, simply use a larger pot.

Garlic is another traditional ingredient that is crushed, rubbed over the inside of the fondue pot or saucepan then discarded. Garlic is added for flavor but many Swiss believe it prevents the cheese from sticking to the pot. Others consider it a digestive aid. Many people love the taste of garlic and prefer to add it to the fondue for more flavor.

SHOPPING FOR CHEESE

The increasing availability of quality domestic and imported cheeses has helped foster the popularity of fondue. Europeans appreciate fine cheese and have a long tradition of serving it in melted cheese dishes. In Switzerland where fondue is practically the national dish, a cheese tray is set out at breakfast, lunch and dinner. American restaurants are beginning to adopt the custom of serving cheese after the entree or dessert course.

A large number of cheeses have excellent melting qualities for fondue. If you are unfamiliar with a cheese used in one of the recipes, refer to the Cheese Glossary (page 209) and learn more. If you live near a specialty cheese store, begin your search there; some offer hundreds of varieties! Gourmet specialty markets keep a well-stocked cheese counter. Local supermarkets may have a separate kiosk for specialty and artisanal cheeses in addition to the regular section stocked with vacuum-packed cheeses. Markets are paying attention to consumers' demands for a larger variety of quality cheeses. If you can't locate a certain cheese, check the listing of stores on page 225; they will be happy to ship to you.

Be selective when buying cheese. Ideally, one should purchase cheese from markets that cut and wrap to order. Some of the best stores display their cheeses with small handwritten signs offering descriptive notes. The staff should be able to share knowledgeable information and provide samples. Flavor and quality can change from cheese to cheese depending on the age, shipping methods, handling and storage. Too often, supermarket specialty cheeses slip quietly into maturity then expire. When past its prime, a piece of cheese can smell like ammonia, taste bitter, mold, be wet and pasty or have a dried-out rind. Don't hesitate to return a piece of cheese displaying any of these characteristics.

Cheese blending is quite an art in Switzerland; cheese shops and dairy stores will offer a variety of blends ready to be melted for fondue. The length of aging affects a cheese's final flavor and melting ability. A young cheese isn't always as tasty melted because it hasn't had time to develop its flavor. Kick up the taste and combine it with a sharper cheese. A mild cheddar is more likely to separate when melted than an aged cheddar. Hard, super-aged cheeses can be grated and added in small amounts as an accent. Avoid low-fat cheeses; fat contributes to the smooth consistency of melted cheese and helps prevent stringiness. For the best results, stick with blocks of premium, naturally aged cheese.

The buzzwords for fine cheese such as artisanal and farmhouse are becoming de rigueur in the American culinary lexicon. Handmade artisanal cheeses are limited in production and can differ slightly in color or shape with each new batch. These little "flaws" are the characteristics that make these cheeses so desirable. The quality is not affected. Until recently, most Americans preferred the uniformity of factory-made cheese. The term "farmhouse" indicates the cheese is handmade in small amounts at a farm using raw, unpasteurized milk. The unpasteurized milk gives the cheese its special character.

That said, cheese tastes are an individual matter and choices are often a matter of personal curiosity and gratification. The most important consideration is that the taste of a particular cheese brings you satisfaction and pleasure.

CHEESE STORAGE

Proper storage is important for maintaining the quality and flavor of cheese. The length of time cheese remains in prime condition in the refrigerator depends on its moisture content and how well it is wrapped. The higher its moisture content, the shorter the shelf life. Hard cheeses like Parmesan or Romano have less moisture; properly wrapped they will keep for months. Natural, semi-firm cheese can remain fresh for four to eight weeks. Softer cheeses should be eaten within one to three weeks. Use shredded cheese within several days; spoilage occurs more rapidly because more surface area is exposed. Unopened packages of pre-shredded cheese last longer. If the end portion of a piece of cheese becomes too hard and dry, trim it off. Don't discard ends or scraps; store in a clean jar and keep for seasoning foods or for making blended cheese spreads.

Cheese sellers recommend wrapping each piece securely in plastic wrap or aluminum foil to prevent surface drying. Plastic wrap does a good job of sealing in moisture, but mold forms rapidly if moisture can't escape. To inhibit mold and allow cheese to breath, change the plastic wrap every few days, or after it is handled. A fresh piece of wrap provides a tighter seal. Packaged cheddar can be left in the original wrapper and given an overwrap. Cheese sealed in wax needs no further wrapping until cut. Some experts recommend soft cheeses be wrapped in waxed paper then stored in a plastic bag to allow more air circulation. Producers of goat cheese recommend storing the cheese in a glass jar or plastic container with a tight-fitting lid; do not use plastic wrap. Fresh cheeses like ricotta or cottage cheese should stay in their airtight containers; they are high-moisture and perishable.

Store cheese in the refrigerator between 35F (0C) and 40F (5C). Most wrapped cheeses can be stored within the same area, preferably in the lower vegetable bin. Do not store cheese near strong-smelling foods; cheese breathes and will pick up odors.

If a piece of firm, natural cheese develops mold, it doesn't mean the cheese is bad. Trim off the mold and the surrounding area. Some cheese sellers retard molding by wiping cheese with a clean cloth dipped into mild vinegar; others shun the practice. Wrap the cheese in fresh wrap and use as soon as possible. In the blue cheese family, including Stilton, Gorgonzola and Roquefort, the development of each strain of mold has been perfected to create a unique flavor and color characteristic. Wrap blue cheese securely in plastic wrap and store in an airtight container or self-sealing plastic bag; push out as much air as possible. Although mold spores are part of our natural environment, if airborne in the refrigerator, they will spread from cheese to other moist foods, enjoying rampant growth. All high-moisture foods should be carefully sealed.

Natural cheese tastes best at room temperature; remove from the refrigerator at least one hour before serving. If you have a large piece of cheese and only need a small portion, cut off the piece you need; rewrap the remainder and return it to the refrigerator. One savvy cheese seller recommends spreading soft butter on the cut portion of the cheese to seal the exposed area.

Freezing Cheese

Cheese keeps naturally for a long period in the refrigerator. Freezing is not an ideal method for maintaining the quality of most types of cheese. Consider it as a last resort. Cow's-milk cheese breaks down under freezing conditions and loses moisture. If cheese must be frozen, cut it into one-half- to one-pound portions. Overwrap the cheese and seal it in a freezer bag with the air pushed out. Some people like to shred the cheese before freezing it. Fresh mozzarella freezes rather well and retains most of its flavor.

Freeze cheese no longer than two months. After slow-thawing in the refrigerator, use the cheese as soon as possible. Thawed cheese becomes crumbly and dry; the longer it freezes, the dryer it becomes. Goat's-milk cheese and sheep's-milk cheese freeze well due to the smaller structure of the milk protein; the quality remains the same. Freeze in portions no larger than eight ounces. Parmesan and Romano cheeses also freeze well; cut in small pieces, wrap in foil and store in airtight plastic bags. Thaw in the refrigerator. Frozen cheese is best used in dishes that do not require cooking. Do not use frozen cheese for making fondue.

SHREDDING AND GRATING CHEESE

To encourage fast, even melting, hard cheese like Parmesan should be grated, semi-soft cheese like Emmentaler (Swiss) or Gruyère should be shredded, blue cheese can be crumbled and soft cheeses like Brie are best cut into small cubes. Trim off the hard rinds from cheeses like Emmentaler, Parmesan and Stilton before grating. The rinds of washed-rind cheeses and natural-rind cheeses do not melt well in fondue. Some rinds may have been treated with antimolding agents. The rinds of soft-ripened cheeses like Brie and Camembert are completely edible.

I suggest processing cheese by hand using the four-sided box grater (tower grater) that goes by the nickname of the "knuckle-buster." This type of grater is a breeze to use, easy to clean and very efficient. I would suggest a deluxe, stainless steel or nonstick model, which features a good grip and larger holes for fast grating. There are variations of this grater with two to six sides; one is flat like a washboard. Box graters are enduring and last for years; they really will leave your knuckles intact.

In general, the harder the cheese, the finer it can be processed. Grate hard, aged cheeses like Parmesan, Dry Jack or Romano with the smallest side of a box grater. The Microplane is a rasp-style plane that is very efficient for finely grating hard cheese. For softer cheese like Swiss or Gruyère, use the side of the grater with the largest holes. Shredding is easy if the cheese is chilled. If shredded ahead, bring the cheese out of the refrigerator about thirty minutes before making the fondue. Grate lemons on the diagonal-hole side of a box grater for more yellow zest and less of underlying bitter pith. Do not use the nail-hole side. Box graters are useful for grating many vegetables; potatoes for Swiss rôsti, cabbage for coleslaw and zucchini for relish.

CHEESE MATH

Cheese amounts for recipes in this book are given by weight (pounds and ounces) and by volume (cups and tablespoons). The weights are for untrimmed pieces of cheese; the volume is for cheese that is trimmed and shredded or grated. In this book, shredded cheese is measured by lightly packing it into a dry measuring cup. Four ounces will measure about one and one-fourth cups; packed more tightly it will measure one cup. Measuring by weight is more efficient and consistently gives the most accurate results. Several factors are at play, such as the type of equipment used, the firmness of the cheese or if it was chilled. A scale's reading will display the correct weight of cheese whether it is shredded, cubed, chilled or at room temperature.

Measuring cheese for fondue is not as critical as

precise measuring for baking, which is essential for consistent results, but weighing is a good habit to get into. Buy a scale that includes metric measurements. Use of the metric system allows cooks to read the "culinary language" of much of the rest of the world. Mechanical or analog scales are easy to use and offer many attractive features at favorable prices. Electronic or digital scales are extremely accurate and provide good readability. New lithium batteries allow the cook to make 100,000 measurements before they must be changed.

High-quality, well-crafted tools for measuring by volume are also important. There can be some variance in the accuracy of different brands of measuring spoons and cups; only use top-quality tools, even if they cost a little more. Use stainless steel or chrome dry measuring cups for cheese and calibrated glass measuring cups for liquids. Place the cup on a flat surface before pouring in the liquid for the most accurate measure.

FONDUE IN THE MICROWAVE

I have discovered the microwave to be an amazing tool for warming leftover fondue. The cheese does not separate and the texture stays smooth and creamy. Although I like to make a fondue shortly before serving, you might try this method if you need to make the fondue in advance. The quality is still very good after it is reheated.

Make the fondue a day or two in advance. Pour it into a glass bowl; cover with plastic wrap. Store in the refrigerator. Remove the bowl of chilled, rubbery fondue from the refrigerator about thirty minutes before heating. Remove the plastic wrap and cover with a piece of waxed paper to prevent splattering. Microwave on 80 percent power in two-minute intervals until the fondue is melted.

Check the consistency after two minutes and give a good stir. When completely melted and warm, whisk the fondue gently for a few seconds and serve at once. Small leftover portions of fondue make a great dip or sauce. Chocolate fondue heats nicely in the microwave, as well.

In her cookbook, *Microwave Gourmet*, Barbara Kafka offers an interesting and handy technique for microwave fondue. She first microwaves wine and garlic before adding the cheese. Ms. Kafka recommends natural Swiss cheese because other cheeses have a tendency to separate.

Need to soften cream cheese in a hurry? Remove it from the foil wrapper and place on a microwave-safe plate. Microwave at 50 percent power for about thirty seconds for a three-ounce package, sixty seconds for an eighty-ounce package. Heating times can vary among different microwave models.

THE "SPIRIT" OF FONDUE

For centuries, the marriage of cheese and wine has been a quintessential food pairing. Both are produced through a process of fermentation and aging. The flavors in cheese come from various cultures and molds, similar to many compounds present in wine.

When choosing a wine to make fondue, select one that matches the flavor intensity of the cheese and complements its taste. The Swiss recommend a complementary wine made in the same region as the cheese. They prefer a dry white wine with a crisp acidity. Switzerland's favorite wine for fondue has been produced from Chasselas, the most dominant grape varietal for centuries. The flavor makeup of the wine changes with each area of production, reflecting the character of the variable soils and climates. In the Canton of Vaud, the largest area of production, the wine is simply called Chasselas. In Valais, it is called Fendant. In Western Switzerland, it is Neuchâtel. Other good choices include dry Alsace Riesling, dry Chardonnay, Sauvignon blanc, dry German Riesling, or Champagne. For the perfect accompaniment, serve the remaining wine at the table.

For a final layer of flavor in a cheese fondue, the Swiss like to add a soupçon of colorless, dry brandy known as *eau de vie* or "water of life." Made from the finest fruits, they are a tribute to the distiller's art. The most popular choice is kirschwasser or kirsch, distilled from cherries and the most familiar choice. Quetsch, a fine plum *eau de vie*, is often favored in the Canton of Valais. Apple brandy, namely Calvados, is distilled from apple pomace and exudes the scent of fresh apples. A specialty of Normandy, France, Calvados is added to fondue in the French-speaking region of Gruyère. Some people enjoy the distinction of a fine Cognac, the most famous brandy of all. Other choices might include American applejack, French pear William, slivovitz (plum brandy) bourbon, grappa, pflumli and marc, a strong brandy made from pomace, the spent grape skins, seeds and stems left over from wine production.

ALCOHOL ALTERNATIVES

Wine is a primary ingredient in the classic cheese fondue and occasionally, in broth fondues. Some versions call for beer, Champagne or hard cider. Many cheese fondues are also flavored with clear brandies. Yet others might not include spirits at all. Many people think all traces of alcohol are eliminated through cooking but this myth isn't true. Studies by the U.S. Department of Agricul-

ture show the approximate amounts left in food after it is cooked. When simmered with other ingredients, wine retains about 40 percent of the alcohol after fifteen minutes. The amount decreases to 25 percent after one hour.

Some people prefer complete abstinence from alcohol and wonder if they can still make a good fondue. The answer is yes! If a small amount of wine or a white brandy like kirsch is added to the recipe as an accent flavor, it can simply be omitted. But wine does play a major role in cheese fondue. As mentioned earlier, it helps prevent cheese from curdling and adds to the overall flavor. Fortunately, you can make a tasty cheese fondue with substitutes such as apple cider, pear cider, sparkling apple juice, apple-cranberry juice, white grape juice, half and half, whipping cream or even light chicken stock. Apple juice is a sweetened apple drink, often made from concentrate. It is too sweet for fondue. You can bring sophistication to the fondue pot without alcohol but don't sacrifice the taste and use plain water. Always go for the flavor. Apple-cranberry juice has the added tang of cranberries and makes an interesting blend with sharp orange cheddar. Try a nonalcoholic wine or Amé, a light sparkling nonalcoholic beverage with fruit juices and herbs. It is sold in bottles like wine and is available in white, red and rosé. Experiment to discover the cheese and beverage pairings you like best.

CHEESE LAGNIAPPE

Lagniappe is a popular term in South Louisiana for "a little something extra." It is like receiving a special little gift. If you enjoy eating cheese and making fondues, you may occasionally end up with a stockpile of hard, leftover pieces of cheese in the refrigerator. The best way to use up these "odds and ends" is to whip up a container of cheese spread the French refer to as *fromage fort* or "strong cheese." There is no particular recipe; just pull out all the extra cheese you have on hand. The fun in this method is that no two batches will taste exactly alike. Leftover blue cheese, goat cheese or soft-ripened cheeses can be blended together or creamed alone with soft butter and fortified with a small amount of Cognac or brandy. Semi-firm and hard pieces of cheese can be shredded or grated and blended with butter or cream cheese to soften the strong flavor. I like to add a very small amount of one or two of the following: minced shallots, minced garlic, minced fresh herbs, pear or apple *eau de vie*, minced sun-dried tomatoes, or chopped toasted nuts. Pack the mixture into a crock and chill overnight to develop the flavors. Use within a week or so for the best flavor. If you prefer, simply grate pieces of leftover semi-firm and hard cheeses, mix them up and store in a jar in the refrigerator for seasoning foods.

SWISS TRADITION

Give a thought to Swiss tradition when planning seating arrangements for fondue parties. One Swiss custom dictates that a lady must offer a kiss to the nearest man if she loses her piece of bread or meat in the pot.

Another tradition is that if your bread slips off the fork into the cheese, you have to pay a penalty of having to buy a bottle of wine or a round of drinks for the table or kiss each fellow diner. Do as the Swiss do and create challenging new penalties as the evening progresses.

Camembert, poetry,
Bouquet of our meals,
What would become of life,
If you did not exist?
—Jean Anthelme, Brillat-Savarin

Savory Camembert with Wild Mushrooms

Serve this warm, savory Camembert as an elegant appetizer with Melba Crisps (page 137), water crackers or slices of French baguette.

Makes 3 to 4 small servings

1 (8-ounce) wheel Camembert

1 tablespoon Cognac or brandy

1 tablespoon unsalted butter

8 ounces fresh wild mushrooms, trimmed, coarsely chopped

1 shallot, minced

1 clove garlic, minced

1 teaspoon fresh marjoram or thyme

Salt and freshly ground black pepper, to taste

Using a small knife, outline a circle on top of the cheese, 1/2 inch from the edge. Carefully trim under the outlined circle, lifting off the top rind. If cheese comes away with the rind, scrap it off and spread it back onto the cheese. Discard the rind. Brush the top and sides of the cheese with Cognac. In a small skillet over medium heat, melt the butter. Sauté the mushrooms for 1 minute; add the shallot and garlic. Cook until aromatic and mushrooms are tender, 2 minutes. Add the marjoram, salt and pepper. Cool the mushroom mixture; spoon on top of the cheese. (You can wrap and refrigerate the cheese overnight; bring to room temperature before heating.)

Preheat the oven to 350F (175C). Place the cheese on a foil-lined baking sheet. Bake for 4 to 5 minutes, or until soft and warm. Watch carefully; don't overheat. Remove from oven. Place on a serving plate; surround with toast, crackers or bread. Serve at once.

Tofu Dill Dip

Silken tofu has a soft texture that blends beautifully into dips, sauces, custards and ice creams. You can use the type that comes packed in small, sealed boxes and lasts on the shelf up to six months. Additional seasonings might include curry powder, miso paste, grainy mustard or prepared wasabi. Select dippers with an Asian theme; brightly colored chips made with exotic vegetables are available at upscale markets and natural food stores.

Makes about 1½ cups or 6 appetizer servings

1 (about 12-ounces) package silken tofu, drained

½ cup regular or low-fat sour cream

½ cup Fresh Mayonnaise (page 157) or good-quality prepared mayonnaise

2 tablespoons chopped green onion

2 tablespoons chopped cucumbers (without seeds)

½ teaspoon Green-Tea Salt (page 159) or plain sea salt

3 tablespoons fresh minced dill or 1 tablespoon dried dillweed

1 tablespoon fresh lemon juice

FOODS FOR DIPPING

Vegetable chips (taro, yucca, parsnips, sweet potato and beet)

European cucumber, cut in ½-inch strips

Baby carrots

Baby ears of corn

Lotus Crisps (page 64) or ¼-inch-thick slices blanched lotus root

Butterfly Crisps (page 124)

Rice cakes

Snow peas, blanched, chilled in iced water, strings removed

Fried shrimp chips

Combine all the ingredients in a medium bowl. Cover and chill overnight for the best flavor. Serve with a selection of the Foods for Dipping.

White-Bean Fondue with Kasseri and Feta

This unconventional fondue is lighter than the all-cheese variety. Fresh-cooked cannellini beans are always delicious but if you cheat and save time with good-quality canned beans, the food police will not show up at your door! Of Greek origin, kasseri and feta are sheep's milk cheeses and give the fondue a snappy, assertive taste. If it is immersed in brine, rinse the feta to remove excess salt. Enjoy this addictive fondue warm or at room temperature as a party appetizer. Well-chilled, it can be spread on

Crostini or Bruschetta (page 138); serve as a light lunch with sliced hard sausage, olives, wine and a fresh fruit dessert.

Makes 8 appetizer or 4 main-course servings

2 (19-ounce) cans cannellini beans (white kidney beans)

2 cloves garlic, crushed

1 tablespoon red wine vinegar

⅛ teaspoon freshly ground black pepper

1½ teaspoons *each* minced fresh rosemary and sage or 1 teaspoon each dried herbs

¼ cup chopped oil-packed sun-dried tomatoes

2 tablespoons oil from sun-dried tomatoes or olive oil

2 ounces kasseri cheese, shredded (about ⅔ cup)

4 ounces feta cheese, crumbled (about ½ cup)

1 tablespoon minced fresh parsley

FOODS FOR DIPPING

Pita bread, warmed and cut in wedges

Herb Croutons (page 137)

2 bell peppers, (1 yellow and 1 red), cut in wedges

Strips of fresh fennel bulb

Bite-size cubes of smoked sausage

Cucumber slices

Baby carrots

Blanched broccoli florets

Cooked bite-sized lamb meatballs

Homemade bread sticks, broken in pieces

Pour 1 can of the beans with juice into the bowl of a food processor fitted with the steel blade. Add the garlic; process until smooth. Drain the second can of beans; discard juice. Add the beans to the bowl. Process, using 2 or 3 quick bursts of power. The beans should retain some texture; do not puree.

Scrape the mixture into a medium heavy saucepan. Stir in the vinegar, black pepper, herbs, sun-dried tomatoes and oil. Heat over medium-low heat, stirring constantly. When mixture begins to bubble around the edge, add the kasseri cheese in 2 portions; stir until melted. Stir in the feta cheese; do not melt completely.

Pour into a warmed cheese fondue pot. Sprinkle with the parsley. Place over a lighted burner adjusted to keep the fondue warm. Serve at once with any of the Foods for Dipping.

Fondue Neufchâtel

This classic fondue originated in the western, French-speaking region of Switzerland. Two essential cheeses, nutty Emmentaler and creamy Gruyère, are melted in Neuchâtel, a white wine from the area. This fondue might be served in Neufchâtel at the annual Vintage Festival honoring local vineyards, cultivated since the tenth century. Swiss cooks experiment with a variety of different cheeses for fondue; cheese shops might offer a half dozen blends. You can intensify the flavor of this mellow fondue by adding a piquant cheese like Appenzeller, which is rubbed with white wine, spices and salt during the aging process. Swiss mountain cheese, similar to aged Parmesan, will enhance the taste, as well. Alongside, serve the Field Greens with Radicchio Ribbons (page 125) or the Alpine Mushroom Salad (page 122). In Swiss tradition, serve small glasses of kirsch, a complementary white wine or hot peppermint tea.

Makes 5 or 6 servings

Jazz Up Your Basic Cheese Fondue
Add a zesty flavor to a basic cheese fondue by mixing in one or more of the following seasonings. Amounts are approximate; vary them according to your own taste.

2 teaspoons curry paste

Freshly ground black pepper, to taste

Red (cayenne) pepper, to taste

2 or 3 dashes hot pepper sauce

Finely grated sapsago (Swiss green herb cheese), to taste

2 to 3 teaspoons grainy mustard

1 tablespoon of dried fine herbs with 1 tablespoon minced fresh parsley

1 to 2 tablespoons minced, fresh herbs (tarragon, basil, sage, chives, chervil, marjoram)

4 to 6 ounces sautéed, chopped fresh mushrooms

Dried mushrooms, rehydrated

Flavoring powders (see Flavoring Powders, page 220)

1 to 2 tablespoons roasted garlic paste

6 shallots, sliced and caramelized

1 to 2 tablespoons olive paste, such as olivada San Remo

3 anchovy fillets, rinsed, dried and mashed to a paste

1/4 cup brine-cured or spicy-hot olives, pitted, chopped

3 to 4 ounces minced ham, prosciutto, capicola, salami or pepperoni

6 to 8 pieces cooked, crumbled bacon

1/3 cup minced, rehydrated sun-dried tomato

---

16 ounces Swiss Gruyère, shredded (about 5 cups, lightly packed)

8 ounces Emmentaler or aged domestic Swiss, shredded (about 2 1/2 cups, lightly packed)

2 tablespoons cornstarch

1 clove garlic, crushed

1 1/2 to 2 cups Neufchâtel, Fendent, Riesling or other dry white wine

1 tablespoon fresh lemon juice

1/8 teaspoon salt

Freshly ground black pepper, to taste

1/4 teaspoon sweet paprika

1/8 teaspoon freshly grated nutmeg

1 to 2 tablespoons kirsch (cherry brandy), to taste

FOODS FOR DIPPING

Crusty French loaf, cut in 3/4-inch cubes (Wrap half the cubes in paper-thin shreds of prosciutto.)

Herb Croutons (page 137)

Soft bread sticks, broken in pieces

Roosted Potatoes with Fresh Herbs, (page 114) or small, boiled new potatoes, in their jackets

Lightly steamed broccoli and cauliflower florets

Bite-size cubes of cooked, smoked sausage

Large poached shrimp

Blanched asparagus, cut in 2-inch lengths, wrapped in prosciutto strips

Bite-size cubes of honey-baked ham

Asparagus Toasts (page 142)

Combine the cheeses with the cornstarch in a large bowl; set aside. Gather remaining ingredients. Rub the inside of a medium, heavy saucepan with the garlic; drop it into the pan. Add 1½ cups wine and the lemon juice. Heat over medium heat until the wine simmers; discard garlic if desired. Add the blended cheese in handfuls. Stir gently after each addition until the cheese melts and becomes smooth. Stir in the salt, pepper, paprika and nutmeg. Stir until the fondue bubbles gently around the edge of the pot, 1 to 2 minutes; do not boil. If fondue seems too thick, warm the remaining wine and gently whisk in. Stir in the kirsch.

Pour into a warm cheese fondue pot. Place over a lighted burner adjusted to keep the fondue barely bubbling. Serve with several of the Foods for Dipping.

REGIONAL VARIATIONS

These variations feature several outstanding Swiss and French cheeses. Vacherin Fribourgeoise, from the Canton of Fribourg resembles Italian Fontina Val d' Aosta with a bigger flavor. Brie may be the "king of French cheeses" but famed French gastronome, Brillat-Savarin, called aristocratic Beaufort d' Alpage the "Prince of Gruyère." French Gruyère de Comté, produced in Franche-Comté near the Swiss border, is aged longer than Swiss Gruyère and has flavor undertones of hazelnuts and toffee. Gomser is an ultra-creamy cheese used for making râclette. All are exceptional for melting. For ordering information, refer to the Mail-Order Resources (page 225).

Fribourg Fondue Prepare 1 recipe Fondue Neufchâtel, but use 12 ounces Vacherin Fribourgeois and 12 ounces aged Swiss Gruyère. Slightly reduce the amount of wine. This fondue is traditionally served with potatoes instead of bread.

Fondue de Savoyarde Prepare 1 recipe Fondue Neuchâtel, but use 1 pound French or Swiss Emmentaler and 8 ounces French Beaufort cheese.

Fondue de Franche-Comté Prepare 1 recipe Fondue Neuchâtel, but use 1 pound Gruyère de Comté and 8 ounces French or Swiss Emmentaler.

Valais Fondue Prepare 1 recipe Fondue Neuchâtel, but use 1½ pounds râclette cheese or Gomser cheese. Omit the wine and kirsch; substitute 2 cups milk. Rub the inside of the pan with garlic before the milk is added then discard.

Ostschweizer Fondue (East Switzerland-Style Fondue) Prepare 1 recipe Fondue Neuchâtel, but use 8 ounces Vacherin Fribourgeois, 8 ounces Appenzeller and 8 ounces Swiss Emmentaler. Omit wine; substitute about 1½ cups hard cider, sparkling cider or Swedish Pear Sparkler (see page 198).

Dutch Cheese Pot Prepare 1 recipe Fondue Neuchâtel, but use 1 pound Gouda or Edam cheese and 8 ounces Leyden cheese or brick. Use Rhone wine and kummel (caraway liqueur) instead of kirsch. Serve with chunks of dark peasant-style bread, sausage or salami bites and boiled, new potatoes.

Cheddar Melt with Smoked Salmon

Salmon is a good source of omega-3 fatty acids, which provide heart-healthy benefits. Select a flavorful, aged cheddar cheese for this recipe. On occasion, I use British Cotswold cheese, a delicious Double Gloucester with onion and chives. If you use Cotswold, omit the chives called for below. Any chilled leftovers makes a delicious spread; bring it out of the refrigerator 20 minutes before serving.

Makes about 2¹/₂ cups or 8 appetizer servings

1 (3-ounce) package cream cheese, softened

1 cup sour cream

12 ounces sharp cheddar, shredded (about 3 cups, lightly packed)

4 teaspoons snipped chives

1 teaspoon whole-grain mustard

1 teaspoon Worcestershire sauce

4 to 5 ounces good-quality, thin-sliced smoked salmon, chopped

FOODS FOR DIPPING

Crusty French loaf, cut in ¾-inch cubes

Herb Croutons (page 137)

Melba Crisps (page 137)

Oven-roasted, small, new potatoes

In a 2-quart saucepan, blend the cream cheese and sour cream. Heat the mixture over medium-low heat. Stir in the cheddar cheese in 2 or 3 batches and cook, stirring until melted and smooth; do not allow mixture to simmer or boil. Stir in 3 teaspoons of the chives, the mustard and Worcestershire sauce. Mix in the smoked salmon.

Pour into a warmed cheese fondue pot. Sprinkle with remaining chives. Place over a lighted fondue burner adjusted to keep the dip warm. Serve with Foods for Dipping.

VARIATIONS

Cheddar Melt with Smoked Trout Omit the smoked salmon; substitute 4 to 5 ounces smoked trout with skin removed and flaked. Omit the mustard; add 2 teaspoons prepared horseradish.

Cheddar Melt with Smoked Oysters Omit the smoked salmon; substitute 4 to 5 ounces smoked oysters, mashed with a fork.

Manys the long night I've dreamed of cheese—toasted, mostly.
—Robert Louis Stevenson,
Pirate Ben Gunn in *Treasure Island*

Welsh Cheddar Rabbit

Welsh Rabbit (rarebit) is a British cousin of Swiss fondue. It is a simple dish of melted cheese over toast and tastes splendid made with traditional Red Leicester, Double Gloucester or Cheshire cheese. Or substitute any full-flavored English or American cheddar that suits your taste. Melt the cheese over gentle heat; if necessary, place a protective heat-diffusing pad over the burner. For bread, choose a rustic, hearth-style loaf. The shallot isn't traditional but adds a great flavor.

Accompaniments might include: poached or fried eggs, crisp bacon strips, marinated anchovies, tomato chutney, sautéed mushrooms, gherkin pickles or sliced, ripe tomatoes. Or, sprinkle a little grated Italian Parmesan on top just before broiling. Spoon the rabbit on baked potatoes, potato skins, Swiss rösti, French fries, steamed vegetables, fritatta or grits. Try the novel variation, Mexican Rabbit, over nachos.

Makes 4 or 5 servings

2 tablespoon unsalted butter

1 small shallot or green onion, finely minced

½ to ⅔ cup whipping cream, half and half or light ale

1 teaspoon Worcestershire sauce

2 teaspoons whole-grain mustard

Dash of ground white pepper

1 pound aged cheddar cheese, shredded (about 5 cups, lightly packed)

1 to 2 tablespoons medium-dry sherry (optional)

8 slices bread or 4 large slices bread, cut in half

Preheat the broiler. Melt the butter in a medium saucepan over medium-low heat. Add the shallot; cook 2 minutes to soften. Stir in ½ cup cream, Worcestershire sauce, mustard and white pepper. When bubbles appear around the edge of the cream, add the cheese in handfuls. Gently stir after each addition until the cheese melts and becomes smooth. Move the pan off the heat, as necessary, to prevent overheating. Thin with remaining cream, if desired. Keep sauce warm.

Toast the bread on one side; place on 4 heatproof serving plates, toasted sides down. Spoon the cheese sauce on top. Place under the broiler for 1 to 2 minutes, or until the cheese sauce becomes puffy and begins to brown. Serve with any of the accompaniments mentioned above. Refrigerate leftover sauce; warm over gentle heat.

VARIATIONS

Cheddar-Rabbit Brunch Increase the cream to ¾ cup. If desired, stir in 1 to 2 tablespoons good-quality apple butter or pear butter. Serve in a warmed cheese fondue pot over a lighted burner adjusted to keep the fondue warm. Serve with breakfast foods such as toasted bread cubes, bite-size pieces of toasted English muffins or crisp waffles, smoked sausage bites, cooked sausage balls, fritatta squares and apple or pear wedges.

Blushing Bunny Stir in 1 chopped, seeded, peeled ripe tomato and 1 tablespoon minced fresh basil.

Buck Rabbit (Golden Buck) Top each serving of Welsh Cheddar Rabbit with 1 or 2 poached or fried eggs.

Scottish Rabbit Use a Scottish Cheddar or Dunlop cheese; omit sherry and substitute a good Scotch whisky.

Mexican Rabbit Stir in 2 tablespoons fresh or prepared chunky salsa, ¼ teaspoon ground cumin and 2 tablespoons minced fresh cilantro.

Border Melt

Queso fundido, or "melted cheese," is a Mexican rendition of fondue and râclette. This gringo version calls for Monterey Jack, popular in Tex-Mex and border cooking. Dry Jack is an aged version, tasty as fine Italian grating cheese. I often toss bits of leftover cheese from my refrigerator into the mix: California Teleme, extra-sharp white cheddar, brick, feta or English Stilton. Avoid an excess of mozzarella-type cheeses that stretch in long strings from the pan to your mouth. I make this dish in a large, shallow platter of "heat-and-serve" Mexican pewter. I pass a basket of tortilla chips or soft, fresh tortillas for scooping up the warm cheese.

Makes 6 to 8 appetizer servings

2 poblano chilies, roasted, peeled and seeded (see Cook's Notes below) or 1 (4-ounce) can green chilies

½ pound large shrimp, grilled 2 to 3 minutes, peeled, deveined, or ⅓ pound cooked, crumbled spicy sausage (optional)

10 ounces Monterey Jack cheese or *queso asadero*, shredded (about 3⅛ cups, lightly packed)

2 ounces freshly grated Dry Jack, *queso cotija* or Asiago cheese (½ cup, lightly packed)

1 large clove garlic, finely minced

1 thin green onion, sliced in thin rings

2 tablespoons minced fresh cilantro

¼ cup chunky hot salsa, homemade or prepared

Corn chips or tortillas

Cut the chilies into ¼-inch strips. Cut shrimp into bite-size pieces. Preheat the oven to 350F (175C). Toss the cheeses and garlic together in a medium bowl; spread over the bottom of a shallow oven-proof casserole or a 10-inch glass pie plate. Scatter the chilies, shrimp, green onion, cilantro and salsa evenly over the top.

Bake for 10 minutes, or until the cheese has melted. Serve with chips or tortillas. If desired,

stick colorful chips upright around the edge of the melted cheese.

VARIATION

Omit the shrimp and add cooked baby artichoke hearts, cut in half.

COOK'S NOTES

Roasted Chilies Place large fresh poblano or Anaheim chilies or bell peppers on a baking sheet lined with foil. Place under a hot broiler. When chilies begin to blister and char, turn with tongs until evenly roasted. Remove from the oven; wrap in the foil or cover with a clean cloth towel. After 15 minutes, peel off the skins, remove the cores and scrape out the seeds. Try to avoid rinsing to preserve flavor. Use at once or refrigerate in a covered container for up to 2 days. Grilled outdoors over a hot charcoal fire, the chilies take on a smoky flavor.

Cheese Blossoms

Trimmed and deep-fried, flour tortillas bloom into a bouquet of edible blossoms. Tortillas come in a colorful variety of flavors: chipotle chili, cilantro and tomato. Filled with warm, melted cheese, these pastry shells make an unforgettable party appetizer. For ten pastries, you will need at least 8 ounces of shredded cheese and about ⅔ cup of topping. Try your hand at creating a custom blend or use the Cheese and Topping Combinations.

Makes 10

10 (6-inch) flavored or plain flour tortillas

About 6 cups vegetable oil, for deep-frying

CHEESE AND TOPPING COMBINATIONS

Mexican: *queso asadero, queso cotija,* **cooked chorizo, minced garlic and cilantro leaves**

Dutch: Gouda cheese mashed with caraway seeds, grainy mustard, shallots and Worcestershire sauce, to taste

French: Cubed Camembert, sautéed wild mushrooms and chives

Italian: 4 ounces Gorgonzola mixed with 4 ounces cream cheese, pear chutney and chopped walnuts

Sonoma: chèvre, Parmigiano-Reggiano and chopped fresh rosemary

California: smoked Gouda, strips of grilled barbecue chicken and shredded red onion

Mediterranean: smoked mozzarella, sliced black olives and strips of sun-dried tomato

Spanish: manchego cheese, quince jelly and chopped, toasted almonds

Using kitchen scissors, cut 1-inch-deep, V-shaped points around the edge of each tortilla.

In a wok or deep pot, heat the oil to 350F (175C), or until a 1-inch cube of bread turns brown in 60 seconds. Place a tortilla inside a 6-inch Chinese wire skimmer. Using a 2-ounce metal ladle to hold it in place, lower the tortilla into the hot oil. The sides will curve up slightly into a flower shape. Ladle oil over the tortilla, if not completely submerged. When barely crisp and golden, remove from oil. Do not overcook; tortilla will brown further in the oven. Drain on paper towels. Use tortilla blossoms at once, or cover lightly for up to 4 hours.

To serve, preheat the oven to 350F (175C). If using more than 1 cheese, toss cheeses together in a medium bowl. Spoon 3 generous tablespoons

cheese into each pastry shell. Top each with 1 tablespoon of topping and $1/2$ teaspoon herbs or nuts if used. Bake for 5 minutes, or until cheese melts. Do not over-brown the tortillas. Serve at once. The recipe can be doubled.

Stuffed Cheese Wheel

Sometimes, reinventing the wheel can be fun. Embellish a wheel of Brie or Camembert and stuff it with a thin layer of savory or sweet filling.

Makes 4 to 8 servings

1 (8-ounce) or 1 (1-pound) Brie or Camembert round

FILLING SUGGESTIONS

Mashed triple-cream blue cheese, softened

Olivada (olive paste)

Fruit chutney

Chopped, oil-packed sun-dried tomatoes blended with fresh herbs

Pesto

Oil-cured olives, pitted and chopped

Smoked salmon cream cheese, softened

Dried tart cherries, cranberries or blueberries, macerated with spirits

Plain or spirited preserves (apricot and Armagnac, cranberry and Cointreau or raspberry and framboise)

Cognac, kirsch, rum or a liqueur (optional)

Chopped fresh herbs or nuts, to decorate

Plain crackers or bread, to serve

Preheat the oven to 350F (175C). Line a baking sheet with foil. Using a small knife, trim a circle in

Cheese Scorpions and Bugs Edible cheese scorpions and bugs taste great and will entertain kids of all ages. Serve them in baskets at Mexican parties or for any occasion. Use medium, colorful, round flour tortillas in flavors like chili, tomato or cilantro. Fold a tortilla in half but do not press and break the fold. With a pair of kitchen scissors, starting on the side in which the folded edges meet, trim a design that resembles half of a scorpion or large bug. Begin at the bottom and cut upwards creating an elongated body, then cut out 2 or 3 legs near the middle. Near the top, trim out a small rounded head. When you open the trimmed tortilla, it should resemble a fat three-legged critter. Place the cut tortillas on a large baking sheet and sprinkle the bodies with your favorite cheese or cheese blend. If you wish, use sliced olives for eyes. Place in a preheated 350F (175C) oven. Bake for 4 or 5 minutes, or just until the cheese melts and the tortillas are crisp. These are fun for kids to make using scissors appropriate to the age group. They are an approved, fun activity for adult parties, as well! Make tortilla-bug crackers by sprinkling the bodies with cheese, then placing them in a low oven until the tortillas are dry and crisp. Eat at once or store in an airtight container.

the cheese, 1/2 inch from the edge and 1/2 inch deep. Use the tip of the knife to trim out and lift off the top.

Spread a thin layer of filling inside the cavity. Fit the lid back into place, pressing gently to restore the shape. The cheese can be brushed with Cognac, depending on the flavor of the filling. Place the cheese on the lined baking sheet. Decorate the top with chopped herbs or nuts.

Heat an 8-ounce wheel for 4 to 5 minutes, a 1-pound wheel for 8 to 10 minutes, or until soft and warm. Serve as an appetizer or dessert with crackers or bread. (Cheese can be filled, wrapped and refrigerated 1 day in advance; unwrap and bring to room temperature 1 hour before heating.)

VARIATION

For an elaborate presentation, fit the small, stuffed cheese into an appropriate-size prebaked pastry shell before heating.

Artichoke, Sun-Dried Tomato and Prosciutto Fondue

This hearty fondue is filled with many irresistible flavors found on the Italian antipasto table. Prosciutto is a fine seasoned, salt-cured and air-dried Italian ham. It has a subtle, just-right salty taste with a hint of sweetness. Cut into thin slices, not quite paper-thin. For fondue, it isn't necessary to buy prosciutto di Parma, the finest grade. Stir the prosciutto into the fondue at the very last minute to prevent toughening. Serve this fondue as a party centerpiece. For a special supper include the Alpine Mushroom Salad (page 122) or Cucumbers with Fennel (page 124).

Makes 6 to 8 servings

8 ounces fontina cheese, shredded (about 2½ cups, lightly packed)

8 ounces sharp provolone, shredded (about 2½ cups, lightly packed)

4 ounces freshly grated pecorino Romano or Parmigiano-Reggiano (½ cup)

2 teaspoons cornstarch

1 tablespoon olive oil or oil from sun-dried tomatoes

⅓ cup finely chopped shallots or onion

2 cloves garlic, finely minced

1 (9-ounce) package frozen artichoke hearts, thawed, chopped

½ cup dry white wine

1 tablespoon red wine vinegar

1 cup half and half

1 teaspoon each minced fresh rosemary, basil and thyme

⅓ cup chopped oil-packed, sun-dried tomatoes

3 ounces prosciutto or salami, finely chopped

8 imported black olives, such as kalamata, pitted and chopped

FOODS FOR DIPPING

Crusty French or Italian loaf, cut in ¾-inch cubes

Potato Focaccia (page 139), cut in bite-size squares

Crostini (page 138)

Large, cooked shrimp, peeled and deveined

Cleaned, steamed mussels, served in the shells

Grilled sea scallops

Large, soft bread sticks

Combine the cheeses with the cornstarch in a large bowl; set aside.

Heat the oil in a medium heavy saucepan over medium heat. Cook the shallots for 2 minutes; add the garlic and artichoke hearts. Cook, stirring, for 1 minute; add the wine. Cook until the wine is almost reduced, 3 to 4 minutes. Add the vinegar, half and half and herbs. When the mixture begins to simmer, add the cheese in handfuls. Gently stir after each addition until the cheese melts. Add the sun-dried tomatoes. Cook until fondue begins to bubble around the edge, 3 minutes; do not boil. Stir in the prosciutto.

Pour into a warmed cheese fondue pot. Garnish with olives. Place over a lighted burner adjusted to keep the fondue barely bubbling. Serve with any of the Foods for Dipping.

Fondue au Fromage Blanc with Lemon and Basil

Fromage blanc is a soft, young chèvre (goat cheese) with a delicate, tangy flavor. In this fondue, it is flavored with fresh basil and oil-rich lemon zest for an intense lemon flavor. This fondue doesn't require any real cooking, just a quick warming over gentle heat. For dipping, serve an assortment of bite-size, skewered, fresh vegetables brushed with olive oil and briefly grilled. Serve as an appetizer, an unusual first course or a light lunch.

Makes about 2 cups

8 ounces fromage blanc (1 cup) or other fresh, young goat cheese

¾ to 1 cup half and half

1 tablespoon finely minced shallot

1 tablespoon minced fresh basil or tarragon

1 tablespoon minced fresh Italian parsley

1 clove garlic, finely minced

1 teaspoon freshly grated lemon zest

¼ teaspoon salt

FOODS FOR DIPPING

Skewered vegetable bites, brushed with virgin olive oil, briefly grilled and served on a platter (mushroom caps, pearl onions, sliced Japanese eggplants, 1½-inch lengths of fresh asparagus, zucchini slices, red bell pepper cubes, baby artichoke hearts, parboiled fingerlings or miniature purple or red potatoes)

Yellow or red grape tomatoes

Steamed broccoli or cauliflower florets

Cleaned grilled or poached shrimp

Hearts of palm wrapped in thin slices smoked salmon, cut in 1½-inch pieces

Asparagus Toasts (page 142)

Cooked bite-sized lamb meatballs

Cucumber slices

Place the goat cheese into small bowl. Whisk in ¾ cup half and half, about 2 tablespoons at a time, until smooth and creamy. Stir in the remaining ingredients. Scrape the mixture into a small saucepan; place over medium-low heat. Whisk gently until warm; do not simmer or boil. If the fondue seems too thick, stir in the remaining half and half.

Pour the fondue into a warmed small ceramic fondue pot. Place over a tea light to keep the fondue warm. Serve with any of the Foods for Dipping.

Smoke 'n' Jack Fiesta Fondue

The winning combination of melted Jack, smoky chilies and beer makes this fiesta fare! *Chipotles en adobo* are smoked jalapeño chilies packed in a reddish sauce of vinegar, ground chilies and herbs. They add an addictive, smoky flavor and plenty of heat. Unless you are a graduate from the school of fire-eating, it would be best to start with a single chili and work your way up. One chipotle makes this a peppery "one-alarm" dish with a mild after-burn. Three or more puts it in the "three-alarm" category, worthy of a "melted spoon award."

Makes 8 to 10 appetizer servings or 6 main-course servings

12 ounces Monterey Jack cheese, shredded (about 3¾ cups, lightly packed)

8 ounces manchego cheese or sharp Tillamook cheddar, shredded (about 2½ cups, lightly packed)

3 ounces freshly grated Asiago, Dry Jack or Parmigiano-Reggiano cheese (about ¾ cup)

2 teaspoons all-purpose flour

2 tablespoons virgin olive oil

1 cup chopped onion

1 small red bell pepper, cut in ¼-inch dice

¼ pound well-seasoned lean bulk sausage, such as Jimmy Dean

2 cloves garlic, finely minced

1 teaspoon ground cumin

1 cup flat lager beer

1 to 3 mashed *chipotles en adobo*, plus some of the sauce, depending on desired heat

¼ cup chopped fresh cilantro

FOODS FOR DIPPING

Cowboy Flat Bread (page 138), torn in small pieces

Tortilla chips

Large corn chips

Fresh soft flour tortillas

Whole cherry or grape tomatoes

Combine the cheeses with the flour in a large bowl; set aside.

Heat the oil in a medium heavy saucepan over medium heat. Sauté the onion and bell pepper, stirring often, until softened, 5 minutes. Add the sausage and cook, stirring to break up, until browned. (Drain off fat if needed.) Add the garlic and cumin; cook, stirring, 1 minute. Add the beer. When the mixture begins to simmer, add the cheese in large handfuls. Stir after each addition until the cheese melts. Mix in the chipotles and cilantro. Cook, stirring, until fondue is smooth and just begins to bubble around the edge, 1 to 2 minutes; do not boil.

Pour into a warmed cheese fondue pot. Place over a lighted burner adjusted to keep the fondue barely bubbling. Serve at once with any of the Foods for Dipping.

Brie Fondue en Croustade

In the sixties, French Brie and crackers were *au fais* at trendy wine-and-cheese parties given by the "smart set." Soft-ripened cheeses are even more popular today as creative party-givers serve them topped, sauced, stuffed, wrapped and heated. In this recipe, Brie is melted in a large edible bread container called a *croustade*. The best part is eating the crusty loaf after the cheese has disappeared. In France, Brie was known as the "king's cheese" up until the French Revolution. The name quickly changed to "the king of cheeses," an appellation still well deserved. Explorateur, a luxurious substitute, is an ultra-creamy, triple-crème French cheese.

Makes 6 to 8 appetizer servings

1 (1-lb) round loaf of crusty bread

3 tablespoons unsalted butter, melted

1 large garlic clove, finely minced

1 pound Brie, Camembert or Explorateur, well-chilled, trimmed, cubed

4 large fresh basil leaves, shredded, plus extra for garnish

¼ cup oil-packed, sun-dried tomatoes, drained, chopped

1 to 2 tablespoons oil from sun-dried tomatoes

¼ cup lightly toasted pine nuts

FOODS FOR DIPPING

Crusty French baguette, cut in ½-inch-thick slices

Apple slices

Water crackers

Melba Crisps (page 137)

Preheat the oven to 350F (175C). With a large sharp knife, cut out the center portion of the bread to form a large cavity. Slice and reserve bread trimmings. Combine the butter with half of the garlic; brush the inside and outside of the bread container with the butter mixture. Place on a foil or parchment-lined baking sheet; bake for 5 minutes, or until lightly crisped.

While heating the bread, combine the Brie, shredded basil, remaining garlic, sun-dried tomatoes and oil. Fill the bread container with the Brie mixture; sprinkle the pine nuts over the top. Return to the oven; bake 10 minutes or until cheese melts. Toast the bread trimmings while heating the cheese mixture. Place the croustade on a large platter; surround with desired Foods for Dipping. Garnish with basil. Serve at once.

Fonduta with Asparagus Toasts

At heart, the Piedmontese specialty *fonduta* is a simple cheese sauce. But the traditional garnish of shaved white truffles turns it into an elegant dish with a flourish of Northern Italian sophistication. This lovely recipe comes from my sister, Dee Bradney, who lived in Italy several years with her family. Since fresh truffles are costly, Dee suggests several substitutions. "Include their essence with a few drops of aromatic white truffle oil or add a small amount of grated Parmigiano or Boschetto al Tartufo cheeses that are laced with truffles. Minced, soaked, dried porcini mushrooms add a superb woodsy flavor or try a crushed clove of garlic for a different but tasty result." Embellished or plain, the fonduta will still be delicious! Just don't

overheat the sauce or the eggs and cheese will become grainy.

Makes 4 or 5 servings

Asparagus Toasts (page 142)

3 large egg yolks

1 cup half and half or milk

1 teaspoon all-purpose flour

12 ounces Italian fontina Val d' Aosta, Swiss Gruyère or French Beaufort, shredded (about 3¾ cups, lightly packed)

1 tablespoon unsalted butter

FOODS FOR DIPPING

Cooked artichoke hearts

Crisp, fresh fennel sticks

Zucchini slices

Cherry or grape tomatoes

Lightly steamed whole radishes

About 30 minutes before serving prepare the Asparagus Toasts. Keep toasts warm; slice just before serving.

In the top of a double boiler, whisk the egg yolks, half and half and flour. Place over simmering water. Cook, stirring, until custard thickens slightly and coats a metal spoon, 6 to 7 minutes. Add the cheese in 1 or 2 handfuls. Gently stir after each addition until the cheese is almost melted. Remove double boiler from the heat; stir in the butter. Keep warm over hot water for up to 10 minutes, stirring occasionally.

Spoon the Fonduta into 4 small, warm bowls; place on service plates with Asparagus Toasts and any other Foods for Dipping. Fonduta can be served in a small ceramic fondue pot placed over a tea light; stir the sauce often.

To Use Dried Mushrooms Place 1 ounce (about 1 lightly packed cup) whole or sliced, dried mushrooms in a bowl; cover with 1½ cups boiling water, consommé or wine; soak for 1 hour or until soft. Press out and reserve soaking liquid. Rinse mushrooms to remove gritty soil. Discard any tough stems or parts. Pour the soaking liquid through a fine strainer lined with a coffee filter or paper towel. Mushrooms can be sautéed in 1 tablespoon unsalted butter or olive oil or simmered briefly in broth or soaking liquid to tenderize. Slice or mince, as desired. Mushrooms can be stirred into a fondue or Fonduta. Use leftover soaking liquid to season fondue, sauces and stocks. Freeze leftover soaking stock for further recipes. One ounce dried mushrooms equals about 4 ounces fresh.

Champagne Brunch Fill baked, puff pastry shells with sliced, sautéed wild mushrooms and chunks of cooked lobster or crabmeat. Top each portion with a poached egg and 2 to 3 spoonfuls of warm Fonduta. Garnish with truffle shavings, truffle oil or fresh, snipped chives. Serve with ripe melon slices, raspberries and a glass of Champagne.

Lipateur Cheese Fondue

The vivid flavors in this piquant fondue resemble those in a Hungarian Lipateur cheese blend. Don't be tempted to leave out the anchovies. This "secret ingredient" creates an interesting, complex taste, not the least bit fishy. Mild-tasting Gouda and Jarlsburg pair up in a Dutch-treat arrangement with the spicy seasonings. For another layer of flavor, stir in some grated *parrano*, a tasty, aged Gouda "that thinks it's a Parmesan." Include gherkin pickles on the side and plenty of cold beer or German Riesling wine.

Makes 8 appetizer servings

> **12 ounces Gouda, Edam, Havarti, brick cheese, shredded (about 3¾ cups, lightly packed)**
>
> **8 ounces Jarlsberg or baby Swiss cheese, shredded (about 2½ cups, lightly packed)**
>
> **2 tablespoons unsalted butter**
>
> **½ cup finely chopped onion**
>
> **1 large clove garlic, finely minced**
>
> **1½ teaspoons caraway seeds**
>
> **1 teaspoon hot or mild Hungarian paprika**
>
> **2 tablespoons all-purpose flour**
>
> **1½ cups lager beer**
>
> **1 teaspoon red wine vinegar**
>
> **2 anchovies, minced almost to a paste**
>
> **1 tablespoon whole-grain mustard**
>
> **2 tablespoons pitted, chopped olives**
>
> **1 tablespoon capers, rinsed**
>
> **1 tablespoon minced fresh parsley**
>
> **2 teaspoons minced fresh chives**

FOODS FOR DIPPING

> **Crusty dark peasant bread, cut in ¾-inch cubes**
>
> **Cooked smoked sausages, cut in bite-size cubes**
>
> **Steamed, boiled or roasted new potatoes, cut in halves or quarters**
>
> **Cherry tomatoes**
>
> **Italian salami, cut in bite-size pieces**

Combine the cheeses in a large bowl; set aside.

Melt the butter in a medium, heavy saucepan over medium heat. Sauté the onion and garlic until soft, 2 minutes. Add the caraway seeds, paprika and flour; cook, stirring, 1 minute. Pour in the beer. Cook, stirring, until the mixture simmers and thickens. Reduce the heat. Add the cheese in handfuls. Gently stir after each addition until the cheese melts. Add the vinegar, anchovies, mustard, olives, capers and parsley. Cook, stirring, until fondue begins to bubble around the edge, 2 to 3 minutes; do not boil.

Pour into a warmed cheese fondue pot. Garnish with the chives. Place over a lighted fondue burner adjusted to keep the fondue barely bubbling. Serve with any of the Foods for Dipping.

The best of all physicians is apple pie and cheese.
—Eugene Field

Smoky Cheddar and Bacon Fondue

The tradition of making cheddar cheese came to the New World with the English colonists; soon it became a New England cottage industry. During the American Civil War, Vermont produced most of the nation's cheese. Vermont cheddar is always white, never dyed orange. Use this fondue as a sumptuous smoky cheddar cheese sauce for a knife-and-fork version of a grilled ham sandwich. You can spoon it over crisp popovers filled with scrambled eggs and chives for a special brunch!

Makes 4 to 6 servings

1 pound smoked or plain cheddar cheese, preferably farmhouse-quality, shredded (about 5 cups, lightly packed)

1 slightly rounded tablespoon all-purpose flour

1½ tablespoons unsalted butter

2 shallots or 1 small onion, minced

1 large clove garlic, finely minced

1 cup hard cider, lager beer or sparkling apple cider

1 teaspoon fresh lemon juice

1 to 2 teaspoons grainy mustard, or to taste

6 slices premium bacon, cooked until crisp, chopped

¼ cup minced, re-hydrated sun-dried tomatoes

FOODS FOR DIPPING

Crisp, tart red and green apple wedges

Herb Croutons (page 137)

Pumpernickel, rye or black olive loaf, cut in ¾-inch cubes

Roasted Potatoes with Fresh Herbs (page 114)

Cooked meatballs

Bite-size cubes of ham

Whole, pitted black olives

Blanched broccoli or cauliflower florets

Sturdy chips

Combine the cheese and flour in a large bowl; set aside.

Melt the butter in a medium heavy saucepan over medium heat. Sauté the shallots and garlic for 2 minutes. Pour in the cider. Simmer for 1 minute. Reduce the heat; discard the garlic. Add the cheese in handfuls. Gently stir after each addition until the cheese melts. Add the lemon juice, mustard, bacon and sun-dried tomatoes. Cook, stirring, until fondue begins to bubble around the edge, 1 to 2 minutes; do not boil.

Pour into a warmed cheese fondue pot. Place over a lighted burner adjusted to keep the fondue hot. Serve at once with any of the Foods for Dipping.

COOK'S NOTES

As a special touch, warm chips, crackers and flatbreads to be dipped into the fondue.

Râclette

There's a chill in the air, the fireplace is lit and good friends have arrived to share a meal of râclette. Everyone takes a turn at serving by scraping the oozing, creamy cheese from the half-wheel melting slowly by the warmth of the cozy fire. For convenience, many people use an electric tabletop râclette oven with individual trays for holding the cheese; small amounts of vegetables, fruits, meat or bread might be added, as well. If you don't have a special oven or even a fireplace, you can still prepare râclette. Heat individual portions of cheese in a hot oven on small, heatproof dishes. If you have them, use those oblong, metal steak plates, once trendy for serving sizzling-hot steaks. Their matching heatproof trays are perfect for transporting the hot plates to the table. Arrange your table near the fireplace and place baskets of giant pinecones on the hearth to create a homespun, Alpine-like setting. Good fellowship, a unique meal and a toast to Swiss tradition will create a mood of euphoria that will leave your guests yodeling for more!

Makes 6 servings

1 (3-pound) piece râclette or other melting cheese

Roasted Potatoes with Fresh Herbs (page 114)

Alpine Mushroom Salad (page 122)

Cucumbers with Fresh Dill (page 123)

1½ pounds smoked German or Polish sausages

½ pound air-dried beef, such as Swiss *bundnerfleisch*, Italian *prosciutto crudo*, Spanish *jamon serrano*, Smithfield ham or hard salami, cut in very thin slices

Cornichons or gherkin pickles, as desired

Pickled cocktail onions, as desired

Small shaker or bowl of sweet Hungarian paprika

Freshly ground black pepper, to taste

French baguette, cut in thin slices

Cut cheese into 12 (4-ounce) portions; place 1 piece into each of 6 heatproof dishes. Cover lightly until needed.

Prepare Roasted Potatoes with Fresh Herbs, Alpine Mushroom Salad and Cucumbers with Fresh Dill. Pan-fry the sausages; keep warm. Arrange the cold cuts on platters. Put cornichons and onions separately in small bowls. Arrange the baguette in a basket.

Preheat the oven to 450F (232C). Arrange all the foods on the table. Place dishes of cheese in the hot oven; watch carefully. When cheese softens and begins to pool, use a hot pad to remove dishes from the oven; place on larger plates. Serve at once. Spread warm cheese over portions of the potatoes and bread. Pass around the accompaniments.

Swiss Râclette

- Heat small portions of cheese; repeat the process for second helpings. Other cheeses to melt for Swiss râclette include: Gomser, Bagnes, fontina, Gruyère, young Teleme or Don Olivo, a new semisoft cheese with black olives from Switzerland.
- If carefully watched, the cheese can be heated under a broiler. Use a tabletop toaster oven; shape small pans from heavy-duty aluminum foil.
- Provide 7 to 8 ounces of cheese for each person. The amount of cheese needed can vary, depending on everyone's appetite. Quality cheese is rich and satisfying; one serving may be just enough.
- Scrape the cheese's outer rind rather than cutting it off for a delicious, crusty exterior.
- Râclette's flavor intensifies when heated but don't melt it completely or the fat will ooze and the texture will turn grainy.
- If you prefer, serve 2½ pounds small, new potatoes, boiled in their jackets. Serve cooked potatoes in a bowl lined with a cloth napkin; wrap to keep warm.
- The amount of food can easily be increased or decreased, depending on the number of diners.
- If all the cheese is not used, wrap it in plastic wrap; refrigerate for another use.
- The Swiss enjoy beer, small glasses of kirsch or hot peppermint tea, a favorite beverage that stimulates digestion. Or serve a light wine: Swiss Neufchâtel Blanc, California Fumé Blanc, a crisp Oregon Pinot Gris or rosé. Serve a light dessert such as fruit sorbet, ice cream or skewered, seasonal fruits with Raspberry Cabernet Sauce (page 156).

VARIATIONS:
RÂCLETTE FOR ALL SEASONS

Spring Râclette: Melt râclette over tender, young steamed vegetables: asparagus, baby carrots, fava beans, new potatoes, spring onions with chervil or marjoram.

Summer Râclette: Melt râclette over grilled, sliced eggplants, tomatoes and red peppers brushed with basil, sage or thyme-flavored oils.

Autumn Râclette: Melt râclette over sautéed wild mushrooms and shallots, sliced baked pears with rosemary, or rösti (boiled, grated, fried potato cake).

Winter Râclette: Melt râclette over fried veal cutlets, grilled sausages, fennel gratin.

FROM MY RECIPE BOX

Quick Strawberry Dip For the ultimate dip, wrap large, plump fresh strawberries in paper-thin narrow strips of prosciutto or Smithfield ham. Serve on a platter surrounding a small bowl of quality balsamic vinegar seasoned with a dash of freshly ground black pepper.

Vidalia Onion and Blue-Cheese Fondue with Cognac

Caramelized Vidalia onions and tangy Maytag or Clemson blue cheese add a delicious touch of Americana to this fondue. It is also delicious made with British Stilton. Vidalia onions, the pride of Georgia, were named Georgia's official state vegetable in 1990. If they are not available at your markets, substitute any other mild, sweet onion like the Walla Walla, Maui or sweet Oso onions from Chile, available here January through March.

Makes 4 to 6 servings

12 ounces fontina or Emmentaler cheese, shredded (3¾ cups, lightly packed)

3 ounces finely grated pecorino Romano, Parmigiano-Reggiano or Asiago cheese (¾ cup, lightly packed)

2 teaspoons cornstarch

1 tablespoon unsalted butter

1 tablespoon extra-virgin olive oil

1 pound Vidalia or other sweet onions, peeled, quartered, thinly sliced

1½ cups dry white wine or Basic Chicken Stock (page 176)

1 tablespoon white wine vinegar

2 teaspoons fresh thyme leaves or fresh marjoram

½ cup crumbled blue cheese (Maytag blue, Clemson blue or Saga blue)

2 tablespoons Cognac or white port

FOODS FOR DIPPING

Crusty French loaf, cut in ¾-inch cubes

Herb Croutons (page 137)

Grilled beef tenderloin, cut in bite-size cubes

Small mushroom caps, wiped clean

Roasted Fingerling potatoes or other small potatoes

Combine the fontina and pecorino cheeses with the cornstarch in a large bowl; set aside.

In a medium, heavy saucepan, melt butter with the oil over low heat. Add the onions; cover and cook 20 minutes to soften, stirring occasionally. Remove the lid; cook 10 minutes more. Raise heat to medium. Add ½ cup of the wine. Cook until liquid is reduced and onions are golden brown, 2 to 3 minutes. Add the remaining wine, vinegar and thyme. When hot, add the cheese mixture in handfuls. Gently stir after each addition until the cheese melts. Add half of the blue cheese. Cook until the fondue begins to bubble around the edge, 1 to 2 minutes; do not boil.

Pour into a warmed cheese fondue pot. Finely crumble the remaining blue cheese; sprinkle on top. Place over a lighted burner adjusted to keep the fondue barely bubbling. Serve with any of the Foods for Dipping.

The kettle soon began to boil, and meanwhile the old man held a large piece of cheese on a long iron fork over the fire, turning it round and round till it was toasted a nice golden yellow color on each side.

—Johanna Spyri, *Heidi*

Fondue in a Box In the autumn, Swiss cows produce less milk and soft cheese production begins. Buttery-rich Vacherin Mont d'Or is produced in the Canton of Vaud, near the French border. Some of its special flavor comes from the spruce cork used for its packing box. Mont d'Or is served as fondue but in a special presentation. Still in the box, a hole is cut in the center of the cheese and filled with dry white wine. Wrapped securely in foil, the box serves as a "baking container" for the cheese; out of the oven, it becomes a serving dish. Bread, potatoes and charcuterie (particularly delicatessen-style pork products) are served on the side. Mont d'Or is available from Specialty Cheese Stores (page 225) in the fall.

Duplicate this dish with Brie or Camembert. Remove the box label and wrapping from the cheese. Using a small knife, outline a circle on top of the cheese, ½ inch from the edge. Trim off the top rind. Place cheese back into the box; top with the lid. Place on a baking sheet.

In a preheated 350F (175C) oven, heat an 8-ounce wheel 4 to 5 minutes; 1 pound wheel 8 to 10 minutes, or until soft and warm. Serve at once with French bread or Melba Crisps (page 137). California Teleme can be ripened for 2 months in the refrigerator; the flavor will intensify and the texture will become ultra-soft and runny. To serve, simply slice off the darkened top rind and serve at room temperature with spoons or chunks of crusty bread for scooping up the cheese.

Sun-Dried Tomato Fondue

This fondue features many of the sunny flavors of Southern Italy. Tomatoes have a red pigment called lycopene, a strong antioxidant, which may inhibit the growth of several types of cancer cells. Cooked in a small amount of fat, the cell walls of the tomatoes break down, releasing more of the beneficial lycopene. Serve this tomato-rich fondue in good health with the Alpine Mushroom Salad (page 122). Leftover fondue can be stirred into a saucepan of crumbled, sautéed Italian sausage then served with pasta.

Makes 5 cups sauce or 4 or 5 servings

2 tablespoons extra-virgin olive oil

1 medium onion, chopped (about ½ pound)

½ red bell pepper, chopped

3 garlic cloves, minced

1 (28-ounce) can diced tomatoes with juices

½ cup rehydrated sun-dried tomatoes, chopped

1 cup Clamato juice, regular tomato juice or water

2 tablespoons tomato paste mixed with ½ cup dry red or white wine or water

¼ teaspoon salt, or to taste

¼ teaspoon coarsely ground black pepper

1 ounce grated pecorino Romano, Asiago or Mimolette (about ¼ cup)

5 or 6 fresh basil leaves, shredded

2 tablespoons chopped brine-packed pitted black olives

FOODS FOR DIPPING

Baby mozzarella balls

Cooked bite-sized beef or sausage meatballs

Sautéed whole mushroom caps

Provolone cheese, at room temperature, cut in 1-inch cubes

Soft breadsticks

Potato Focaccia (page 139), cut in bite-size squares

Whole, large pitted olives

Grilled, spicy Italian sausages, cut in bite-size pieces

Cooked tortellini

Heat the olive oil in a medium saucepan. Sauté the onion, bell pepper and garlic on medium-low heat, stirring occasionally, until soft, about 10 minutes. Add the canned tomatoes, sun-dried tomatoes, juice, tomato paste and wine. Simmer the mixture, stirring occasionally, over low heat for 20 to 25 minutes.

Pour the sauce into a food processor bowl fitted with the steel blade. Process, in bursts, 30 seconds or until fairly smooth. For a smoother texture, process in a blender. (The blended sauce still retains a pleasant, rustic texture.)

Pour sauce back into the pot; add salt and pepper. Stir in the cheese, basil and black olives. Warm over low heat; pour into a warm cheese or meat fondue pot. Place over a lighted burner adjusted to keep the fondue warm. Serve at once with any of the Foods for Dipping. (The sauce can be made 1 to 2 days ahead and refrigerated.)

Broth-Based Fondues

Switzerland, the birthplace of fondue, has a diverse cuisine that is heavily influenced by the border countries of Italy, Germany and France. The culinary traditions of these countries are woven into the pattern of everyday life, touching every village, city and town. As a result, Switzerland is the domicile of three exceptional cuisines; each represented in a different Swiss region and constituting a different culture.

Switzerland has never had a royal court cuisine; food is deeply connected to the people. The French-influenced cheese fondue (*fondue au fromage*) is a centuries-old dish that was born of circumstance and necessity. Broth-based fondues are a modern spin-off, ingeniously devised as a lighter and healthier version.

Swiss cooks are savvy about many ethnic cuisines. The method for preparing broth fondues was adapted from the ancient Chinese technique of hot-pot cooking. Judiciously paired with quality ingredients, the Swiss infused fresh, new flavors into their signature pot of fondue. Fondue Chinoise is the classic example of a broth fondue. The recipe features paper-thin slices of tender, succulent beef simmered in a flavorful homemade stock.

A broth fondue can be made with a single type of meat or seafood or a crazy quilt of seafood, meats and vegetables. Serve your favorite dipping sauces on the side. For a surf-and-turf combination, pair lobster or shrimp with tender cubes of beef tenderloin; round out the meal with two or three fresh vegetables. For a vegetarian version, cook meaty portobello mushrooms with other vegetables in a flavorful court bouillon. Less common but delicious meat versions include the Lamb Fondue with Sun-Dried Tomato and Rosemary Mayonnaise and Venison Fondue with Dried Cherry and Port Sauce. The French Quarter Fondue includes a potpourri of sausages, chicken, oysters and shrimps. Follow the Chinese culinary philosophy and choose ingredients that are very fresh; cook them briefly to retain their natural tastes and textures.

A well-seasoned beef or chicken stock, broth, court bouillon or fish stock can be used for the cooking liquid. The foods absorb the taste of the piquant cooking liquid as they simmer in the fondue pot. In turn, the cooking liquid becomes greatly enriched. The Bouillabaisse Fondue features a golden saffron-spiced chicken stock that is infused with another layer of flavor from the medley of seafood cooked in the pot. At the end of the meal, the tasty broth can be ladled into small cups and passed for sipping. A small amount of cooked rice or noodles can be added to stretch the broth.

For a *fondue de vin*, the cooking liquid is infused with wine, which adds a depth of flavor and character. When selecting a wine, choose one that you enjoy drinking. A good deal of the alcohol evaporates in cooking, leaving behind a concentrated flavor. It isn't necessary to select the most expensive wine, but a mediocre wine will result in a mediocre dish. For a lively flavor, heat the wine and cooking liquid in the fondue pot shortly before you begin cooking. Avoid cooking wines; they may be high in sodium and are inferior for drinking or cooking.

You can rely on color-coding to choose the right wine. A young, dry red wine is a good choice for a hearty beef stock or broth. For a taste of Switzerland, try a Swiss Pinot Noir or Dôle des Monts, a light, blended wine comprised of Pinot Noir and Gamay. For a lighter chicken stock or broth, court bouillon or fish stock, select a dry, white wine. Try a Swiss Neuchâtel, pinot blanc or a quality, dry French vermouth.

Wine can improve the taste of a canned stock, broth or bouillon. Make a quick fondue broth by fortifying canned chicken broth with a small amount of canned beef stock or bouillon, then simmering the blend with chopped vegetables and some dry white wine. Knorr brand bouillon cubes from Unilever Bestfoods in Holland come in a variety of excellent European and Asian flavors. They can be used as a quick stock for fondues and hot pots. Add to canned or homemade stocks for extra enrichment. These bouillon cubes are available in some ethnic markets. Several flavorful varieties are made and sold throughout the United States.

When adding wine, taste as you go. One-half cup might be just enough or you might prefer equal parts wine and stock. If you don't use alcohol but want to add the flavor, try adding some Wolffer Estate verjus, an unfermented, nonalcoholic juice from grapes picked at half ripeness. Refer to the Stock chapter (page 173) for a variety of recipes for stocks and broths.

Inland waterways and surrounding seas provide limitless opportunities for South Carolina "Sandlappers" to socialize, eat and throw parties. Seafood social clubs, crabbing parties and seafood boils are some of the more popular entertainments. South Carolina Beaufort Stew is quintessential Lowcountry Creole cuisine. Just as the Swiss consider fondue to be their national dish, South Carolinians have declared Beaufort Stew the "unofficial" seafood dish of South Carolina. No one knows the exact spot, but the dish originated around the Beaufort area or St. Helena Island.

Beaufort Stew is also known by the names Lowcountry Stew and Frogmore Stew; Frogmore being one of the communities of St. Helena Island. The dish is said to have been the invention of local shrimpers who created it from items on hand. Diners gather around the table to feast on a mouthwatering pile of seafood, smoked sausage, corn on the cob and potatoes. The food is served in a communal, down-home, eat-with-your-elbows-on-the-table atmosphere. Don't worry about leftovers; they are well seasoned and taste just as good the second day. You can even recycle them into a variety of other tasty dishes. The flavorful broth can be strained, defatted and added to soups or stews.

Foods cooked in a broth fondue are dipped into a variety of terrific, easy sauces that lend a contrasting burst of flavor. The complimentary sauces can give the fondue an ethnic profile, offering the diners a variety of exciting new tastes to dip into. The Pork Fondue with Guacamole Sauce also features the Mexican-influenced Black Bean Sauce and a Smoky Tomato Salsa. You can choose to serve one favorite sauce or four or five, depending on your time and budget. Most of the dipping sauces in this book are interchangeable; pair them with a thought to flavors, textures and colors.

SEAFOOD SAVVY

Mollusks (clams, oysters, scallops and mussels) and crustaceans (shrimp, crab and lobster) are two of the most popular additions to broth fondue and hot pot. When mollusks are purchased in the shell, they should be alive. The shells may open naturally but should close tightly when tapped. Discard any that do not respond; they are dead.

Mussels and clams live in sandy waters and take in sand as they feed. To purge them, soak in cold water with a little salt and oatmeal or flour for several hours. Scrub the shells well after soaking. Littleneck clams, among the smallest type, are tender and have a sweet flavor. You will get 7 to 10 clams per pound. Medium-size cherrystone clams will yield 5 to 7 per pound.

Freshly shucked scallops and oysters should have a clean, sea-breeze odor. Scallops can overcook quickly; remove them from the broth when they turn white, opaque and become firm. A clear milky or light grayish liquid surrounds freshly shucked oysters; rinse in cool water before use. Oysters cook in about 3 minutes; when done, the edges begin to curl. When simmered in the shell, cook mussels and clams two to three minutes after they open. Live lobsters curl their tails tightly beneath them when handled; when cooked, they turn bright red.

Shelled shrimp cook in two to three minutes; when done they turn pink and become firm. If purchased frozen, shellfish should be packed in tight, moisture-proof containers.

Fondue Chinoise

This Asian-influenced beef fondue is inspired by a favorite fondue of Chef Josef Ruckstuhl and his wife Monika. They make it often for family and friends when not busy with their popular Swiss pastry shop in Columbia, South Carolina. Chef Ruckstuhl is from Klosters, Graubünden, Switzerland. He says this fondue is quite popular with the Swiss and a great way to bring people together for two or three hours of good food and great conversation. Monika, also Swiss, shared ideas for three delicious, easy sauces and for a fourth suggests mixing anchovy paste into homemade mayonnaise. She suggests side dishes like the Celery Root Rémoulade (page 125), crusty rools and plain potato chips, popular in Switzerland with beef fondue. I like to serve the Alpine Mushroom Salad (page 122). The beef can be partially frozen for easy slicing.

Makes 6 servings

5 cups Basic Beef Stock (page 178) or Enriched Beef Consommé (page 180), seasoned, to taste

Parsley and Cognac Mayonnaise (page 159)

Bull's-eye Sauce (page 159)

Zesty Tomato Sauce (page 159)

2 pounds beef tenderloin, cut into thin slices between 1/8 inch and 1/4 inch thick

Salt and freshly ground black pepper, to taste

Prepare the stock and sauces.

Cut each slice of beef in half or into thirds, if large. For each diner, arrange a portion of the beef on a small plate. Place on the table with the dinner plates, forks, dipping sauces and any side dishes.

In the kitchen, pour $3^1/_2$ cups of broth into a metal or porcelain enameled fondue pot. Place over medium-high heat. When the stock comes to a boil, carry the fondue pot to the table and place over a lit burner adjusted to the highest setting. Keep the remaining broth warm on low heat to replenish the pot.

Diners should use fondue forks to swish each piece of beef through the broth for a few seconds until it loses its pink color. Use a regular fork for dipping and eating.

South Carolina Beaufort Stew

Each fall when the shrimp are a decent size, Jodi and Don Phillips head to the Ace Basin in South Carolina's Lowcountry for a week of serious shrimping and fun. Everyone reaps the rewards when the Phillips cook up a huge pot of Beaufort Stew. The concoction of shrimp, vegetables and sausage chunks is served at the table in a huge communal bowl from which diners continually replenish their plates. Serve this scaled-down version with Hot and Spicy Thai Coleslaw (page 128), crusty bread, cold tea and beer. Some cooks like to add a few bottles of beer to the stockpot. When you add the shrimp, stay close to the pot to prevent overcooking. One or more types of seafood can be included such as partially cleaned hard-shelled blue crabs, clams,

oysters, crawfish and lobsters. A larger pot and extra water may be necessary to accommodate the additional seafood.

Makes 6 servings

Cocktail Sauce (page 161)

Dill Butter (page 160)

Tartar Sauce (page 159)

1 (3-ounce) bag Zatarain's Crawfish, Shrimp and Crab Boil Seasoning, or other similar seasoning

2 large onions, peeled and cut in half

4 large cloves garlic, mashed

2 red bell peppers, cut in large cubes

2 ribs celery, cut in 1-inch pieces

2½ pounds small, new potatoes, scrubbed

Salt and coarsely ground black pepper, to taste

8 ears fresh corn, shucked, broken in 2 or 3 pieces

2 pounds spicy smoked sausage links, cut in 2-inch pieces

3 pounds large shrimp, in the shell, rinsed

Butter for corn, at room temperature

Hot pepper sauce, to taste

Prepare the Cocktail Sauce, Dill Butter and Tartar Sauce.

Pour $1^1/_2$ gallons water into a 3-gallon stockpot. Cut a slit halfway down one side of the seasoning bag. Add the seasoning bag, onions, garlic, bell peppers and celery to the water. Bring to a boil and simmer for 10 minutes. Add the potatoes; simmer for 8 minutes. Raise the heat slightly; season the water with salt and pepper. Add the corn and sausage; cook on a low boil until potatoes and corn are tender, 10 minutes. (Potatoes can be removed at any time if in danger of overcooking.) Add the shrimp; press under the liquid. Cook 3 to 5 minutes. Turn off heat.

With a large slotted spoon, scoop ingredients, coated with some of the spices, onto one or two large serving platters. Place on the table with serving plates, forks, dipping sauces, butter for corn, hot sauce and any side dishes. Diners can help themselves. Provide large, empty bowls to hold the discarded shrimp shells and corn cobs.

COOK'S NOTES

Lemon Wraps When serving seafood, Jody Phillips uses pinking scissors to cut circles from bright-yellow net produce bags. She puts a lemon half, cut side down, on each circle. The edges are pulled up around the lemon, gathered at the top then tied with yellow ribbons. The net holds the seeds in place when the lemon halves are squeezed on seafood.

FROM MY RECIPE BOX

Beaufort Salad Any leftover Beaufort Stew can be recycled the next day. In a large bowl, combine leftover cleaned, chopped shrimp, diced potatoes, diced sausage, and corn kernels cut from the cobs. Mix in sliced green onions, strips of oil-packed sun-dried tomatoes and diced pieces of Emmentaler or provolone cheese. Dress with Thyme Vinaigrette (page 126). Spoon over crisp butter lettuce leaves; drizzle with additional dressing. Serve with Melba Crisps (page 137).

Lamb Fondue with Sun-Dried Tomato and Rosemary Mayonnaise

Sheep came to the New World with Columbus on his second voyage in 1493. Eventually, the Spanish established a breeding center in St. Augustine, Florida. Leg of lamb is a tender cut for fondue, especially the sirloin end. In this recipe, strips of lamb and vegetables are simmered in a golden, aromatic saffron broth.

Makes 4 to 6 servings

5 cups Saffron Chicken Broth (page 178), or Basic Chicken Stock (page 176)

Sun-Dried Tomato and Rosemary Mayonnaise (page 159)

Basil Dijon Aïoli (page 158)

Peppered Peanut Sauce (page 151)

2 pounds boneless leg of lamb, cut into very thin 2-inch strips or 3/4-inch cubes

Freshly ground black pepper, to taste

3 leaves from sprigs of fresh rosemary or thyme

5 small long Asian eggplants, cut in 1/4-inch-thick diagonal slices

2 red bell peppers, cut in 1-inch squares

5 zucchini, cut in 1/4-inch-thick diagonal slices

Prepare the Saffron Chicken Broth, Sun-Dried Tomato and Rosemary Mayonnaise, Basil Dijon Aïoli and Peppered Peanut Sauce.

For each diner, arrange a portion of lamb and vegetables on a small plate. Season each portion with rosemary and black pepper. Place the plates, forks, dipping sauces and any side dishes on the table.

In the kitchen, pour 3 1/2 cups of broth into a metal or porcelain enameled fondue pot. Place over medium-high heat. When the broth comes to a boil, carry the fondue pot to the table and place over a lit burner adjusted to the highest setting. Keep the remaining broth warm on low heat to replenish the pot.

Diners should use fondue forks to spear and cook the lamb and vegetables in the simmering broth. Cook lamb to the desired degree of doneness. Use a regular fork for dipping and eating.

Lobster Pot Fondue with Kiwi-Mango Salsa

Native Australian cuisine includes exotic dishes like emu curry, crocodile spring rolls and kangaroo carpaccio prepared with ingredients like wattle seeds, eucalyptus oil and bush tomatoes. Australian cooks serve up some of the finest seafood in the world. This fondue calls for several favorites: lobster, shrimp and scallops served with kiwi, mango and macadamia-nut salsa. The Australian vocabulary is as colorful as the cuisine. Spiny lobsters are referred to as Balmain "bugs." To enjoy a taste of Australian "bugs" and salsa, be sure and give this recipe a "Captain Cook" or very close look!

Makes 4 servings

5 cups Fish Stock (page 181), Court Bouillon (page 181), or Saffron Chicken Broth (page 178)

Kiwi-Mango Salsa (page 171)

Dill Butter (page 160)

Apple and Curry Cream (page 158)

Cocktail Sauce (page 161)

4 (about 6-ounces) fresh or frozen lobster tails, if frozen, thawed in the refrigerator

Fresh herbs of choice, baby greens or shredded cabbage

Lemon slices

½ pound scallops, cut in half horizontally

½ pound squid, cleaned, cut into ¼-inch rings

½ pound large shrimp, peeled, deveined

Prepare the Fish Stock, Kiwi-Mango Salsa, Dill Butter, Apple and Curry Cream and Cocktail Sauce.

Place a sharp, thin knife between the undershell and the meat of a lobster tail; cut around the edges of the undershell and hard upper shell then lift it off. Or use sturdy kitchen scissors. Using the tip of the knife, carefully remove the lobster meat; cut it into bite-size chunks. Prepare remaining lobsters; chill the meat until served. Drop the shells into boiling water to turn bright red; rinse in cold water and chill until needed.

To serve, make a nest of fresh herbs inside each lobster shell. Arrange the lobster meat back in the shells; garnish with lemon slices. For each diner, arrange a lobster tail and a portion of the other seafood on a small plate. Place on the table along with serving plates, forks, sauces and any side dishes. In the kitchen, pour 3½ cups of stock into a metal or porcelain enameled fondue pot. Place over medium-high heat. When the stock comes to a boil, carry the fondue pot to the table and place over a lit burner adjusted to the highest setting. Keep the remaining broth warm on low heat to replenish the pot.

Diners should use fondue forks to spear and cook each piece of seafood in the simmering stock 1 to 1½ minutes. Use a regular fork for dipping and eating.

French Quarter Fondue

The cuisine of New Orleans began with the citified Creoles who combined French techniques with native ingredients used by the Indians, Spanish and black cooks in the area. At the same time, the country Cajuns threw their own culinary talent into the mix, resulting in the slow convergence of two of America's oldest and most developed regional cuisines. Even Chef Paul Prudhomme says it's becoming hard to define the characteristics that set them apart. One sure thing is that Louisiana cooks produce some of the finest food in the country. In the spirit of New Orleans, celebrate Mardi Gras with this "mixed grill" fondue. If you want to add a little Cajun spice to your party, include some crawfish tail meat, breast of game birds or white alligator jaw meat! Add a starch from the side-dish chapter and the Creole Cucumber Salad (page 157), or a lettuce salad with the Green Onion Dressing (page 122). The shrimp are especially good wrapped in strips of half-cooked lean bacon. Don't use raw bacon; when those shrimp hit the fat, it will sound like the Battle of 1812.

Makes 6 servings

4 to 6 cups Basic Chicken Stock (page 176)

Creole Honey-Mustard Sauce (page 171)

Sauce Rémoulade (page 159)

Mignonette Sauce (page 165)

1 pound spicy smoked sausage, cut into bite-size pieces

1 pound boneless chicken breasts, cut in 3/4-inch cubes

1 pound large shrimp, peeled and deveined

12 shucked oysters

Prepare the Basic Chicken Stock, Creole Honey-Mustard Sauce, Sauce Rémoulade and Mignonette Sauce.

For each diner, arrange a portion of the sausage, chicken, shrimp and 2 oysters on a small plate. Place on the table along with the dinner plates, forks, dipping sauces and any side dishes. In the kitchen, pour 3 1/2 cups of stock into a metal or porcelain enameled fondue pot. Place over medium-high heat.

When the stock comes to a boil, carry the fondue pot to the table and place over a lit burner adjusted to the highest setting. Keep the remaining broth warm on low heat to replenish the pot. Diners should use fondue forks to spear and cook the meats and seafood in the simmering stock. Use a regular fork for dipping and eating.

Veal Fondue with Cremini Mushrooms

A cremini or "brown" mushroom is a baby portobello mushroom. The caps are about 2 inches wide; mature portobello caps can measure up to 6 inches wide. Always rinse mushrooms gently and briefly in cool water just before they are used; drain and pat dry. Veal is very young beef and low in fat. Simmered briefly in a fondue broth, it stays tender and tastes especially flavorful. At the end of the meal, serve the rich broth in small demitasse cups.

Makes 4 to 6 servings

5 cups Basic Beef Stock (page 178), or Enriched Beef Consommé (page 180)

Zesty Tomato Sauce (page 159)

Beef and Wine Dipping Broth (page 172)

Creamy Artichoke and Parmesan Sauce (page 167)

2 pounds veal top or bottom round, cut in thin scaloppine slices, less than 1/4 inch thick (about 12 slices), each cut in 2 to 3 pieces

1 (12-ounce) package refrigerated herb-chicken, portobello or cheese-filled tortellini, cooked half the suggested time on the package, rinsed in cool water, drained

8 ounces fresh cremini mushrooms or shiitaki mushrooms (or a blend), sliced 1/3-inch thick

Prepare the Basic Beef Stock, Zesty Tomato Sauce, Beef and Wine Dipping Broth, and Creamy Artichoke and Parmesan Sauce.

For each diner, arrange a portion of the veal, tortellini and mushrooms on a small plate. Place on the table along with dinner plates, forks, sauces and any side dishes.

In the kitchen, pour 3 1/2 cups of stock into a metal or porcelain enameled fondue pot. Place over medium-high heat. When the stock comes to a boil, carry the fondue pot to the table and place over a lit burner adjusted to the highest setting. Keep the remaining broth warm on low heat to replenish the pot.

Diners should use fondue forks to spear and cook the veal, pasta and mushrooms in the simmering stock. Use a regular fork for dipping and eating.

Peruvian Sea Bass with Inca-Gold Sauce

Tomatoes, corn, chilies, potatoes, chocolate and beans are foods native to South America. Peru, once part of the vast Inca Empire, has a colorful Creole cuisine that often calls for corvina, a pacific sea bass.

Serve this fondue with Roasted Potatoes with Fresh Herbs (page 114), using small Peruvian blue potatoes and a green salad with hearts of palm. The Sesame-Miso Sauce lends an Asian touch reflecting the large influx of Japanese immigrants to Peru.

Makes 4 to 6 servings

5 cups Fish Stock (page 181) or Court Bouillion (page 181)

Inca-Gold Sauce (page 170)

Sesame-Miso Sauce (page 166)

Smoky Tomato Salsa (page 155)

2 pounds pacific sea bass or other white, firm fish like swordfish or cod

1 large red bell pepper, cut in wide strips

1 medium carrot, cut in thin diagonal slices

6 green onions, trimmed, cut in 2-inch pieces

Fresh cilantro sprigs

Prepare the Fish Stock, Inca-Gold Sauce, Sesame-Miso Sauce and Smoky Tomato Salsa.

For each diner, arrange a portion of the fish, bell pepper, carrot and green onion on a small plate. Garnish with cilantro. Place on the table along with dinner plates, forks, sauces and any side dishes.

In the kitchen, pour 3 1/2 cups of stock into a metal or porcelain enameled fondue pot. Place over medium-high heat. When the stock comes to a boil, carry the fondue pot to the table and place over a lit burner adjusted to the highest setting. Keep the remaining broth warm on low heat to replenish the pot. Add some of the cilantro sprigs to the stock.

Diners should use fondue fork to spear and cook the fish, in the simmering stock. Use a regular fork for dipping and eating.

Venison Fondue with Dried Cherry and Port Sauce

In America, almost any food can end up in a fondue pot. One innovative West Coast restaurant offers fondues of alligator, ostrich, wild boar and buffalo meat. Quality, free-range venison doesn't taste overly gamy and can hint of wild herbs from the deer's natural habitat. Or try antelope, which has a rich, delicate flavor. Simmered in fondue broth, lean game meat stays moist and tastes especially flavorful. Be sure to buy game that has been denuded, or had the tough silver skin removed. Serve this fondue with Pecan Rice with Sausage and Sage (page 113) and Orange-Caraway Beets with Spinach (page 127). Refer to the Mail-Order Resources (page 225) for sources of fine game.

Makes 4 to 6 servings

Basic Beef Stock (page 178) or Basic Chicken Stock (page 176)

Dried Cherry and Port Sauce (page 164)

Parsley and Cognac Mayonnaise (page 159)

Shoyu and Ginger Steak Sauce (page 152)

About 2 pounds boneless leg of venison or loin or boneless antelope loin, cut in ³/₄-inch cubes or in thin strips

Prepare the Basic Beef Stock, Dried Cherry and Port Sauce, Parsley and Cognac Mayonnaise and Shoyu and Ginger Steak Sauce.

For each diner, arrange a portion of the venison on a small plate. Place on the table along with dinner plates, forks, sauces and any side dishes. In the kitchen, pour 3¹/₂ cups of stock into a metal or porcelain enameled fondue pot. Place over medium-high heat. When the stock comes to a boil, carry the fondue pot to the table and place over a lit burner adjusted to the highest setting. Keep the remaining broth warm on low heat to replenish the pot.

Diners should use fondue forks to spear and cook the venison in the simmering stock until medium or to the desired degree of doneness. Use a regular fork for dipping and eating.

VARIATION

Substitute beef tenderloin for the venison.

Bouillabaisse Fondue

Bouillabaisse is an elaborate fish and shellfish soup from the south of France. Without careful timing the seafood can quickly overcook. Prepared in a fondue, every bite can be simmered to perfection. Bouillabaisse is a versatile dish; substitute other seafood such as lobster-tail meat, rockfish, monkfish, squid rings, shucked mussels, shucked cherrystone clams or littleneck clams for the ingredients below. Bouillabaisse is traditionally served with a hot pepper sauce called *rouille* (rust) and sometimes a high-octane, garlicky mayonnaise called *aïoli*; the version below includes basil and garlic. Many savvy cooks season bouillabaisse with a few drops of the anise-flavored liqueur called Pernod. Fondue forks work well for cooking firm cubes of fish but long-handled Asian basket spoons used in hot pots come in handy, as well.

Makes 4 to 6 servings

5 cups Saffron Chicken Broth (page 178), or Fish Stock (page 181)

Mignonette Sauce (page 165)

Basil-Dijon Aïoli (page 158)

Sun-Dried Tomato and Rosemary Mayonnaise (page 159), seasoned with 3 to 4 teaspoons hot Asian chili sauce or other hot pepper sauce, to taste

1½ to 2 pounds firm, mild fish such as cod, halibut, sea bass or swordfish, cut in 1-inch cubes

1 pound large shrimp, shelled, deveined, butterflied

12 shucked oysters

½ pound sea scallops, sliced in half

12 small new potatoes, parboiled, cut in half

Sprigs of fresh thyme, (for the broth and garnish)

Prepare the Saffron Chicken Broth, Mignonette Sauce, Basil-Dijon Aïoli, and Sun-Dried Tomato and Rosemary Mayonnaise.

For each diner, arrange a portion of the seafood and potatoes on a small plate; garnish with thyme. Place on the table along with dinner plates, forks, sauces and any side dishes.

In the kitchen, pour 3½ cups of stock into a metal or porcelain enameled fondue pot; add 2 thyme sprigs. Place over medium-high heat. When the stock comes to a boil, carry the fondue pot to the table and place over a lit burner adjusted to the highest setting. Keep the remaining broth warm on low heat to replenish the pot.

Diners should use fondue forks to spear and cook the seafood and potatoes in the simmering stock. Use a regular fork for dipping and eating.

Pork Fondue with Guacamole Sauce

Celebrate the Mexican holiday, Cinco de Mayo, with a festive pork fondue. The pork is delicious with the Roasted Potatoes with Fresh Herbs (page 114). Dust the potatoes lightly with pure Mexican chili powder before baking; top with shredded Jack cheese 5 minutes before they are ready to come out of the oven. Serve with a platter of peeled jicama strips and navel-orange segments with lime and chili powder. This fondue is good with chicken, large shrimp and cubes of beef tenderloin. The Chipotle-Orange Sauce (page 158) is another tasty sauce that can be served in this recipe.

Makes 4 to 6 servings

5 cups Basic Chicken Stock (page 176) or Quick and Easy Chicken Broth (page 177)

Guacamole Sauce (page 165)

Spicy Black Bean Sauce (page 154)

Smoky Tomato Salsa (page 155)

Hot Pepper Jelly Sauce (page 154)

2 pounds pork tenderloin, cut in ⅛-inch-thick slices

1 cup sour cream

Prepare the Basic Chicken Stock, Guacamole Sauce, Spicy Black Bean Sauce, Smoky Tomato Salsa and Hot Pepper Jelly Sauce.

For each diner, arrange a portion of the pork on a small plate. Place on the table along with dinner plates, forks, sauces and any side dishes.

In the kitchen, pour 3½ cups of stock into a metal or porcelain enameled fondue pot. Place over medium-high heat. When the stock comes to a boil, carry the fondue pot to the table and place over a lit burner adjusted to the highest setting.

Keep the remaining broth warm on low heat to replenish the pot.

Diners should use fondue forks to spear and cook each piece of pork in the simmering stock until no longer pink. Use a regular fork for dipping and eating. Spoon a dollop of sour cream on each portion of Spicy Black Bean Sauce.

Chicken and Tortellini Fondue with Red Bell Pepper Sauce

This fondue works beautifully as a spring menu. Serve with the Sugar Pea and Shrimp Salad with Creamy Strawberry Vinaigrette (page 131). The tortellini are especially good dipped into the Red Bell Pepper Sauce. This dish is very pretty with three colors of tortellini made with red, green and white pasta.

Makes 4 to 6 servings

5 cups Basic Chicken Stock (page 176) or Quick and Easy Chicken Broth (page 177)

Red Bell Pepper Sauce (page 166)

Cucumber-Dill Sauce (page 169)

Lemon-Parsley Sauce (page 159)

1 (12-ounce) package refrigerated spinach tortellini with portobello or cheese filling, cooked half the time suggested on the package, rinsed in cool water, drained

2 pounds boneless, skinless chicken breasts, cut into ³/₄-inch cubes

1 bulb fennel, cut into 1-inch strips

Prepare the Basic Chicken Stock, Red Bell Pepper Sauce, Cucumber-Dill Sauce and the Lemon-Parsley Sauce.

For each diner, arrange a portion of the pasta, chicken and fennel on a small plate. Place chicken on the table along with serving plates, forks, sauces and any side dishes.

In the kitchen, pour 3¹/₂ cups of stock into a metal or porcelain enameled fondue pot. Place over medium-high heat. When the stock comes to a boil, carry the fondue pot to the table and place over a lit burner adjusted to the highest setting. Keep the remaining broth warm on low heat to replenish the pot.

Diners should use a fondue fork to spear and cook the chicken, pasta and fennel in the simmering stock. Cook chicken until no longer pink. Use a regular fork for dipping and eating.

Shrimp and Grits Fondue with Southern Comfort Barbecue Sauce

Shrimp and grits is a popular breakfast dish in Charleston, South Carolina, but it is eaten just as often at the evening meal. This fondue was inspired by a dish that restaurateur and chef, Steven G. Kish serves at his Charleston restaurant, 82 Queen, in the heart of the historic district. Chef Kish serves the Southern Comfort Barbecue Sauce over grilled shrimp placed on a bed of grits. Serve this fondue with a side salad of Fried Green Tomato and Goat Cheese Stacks (page 130) and tall glasses of iced tea with fresh mint—the wine of the South!

Makes 4 to 6 servings

5 cups Basic Chicken Stock (page 176) or Quick and Easy Chicken Broth (page 177)

Lowcountry Grits (page 112)

Southern Comfort Barbecue Sauce (page 161)

Dill Butter (page 160)

Zucchini and Mango Relish with Ginger (page 163)

2 pounds large shrimp, shelled and deveined, or cubed salmon

1 pound smoked sausage links, cut into bite-size pieces

Prepare the Basic Chicken Stock, Lowcountry Grits, Southern Comfort Barbecue Sauce, Dill Butter and Zucchini and Mango Relish with Ginger.

For each diner, arrange a portion of the shrimp and sausage on a small plate. Place on the table with the dinner plates, forks, bowls of grits, dipping sauces and any side dishes.

In the kitchen, pour $3^1/_2$ cups of broth into a metal or porcelain enameled fondue pot. Place over medium-high heat. When the broth comes to a boil, carry the fondue pot to the table and place over a lit burner adjusted to the highest setting. Keep the remaining broth warm on low heat to replenish the pot.

Diners should use fondue forks to spear and cook the shrimp and sausages in the simmering broth. Use a regular fork for dipping and eating.

Hot Oil Fondues

When most people think of Swiss fondue, cheese immediately comes to mind. Sitting at the heart of Europe, Switzerland's lush Alpine pastures are naturally suited to dairy farming and cheese production. What better way to use all that hearty Swiss mountain cheese? But sometime after World War II, a new type of fondue was introduced to the Swiss by a respected women's magazine. The dish was Beef Bourguignonne, an offshoot of cheese fondue. Tender cubes of beef were skewered on fondue forks and cooked in a pot of hot oil. The dish was created by the French-speaking Swiss, descendants of the Burgundians. According to legend, this style of cooking meat originated in France in the Middle Ages. During the grape harvest, the pickers would gather around a makeshift fire in the vineyards to prepare a hot meal.

The Swiss philosophy is to keep the dish simple. Bare cubes of beef are fried in a communal pot of hot oil, unfettered by batters, crumbs or coatings. The taste of the fried meat is enhanced by a variety of mouthwatering dipping sauces, one of the best reasons for making hot oil fondue. The original recipe has evolved into numerous variations using boneless chicken, pork, lamb, shellfish, fish and vegetables.

My version of the classic Swiss dish is served with three mouthwatering sauces: Creamy Artichoke and Parmesan Sauce, Stilton and Red Bell Pepper Dip and Horseradish and Tarragon Cream Sauce. The recipe for Argentine Beef Fondue with Chimichurri Sauce is a lively Latin variation that showcases a vivid emerald-green herb and garlic sauce. Chicken is the number one choice for dinner in America and one of the most versatile meats to cook with. Peanutty-Chicken Fondue features cubes of tender, fried chicken thighs dipped into a complementary Brandied Hoisin Sauce.

Fried foods are popular throughout Asia. Few cultures have perfected the art of hot oil frying like the Japanese. Around 1543 during the Muromachi period (1333–1568), Spanish and Portuguese missionaries sailed into southern Kyushu. In the following years, they introduced matchlock muskets, religion, spongecake, sugary confections and deep-fried fish in batter. The "southern barbarians" fried-fish recipe was refined by the Japanese into today's tempura. The word *tempura* is believed to be a corruption of the Portuguese word, *tempero* or "Lent." Tempura features a variety of seasonal foods dipped into a floury batter then deep-fried. The lacy, grease-free coating allows the natural textures, colors and flavors of the foods to shine through. Tempura is a perfect dish for tabletop dining because the foods are at their best immediately after being fried. The recipe and tips in this chapter will tell you everything you need to know to successfully make and serve this classic Japanese dish.

Use a good-quality, mild-flavored oil with a high smoke point for deep-frying. The smoke point is reached when oil decomposes enough to burst into flames. Below I have included the approximate smoke points of each oil when fresh and unused; after a single use this number can drop considerably. Refined oils are more stable and have a higher smoke point. But refinement can cause the loss of some nutrients, flavor and aroma.

SMOKE POINTS OF FATS

Safflower oil	450F (230C)
Canola oil	437F (225C)
Corn oil	410F (210C)
Peanut oil	410F (210C)
Pure olive oil	410F (210C)
Lard	375F (190C)
Solid vegetable shortening	370F (190C)
Virgin and extra-virgin olive oils	250F (120C)

Canola oil and peanut oil are predominantly monounsaturated and have a healthier effect on blood cholesterol levels. Some cooks deep-fry in pure olive oil. Do not use virgin and extra-virgin olive oils; their low smoking points make them an unsuitable choice. There are several oil blends that are ideal for deep-frying. Canolive is a blend of canola and olive oil. Two other combinations

are canola-corn oil and canola-soybean oil. Corn oil and vitamin E–rich safflower oil are high in polyunsaturated fatty acids. They are fine for deep-frying, but not quite as heart-protective. Safflower oil is less heat stable; it can oxidize and become rancid quickly; refrigerate after opening and use within two months. Polyunsaturated oils stay in liquid form even when refrigerated.

Asian or toasted sesame oil smokes at high temperatures and has a strong nutty flavor. Used in Japan since the eighth century, it was once the favored oil for tempura. Japanese chefs now prefer a lighter taste and use it sparingly in frying-oil blends. To give your fried foods a special nutty taste, blend 20 percent to 25 percent toasted sesame oil into your regular frying oil.

Do not fry with saturated animal fats, which have a smoke point around the temperature required for deep-frying. Solid vegetable shortening is not the best choice either. Shortening and animal fat blends are more stable for frying but contain unhealthy hydrogenated fats, saturated fats and preservatives.

HEATING THE OIL

In the kitchen, heat 2 to 3 cups of vegetable oil in a sturdy stainless steel or porcelain enamel cast-iron fondue pot. Fill the pot no more than half full. Wearing oven mitts, carefully transport the filled pot to the table and place it securely over the lit burner. Adjust the fuel burner to high heat.

A quality candy or deep-frying thermometer takes the guesswork out of regulating oil temperatures for fondue or tempura. Optimum temperatures range from 350F (175C) to 375F (190C). Use a thermometer while heating the oil on the stove and again at the table. My thermometer has a metal clip that holds it securely onto the side of the pan. If you don't have a thermometer, test the oil by frying a cube of bread. When the oil is heated to 350F (175C), the bread will brown in about 1 minute. Drops of batter will splatter near the oil's surface. Alcohol is the most efficient fondue fuel and can heat the oil to 375F (190C) as long as a fondue pot is not overfilled.

Remove meats and seafood from the refrigerator about twenty minutes before cooking. Vegetables should be at room temperature. Chilled foods can lower the oil temperature suddenly. The initial oil temperature should be ten degrees higher than suggested in the recipes to compensate for this drop. Keep oil heated to the proper temperature to minimize the absorption of oil.

Six diners is the maximum number for one fondue pot. The amount of food needed for more will crowd the pot, reducing the oil temperature to the "soggy food level." Tempura vegetables are fried whole, in strips, in wedges and large diagonal slices. They need ample surface space to fry evenly so they don't end up becoming steamed. Use your metal fondue pot to prepare three or four tempura-style ingredients for four. To efficiently prepare a complete seafood and vegetable meal for more, use a Japanese *tempura-nabé* or heavy, flat-bottom pot with a portable butane canister stove. A sturdy electric wok is also a good choice; tuck the electrical cord safely out of the reach of legs and feet.

RECYCLED OIL

Fresh cooking oil is essential for fried fondues; do not use if it is recycled. Because of the social nature of a fondue meal, the relatively small amount of oil heats for a longer period, which can cause rapid darkening, foaming and structural breakdown. The smoking point is irreversibly lowered. This decomposition eventually creates a malodorous compound called acreolein. Oxidized, rancid oil causes fried foods to taste bad. According to scientific studies, it may contain toxic compounds and lead to heart disease. In favor of the metal fondue pot, food scientists explain that tall, narrow pots help delay the oil's rate of decomposition by reducing its surface exposure to the atmosphere.

If you do choose to recycle a larger amount of briefly used frying oil only consider oil that is still very light in color. Pour it through a fine mesh strainer into a bowl to remove impurities. Refrigerate in an airtight container; use within a month. You can blend in some fresh oil but the entire batch will deteriorate more quickly. Asian cooks refresh cooking oil by slowly heating 1 or 2 green onions or slices of fresh ginger until the temperature reaches 350F (175C). European cooks might fry several slices of potato. Discard the vegetables after they turn golden brown. Recycled oil that has been refreshed does create a crispy, attractive brown crust on batter fried foods. Do not use recycled oil more than once.

When discarding used oil, allow it to cool completely in the pot then pour it into a disposable container or thick plastic kitchen bag that self-seals. Torn, crumpled pieces of paper towels or newspapers stuffed into the container help soak up the oil, making it less precarious to handle.

TIPS FOR HOT OIL FONDUE

Frying techniques, the choice of cooking oil and the ingredients differ around the world, from cook to cook. But all agree there are two major classifications of fried foods—extremely good and extremely bad! These guidelines will help you to avoid the latter.

- For best results in making hot oil fondue, use high-quality, fresh seafood, poultry and meats, which need little preparation except cutting and cooking.

- Marinades are not necessary for tender beef and pork tenderloin, the recommended cuts for fondue. Trim away excess fat then cut the meat into even-size cubes, 3/4 to one inch. If too large, the longer frying time will toughen and dry out the meat.

- You can marinate a less tender cut like flank steak. Marinades can add flavor to poultry and seafood. High-acid marinades can toughen instead of tenderize. Use a proportion of two tablespoons vinegar or lemon juice to 1/2 cup oil. Add seasoning liquids or pastes for flavor. Commercial meat tenderizers contain enzymes that can make meat textures mushy. Yogurt is an excellent tenderizer and won't toughen meats. Marinate fish and seafood 10 to 15 minutes with a low-acid marinade. Dry marinated foods thoroughly with paper towels before frying.

- Do not salt foods just before frying.
  1. Moisture is drawn to the surface causing hot oil to splatter.
  2. Moisture within the meat is beneficial; it helps prevent burning and excess oil absorption.
  3. Salt on the meat lowers the oil's smoking point and contributes to quicker deterioration.

4. Don't sprinkle foods with dry herbs and spices; they will burn in the oil. Dipping sauces and condiments provide the necessary flavor boost after cooking.

- Hot oil fondue is a quick-cook method, requiring from one to three minutes for each bite of food. After cooking one or two pieces, you will gain a better feel for how much time is needed. Beef is best cooked until moderately pink inside or to suit your taste. Cook shrimp about 1 minute until pink and firm and poultry and pork until lightly browned around the edges and no longer pink inside.

TIPS FOR TEMPURA

- Japanese esthetics demand that the dinnerware be as interesting as the food. Artistic sensibilities like texture, color, form and arrangement come into play when selecting a table setting. Gather for each place setting: a plate or flat basket for the fried food, a sauce bowl, a condiment dish, a rice bowl, a soup bowl, a small salad dish, saké cup or other beverage container and a dessert dish, if desired. Oriental shops and stores like Pier One Imports often carry a variety of attractive small Asian plates, bowls, cups and chopsticks. Japanese dishes do not have to match; choose the pieces to reflect the season and complement the foods they hold. A unique tablesetting adds to the ambience and fun of the meal.

- Provide each diner with a pair of chopsticks. Disposable wooden chopsticks are called *warabashi* in Japan. Chopsticks rests are used in more formal settings, but they are fun to use casually. You can use a pretty flower, a seashell or an origami bow made from the chopstick's paper wrapper. Consider joining the crusade sweeping through Asia to ban the rampant use of disposable chopsticks. It began during the 1990s by China's environmentalists as a response to statistics that more than twenty-five million trees are being cut down for *warabashi* yearly; by the end of this decade the remaining forests could be depleted. Instead of birch or poplar throwaway chopsticks, choose reusable chopsticks of bamboo, farmed teak, cedar or sandalwood. Plastic, ivory and silver chopsticks, preferred in Korea, are not suitable for dipping into hot broth or hot oil.

- Japanese attention to tabletop detail is never lacking. Place a piece of folded absorbent paper or a doily on individual plates to absorb the oil from the fried foods. This is a nice touch that can be used with other fried fondues, as well. Japanese markets carry coated sheets of paper (*shiki shi*) for this use.

- Arrange all the ingredients and utensils in advance before starting to fry. Bring everything to the table. Place a covered container of cooked rice nearby for easy refills. Heat the oil then make the batter. When the oil is hot, begin dipping and frying. Guests can sip on miso soup as the first batch goes in.

- It is much more efficient for the host or hostess to be responsible for the job of dipping and frying. If they wish, the diners can take turns and assume the cooking duties. Everyone takes food from the pot or the draining rack.

- Begin frying fiberous foods that need more cooking time (squash, potatoes, carrots); fin-

ish with foods that require less cooking times (shellfish, mushrooms, tofu).

- Retrieving the food is part of the fun, unless you are not proficient with cooking chopsticks. Provide spring-loaded chopsticks or spring-loaded tongs in addition to the eating chopsticks or fork. Bamboo skewers can come in handy for removing the foods, as well.

- Keep a mesh skimmer on the side to remove pieces of fried batter to prevent them from burning. Skim the oil regularly. Many woks and frying pots have a handy, curved, detachable wire rack for draining the fried foods.

- Use chopsticks, tongs or your hands to dip the foods in the batter. Keep damp paper towels nearby to wipe up drips. Lower the foods into the hot oil gently to prevent splattering. Fry five or six pieces at a time; use wooden chopsticks to keep the pieces separated and remove them from the pan.

- Beverages can include small cups of warm saké, hot green tea or cold beer.

FIRE SAFETY HINT

Never use water to extinguish an oil fire; burning oil will splatter and spread. Smother flames in the pot by covering it with a tight-fitting lid or sheet of heavy foil carefully applied while wearing protective mitts. If the flames are outside the pot, smother with baking soda or a fire extinguisher formulated for oil fires.

Steak Fondue Hoedown

One of the most innovative fondue dinners you will ever hear about is a "pitchfork fondue" held by the Northwest Iowa Republican party during an old-fashioned grassroots political rally. The concept is simple; Black Angus ribeye steaks are skewered on the end of stainless steel pitchforks and lowered into a huge iron pot of oil bubbling over a wood fire. In 2 minutes flat, the steaks are cooked; crusty on the outside; pink and juicy throughout. Enjoy the thought as you feast on this mini "pitchfork fondue" of tender steak with all the trimmings. Serve the beef and sauces with big bowls of the creamy Garlic Mashed Potatoes (page 113). They are really delicious with the tender fried beef and trio of sauces.

Makes 4 to 6 servings

Tomato and Red Onion Chutney (page 162)
Mustard and Tarragon Sauce (page 162)
Shoyu and Ginger Steak Sauce (page 152)
2 pounds beef tenderloin cut into 3/4-inch cubes
Canola oil, for deep-frying

Prepare the Tomato and Red Onion Chutney, Mustard and Tarragon Sauce and Shoyu and Ginger Steak Sauce.

For each diner, arrange a portion of the beef on a small plate. Place on the table with dinner plates, forks, dipping sauces and any side dishes. In the kitchen, pour oil into a metal or porcelain enameled fondue pot until about half full. Place on the stove and heat until the temperature reaches 375F (190C).

Carry the fondue pot to the table and place over a lit burner adjusted to the highest setting. Diners should use fondue forks to cook the beef to the desired degree of doneness. Use a regular fork for dipping and eating.

Argentine Beef Fondue with Chimichurri Sauce

This fondue offers a taste of Argentina's culinary obsession—savory grilled beef. For a hearty meal that will satisfy even a *gaucho*, serve this fondue with the Coconut Rice Pilaf (page 116), topped with black beans and Mango, Cucumber and Cashew Relish (page 163). Besides the lively Chimichurri Sauce, other dipping sauces you might try are Basil Dijon Aïoli (page 158) and Chipotle-Orange Sauce (page 158).

Makes 6 servings

2 to 2 1/2 pounds beef top sirloin
1/4 cup olive oil
2 tablespoons red wine vinegar
1/2 teaspoon ground cumin
Chimichurri Sauce (page 170)
Canola oil, for deep-frying

In a shallow pan, marinate the beef in the olive oil, vinegar and cumin in the refrigerator for at least 6 hours.

Prepare the Chimichurri Sauce. Drain the beef and pat dry with paper towels; cut into 3/4-inch cubes. For each diner, arrange a portion of the beef on a small plate. Place on the table with dinner plates, forks, dipping sauces and side dishes.

In the kitchen, pour the canola oil into a metal or porcelain enameled fondue pot until about half full. Place on the stove and heat until the temperature reaches 375F (190C).

Carry the fondue pot to the table and place over a lit burner adjusted to the highest setting. Diners should use fondue forks to cook the beef to the desired degree of doneness. Use a regular fork for dipping and eating.

Spicy Korean Meatball Fondue in Lettuce Wraps

Small appetizer-size dishes are not served as a first course in Korean meals, but are viewed as alternative little meals in which socializing is the most important consideration. When in Korea, I grazed on foods like this tasty dish of lettuce-wrapped meatball and rice bundles. Serve this fondue as a unique appetizer or light lunch with bowls of Mushroom and Fried Tofu Chowder (page 186), pickled *kim chee* and a fresh fruit platter. You can increase the amounts, as desired.

Makes 6 appetizer or luncheon servings

Soy Sauce and Sesame Dip (page 166)

Chili-Sesame Sauce (page 152)

Cooked Medium-Grain Rice (page 117)

6 or 7 small butter lettuce leaves, per person, rinsed and dried

1/2 pound ground pork or beef

2 garlic cloves, minced

1 green onion, minced

1 teaspoon fresh ginger, minced

1 large egg yolk

1 tablespoon dry white wine

2 teaspoons Japanese soy sauce (shoyu)

1/2 teaspoon sesame seed oil

1/8 to 1/4 teaspoon red (cayenne) pepper, to taste

Salt and black pepper, to taste

Canola oil, for deep-frying

Prepare the Soy Sauce and Sesame Dip, Chili-Sesame Sauce and Cooked Medium-Grain Rice. Rinse the lettuce leaves.

In a medium bowl, blend the ground pork with all the remaining ingredients except the canola oil. Shape into small meatballs, using a scant tablespoon of the mixture per meatball. For each diner, arrange a portion of the meatballs and lettuce leaves on a small plate. Place on the table with dinner plates, a large bowl of rice, dipping sauces and any side dishes.

In the kitchen, pour the canola oil into a metal or porcelain enameled fondue pot until about half full. Place on the stove and heat until the temperature reaches 375F (190C).

Carry the fondue pot to the table and place over a lit burner adjusted to the highest setting. With a fondue fork, skewer a meatball and cook it 2 minutes or until no longer pink inside. Place a small spoonful of rice on a lettuce leaf then add a meatball. Top with a small amount of either of the sauces. Fold the lettuce leaf over the filling into a packet and eat out of hand.

Obi-Wrapped Tuna Fondue

Each piece of tuna is wrapped around the middle with an obi, "sash," cut from a sheet of nori, which is an iridescent black seaweed sheet used for making rolled sushi. An alternate obi wrap can be made with strips of flavorful *kaipen*, a nutritious algae from Laos that is dried into beautiful green textured sheets and seasoned with sesame seeds and tamarind juice. When fried, *kaipen* is crisp and very flavorful. The sheets are so attractive they could be fashioned into place mats (See Mail-Order Resources, page 225). Sashimi-quality tuna is best cooked rare, but even well-done, it tastes delicious dipped into this medley of sauces.

Makes 4 servings

Sesame-Miso Sauce (page 166)

Wasabi Crème Sauce (page 164)

Daikon Dipping Sauce (page 155)

2 pounds sashimi-quality tuna steaks, 1-inch thick or swordfish steaks, with bloodline trimmed

2 tablespoons virgin olive oil

2 tablespoons fresh lemon juice

2$^1/_2$ sheets pre-seasoned nori (laver), cut in 4 × 1-inch strips

Canola oil or soybean oil, for deep-frying

Prepare the Sesame-Miso Sauce, Wasabi Cream Sauce and Daikon Dipping Sauce.

Place the tuna steaks, olive oil and lemon juice in a shallow glass dish. Marinate for up to 1 hour. Drain the tuna and pat dry with paper towels. Cut into strips, $^1/_2$-inch to $^3/_4$-inch wide. Cut the strips into rectangular pieces 2$^1/_4$-inches long. Wrap a band of nori around the center of each tuna strip, sealing with a tiny bit of marinade or oil. For each diner, arrange a portion of the wrapped tuna on a small plate. Place the fish, serving plates, sauces and any side dishes on the table.

In the kitchen, pour oil into a metal or porcelain enameled fondue pot until about half full. Place on the stove and heat until the temperature reaches 375F (190C).

Carry the fondue pot to the table and place over a lit burner adjusted to the highest setting. Diners should use fondue forks to skewer the pieces of tuna on the sides the nori is sealed on. Cook 30 seconds for rare or to the desired degree of doneness. Use a regular fork for dipping and eating.

VARIATION

For 6 people, increase the tuna to 2$^1/_2$ pounds and use 3$^1/_2$ sheets nori.

Banana-and-Ginger Spring Rolls

Banana spring rolls might be served for *merienda*, or afternoon tea, in the Philippines. They make unique fondue dippers with a fruity dipping sauce or big bowls of banana ice cream drizzled with Hot Buttered Rum Fondue (page 203). Spring rolls are made with special paper-thin wrappers but extra-thin egg roll wrappers work fine, too. Make egg roll wrappers thinner by feeding them through the roller blade of a pasta machine; narrow the roller spacing one or two times. Trim the rolled wrappers into 6-inch squares. These spring rolls are especially good made with tangy, red Cuban bananas; use one banana for each wrapper.

Makes 20 rolls; 10 servings

5 firm, ripe large bananas, peeled, cut in half crosswise

1 (1-pound) package thin egg roll wrappers (20 wrappers) or 10 spring roll wrappers, cut in half

1/2 cup crystallized ginger, cut in thin shreds, 1/2 cup toasted chopped walnuts or 1/2 cup miniature chocolate chips (use one or more)

Peanut or canola oil, for deep-frying

Cut each banana half lengthwise, forming 2 strips. Lay a wrapper diagonally with one of the corners pointing toward you. Lay a banana strip in the center of the wrapper; sprinkle with a few shreds of ginger. Fold up the bottom corner to cover the banana strip. Fold up sides snugly against the banana. Moisten edge of remaining flap; roll up to form a package.

When all the spring rolls are made, cook at once or place on a tray and cover with plastic wrap; cook within 2 hours.

At the table, heat oil in an electric wok to 365F (185C). Deep-fry the banana rolls, 3 or 4 at a time, until the wrappers are crisp and golden brown, 1 to 2 minutes. Drain on paper towels then cut diagonally in half; serve with dipping sauces. Half of the recipe can be fried in a fondue pot.

Drunken Shrimp Fondue

The magic in this light, crispy batter is that it can be made hours in advance. Use it for frying scallops, squid rings, fish fillets such as red snapper, Brie, vegetables or fruit. At the table, you can use metal shakers with fine mesh lids to dust the foods with flour.

The batter is versatile; omit the paprika and substitute 1/2 teaspoon curry powder, powdered green tea, sesame seeds, coconut or a pinch of saffron.

Besides the sunny Five-Spice Orange Sauce, the fried shrimp are delicious dipped into Horseradish and Tarragon Cream Sauce (page 163), Sauce Rémoulade (page 159) or the Tempura Dipping Sauce (page 168).

Makes 4 servings

Five-Spice Orange Sauce (page 167)

1 (12-ounce) bottle light domestic beer

2 teaspoons sweet Hungarian paprika

1 rounded teaspoon salt

1 1/2 cups cake flour, plus extra for dusting

1 1/2 pounds large shrimp, peeled and deveined, with tails intact

2 medium zucchini, cut diagonally in 1/4-inch slices

1 or 2 small tart green apples, cut in 1/8-inch rings

Canola or peanut oil, for deep-frying

Prepare the Five-Spice Orange Sauce.

In a medium bowl, whisk together the beer, paprika and salt. Slowly whisk in the flour until blended. Let the batter rest for at least 30 minutes; whisk briefly to blend. Divide batter between 2 medium bowls.

Make several cuts on the inside curve of each shrimp to help prevent curling. Divide the shrimp, zucchini and apple rings between 2 platters. Arrange the platters on the table with 4 small plates, dipping sauce, batter, extra cake flour and any side dishes.

In the kitchen, pour the oil into a metal or porcelain enameled fondue pot until about half full. Place on the stove and heat until the temperature reaches 375F (190C). Carry the fondue pot to the table and place over a lit burner adjusted to the highest setting.

Dust each food lightly with flour. Each diner should use fondue forks to skewer a shrimp near the tail and dip it into the batter. Tap off excess batter and lower it into the hot oil. Cook until golden and crisp, 2 minutes. Tap off excess oil; place shrimp on a plate lined with absorbent paper. Use a regular fork or fingers for dipping and eating. Fry the remaining foods along with the shrimp.

Brie Fritters with Raspberry Cabernet Sauce

Cheese fondue appears in many forms. Delicious Brie oozes with every bite of these crispy wedges. Make bread crumbs in the food processor, but don't process too finely. For extra-crispness, use *panko*, the large, dried Japanese bread crumbs, mixed with 1/4 cup white sesame seeds. Breaded, fried cubes of Brie can be served with a small pot of warm Raspberry Cabernet Sauce for dipping. For a luncheon, serve each wedge on a bed of dressed salad greens; omit the sauce.

Makes 6 servings

Raspberry Cabernet Sauce or Blackberry Cabernet Sauce (page 156)

3 cups fresh bread crumbs from French bread or sourdough

2 large eggs

Canola or safflower oil, for deep-frying

6 (about 2-inch-wide) wedges chilled Brie cheese (about 1 pound)

Confectioners' sugar (optional)

Prepare the Raspberry Cabernet Sauce. Put the bread crumbs into a shallow pan. Place the eggs in another shallow pan; blend with a fork. In a wok or shallow, heavy saucepan, heat 2 inches of oil to 375F (190C).

Dip the cheese wedges into the beaten egg, moistening all sides. Roll in crumbs until completely coated. Place wedges on a baking sheet. Fry 2 pieces of cheese at a time until the coating is crisp and medium-golden brown, 1 minute. Drain on paper towels. If necessary, skim oil to remove crumbs during frying.

Spoon some sauce on each of 6 small serving plates; top with a cheese wedge. Dust lightly with confectioners' sugar, if desired. Serve at once. The breaded cheese fritters can be refrigerated 1 hour before frying.

Peanutty Chicken Fondue

Asian cooks prefer chicken thighs, because they stay wonderfully moist and are economical. They become extremely flavorful when soaked overnight in a peanut marinade. The chicken can also be cut into 3/4-inch cubes and cooked in hot oil or chicken broth using fondue forks. The menu rounds out nicely with fried rice and the Cucumber Salad with Fresh Mint and Red Chili Vinaigrette (page 128). Two additional dipping sauces you might like to include are the Apple and Curry Cream (page 158) and the Peppered Peanut Sauce (page 151), especially if you are one of those people who just can't get enough peanut butter.

Makes 4 servings

Brandied Hoisin Sauce (page 151)

Sichuan Pepper Salt (optional, page 160)

¼ cup Japanese soy sauce (*shoyu*)

1 tablespoon sugar

1 rounded tablespoon peanut butter

1 rounded teaspoon minced fresh ginger

½ teaspoon Asian sesame oil

1 teaspoon hot chili sauce with garlic

2 cloves garlic, finely minced

1 green onion, chopped

2½ pounds chicken thighs, skinned, boned (8 or 9 pieces) or chicken tenderloins

Peanut or canola oil, for deep-frying

Prepare the Brandied Hoisin Sauce and Sichuan Pepper Salt if using. To make the marinade, blend all the remaining ingredients, except the chicken and peanut oil, in a medium bowl. Add chicken to the marinade; turn to coat. Cover and refrigerate for 6 hours or overnight.

Drain the chicken and pat dry with paper towels. Cut each thigh into 5 or 6 strips. Thread each strip near the end of a 10-inch wooden skewer. (You can cover and refrigerate chicken skewers up to 2 hours.) Divide the skewers between 2 platters. Place on the table with 4 small plates, dipping sauce and any side dishes.

In the kitchen, pour the oil into a metal or porcelain enameled fondue pot until about half full. Place on the stove and heat until the temperature reaches 375F (190C).

Carry the fondue pot to the table and place over a lit burner adjusted to the highest setting. Diners should place skewers of chicken in the hot oil and cook until no longer pink inside. Use a regular fork for dipping and eating.

Lotus Crisps

Exquisite pink-and-white water lily flowers have amazing underwater roots that resemble plump, linked sausages. Open canals run the length of the roots, creating a pretty paper-chain design when sliced. Deep-fried lotus root slices make a unique accompaniment for salads or a delightful cocktail nibble. Peeled, boiled lotus root is available in the produce section of many supermarkets or Asian markets. A French mandoline or Japanese Benriner cutting box would be helpful in making ultra-thin slices, about ¹⁄₁₆-inch thick, the thinner the slice, the crisper the chip.

Makes about 2½ dozen

1 section of peeled, boiled lotus root, about ½ pound

Canola or peanut oil, for deep-frying

Herb salt, seasoning salt or Kosher salt

With a sharp knife, cut the lotus root into ¹⁄₈-inch to ¹⁄₁₆-inch-thick slices. Soak in salted water for 1 to 2 hours. Dry the slices carefully on paper towels. In a wok or shallow, heavy saucepan, heat the canola oil to 365F (185C). Fry several lotus slices, turning occasionally, until crisp and light brown, about 3 minutes. Drain and immediately sprinkle with salt. Cool completely, then store in an airtight container for 1 to 2 days. If desired, warm in a medium oven before serving.

Edible Lace Japanese cooks create a lacy network of batter around pieces of tempura by dipping their fingers into the thin batter and sprinkling them on the hot oil. This is repeated several times to make a lacy background. Several shrimp are dipped into the batter then placed on top of the lacy batter. More batter is sprinkled on top. After about 1 minute, the shrimp are turned to cook on the other side. When cooked, they are drained and served. The delicious crispy bits of loose fried batter (*agédama*) floating in the pan are scooped out and saved to sprinkle on noodle bowls, soups or added to *okonomiyaki*, Japanese-style pizza.

Tempura

Tempura is a dish for all seasons. Serve it year-round, choosing your favorite fresh ingredients. When fried, the essence of each ingredient should still be clearly defined. Tempura is a dish best cooked in front of the diners. In Tokyo at the famous tempura restaurant, Ten-ichi, each piece is skillfully fried and quickly passed across the counter to the customer or rushed by the plateful to a table. Behind the counter, Ten-ichi chefs keep a discreet tally of the pieces sold with strategically placed grains of rice.

Tempura is delicious dipped into the accompanying sauce but some epicures prefer a squeeze of fresh lemon and sprinkle of salt. I have included the recipe for a special Green Tea Salt for you to sample this delicacy for yourself. To serve a complete meal (*teishoku*), include bowls of seasoned Dashi broth or Hearty Miso Soup (page 185), Cooked Medium-Grain Rice (page 117) and the Spinach and Cabbage Rolls (page 134) sprinkled with a light rice vinegar or balsamic vinegar dressing.

Makes 4 to 6 servings

Tempura Dipping Sauce (page 168)

Green Tea Salt (page 159) or other flavored salt

3/4 to 1 pound large shrimp, peeled with tails intact

1 to 1 1/2 pounds thin fish fillets, cut into 1 1/2-inch pieces

1 large red bell pepper, cut in wedges

1 sweet potato, peeled, cut in 1/4-inch-thick slices

6 medium fresh shiitaki mushrooms, stems trimmed

1 medium sweet onion, peeled, halved and sliced 1/3-inch thick (secure slices with a wooden pick)

Canola or soybean oil, for deep-frying (with 10 to 20 percent sesame oil, if desired)

Yuri's Tempura Batter (page 66)

Flour, for dusting

1 or 2 lemons, cut into wedges

Prepare the Tempura Dipping Sauce and Green Tea Salt. Slit open the backs of the shrimp, three-fourths of the way through. Do not cut into the tail sections. Remove veins. Place on a flat surface, cut sides down; pound gently 2 or 3 times to slightly flatten.

Arrange the shrimp, fish, bell pepper, sweet potato, mushrooms and onion; arrange on 1 or 2 platters. Place on the table with the dipping sauce, Green Tea Salt, and serving container of rice.

At the table, pour the oil into a *tempura-nabé* or electric wok until about half full. Heat to 360F

Ingredients for Tempura

Sliced Japanese eggplant

Chicken tenderloin strips, cut in half

Pencil-thin whole green onions, trimmed

Tender small green beans

Small asparagus stalks, trimmed

Scallops, cut in half horizontally

Peeled lotus root, cut in 1/8-inch-thick slices

Zucchini, cut in diagonal slices

Fresh shiso leaves

Calamari, cleaned and cut in rings

Whole small tender okra

Fresh cultivated or wild mushrooms

Gobo (burdock)

Fennel stalks

Large sprigs of herbs with long stems

Pea pods

Diagonally-cut, paper-thin slices of young fresh ginger

Banana slices

Whole strawberries

1/2 small kabocha or acorn squash, halved, cut in 1/4-inch slices

Pressed tofu, cut in cubes or flower-shapes with large flower-shaped vegetable cutters or cookie cutters

Carrots, cut in thin diagonal slices

Small fish, butterflied

(180C). Just before cooking, prepare the tempura batter; carry to the table on a tray.

Dust 4 or 5 shrimp with flour. Hold a shrimp by the tail and dip it into the batter. Lower it into the oil and hold a few seconds to set the shape. Fry until crisp, 2 to 3 minutes. (Japanese cooks like to drizzle thin streams of extra batter over the shrimp in the oil to create a lacier batter.) Dip and fry the remaining ingredients, 4 or 5 pieces at a time. Cooking times can vary with each ingredient. Drain fried foods on a rack placed on a tray or fitted on the wok.

Dip the tempura into the sauce seasoned with condiments or sprinkle with lemon juice and salt. Diners can sip on miso soup while waiting for the first batch of tempura to cook.

Yuri's Tempura Batter

Tempura is made with a thin, undermixed batter that is transformed into a crisp, lacy coating when deep-fried. It is known as *koromo* or clothing. Tempura chefs say smooth batters trap excess moisture, creating air pockets between the batter and food that cause the batter to fall off. The fried coating should be as ethereal and delicate as a "woman's veil."

This excellent batter is all that and more. It comes from my good friend, Yuri Kita, from West End, North Carolina. Yuri is a culinary artist and an expert in preparing Japanese cuisine. It is helpful to have additional ingredients nearby in case you want to mix up more batter at the table.

A pair of *ryoribashi* or 14-inch-long cooking chopsticks is useful for undermixing the batter. In Japan, many tempura masters make their own chopsticks. You can buy pairs that are cleverly attached at the top so one can't become lost. Have fun with the batter and experiment with additional flavor enhancers such as powdered green tea, sesame seeds, powdered dried seaweed, curry powder or fresh minced herbs.

Makes about 1¼ cups batter

1 large egg yolk

1 cup ice water

1 cup plus 4 tablespoons plain cake flour

⅛ teaspoon baking soda

In a medium bowl, blend the egg yolk and ice water with a pair of cooking chopsticks or a fork. Sprinkle in 1 cup of the flour and the baking soda. Stir roughly just to blend in half the flour. The batter should be lumpy and undermixed, with flour visible. Set the bowl of batter inside a larger bowl ⅓ full with water and ice. As the flour disappears and the batter smoothes out, sprinkle in the extra 4 tablespoons flour, as needed, 1 tablespoon at a time. The combination of ice-cold, floury batter and hot oil creates the lacy, crisp coating.

Fondue Bourguignonne with Creamy Artichoke and Parmesan Sauce

Do as the Swiss do *aprés ski* or after a hard day of work and gather with friends around a fondue pot. Beef tenderloin is the top choice for this classic dish. Serve with the Roasted Potatoes with Fresh Herbs (page 114) and the Alpine Mushroom Salad (page 122).

Makes 6 servings

Creamy Artichoke and Parmesan Sauce (page 167)

Stilton and Red Bell Pepper Dip (page 156)

Horseradish and Tarragon Cream Sauce (page 163)

2 to 2¼ pounds trimmed beef tenderloin, cut in ¾-inch cubes

Peanut or canola oil, for deep-frying

Prepare the Creamy Artichoke and Parmesan Sauce, Stilton and Red Bell Pepper Dip and Horseradish and Tarragon Cream Sauce.

For each diner, arrange a portion of the beef on a small plate. Place on the table with the dinner plates, dipping sauces, and any side dishes.

In the kitchen, pour oil in a metal or porcelain enameled fondue pot until about half full. Place on the stove and heat until the temperature reaches 375F (190C).

Carry the fondue pot to the table and place it over a lit burner adjusted to the highest setting. Diners should use fondue forks to spear and cook the beef to the desired degree of doneness. Use a regular fork for dipping and eating.

Fried Tofu Wedges

Japanese-style fried tofu (*atsuagé or namaagé*) can be purchased in blocks and wedges in markets near sizeable Asian communities. Japanese cooks add them to one-pot dishes and soups. In long-simmered dishes, fried tofu doesn't disintegrate like plain tofu. It is highly perishable and you may not be able to find it at your local market. Here is an easy substitute to make at home that is fresh and tasty.

For a vegetarian fondue lunch for four, double the recipe and fry the tofu in a fondue pot. Complete the meal with bowls of Hearty Miso Soup (page 185) and Cooked Medium-Grain Rice (page 117). For dipping sauces try the Daikon Dipping Sauce (page 155), the Peppered Peanut Sauce (page 151) or the Chili-Sesame Sauce (page 152).

Makes 2 to 4 servings

1 (10- to 16-ounce) block firm tofu
Peanut oil, for deep-frying

Open the tofu and drain. Rinse and pat dry. Slice tofu in half horizontally. Pat off the water with paper towels. Wrap in several layers of paper towels and place a light weight on top to help press out more water. After 30 minutes, unwrap the tofu. Cut each piece in half crosswise. Cut the 4 blocks in half diagonally to form 8 wedges. Pat the tofu again with paper towels to remove any moisture.

Heat the oil in a wok or heavy shallow pan to 350F (175C). Deep-fry the tofu wedges, turning occasionally, until they are crisp and golden brown, 2 to 3 minutes. Drain on paper towels.

VARIATION

Agédashi-Dofu To make this crispy fried tofu appetizer or snack, dredge the tofu wedges in potato starch (*katakuri-ko*) or cornstarch. Fry in the hot oil, as directed. Drain on paper towels. Divide the tofu among 3 or 4 small bowls. Pour a portion of the warm Daikon Dipping Sauce (page

155) over each serving. Garnish with paper-thin rings of green onion and grated daikon. The sauce can be thickened slightly with about 1 teaspoon potato starch or cornstarch.

Lamb Fondue with Banana-and-Cilantro Sauce

The symphony of tropical flavors in this fondue hints at the sophistication and versatility of the addictive cuisines of Southeast Asia. The tropical banana sauce, Peppered Peanut Sauce and Fresh Mint Sauce are a perfect flavor match for the tender slices of lamb. I would suggest a platter of Thai-Style Coconut Rice Pilaf (page 116) and a platter of sliced tropical fruits on the side. As dessert, keep the fun going with a pot of the Tropical Lime Fondue (page 200) with Coconut Logs (page 201).

Makes 6 servings

Banana-and-Cilantro Sauce (page 168)
Fresh Mint Sauce (page 155)
Peppered Peanut Sauce (page 151)
2 to 2¼ pounds trimmed boneless leg of lamb, cut in ¾-inch cubes
Peanut or canola oil, for deep-frying

Prepare the Banana-and-Cilantro Sauce, Fresh Mint Sauce and Peppered Peanut Sauce.

For each diner, arrange a portion of the lamb on a small plate. Place on the table with dinner plates, dipping sauces, and any side dishes.

In the kitchen, pour the oil in a metal or porcelain enameled fondue pot until about half full. Place on the stove and heat until the temperature reaches 375F (190C).

Carry the fondue pot to the table and place it over a lit burner adjusted to the highest setting. Diners should use fondue forks to spear and cook the lamb to the desired degree of doneness. Use a regular fork for dipping and eating.

Three-Star Pork Fondue with Cucumber-Dill Sauce

Fondue cooking is appealing for small, intimate parties because most of the prep can be done ahead and the ingredients pre-cut into bite-size portions for quick cooking at the table. You will stay cool as a cucumber when you serve this easy fondue with Kathy McCorkle's refreshing Cucumber-Dill Sauce and flavorful Apple-Raisin Sauce. As the wife of a Marine Corps lieutenant general, entertaining has been part of the fabric of Kathy's life. She can successfully plan and orchestrate parties for groups from 20 to 200.

Makes 6 servings

Cucumber-Dill Sauce (page 169)

Apple-Raisin Sauce (page 153)

Hot Pepper Jelly Sauce (page 154)

2 to 2¼ pounds pork tenderloin, cut in ¾-inch cubes

Peanut or canola oil, for deep-frying

Prepare the Cucumber-Dill Sauce, Apple-Raisin Sauce and Hot Pepper Jelly Sauce.

For each diner, arrange a portion of the pork on a small plate. Place on the table with the dinner plates, dipping sauces and any side dishes.

In the kitchen, pour oil in a metal or porcelain enameled fondue pot until about half full. Place on the stove and heat until the temperature reaches 375F (190C).

Carry the fondue pot to the table and place it over a lit burner adjusted to the highest setting. Diners should use fondue forks to spear and cook the pork until no longer pink inside. Use a regular fork for dipping and eating.

Turkey Fondue with Jalapeño-Cranberry Port Sauce

Pairing meat with fruit sauce is a culinary tradition begun centuries ago in "merry old England" but the spicy taste of the jalapeño chili would have caused quite a stir! To create a special harvest meal, include a salad of Fried Green Tomato and Goat Cheese Stacks (page 130) and Baked Sweet Potatoes with Honey-Spice Butter (page 172). For a touch of seasonal fun, finish with one of the desert fondues served in the adorable Jack-Be-Little Pumpkin Bowls (page 207).

Makes 4 to 6 servings

Jalapeño-Cranberry Port Sauce (page 169)

Apple and Curry Cream (page 158)

Herb Mayonnaise (page 158)

2 pounds turkey cutlets

Salt and freshly ground black pepper, to taste

Peanut or canola oil for deep-frying

Prepare the Jalapeño-Cranberry Port Sauce, Apple and Curry Cream and Herb Mayonnaise.

With a rolling pin, pound each turkey cutlet between 2 sheets of plastic wrap until thin; cut in 2 or 3 pieces.

For each diner, arrange a portion of the turkey on a small plate. Place on the table with the dinner plates, dipping sauces, salt and pepper and any side dishes.

In the kitchen, pour the oil in a metal or porcelain enameled fondue pot until about half full. Place on the stove and heat until the temperature reaches 375F (190C).

Carry the fondue pot to the table and place it over a lit burner adjusted to the highest setting. Diners should use fondue forks to spear and cook the turkey in the hot oil until no longer pink inside. Use a regular fork for dipping and eating.

Buffalo-Style Chicken Fondue with Zestful Blue Cheese Dressing

This fondue features pieces of chicken breast that taste like buffalo chicken wings. Use chicken breasts, strips of chicken tenderloin, or thin strips of moist meat from boned chicken thighs or chicken legs. Serve with the Celery Root Rémoulade with Dried Blueberries and Hazelnuts (page 125) and spicy sweet potato chips or your favorite coleslaw and chips.

Make 4 to 6 servings

Zestful Blue Cheese Dressing (page 167)
Buffalo Wing Sauce (page 169)
2 pounds boneless, skinless chicken breasts cut into 2-inch strips or $3/4$-inch cubes
Ribs of celery, cut in half lengthwise, then cut in 3-inch sticks
Peanut or canola oil, for deep-frying

Prepare the Zestful Blue Cheese Dressing and the Buffalo Wing Sauce.

For each diner, arrange a portion of the chicken on a small plate. Place on the table with the celery sticks, dinner plates, dipping sauces, salt and pepper and any side dishes.

In the kitchen, pour the oil in a metal or porcelain enameled fondue pot until about half full. Place on the stove and heat until the temperature reaches 375F (190C).

Carry the fondue pot to the table and place it over a lit burner adjusted to the highest setting. Diners should use fondue forks to spear and cook the chicken in the hot oil until no longer pink inside. Use a regular fork for dipping and eating. Serve the celery sticks on the side.

Chinese Hot Pots

APPETIZER AND STARTERS
FOR HOT POT MEALS

Butterfly Crisps (page 124) with Tofu Dill Dip (page 22)

Edamamé Appetizer (page 94)

Lotus Crisps (page 64)

Sugar Pea and Shrimp Salad with Creamy Strawberry Vinaigrette (page 131), served as a small salad or as dippers with dipping sauce

Small portions of Kayoko's Spring Rain Salad (page 132)

Fried Tofu Wedges (page 67) with Soy Sauce and Sesame Dip (page 166)

Small portions of Mixed Greens with Pear and Ginger Vinaigrette (page 129)

Chinese Roast Pork Tenderloin (page 87), thin-sliced in a cold plate

Sautéed meatballs from Spicy Korean Meatball Fondue in Lettuce Wraps (page 60)

Hot and Spicy Thai Coleslaw (page 128)

Cucumbers with Fresh Dill (page 123), or substitute cilantro, basil or mint

Cucumber Salad with Fresh Mint and Red Chili Vinaigrette (page 128)

Pear Fans (page 130) or sliced Asian pears with Indochine Sauce (page 170)

Orange-Flavored Carrot and Pear Salad Rolls (page 133)

Spinach and Cabbage Rolls (page 134), with dressing

Neri Seihin (page 98), with prepared wasabi, soy sauce and Hot Chinese Mustard (page 154)

Edible Rice Plates (page 78)

Sliced Marinated Lotus Root (page 74)

The way you cut your meat reflects the way you live.

—Confucius

A hot pot is a unique style of communal dining enjoyed throughout Asia. It is fun-filled and satisfying, especially when the weather turns cold. In northern China, *huo guo* means "fire pot" or "fire kettle." The oldest, most popular version is the Mongolian fire pot. When freezing winds from Mongolia begin to blow, people flock to public dining stalls and steamy, crowded restaurants to congregate around these large, metal workhorses. As the diners bask in heat radiating from the pot's broad, charcoal-fueled smokestack, water or broth in the cooking bowl begins to boil. Diners use chopsticks to dip paper-thin sliced mutton or lamb into the bubbling liquid. Cooked within seconds, the meat is then dipped into a spicy, custom-blended sauce to enliven its plain taste. Baked buns are passed on the side. Finally, the savory broth is ladled into bowls as a soup course and digestive.

Throughout Asia, hot-pot meals go by lyrical names such as the steamboat, volcano soup or chrysanthemum pot. The handsome metal pot is the centerpiece, surrounded by plates of thinly-sliced meats, fresh seafood, vegetables, noodles and at least six condiment bowls covering the table. Counting empty plates is the traditional way to tally the bill.

Businessmen gather around the communal pot to demonstrate goodwill and build cooperative relationships. It is the "social cement" for strengthening old friendships and bonding new acquaintances. The hot pot ritual serves as a therapeutic roundtable for family gatherings and creates a festive ambience for special celebrations. In public settings or at home, hot-pot meals should be leisurely enjoyed in an atmosphere of convivial informality. Lively conversation and a sense of togetherness have profound meaning to the gregarious Chinese, especially when bolstered with good food.

Ghengis Khan united nomadic Mongolian tribes and invaded neighboring China to establish the Yuan dynasty (A.D. 1280 to 1368). From early times, warring Mongols gathered around a fire to plunge mutton into pots of boiling water or cook it on metal fire-grills. The campfire evolved into the fire pot, typical of the lighter, refined imperial cuisine of the ancient capital. In Beijing, this cooking method, called *chün* or "lamb rinsing," is often found in Hui Muslim restaurants.

Sichuan province is called the center of Chinese hot-pot cuisine. The yin-yang pot is popular in the provincial capitol, Chengdu. The unusual pot is divided down the middle by a metal strip curved to resemble the yin-yang symbol. The dish is a dichotomy of traditional and esoteric tastes. One side holds a savory, mild broth—the other, a reddish broth, charged with chilies. Wildly popular in Taiwan and Hong Kong, the dish is an offshoot of the *mala tang* hot pot featuring a chili-laced broth that could pass for bubbling brimstone. *Ma* refers to the numbing effect of Sichuan peppercorns; *la* refers to the spicy sting of red chilies. The mild broth is best for cooking dumplings, seafood and fish balls; the spicy broth is well suited for hearty meats and vegetables.

The Southern Cantonese hot pot is lighter than the northern version; mutton and lamb are rarely included. It is a gustatory delight filled with seafood, seafood dumplings, meats, colorful fresh vegetables and meatballs. Waste-not, want-not! Almost every imaginable part of a fish is used, along with a few unimaginable ones!

Hot pots come in copper, brass, pewter, stainless steel or aluminum. Six can comfortably gather around a twelve-inch pot; in an Asian household it might accommodate eight to ten. Inexpensive, lightweight aluminum pots from Thailand come in three sizes, serving two to ten people. All pots have a deep, metal cooking bowl built around a chimney. The bowl and lid have sets of handles. Lift the bowl off the broad base to uncover a tin-lined container for housing charcoal. The base has a set of handles for lifting the entire pot. In another style, the bowl is fused onto a narrow base forming a single unit. It has a removable liner. Charcoal is added through the chimney. All hot pots have cutout sections in the base for draft and access to the ashes.

Fire was the first essential for the Yuan dynasty housewife, but today we use charcoal briquettes, the pillow-shaped carbon composites found in any supermarket or hardware store. Some contain chemical additives for easy lighting. Borax may be added to bind the charcoal; lime for whitening the ash to indicate they are ready for use. Stick with top-quality brands, which are dense and burn longer.

To use, light fifteen to twenty charcoal briquettes outdoors in a barbeque grill. (I do not recommend heating charcoal under an oven broiler.) You can cut the briquettes in half to fit into the chimney. Heat past the smoking stage until completely covered with gray/white ash. It is important to burn off the chemicals before placing the briquettes into the pot, especially if cooking indoors. To boost the fire in the pot, don't add fresh charcoal. Keep a few heated briquettes on the grill, ready if needed. Lump charcoal burns hotter but is messy and creates more sparks.

Smoldering charcoal needs plenty of ventilation. The U.S. Consumer Product Safety Commission warns ". . . never light and burn charcoal inside your home or camper because of the danger of carbon monoxide poisoning in a closed environment."

On the table, place a wide, shallow pan with one inch of water on a fireproof pad. Set the fire-pot base in the water to insulate and extinguish stray sparks. Heat the stock to boiling; fill the bowl about half full. Use hot pads to carry it to the base; add the lid. Carry hot briquettes to the table on a heavy foil-lined pan. With tongs, drop them down the chimney, partially filling the chimney walls. In some pots, briquettes must be added before the bowl is put into place. Invite the diners to sit down and enjoy an appetizer until the broth bubbles. Remove the lid and begin cooking.

Chinese hot pots lend an unmatched ambience and can be used outdoors safely in the spring, summer and fall. Chinese restaurant and home cooks often use a Japanese shabu shabu pot (*hokonabé*), which is heated on a tabletop burner. It is the most efficient substitute. Or use a Japanese earthenware casserole (*donabé*), an enameled cast-iron casserole, electric wok or deep electric skillet. The substitute pot should hold at least three inches of liquid. A fondue pot isn't practical for a large group but works fine with a scaled-down menu for four. Read more about Japanese equipment in the Nabémono chapter (page 89). All this cooking equipment can be purchased online; look for addresses in the Mail-Order Section (page 225). Locating and purchasing this type of cookware has never been easier.

CHINESE KNIFE SKILLS

The success of a Chinese hot pot meal partly depends on how the meat is cut. The thinner the slice, the faster it will cook in the broth and the sooner everyone gets to eat. To facilitate slicing, wrap and freeze meat and poultry until about half frozen. With a sharp, lightweight Chinese vegetable cleaver or large chef's knife, cut or shave the meat across the grain diagonally into 1/8-inch-thick slices or thinner. Chicken can be cut slightly thicker. Beef tenderloin slices can be cut in half. Cut a flank steak in half lengthwise then cut each half into paper-thin slices. Cut a thick steak diagonally into thin strips, about three inches long. Arrange the slices overlapping in a circle on plates or platters. Garnish the center with edible flowers, scallions or sculpted vegetable flowers. Each piece of meat should take thirty seconds to one minute to cook, depending on the thickness. If the slices seem large, don't worry; they shrink quickly when dipped into boiling broth. Tougher cuts like flank steak or top round benefit from marinating. Chinese cooks may marinate the meat after it is arranged on the platter. Pour some soy sauce and a little dry sherry into a clean plastic spray bottle. Spray the meat lightly or brush on the mixture with a pastry brush. Tender meats can be marinated for thirty minutes for flavor; tougher cuts need at least two hours up to overnight in the refrigerator.

CHINESE HOT-POT ETIQUETTE

Eating Chinese-style at a round table compels the diner to repeatedly practice his boardinghouse reach. Etiquette permits one to reach politely across the table with chopsticks to select each bite from a set of communal platters. Foods are never passed around. For this reason, serving chopsticks can cause great confusion. But good etiquette dictates that we offer two sets of chopsticks per diner for tabletop dining—one pair for cooking foods and removing them from the pot and a pair for eating. For diners not adept at chopsticks, provide Chinese wire basket spoons that securely hold the foods or a fondue fork. Use chopsticks to put foods into the wire spoon and to take them out, or just tap the foods out on the plate. Asian diners often turn their chopsticks and use the clean ends to transfer foods to their plate. Extra long chopsticks are provided in "lamb-rinsing" restaurants. Juicy dumplings are placed into a porcelain spoon and held up to the mouth with one hand and eaten with chopsticks in the other hand. Other points of etiquette: You can lift your bowl and shovel the rice into your mouth or eat the noodles with chopsticks. Slurping hot soups and noodles is acceptable and a sign of real enjoyment. During a Chinese meal, perfumed, steaming hot towels are served at the end of the meal to wipe greasy hands. A curious dining custom: Northern Chinese may display a particular stance while eating lamb hot pot. They prefer to stand while eating, with one foot placed upon a bench. According to legend, this is a compromise; Mongolians prefer to eat sitting on the ground; Chinese prefer to eat while sitting in chairs.

SLICED MARINATED LOTUS ROOT

Thin slices of marinated lotus root make an excellent appetizer or side-dish for Asian one-pot meals. Cut one pound peeled lotus root into $1/8$- to $1/16$-inch-thick slices. Thin slices are easy to cut with a Benriner slicer. Blanch one minute in salted, boiling water. Drain; chill in iced water. With a paring knife, cut scalloped edges around the natural openings of each slice to create a flower design, if desired. Marinate the slices in a mixture of two tablespoons rice vinegar, two tablespoons sugar, one teaspoon light soy sauce, $1/2$ teaspoon salt, two teaspoons sesame oil and one teaspoon Firepot Oil (page 153) or hot chili sauce. Cover and chill until served. Makes 6 servings.

Vietnamese Beef and Rice Noodle Hot Pot

Pho is the ubiquitous North Vietnamese soup and salad in a bowl that evolved from the Mongolian hot pot. It is a popular street-vendor food and often eaten for breakfast. A boiling-hot fragrant, spiced stock is poured into a large bowl of chewy rice noodles and tissue-thin raw beef, which is quickly cooked. Tender meat from the stockpot and tripe might also be included. The diner customizes his meal with fresh herbs, bean sprouts and tasty sauces. The name *pho* translates to "your own bowl," which means the diner receives his own portion instead of sharing food from communal platters. Serve this hot pot as a light, satisfying lunch or supper with Orange-Flavored Carrot and Pear Salad Rolls (page 133) on the side. Offer a chilled Asian beer such as Chinese Tsingtao or glasses of Iced Lemongrass Tea (page 143). For dessert, pass a tropical fruit platter or Perfumed Oranges (page 206).

Makes 6 servings

Asian Beef Stock (page 179)

Salt, to taste

Brandied Hoisin Sauce (page 151)

1¹⁄₂ to 2 pounds beef tenderloin, sirloin or flank steak, partially frozen, cut into ¹⁄₈-inch-thick slices

1 red onion, peeled, halved, cut in thin slices

Vietnamese Table Salad (page 124)

1 (1-pound) package ¹⁄₄-inch thick, dried, flat rice noodles, soaked in a large bowl of water 45 minutes

Siracha hot chili sauce, to taste

Vietnamese fish sauce (*nuoc mam*), to taste

Prepare the Asian Beef Stock; season with salt. Prepare the Brandied Hoisin Sauce. Slice the beef and arrange the beef on 3 plates in overlapping slices. Garnish with the onion. Prepare the Vietnamese Table Salad.

Bring a large pot of water to boil. Drain the noodles, add to the boiling water and boil about 1 minute. Drain and rinse with tepid water. Gently press out water. Arrange the noodles in 6 deep soup bowls. Carry the plates of meat, salad and a soup ladle to the table. Provide a small plate, a small bowl of each sauce, a soup spoon, fondue fork and chopsticks for each diner.

In the kitchen, pour 3¹⁄₂ cups of the broth into a metal or porcelain enameled fondue pot. Bring to a boil over medium-high heat.

Carry the fondue pot to the table and place over a lit burner adjusted to the highest setting. Bring the remaining broth to a boil; ladle about 1¹⁄₂ cups broth into each bowl of noodles. Keep remaining broth warm. Serve noodles; each diner can add ingredients from the salad and any of the sauces.

Diners can use chopsticks or fondue forks to dip 1 or 2 slices of meat and some onion into the hot broth. Cook 30 seconds; add to the noodles and broth. The Vietnamese use chopsticks in one hand to grasp the noodles and a spoon in the other hand to help with the lift. The meat can be dipped into the Brandied Hoisin Sauce before eating. Replenish the fondue pot with stock, as needed. When the meat is eaten, ladle the rich broth into the soup bowls; season to taste.

COOK'S NOTES

Eating noodles is serious business for the Vietnamese. In America, at noodle shops where *pho* is served, the smallest size serving would be considered large by American standards. The largest size could easily feed four in the average American restaurant. To serve large portions of *pho* and other one-bowl noodle meals, I like to use Japanese noodle bowls or *donburi* bowls used for one-bowl rice meals. These bowls hold 3¹⁄₂ to 4 cups liquid. They are available in Asian markets and department stores or through the Mail-Order Resources (page 225).

Vietnamese Beef Fondue with Indochine Sauce

Centuries of Chinese and French rule left permanent, distinguishing marks on Vietnam's cuisine. Beef is expensive, but the Vietnamese have been fond of it since the thirteenth-century Mongolian invasions. Beef fondue is served at Bo Bay Mon restaurants where it appears as the first course in a special seven-course feast that features beef in every dish. The final dish is a rice and chopped-beef soup with fried noodles and peanuts made from the leftover lemon-vinegar broth. At home, use the broth to make a simple soup with cabbage, rice or noodles and seasonings, as desired. This fondue is light and refreshing; strips of beef are enclosed in a salad wrap. I like to serve it as a participation appetizer followed with a menu of grilled salmon with kaffir lime sauce, Coconut Rice Pilaf (page 116) and Hot and Spicy Thai Coleslaw (page 128). Caramel flan and sliced mangoes make a lovely dessert.

Makes 6 appetizer servings

1 tablespoon extra-virgin olive oil or canola oil

2 shallots, thinly sliced

1 (14-inch) stalk lemongrass, smashed and cut into 2-inch strips or the zest from 1 large lemon

2 cloves garlic, chopped

2 (1/8-inch-thick) diagonal slices fresh ginger

1 (25-ounce) bottle mineral water with natural lemon flavor or plain

1 teaspoon sea salt

1/4 cup cider vinegar

2 tablespoons sugar

Indochine Sauce (page 170)

1 pound beef tenderloin, or sirloin, partially frozen, cut into 1/8-inch-thick slices

Vietnamese Table Salad (page 124)

Small butter lettuce leaves, rinsed and dried

1 medium red onion, peeled, halved, cut in paper-thin slices, soaked in 1/2 cup rice vinegar 10 minutes, drained

24 (6-inch) round rice papers

To make the broth, heat the olive oil in a 2-quart saucepan over medium heat. Sauté the shallots, lemongrass, garlic and ginger for 2 to 3 minutes, stirring constantly. Reduce the heat to low; pour in the water. Mix in the salt, vinegar and sugar. Simmer over low heat for 10 minutes. (The broth can be made 1 or 2 hours ahead; cover and set aside.)

Prepare the Indochine Sauce. Arrange the beef on 3 plates. The beef can be covered with plastic wrap and refrigerated for up to 1 hour. Prepare the Vietnamese Table Salad and lettuce. Divide ingredients for the table salad, the lettuce and drained red onion among 3 large plates. Two people will share each plate of meat and salad.

At serving time, dip each rice paper into a bowl of hot tap water. Remove at once and place on a clean cloth towel. Turn after 1 minute. The rice papers should be moist and slightly elastic but not soggy. Stack on 2 plates; keep covered. Carry the plates of meat and salad, bowls of sauce and rice papers to the table. Provide a salad plate, fondue fork, and chopsticks for each diner.

In the kitchen, bring the broth to a boil over medium-high heat. Strain it into a metal or porcelain enameled fondue pot.

Carry the fondue pot to the table and place over a lit burner adjusted to the highest setting. Each diner should place a rice paper on his plate; top with a piece of the lettuce. With chopsticks or a fondue fork, dip 1 or 2 slices of meat into the hot broth. Cook 30 seconds; place it on the rice paper and lettuce. Add ingredients from the table salad. Roll up the packet, folding in the sides. Dip into the sauce before eating.

Food has no taste if you eat too much.
—Ancient Chinese Proverb

Thai Seafood Hot Pot

A steamboat, or hot pot, is the traditional serving container for hearty Thai soups. This meal-in-a-bowl features a spicy, lemon-scented, coconut milk broth that is the base for a popular soup in Thai restaurants. Here, seafood is cooked in the fragrant broth at the table then ladled into bowls of chewy rice noodles. You can mix up a zesty dipping sauce for the seafood by blending freshly squeezed lime juice with cilantro, green onion, ginger and hot chili paste, to taste. The seafood mix can be varied; substitute other types such as cooked, in-shell lobster tails, cut into 1½-inch pieces, or salted, quickly blanched oysters rinsed in cool water. A nice way to present the oysters is to wrap each one in a large blanched spinach leaf to form oyster bundles. Serve this dish for lunch or as a light supper. For a heartier meal, you might add an additional course of grilled steak or poultry and a side dish of Cucumber Salad with Fresh Mint and Red Chili Vinaigrette (page 128).

Makes 4 servings

Thai Coconut Broth with Lemongrass (page 183)

2 pounds live mussels, scrubbed, debearded

½ pound large shrimp, peeled, deveined, with tail intact

1 pound skinned sea bass, red snapper, mahi mahi or salmon fillets, cut into 1-inch pieces

½ pound scallops, cut in half

2 medium cleaned squid, cut into rings

4 ounces small cultivated mushrooms, wiped clean, cut in half

4 green onions, white parts cut into 2-inch pieces (reserve green parts)

¼ pound fresh snow peas, blanched in salted, boiling water 30 seconds, rinsed in ice water, strings removed

12 ounces ⅛-inch-thick medium-width dried rice noodles (*sen chan*), soaked in a large bowl of water 45 minutes

CONDIMENTS

4 limes, cut into wedges

1 cup fresh, rinsed, torn cilantro leaves

½ cup minced green onion

2 tablespoons matchstick strips fresh ginger (See Matchstick Strips, page 133)

⅓ cup roasted, salted peanuts, finely chopped

Hot chili paste (*sambal oelek*), to taste

If using a Chinese hot pot, heat the charcoal briquettes outdoors on a grill about 40 minutes before time to cook.

Prepare the Thai Coconut Broth with Lemongrass. Put the mussels into a large pot with 1 cup water. Cover and cook on medium-high heat until the shells open, 3 to 5 minutes. Discard any mussels that stay closed. Remove mussels from shells; place each into a half shell. Arrange seafood on plates or platters.

Arrange the mushrooms, green onions and snow peas on 2 small plates. Drain the noodles.

Place each condiment into a small separate bowl. Bring a large pot of water to boil. Add the noodles; cook 1 to 2 minutes. Drain and rinse with tepid water. Arrange in 6 deep noodle or soup bowls. Carry the noodles, plates of seafood and vegetables, condiments and a soup ladle to the table. Provide a small plate, a sauce bowl, a Chinese soup spoon, a wire basket spoon and chopsticks for each diner.

In the kitchen, heat the broth to boiling. Pour broth into the hot-pot bowl; add the cover. With tongs, place the briquettes into the fire chamber; cover bowl if added through the chimney.

Carry the hot pot to the table; set into a shallow pan of water. If using a substitute pot, add the broth in the kitchen; carry to the table and turn on the heat source. (As the broth heats, the diners can nibble on appetizers.) Add a portion of the seafood and vegetables to the broth. After 1 or 2 minutes, everyone can scoop out the foods, placing them into the noodle bowls. Ladle in some of the broth. Season with the condiments, to taste. Continue adding the foods to the pot.

COOK'S NOTES

Edible Rice Plates Dry rice-paper rounds, 6 to 8 inches in diameter, are usually moistened and used for rolling up cooked meats and salads or for making spring rolls. They can be deep-fried in oil heated to 400F (205C) and will instantly puff and become crispy. The tender wrinkled white discs can be used as an edible plate for salads and stir-fries. Serve a basket full as a tasty appetizer before a hot-pot meal.

Serve with hot mustard sauce, Five-Spice Orange Sauce (page 167) or canned Chinese plum sauce enhanced with a small amount of orange juice, chili sauce and grated orange zest. Sprinkle each bite with finely chopped peanuts if desired.

Korean Steak Pot with Sesame Noodles

Koreans love to cook foods at the table. The Confucian order of stylized dining and Lao-se's Taoist principles of freshness and simplicity have been major influences on Korean cuisine. A Mongolian influence is clearly seen in the Korean's love of beef and spicy seasonings. In Korean soups and hot-pot dishes, the beef is thinly sliced, marinated and usually precooked. I like to precede this dish with a western salad of Mixed Greens with Pear and Ginger Vinaigrette (page 129) or with small bowls of the marinated carrot and pear mixture from the recipe, Orange-Flavored Carrot and Pear Salad Rolls (page 133). Sprinkle each salad with sesame seeds. Of course, don't forget to include a side dish of cabbage kim chee!

Makes 6 servings

6 cups Asian Beef Stock (page 179), omit star anise, lemongrass and cilantro, or Basic Chicken Stock (page 176)

Chili-Sesame Sauce (page 152)

Soy Sauce and Sesame Dip (page 166)

1/3 cup soy sauce

2 tablespoons saké or dry white wine

2 cloves garlic, minced

1 teaspoon minced fresh ginger

1/8 teaspoon ground black pepper

1 1/2 to 2 pounds beef sirloin steak or flank steak, partially frozen, cut in half lengthwise, cut crosswise into 1/8-inch-thick slices

3/4 pound dried Korean wheat-flour noodles or Japanese udon or soba, boiled 4 minutes or until al dente, rinsed in cool water, drained, tossed with 1 tablespoon sesame oil

2 tablespoons vegetable oil

1 pound Napa cabbage, cut into 2-inch pieces

¼ pound bean sprouts, blanched 30 seconds in boiling water, rinsed in cold water, drained

1 bunch green onions, cut diagonally into 2-inch lengths

6 dried black mushrooms, softened in water until soft, stems trimmed, cut in half (see Cook's Note below)

2 zucchini, cut in julienne strips

2 carrots, peeled, cut in julienne strips

1 large red bell pepper, cut in julienne strips

1 (10- to 16-ounce) block tofu, cut into 1-inch squares

If using a Chinese hot pot, heat the charcoal briquettes outdoors on a grill about 40 minutes before time to cook. Prepare the Asian Beef Stock, Chili-Sesame Sauce and Soy Sauce and Sesame Dip.

In a shallow glass bowl, combine the soy sauce, saké, garlic, ginger and black pepper. Lightly dip each piece of beef into the marinade; shake excess back into the pan. Place on a platter. Cover lightly; marinate for 30 minutes. Divide noodles among 6 large bowls.

Add 1 tablespoon of the oil to a large nonstick skillet over high heat. Add a few beef slices; cook 30 seconds or until half done. The beef should still be red inside. Place on a platter; cook the remaining beef in small batches. Add oil, as needed. Drain the beef well.

Heat the stock to boiling. Layer the ingredients in the hot pot in this order: cabbage, bean sprouts, green onions, mushrooms, zucchini and sautéed beef. Scatter the carrot, bell pepper and tofu on top. Ladle in enough stock to reach the top of the layered vegetables and beef. Add the lid. With tongs, pack the briquettes into the fire chamber; cover bowl if added through the chimney.

Carry the hot pot to the table; set into a shallow pan of water. If using a substitute pot, add the foods and stock in the kitchen; carry to the table and turn on the heat source. Carry the bowls of noodles, sauces, tongs and soup ladle to the table. Provide a small plate, a soup spoon, two sauce bowls and chopsticks for each diner. (As the broth heats, the diners can nibble on appetizers.) Spoon Chili-Sesame Sauce and Soy Sauce and Sesame Dip into each sauce bowl. Simmer ingredients for 5 minutes. The diners can use chopsticks to help themselves to the ingredients in the pot. Ladle the broth into the noodles; dip meat into the sauces. Any remaining broth can be added to the pot.

COOK'S NOTE

Chinese Black Mushrooms They are also known as winter mushrooms and are mainly used dried in Chinese cooking. They are known as shiitaki mushrooms in Japan where they are often used fresh. Purchase high-quality mushrooms with thick caps with white cracks for hot-pot dishes. Expensive mushrooms should be used whole or cut in half. Lesser quality mushrooms are fine for stir-fry, noodle or rice dishes. Cost is often an indication of quality. Mushrooms will soften within 20 minutes in hot water but for the finest flavor, soak in tap water 3 hours or overnight. Discard stems; strain soaking liquid for stocks and sauces.

Though lamb may be good,
it is difficult to cook it to suit everyone's taste.
—**Ancient Chinese Proverb**

Mongolian Lamb Fire Pot

Mongolian hospitality is legendary. To establish friendly relationships, Mongolians share food from a common plate and pass a friendship cup, often filled with a bracing beverage of fermented mare's or camel's milk called *koumiss*. During the bitter winters, people gather in companionship around a fire-breathing, funneled hot pot filled with boiling water or broth. Each person cooks his portion of thinly sliced mutton, to taste. Some cooks are so skillful with knives, they can slice 1 pound of meat thin enough to feed a dozen people. If available, you can use the lamb bone, meat scraps, fresh ginger and green onion to make a light stock for this dish.

In the north, chopped, sour, pickled greens might be added to hot-pot broth at the table. You can substitute canned red-in-snow (snow pickle), which is similar to young turnip greens. Begin the meal with roasted, salted pecans or honey walnuts and marinated cucumbers, substituting fresh mint for the dill in Cucumbers with Fresh Dill (page 123), or an elaborate appetizer like spring rolls. The meat is especially delicious stuffed into Sesame-Peanut Pockets, flat buns layered with sesame paste and peanut butter (page 140). The paste mixture gives the bread a special nutty flavor.

Makes 6 servings

8 cups Asian Chicken Stock (page 176) or Asian Beef Stock (page 179), omitting lemongrass

Hot-Pot Dipping Sauce and Condiments (page 150)

Sesame-Peanut Pockets (optional, page 140)

Brandied Hoisin Sauce (optional, page 151)

2 to 2½ pounds trimmed, boned leg of lamb, partially frozen, cut into thin slices, about ¹⁄₁₆-inch thick

2 to 3 (2-ounce) skeins Chinese bean threads (see Bean Threads, page 219), soaked 20 minutes in hot tap water, rinsed in cold water, drained, cut 1 or 2 times

1 (1½-pound) Napa cabbage, quartered, cut in 1½-inch slices, or 4 baby bok choy, leaves separated, sliced diagonally

6 dried black mushrooms, soaked in water until soft, stems trimmed, cut in half (see Cook's Note, page 79)

1 (10-ounce) bag fresh spinach, rinsed, large stems removed

2 (10- to 16-ounce) blocks tofu, cut in 1-inch cubes

If using a Chinese hot pot, heat the charcoal briquettes outdoors on a grill about 40 minutes before time to cook. Prepare the Asian Chicken Stock, Scallion Brushes, Hot-Pot Dipping Sauce and at least 10 condiments, and Sesame-Peanut Pockets and Brandied Hoisin Sauce, if using.

Arrange the sliced lamb on plates or platters in overlapping circles; garnish with some slivered green onions from the condiments. Arrange the bean threads, cabbage, mushrooms, spinach and tofu on plates or platters. Carry the plates of food, dipping sauce, condiments, bread and soup ladle to the table. Provide a small plate, a soup bowl with saucer, Chinese porcelain spoon, wire basket spoon and chopsticks for each diner.

In the kitchen, heat the stock to simmering. With tongs, place the briquettes into the fire chamber; cover bowl if added through the chimney. Pour 6 cups of the hot stock into the bowl.

Carry hot pot to the table and set into a pan of water. If using a substitute pot, add stock in the kitchen; carry to the table and place on the heat source. Turn on the heat source. (As the stock heats, the diners can nibble on appetizers.) Pour about 2 tablespoons dipping sauce into each sauce bowl. Pass the condiments for each person to season his sauce, as desired.

The diners can use chopsticks to pick up 1 or 2 slices of meat and "rinse" them through the bubbling stock. Dip cooked meat into the sauce and eat. Or stuff into split Sesame-Peanut Pockets spread with Brandied Hoisin Sauce; garnish with slivered green onions and cilantro sprigs from the condiments. Add the bean threads and vegetables as the meat is cooked. Or reserve bean threads for the soup course. Replenish the pot with warm stock or boiling water, if needed. After the food is eaten, pour in any remaining stock. Season to taste then ladle into soup bowls.

VARIATION

You can include ¹/₂ recipe Turkish Borek, Tartar Style (page 88) in this hot pot, along with the accompanying Clarified Butter (page 160) and Yogurt Sauce for dipping. Or, omit sliced lamb and Sesame-Peanut Pockets entirely and substitute 1 recipe Turkish Borek, Tartar Style. Makes 5 or 6 servings.

Five-Flavor Pork Balls

These spicy, gingery meatballs can be added to any hot-pot dish or soup. They are cooked ahead for fast reheating in the hot pot. You can poach the meatballs 1 day in advance, wrap well and refrigerate overnight. Remove from the refrigerator 30 minutes before serving. The meatballs can also be dusted lightly with cornstarch and deep-fried.

Makes 12 to 13 meatballs

1 large egg

1 tablespoon Chinese rice wine (*shaohsing*) or dry sherry

1 slice bread, crusts trimmed, torn into shreds

¹/₂ pound ground pork, chicken or turkey

2 green onions, minced

2 teaspoons finely minced fresh ginger

1 teaspoon Chinese mushroom soy sauce or plain soy sauce

1 clove garlic, finely minced

¹/₄ teaspoon hot chili paste, or to taste

Pinch salt and freshly ground black pepper, to taste

In a medium bowl, mix the egg, wine and bread into a paste. Mix in the pork until smooth. Stir in the green onions, ginger, soy sauce and garlic. Season with chili paste, salt and black pepper. With a measuring tablespoon, scoop up ¹/₂ tablespoon of the pork mixture. Using a second spoon, form it into a meatball. Push off spoon onto a plate. Shape the remaining mixture in meatballs.

Bring a medium pot of water to boil. Add the meatballs; cook until barely done, 1 to 2 minutes. Remove with a slotted spoon. Cool; add to a hot-pot platter for 2 to 3 minutes of additional cooking. Or cool, cover and refrigerate overnight. Remove from refrigerator 30 minutes before using.

Eat too much at one meal and
you will have to drink soup at ten meals.

—Ancient Chinese Proverb

Genghis Khan Fire-Grill

When Genghis Khan and his famous horsemen-warriors swept into China they brought the fire-grill method of cooking. Sliced mutton was cooked over an open fire, perhaps on a warrior's discarded breastplate or metal helmet. Swords were laced with chunks of meat for quick grilling.

Treat your guests to a Chinese-style barbecue as they gather around a tabletop grill, electric wok or electric skillet. The tender meat is brushed with the marinade for flavor. For a less tender cut like flank steak or top round, marinate meat strips at least 1 hour. Stuff the meat into Sesame-Peanut Pockets (page 140), or wrap in small, steamed flour tortillas. A bowl of hearty millet soup is the usual accompaniment. Season with any condiment listed below. Serve Sliced Marinated Lotus Root (page 74) on the side. This is good with rice. The Koreans are descendants of the Mongol tribes and adore charcoal-grilled meats. Be sure and try the succulent Korean-Style Barbecue variation.

Makes 4 or 5 servings

---

2 pounds trimmed beef tenderloin or sirloin, boned leg of lamb, pork tenderloin or boneless leg of venison, partially frozen, cut into thin slices, 1/8-inch thick

1/2 cup Japanese soy sauce (*shoyu*)

1/4 cup dry sherry or dry vermouth

1 tablespoon sugar

1/2 cup peanut or canola oil, or as needed

2 small leeks, slit lengthwise, well rinsed, shredded diagonally

3 long, thin Chinese eggplants, cut diagonally in 1/4-inch-thick slices

2 small red bell peppers, seeded, cut in thin strips

1 pound Napa cabbage, cut in 1/2-inch strips

1/2 pound fresh bean sprouts

Condiments from Hot Pot Dipping Sauce and Condiments (page 150)

Peppered Peanut Sauce (page 151)

Arrange the sliced beef on 3 plates in overlapping circles. To make the marinade, combine the soy sauce, sherry and sugar; brush lightly on meat. Cover lightly; use within 30 minutes.

Pour the oil into a small cup. Arrange the leeks, eggplants, bell peppers, cabbage and bean sprouts on plates or platters. Prepare the first 6 condiments listed in the recipe Hot Pot Dipping Sauce and Condiments. Carry the plates of food, cooking oil, pastry brush, condiments, peanut sauce and any side dishes to the table. Provide a small plate, a sauce bowl and chopsticks for each diner.

Heat an electric tabletop grill or substitute a skillet on high heat. Brush with a small amount of the oil. Instruct guests to add slices of meat to the grill, seasoned with any of the condiments. Cook about 1 minute, turning often, or to taste. Dip meat into peanut sauce; garnish with slivered onion and cilantro sprigs from the condiments. Add a portion of vegetables to the grill, beginning with the leeks, eggplants and bell peppers. Turn meat and vegetables with chopsticks as they cook. If the grill is nonstick, the meat may stick; add more oil or a few drops of broth or water. Scrape grill, as necessary. When the meat has been eaten, any remaining vegetables can be cooked together with the condiments.

VARIATION

Korean-Style Barbecue Omit the marinade. Lightly dip thin slices of rib eye or sirloin into this marinade blend: 1/2 cup soy sauce, 2 tablespoons brown sugar, 2 tablespoons dry white wine, 2 minced cloves garlic, 2 teaspoons minced fresh ginger, 1/3 cup slivered green onion, 1 1/2 tablespoons sesame seeds, 2 teaspoons sesame seed oil and 2 dashes of black pepper. Place on a platter; marinate 30 minutes. Cook meat and vegetables on the grill. Serve with Cooked Medium-Grain Rice (page 117).

Chinese Millet Congee Millet is more than birdseed. This protein and magnesium-rich crop has been a Chinese staple since antiquity. The tiny golden grains have an intriguing fragrance and flavor. Millet soup is popular in Northern China and often served with Mongolian grilled meats. To make congee, a slightly thickened porridge, toast 1/2 cup hulled dry millet in a hot skillet until fragrant, 1 or 2 minutes, stirring constantly. In a saucepan, simmer the millet with 6 cups chicken stock until tender, about 20 minutes. Season to taste; eat plain or add any of the Condiments in the recipe for Genghis Khan Fire-Grill (above).

Everyone's tastes in foods are different.
—Ancient Chinese Proverb

Chrysanthemum Pot

Chrysanthemums and hot pots herald the appearance of autumn in China. Hot pots occasionally contain foods not part of the average Western diet. Consider pig intestine, pork kidney, goose gut, fish maw (bladder), and live shrimp that wiggle and jump out of the pot. This delicious dish is filled with familiar tastes, perfect for special occasions. In China, the dish is cooked in a charming chrysanthemum pot. Hard to come by, this pot has a wide, shallow metal bowl, similar to a wok. It has a lid but no chimney. The pot sits on an attractive round brass ring with decorative cutouts that resemble latticework. A cup with denatured alcohol or fuel sits inside the ring. Flames reach through the lattice to dance around the pan; the imagery inspires the Chinese to think of beautiful Asian spider mums. The flames appear green from the reaction of copper in the brass pot. After the foods are eaten, leftover broth in the pot is sprinkled with white chrysanthemum petals and served as soup. Cooked Long-Grain Rice (page 115) can be served with this hot pot. Hot Chinese Mustard and dipping sauce made with light soy sauce and fresh ginger go well with the meats and seafood.

Makes 6 servings

8 cups Asian Chicken Stock (page 182)

Fried Tofu Wedges (page 67)

Five-Flavor Pork Balls (page 81)

1/2 pound beef flank steak, halved lengthwise, partially frozen, cut into 1/8-inch strips

2 chicken breast halves, skinned, boned, partially frozen, cut in half, then into 1/8-inch-thick slices

1 pound skinned sea bass, red snapper or mahi mahi fillets, cut in 1-inch pieces

1/2 pound large fresh shrimp, peeled, deveined, cut in half lengthwise

1 pound Napa cabbage, cut in 1 1/2-inch strips

1/2 pound bundle of spinach leaves, rinsed, stems trimmed

6 dried black mushrooms, soaked in water until soft, stems trimmed, cut in half (see Cook's Note, page 79)

1 bunch green onions, cut diagonally into 2-inch lengths

Hot-Pot Dipping Sauce and Condiments (page 150)

2 to 3 (2-ounce) skeins Chinese bean threads (see Bean Threads, page 219), soaked 20 minutes in hot tap water, rinsed in cold water, drained

If using a Chinese hot pot, heat the charcoal briquettes outdoors on a grill about 40 minutes before time to cook.

Prepare the Asian Chicken Stock, Fried Tofu Wedges, and Five-Flavor Pork Balls. Arrange the tofu, pork balls and sliced meats and seafood separately on plates or platters; decorate the centers with spider mums. Arrange the cabbage, spinach, mushrooms and green onions on small plates or platters.

Prepare the Hot-Pot Dipping Sauce and Condiments. Carry the plates of food, dipping sauce, condiments, bean threads and soup ladle to the table. Provide a small plate, a sauce bowl, a soup bowl with saucer, a Chinese porcelain spoon, a wire basket spoon and chopsticks for each diner.

In the kitchen, heat the stock to boiling. Pour 6 cups of the stock into the bowl; add the cover. With tongs, place briquettes into the fire chamber.

Carry the hot pot to the table; set into a shallow pan of water. If using a substitute pot, add stock in the kitchen; carry it to the table and turn on the heat source. Add some of the green onion. (As the stock heats, the diners can nibble on appetizers.)

Pour 2 tablespoons dipping sauce into each sauce bowl. Pass the condiments for each person to season his sauce, as desired. The diners can use chopsticks to pick up slices of beef, chicken, fish or shrimp and cook them in the bubbling stock. Add

the vegetables and noodles as the meat cooks. Meatballs will be ready in 2 to 3 minutes. Replenish the pot with warm stock. After the food is eaten, season the remaining stock and ladle into soup bowls.

Eight Precious Hot Pot

The southern Chinese name for hot pot is *da-bin-lo*, loosely meaning, "to bang the side of the pot." It refers to all the clacking sounds people make when they touch the sides of the pot with their chopsticks.

Chinese water dumplings like boiled wontons and *chiao-tzu* are adored throughout Asia. When dumplings are featured in a hot pot, it can sound like a concerto. A hot-pot party may not be a Chinese banquet, but the fun will last as long as one. These irresistible mouthfuls are not hard to make, but producing this number can take some time. The solution is to invite eight special friends or family members to come help out. In China, stuffing dumplings is a family affair and often, an important holiday activity. All you need is the dumpling stuffers, a table, bowls of filling, spoons and wrappers. Red and green wonton wrappers are now available; an array of colorful dumplings adds to the fun. The dumplings are briefly poached in the kitchen; the guests finish cooking them in the hot pot for a casual evening of fun.

To boost the flavor of the chicken stock, include ¾ to 1 pound of meaty raw pork-chop bones in the stockpot. Chinese lettuce is popular in soups and hot pots; romaine, Boston or sturdy iceberg lettuce would make a good substitute. For a more substantial meal, you could include a platter of fried rice. Serve Plum Blossom Sherbet (page 118) for dessert.

Makes 8 servings

8 cups Asian Chicken Stock (page 182)

Shrimp and Ginger Dumplings (page 87)

Pork and Spinach Dumplings (page 88)

Hot Chinese Mustard (page 165)

Hot Pot Dipping Sauce and Condiments

Leaf lettuce leaves or head cabbage leaves

4 green onions, slivered

1/4 pound thinly sliced Smithfield ham, cut in 2 × 1-inch strips

6 dried black mushrooms, softened in water until soft, stems trimmed, cut in half (see Cook's Note, page 79)

1 head Boston (butter) lettuce, leaves rinsed, torn in 2 or 3 pieces

1/4 pound small fresh snow peas, strings removed, cut in julienne strips

2 carrots, cut in julienne strips

1/2 bunch cilantro, rinsed, stems trimmed, torn into sprigs

Salt, to taste

If using a Chinese hot pot, heat the charcoal briquettes outdoors on a grill about 40 minutes before time to cook.

Prepare the Asian Chicken Stock, the Shrimp and Ginger Dumplings, Pork and Spinach Dumplings, Hot Chinese Mustard and Hot Pot Dipping Sauce and Condiments. Arrange the cooked dumplings on several plates or platters lined with lettuce or cabbage leaves. Arrange the remaining ingredients on plates.

Carry the plates of food and a soup ladle to the table. Provide a small plate, a bowl of each sauce, a soup bowl with saucer, a Chinese porcelain spoon, a wire basket spoon and chopsticks for each diner.

In the kitchen, heat the stock to boiling. Season with salt. Pour 6 cups of the broth into the hot-pot bowl; add cover. With tongs, place the briquettes into the fire chamber.

Carry the hot pot to the table; set into a shallow pan of water. If using a substitute pot, add the stock in the kitchen; carry to the table and turn on the heat source. Add some of the vegetables to the pot. (As the stock heats, the diners can nibble on appetizers.)

Use chopsticks or a wire basket spoon to begin placing dumplings into the simmering stock. Cook 1 to 2 minutes; then scoop out and place into the soup bowls with some of the stock. Dip dumplings into the sauces. Replenish the pot with warm stock, as needed. Refrigerate leftover dumplings; deep-fry the second day. The recipe can be cut in half.

Cantonese Sha-Cha Hot Pot

At the northeastern border of Guandong Province, the Teochiu people are famous for their light, elegant cuisine. In Hong Kong, this region is known as *Chiuchow* (*Chauzhou* in Mandarin). The cuisine is influenced by the Cantonese of Quandong and the Hokkien from the bordering eastern province of Fukien. Careful attention is paid to freshness and presentation. Soups, dumplings, fresh vegetables, minced seafood balls and fried bean curd are among the favorite foods. The local kung-fu tea received its name because it requires special skills to prepare. Teochiu people have a long tradition of immigrating to Southeast Asia. Many returned bringing techniques for preparing Malay and Indonesian foods. Teochiu cooks thread bites of seafood on bamboo skewers like *saté*; after a brief simmer in a hot pot, the seafood is often dipped into a fish sauce that is a variant of *saté* sauce. In the local dialect, *saté* means "sand tea"; pronounced Sha-Cha in Mandarin. Sha-Cha jiang (sauce) is often used as a Chinese barbecue sauce and served as a dipping sauce with hot pots in Taiwan. Sometimes a raw egg is beaten into each portion. Purchase sha-cha sauce in Asian markets or serve the equally delicious peanut sauce below.

To make a delicate shrimp stock for this dish, simmer the chicken stock with the shrimp shells from the recipe for 30 minutes. Add a few moist, coral-colored dried shrimp for extra flavor. Strain and use as directed below.

Makes 6 servings

Southeast Asian Chicken Broth (page 183)

Shrimp and Ginger Dumplings (page 87), made with red or white wrappers

Poached gingery chicken meatballs from Country Chicken Hot Pot (page 97)

1/2 pound Chinese Roast Pork Tenderloin (page 87), cut in thin slices

Fried Tofu Wedges (page 67), cut into 1-inch cubes instead of wedges

Peppered Peanut Sauce (page 151)

Mignonette Sauce (page 165)

1/2 pound scallops, cut in half

1/2 pound shrimp, shelled, deveined

1/2 pound good-quality smoked mussels or raw, shucked mussels

Lettuce or cabbage leaves

3 baby bok choy, halved lengthwise, well rinsed, or Swiss chard leaves, cut in 2-inch pieces

1 bunch green onions, cut in 2-inch shreds

3/4 pound Shanghai egg noodles or other Chinese egg noodles, cooked al dente, rinsed in cool water

1/2 bunch cilantro, well-rinsed, large stems removed

3 limes, cut into wedges

If using a Chinese hot pot, heat the charcoal briquettes outdoors on a grill about 40 minutes before time to cook.

Prepare the Southeast Asian Chicken Broth, Shrimp and Ginger Dumplings, chicken meatballs, Chinese Roast Pork Tenderloin and Fried Tofu Wedges. Prepare the Peppered Peanut Sauce and Mignonette Sauce. (All these can be prepared 1 or 2 days ahead and refrigerated.) Thread the scallops, shrimp and smoked mussels on 6-inch bamboo skewers, if desired. Arrange dumplings, meatballs and seafood skewers on lettuce or cabbage-lined plates. Place the roast pork, fried tofu, bok choy, green onions and noodles on plates or platters. Garnish with cilantro and lime wedges.

Carry the plates of food, dipping sauces, tongs and a soup ladle to the table. Provide a small plate, a soup bowl with saucer, a Chinese porcelain spoon, a wire basket spoon, sauce dishes and chopsticks for each diner.

In the kitchen, heat the stock to boiling. Season with salt. Pour 6 cups of the broth into the hot-pot bowl; add cover. With tongs, place briquettes into the fire chamber.

Carry the hot pot to the table; set into a shallow pan of water. If using a substitute pot, add the stock in the kitchen; carry to the table and turn on the heat source. Add some green onion to the pot. (As the stock heats, the diners can nibble on appetizers.)

The diners can use chopsticks or wire basket spoons to place the dumplings and meatballs in the bubbling stock. Add seafood skewers. Cook for 2 to 3 minutes or until the scallops and shrimp are cooked. Dip foods into the sauces and season with lime juice. Add the tofu, cabbage and cilantro, as desired. When most of the foods are eaten, add any remaining stock and the noodles to the pot; when hot, ladle into the soup bowls.

FROM MY RECIPE BOX

Chinese Roast Pork Tenderloin Use this tasty meat as an entree in hot pots, soups, fried rice or in fillings for Chinese steamed buns. Marinate 2 pounds pork tenderloin in the following marinade 3 hours or overnight; 2 tablespoons Brandied Hoisin Sauce (page 151), 2 tablespoons soy sauce, 2 minced cloves garlic, 1 teaspoon minced fresh ginger, 1 tablespoon dry sherry, 1 tablespoon brown sugar and $1/4$ teaspoon five-spice powder. Remove the pork from the marinade; roast in a 400F (205C) oven for 25 minutes, or until an instant-read thermometer registers 160F (70C). Cool for 10 minutes; cut into thin slices. For hot-pot dishes, the meat can be made 1 or 2 days ahead.

Grilled Tofu (Yakidofu) Grilled tofu will not fall apart when simmered in one-pot dishes. It can usually be purchased at Japanese markets. If unavailable, make it using this easy method. Cut 1 or 2 blocks of firm (momen) tofu in half horizontally. Wrap in paper towels and top with a

plate and 1 pound of weight for at least 1 hour. Unwrap and pat dry again. Sear the tofu slices in a lightly oiled, cast-iron skillet with raised ridges for stovetop grilling. Or use a regular cast-iron skillet. Sear each side until grill marks are medium golden brown, 1 to 2 minutes. Cool slightly and use at once or cover, refrigerate and use within 1 to 2 days.

Shrimp and Ginger Dumplings

The Chinese characters for wonton loosely translates to "swallowing clouds." These plump, poached dumplings are almost as light as clouds and float lazily in hot pot broths, broth-based fondues and soups. If necessary, poach and refrigerate dumplings 1 day in advance. Use thicker, sturdier dough wrappers for boiled wontons so they won't disintegrate when cooked. When boiled, the Chinese name for these half-moon dumplings is *chiao-tzu*. The wrapper fold in this recipe is often used for fried wontons. These dumplings can be deep-fried and served as an appetizer or side dish with a hot-pot meal. The versatile filling can be shaped into shrimp balls and poached for 2 minutes or dusted with cornstarch and deep-fried; add to hot pots, soups or stir-fry dishes.

Makes 40 to 50 dumplings.

1 pound shrimp, shelled, deveined, chopped to a chunky paste with a cleaver or in a food processor

1 to 2 tablespoons finely minced Smithfield ham, baked ham or bacon fat

1 tablespoon finely minced fresh ginger

1 tablespoon minced fresh cilantro

2 tablespoons finely minced green onions

2 tablespoons Chinese rice wine (*shaohsing*) or dry sherry

2 teaspoons cornstarch

1 teaspoon salt

1 large egg

1 pound (about 50) fresh, plain or colored wonton wrappers or egg-roll wrappers, cut into quarters

Place all the ingredients in a medium bowl except the egg and wonton wrappers. Separate the egg. Add the white to the shrimp mixture. Put the yolk into a bowl; beat in 1 teaspoon water. Set aside. With chopsticks, stir the shrimp mixture in one direction until blended.

To fill dumplings, place a wonton wrapper in a diamond position with the corner pointing toward you. Place 1 teaspoon filling or less at the center. Fold down the bottom half of the wrapper to form a triangle. Brush beaten egg on the inside wrapper edges to seal. Gently press around the filling to seal and hold it into place. Bring the side points up and cross them. Brush the areas that will touch with some of the egg. Press firmly to seal. Place, not touching, on a baking sheet lined with waxed paper. Keep lightly covered. Form remaining dumplings.

Fill a large saucepan with water and bring to a boil over high heat. Add about half of the dumplings. When the water boils, add 1 cup cold water. When water boils again, reduce heat slightly and cook 1 minute. Remove dumplings with a slotted spoon.

Place on a waxed paper-lined baking sheet. Cook the remaining dumplings. For the best taste and texture, use at once. Or cool and place in a single layer in a sealed container; refrigerate overnight. Simmer dumplings in the hot-pot broth 1 or 2 minutes to finish cooking. Cut open a dumpling to determine if it is done.

VARIATIONS

Pork and Spinach Dumplings In a large bowl, blend ¾ pound ground pork, 6 minced water chestnuts and ½ cup frozen chopped spinach thawed with water squeezed out. Mix in 1 tablespoon soy sauce, 2 minced green onions, 1 minced clove garlic, 2 teaspoons minced gingerroot, 2 tablespoons dry sherry, 1 tablespoon chicken stock or water, 2 teaspoons cornstarch, ½ teaspoon salt and ground black pepper, to taste. Shape dumplings and cook as instructed above.

Turkish Borek, Tartar Style In a large bowl, blend 1 pound ground lamb, 2 tablespoons chicken stock or water, 1 tablespoon soy sauce, 2 tablespoons minced fresh dill, 1 large minced clove garlic, ⅓ cup fresh minced parsley, ½ teaspoon salt and ⅛ teaspoon black pepper. Shape dumplings and cook as directed above. Serve with ½ cup Clarified Butter (page 160) heated with ½ teaspoon hot red pepper flakes. For a Yogurt Sauce, combine 1½ cups rich plain yogurt, ½ teaspoon salt, 2 minced cloves garlic and 2 minced green onions.

Nabémono

In Japan, *nabé ryori* is an informal, congenial style of cold-weather dining. It features a variety of one-pot dishes known as *nabémono* or "things in a pot." A nabémono shares some of the charming characteristics of Swiss fondue. The diners experience camaraderie as they gather around a central pot to cook and eat and share a cup of saké or glass of wine. Both meals feature hearty, warming dishes that originated in cold, snowy regions. Always appreciative of good food, the Japanese begin the meal by saying, *"itadakimasu,"* an expression of thanks to the cook. Afterwards, the diners say *"gochiso sama deshita,"* to again express their thanks and say, "a job well done."

For a nabémono, platters of fresh seasonal seafood, meat, poultry and vegetables resemble a kaleidoscope of bright colors, textures and shapes. They should be cooked briefly in the bubbling pot to enhance their natural tastes. The liquid might be an infusion of konbu seaweed and water, weak Dashi (page 184) or Asian Chicken Stock (page 182); it isn't necessary to start with a rich stock. Interesting regional variations might call for saké or milk. A flavorful nabémono broth can be fortified with noodles or rice and served as a final soup course.

When you gather foods for a nabémono, select those that complement each other in taste and texture. Asian diners prefer twice as many vegetables as meat. Cut the foods into equal sizes and shapes for even cooking. Tough or strong-tasting vegetable chunks can be briefly parboiled or blanched. Specialty versions of nabémono feature duck (*kamo-nabé*), turtle (*suppon-nabé*), horsemeat (*sakura-nabé*) and wild boar (*botan-nabé*). Most of the ingredients and sauces can be prepared in advance, wrapped tightly and refrigerated until time to cook.

Japanese culinary scholars believe present-day *nabé ryori* is an offshoot of the cooking once encountered in the *irori* or sunken open-hearth firepits in rustic farmhouses tucked in Japan's mountain villages. Life for the farmer's family revolved around the *irori*. Whatever food was available went into a *tetsunabé*, a deep cast-iron pot with a wooden lid and curved handle. The pot was hung over the fire on a pothook attached to a tripod or a tube of bamboo that hung from a rafter. Family members helped themselves from the pot whenever they were hungry. The nostalgic tradition of eating from a central cooking pot survives in nabémono dishes.

SUKIYAKI

Sukiyaki (SKEE yaki) is a relatively modern dish. A Buddhist mandate effectively discouraged beef eating for more than a thousand years of Japan's history; it became widespread at the turn of the twentieth century. Two exceptions were the Chinese-influenced Okinawans who ate pork and the Northern Ainu who were hunters. There are different theories on the origin of sukiyaki. Early nineteenth century writings indicate it was being prepared by hunters and farmers with a cooking utensil made from a common farming tool; probably a plowshare or type of *fumisuki* or shovel spade. The broad blade of the tool held pieces of venison, chicken or duck over the fire. The meat was seasoned with a thickened soy mixture like tamari. Another theory is that Japanese warriors were fed meat to strengthen them for battle but after returning home, the village elders objected to their carnivorous appetites on the grounds that meat eating desecrated their homes and was an insult to the ancestors. The young men had developed an appetite for meat and were forced to cook it outdoors on a plowshare. Both theories probably contain an element of truth and the fact that the succulent meat was forbidden, no doubt, made it taste even better.

Everything changed when Commodore Perry and his black ships sailed into Kanagawa (Yokohama Bay) in 1854 and secured the Kanagawa treaty that ended over two hundred years of Japan's national seclusion. Townsend Harris, the first American council to Japan, dined on the first slaughtered cow around 1856. Years later, Tokyo butchers erected a monument near Shimoda where the martyred cow died. Beef eating didn't catch on quickly; cows were often treated like family pets. Encouraged by Japanese progressives, the Meiji-era emperor (1868–1912) endorsed beef eating in 1872 to encourage modernization and strengthen the country's youth. Beef was the first

foreign food to become popularized. Thinly sliced and simmered in a small amount of *warashita*, a mixture of soy sauce, mirin and sugar, beef came to suit the Japanese's tastes. Restaurants sprung up everywhere featuring cow-pot dishes (*ushinabé*).

At it's finest, sukiyaki is a luxury dish made with expensive, highly marbled Kobe beef. It is cooked in a flat-bottom, shallow cast-iron pot (*sukiyaki nabé*)that sits on a tabletop stove.

A *tetsunabé*, the deeper iron pot mentioned above, is also used. There is a theory that the tetsunabé is a holdover from the days when people were not accustomed to the taste of beef. They preferred to cook it in a separate pot. If using a *sukiyaki nabé* or *tetsunabé*, season it like a cast-iron skillet; dry thoroughly after washing to prevent rusting. You can substitute a cast-iron skillet, electric skillet or electric wok.

SHABU SHABU

Another beef dish that was popularized in the early twentieth century through Western influence is shabu shabu. The origin of this dish can be traced to the Mongolian hot pot of Northern China. My first taste was when my young son and I visited friends in mountainous Gifu Prefecture. The evening we arrived at their farmhouse, snowflakes were softly falling and had covered the thatched roof and surrounding landscape. A welcome feast in our honor was served in a cozy central room; shabu shabu was the centerpiece spread over a long, low table. The arrangement of meat and vegetables were works of art. Paper-thin slices of *shimofuri* beef were fashioned on a platter into a giant rose. (*Shimofuri* means snow or frost-covered; the meat had so much marbling, it appeared to be dusted with snow.) Shabu shabu is traditionally prepared in a *hokonabé* (small fire-pot) or shabu shabu pan, similar to the Mongolian hot pot. Think of an angel-food cake pan with a cover and small handles attached to gently flaring sides. But unlike the charcoal-fueled Mongolian pot, a shabu shabu pan is designed to sit on top of a portable gas ring or butane canister stove. Heat rises up through the chimney to heat the liquid. You can substitute a large earthenware *donabé*, a French porcelain cast-iron casserole like those produced by Le Creuset or an electric wok.

ODEN

In early November when winter officially arrives in Japan, the weather is quite cold. The *yaitai*, or portable street stalls, are a welcome sight. *Oden-yaitai* specialize in *oden*, a hearty fish-cake stew that originated in Edo or Rivergate, as Tokyo was called from 1180 to 1868. Beside many types of delicious chewy, spongy fish cakes, it includes dozens of other ingredients such as fried tofu, vegetable chunks, boiled eggs, meatballs and jellylike *konnyaku*. Simmered for hours in a flavorful broth, the foods absorb all the surrounding flavors. Small pieces of foods are often laced on skewers. The street stall may have a few seats that quixotically beckon the worker to stop and enjoy a brief respite after a hectic day. The customer picks his favorite ingredients and receives them in a shallow bowl moistened with the broth. Spicy-hot mustard, offered on the side, and a warm cup of saké complete the meal. Oden Nabé takes longer to cook than other nabémono, but the recipe is easy and requires little attention as it simmers in a modern slow cooker. The slow cooker is not an ideal method for cooking fish, but Japanese fish cakes are designed for long, slow simmering, making

them a perfect candidate. Add seafood like shrimp, skewered squid tentacles or pieces of octopus about 30 minutes or so before the dish is done.

JAPANESE DONABÉ

Most nabémono are cooked in an earthenware casserole called a *donabé*, which shares a few characteristics with the earthenware Swiss fondue pot or *caqualon*. The *donabé* can be used on low heat for making cheese fondue. It is also useful for other types of Asian hot-pot dishes. Essential for tabletop cooking, a *donabé* is made from a special porous clay fired at a high temperature. It can be placed over direct heat, holds heat well and distributes it evenly. The *donabé* comes in small, medium and large sizes. Small seven- to eight-inch casseroles can be used for one or two people. A ten-inch casserole will serve five people; a twelve-inch casserole serves six to eight people. The largest size is the most useful. Six is an ideal number for nabémono; for eight or more, I add a second pot. When you arrange your table, make sure everyone can comfortably reach the cooking pot. A *donabé* can be used for any recipe in this chapter except Sukiyaki and the Teppan Yaki Party. At a *teppan yaki* restaurant, a samurai chef cooks the food on a tabletop grill with lightning speed then serves the diners seated around the grill. While there is a distinction between simmering and grilling, the two are inexorably linked in many hot-pot restaurants, where the cooking pot is often built into the grill.

To prepare a new *donabé* for cooking, fill it with water and whisk in two tablespoons flour. The outside bottom is unglazed and must be completely dry or it can crack when heated. Place on a cold burner and turn the heat to low. When the water is hot, heat for one hour. This tempers and seals the casserole to prevent cracking. Pour out the floury water, wash and dry. The glazed lid doesn't require any special attention; the tiny round hole in the top acts as a steam vent. To use the casserole for cooking, add the water or stock. Place on a cold burner; turn the heat to low. When hot, raise the heat to medium. When the liquid begins to bubble, use potholders to immediately transfer the hot casserole to a lit tabletop burner. Begin cooking when the liquid bubbles. Adjust the heat, as necessary. Cool the casserole gradually after you have finished cooking; avoid sudden temperature changes. Do not place it on a cold or wet surface; if hot, it could develop hairline cracks. Never place the empty casserole on a hot burner. Buffer the heat of a professional gas or electric cooktop with a protective heat-diffusing pad. If hairline cracks develop, cook some rice or rice porridge (*okayu*) in the pot to help seal the cracks. Or, use the water and flour mixture described above.

If you don't have a donabé, substitute a porcelain cast-iron casserole or a heavy cast-iron Chinese casserole, a new import to this country. An electric wok or deep electric skillet will work as well. To heat a casserole, you will need a portable tabletop gas ring, butane canister stove, electric burner or efficient induction burner. Induction cooking is flame-free, cool, safe and more efficient than gas or regular electricity. Although the tabletop induction range is expensive, it is state-of-the art with instant temperature control. It is fast becoming the top choice for tabletop cooking in many Asian restaurants. Heavy-gauge metal butane canister stoves (*takujo konro*) are very economical and popular. Ideally, they should be fitted with an electric spark generator for easy and safe burner ignition, a safety shut-off device and easy-to-clean oven pans. The knob should allow for heat adjustment. Com-pressed propane gas cans heat the stove and burn about three hours. Some models come with a handy carrying case for toting outdoors.

KNIVES

Quality, sharp knives are a necessary investment; select a good all-purpose knife such as a Japanese *bunka bocho*. This knife can be used to cut vegetables, meats and fish. A *nikkari bocho* or vegetable knife is also a good choice.

CHOPSTICKS

Chopstick Chatter
The first ancient Japanese chopsticks (*maboroshi* or imaginary chopsticks) resembled bamboo tweezers attached at the top. Similar "training chopsticks" are available for people who lack chopstick prowess. Japanese chopsticks (*o'hashi*) have pointed ends and are shorter than the Chinese kind. They come in bamboo, lacquer and imported hardwoods like ebony, rosewood, cherry and mulberry. Some chopsticks are designed specifically for eating noodles and slippery foods.

Types of Chopsticks
Personal chopsticks: *meimeibashi*

Wooden disposable chopsticks: *warabashi*

Serving chopsticks: *toribashi*

Cooking chopsticks, attached at the top: *saibashi* or *ryoribashi*

Chopstick Etiquette
Eating from shared dishes with one's personal chopsticks is frowned on in polite Japanese society, but the habit does prevail among family and close

friends. Diners often turn their chopsticks and use the thicker, unused ends for removing foods from the pot. You can provide each diner with an extra pair of chopsticks, a fondue fork, a small pair of tongs or a Chinese wire basket spoon. Never spear the foods with chopsticks or stand the chopsticks upright in your bowl of rice. Do not point with your chopsticks or wave them around.

JAPANESE HOT TOWELS

Offer your dinner guests a small, steaming-hot towel (*oshibori*) to wipe their hands and face, Japanese-style, just after they sit down at the table.

Oshibori are offered to guests in private homes and restaurants throughout Japan. Purchase the small towels in Japanese stores or use small, thin white washcloths. Before the guests arrive, wet the towels, squeeze dry then fold in half and roll up. Sometimes I add a drop or two of jasmine or rose essence to the water. Just before the guests sit down, steam the towels or put them in the microwave for two or three minutes, or until hot. In Japan, the hot towels are presented on small bamboo trays. You could serve them on a tray with tongs. Cold towels are served in the summertime.

KOBÉ BEEF

Japanese Kobé beef is legendary for being the most expensive and delicious beef in the world. It is served in top restaurants in dishes like Shabu Shabu, Sukiyaki Nabé, Teppan Yaki and beef sashimi. The exorbitant high-end price for a meal of shabu shabu made with Kobé beef can be two hundred dollars or more. Kobé beef comes from Wagyu, a pure breed of black cattle similar to Black Angus that dates back to 1830. Wagyu, or "Japan-

ese beef" evolved into three predominant bloodlines. The Tajima (or Taijiri) bloodline in Hyogo Prefecture in Western Japan is a leading source for the super-prime Kobé and Matsuzaka beef. The restaurants of Kobé, capital of Hyogo Prefecture, specialize in its preparation. Extreme marbling qualifies this particular beef for a top grading. The most desirable grade has 50 percent more marbling than American prime beef. Wagyu is renowned for its "melt in your mouth" quality and superb flavor. Some connoisseurs say it rivals *foie gras* in richness. High marbling enables the flavorful meat to be thinly sliced; when cut and cooked properly, it has an unmatched, buttery texture and succulent flavor. University test results find Wagyu to be slightly healthier than American beef with a lower ratio of saturated to unsaturated fatty acids in the intramuscular marbling. Wagyu is said to contain all the essential amino acids in the correct ratio to build protein for good health. Wagyu came to America in 1976; demand now outstrips supply, especially in the restaurant trade catering to Japanese businessmen. Washington State University and Kobé Beef America Inc. in Oregon are leaders in American Wagyu production. In Virginia, Wagyu production aimed at the home consumer is underway. To try this special beef at home, refer to the Mail-Order Resources (page 225). Many upscale markets in large cities carry Wagyu beef.

THINLY SLICED MEATS

When recipes like Sukiyaki Nabé, Shabu Shabu or Teppan Yaki call for thinly sliced meat, place the wrapped meat in the freezer until about three-fourths frozen. The meat will be much easier to cut in ultra-thin slices. Use a large, well-sharpened knife. If you prefer, ask your butcher to freeze and slice the meat for you. For sukiyaki, request the meat be sliced 1/8-inch thick. Meat for Shabu Shabu is cut thinner, about 1/16-inch thick. (Korean beef for bulgogi is usually cut thicker than sukiyaki meat, between 1/8- and 1/4-inch thick.) Many large Asian markets carry quality sliced meats and will know exactly what you need. The thickness of the meat will vary from market to market, depending on its ethnic background. If buying frozen meat, examine it carefully for freezer burn. Avoid buying frozen sliced meats.

FROM MY RECIPE BOX

Edamamé Appetizer Protein-rich soybeans contain phytoestrogens, compounds that may help reduce the risk of breast and prostate cancers. Soybeans are a popular snack with cold beer in bars throughout Japan. Fresh-frozen soybeans in the pod can be purchased at most Asian markets. Even if the package notes that they are precooked, dump the bag into a large pot of well-salted, boiling water and cook about 3 minutes. Rinse soybeans in cool water; drain well. Serve in bowls at the table along with empty bowls to hold the shells. Fondue diners can pop the delicious soybeans from the shells and nibble on them while waiting for their foods to cook. The soybeans can be shelled and tossed into rice dishes, salads or mashed to make dipping sauces.

Sukiyaki Nabé

When the Japanese invite friends to come and "dip chopsticks together" into a pot of sukiyaki, it's an expression of friendship. Sukiyaki Nabé is a gregari-

ous meal. The man of the household adeptly cooks the thinly sliced meat and vegetables even though he may not otherwise be accustomed to wielding a pair of cooking chopsticks. There are as many subtle variations for making sukiyaki as there are cooks. In eastern Japan (the Tokyo area), the meat and vegetables are cooked together with a preblended sauce. In western Japan (Osaka and Kyoto) the meat might be eaten first; the sauce ingredients added separately, to taste. Either way, the tastes become complex and delicious when the succulent meat simmers in the enzyme-rich soy sauce mixture.

Each bite is traditionally dipped into raw egg, which cools the hot food and enhances the taste. Use pasteurized eggs, or if you don't like the thought of raw eggs, omit them entirely. As the diners wait for the foods to cook, serve bowls of Dashi (page 184) or Hearty Miso Soup (page 185). On the side, offer Cooked Medium-Grain Rice (page 117), and Plum Blossom Sherbet (page 118) for dessert.

Makes 6 servings

2 cups Dashi (page 184), Kelp Stock (page 184) or canned beef broth

1 cup Japanese soy sauce (*shoyu*)

1/2 cup saké

1/3 to 1/2 cup sugar, or to taste

7 to 8 ounces shirataki noodles (see page 223) or 4 ounces mung bean harusame (see page 221)

1 block Grilled Tofu (page 87), cut in 1 1/2-inch squares

2 to 2 1/4 pounds beef tenderloin or well-marbled sirloin or rib eye beef, sliced about 1/8-inch thick (see Thinly Sliced Meats, page 93)

2 medium sweet onions, halved, cut in thin wedges

1 to 2 bunches green onions, mostly the white parts, diagonally cut in 2-inch pieces

2 medium carrots, peeled, cut in thin flower shapes or diagonal slices

12 fresh shiitaki mushroom caps, rinsed, star-design cut in the top, if desired

1 bunch chrysanthemum leaves, trimmed, cut in half or ½ head Napa cabbage, cored, cut in 2½-inch squares

1½-inch piece beef suet or 2 tablespoons vegetable oil

4 to 8 eggs (optional)

In a large pitcher, combine the Dashi, soy sauce, saké and sugar. Stir until the sugar is dissolved. Drain the shirataki. Boil in boiling water 1 to 2 minutes; drain and rinse in cool water. If using harusame, soak in boiling hot water for 10 minutes; drain well.

Prepare the Grilled Tofu. Arrange all the ingredients attractively on 1 or 2 large platters. The meat slices should be neatly overlapping; add the suet. Carry the platters, the cooking sauce and the eggs to the table. Provide a bowl, a rice bowl, a sauce bowl and chopsticks for each person.

At the table, place a sukiyaki nabé or alternate pan over a lit portable tabletop burner and adjust it to high heat. Add the suet; use cooking chopsticks to rub the bottom of the pan with the suet. Add a portion of the onions and 6 slices of meat. Cook for 1 to 2 minutes. Pour in about one-third of the sauce. If too hot, reduce the heat slightly. Add small portions of the remaining ingredients. The chrysanthemum leaves, tofu and shirataki cook quickly so add them last. If used, each diner should break 1 egg into the sauce bowl; whisk with chopsticks.

Each diner selects foods from the pot and puts them into the individual bowl. Dip each bite into the egg if desired. Replenish the pot as the foods are eaten and add more sauce. The broth continues to become more flavorful. Some people like to spoon it over rice.

Custom Sukiyaki Sukiyaki can be made with as few ingredients as sliced beef and onion. Regional variations might call for thinly sliced chicken breast, pork or even seafood. Japanese beef is expensive; cooks occasionally use seasoned ground beef or chicken patties for an economical version. Sukiyaki can be enjoyed year round using a variety of fresh seasonal vegetables. Substitutes can include fresh bamboo shoots, baby spinach, enokitaké mushrooms, thinly shaved gobo (burdock root), small diagonally sliced leeks, water chestnuts or wheat gluten (*fu*). Don't include too many watery vegetables like spinach and mushrooms, which make the sauce thin.

Shabu Shabu

When Shabu Shabu appears on the table, the stage is set for a festive meal and stimulating conversation. Each diner uses chopsticks to swish paper-thin slices of beef through the simmering broth in a tempo that creates the onomatopoetic sound of shabu shabu to the Japanese ear. The success of this dish is ensured if the tender meat is cut thin enough to cook within seconds after being dipped into the stock. A konbu stock is most often used, but some cooks use Niban Dashi (page 184), a weak fish and sea vegetable stock. If you prefer, use the

Quick Asian Chicken Broth (page 183). Enokitaké are delicate, seasonal mushrooms with long thin stems and tiny creamy-gold colored caps. Shabu Shabu is often served with an appetizer of sashimi. A well-known Tokyo Shabu Shabu chain that I visited offered a special holiday meal with a starter of green salad topped with cheese fritters like those on page 190. Cooked Medium-Grain Rice (page 117) is the perfect side dish or serve the Hot Pot Noodles (page 107).

Makes 6 servings

Sesame Sauce (page 146)

Citrus Dip (page 147)

1 block Grilled Tofu (page 87), cut in 1-inch squares

2 small leeks, slit lengthwise, well rinsed, cut in 2-inch-diagonal pieces, or 12 green onions

1 medium carrot, peeled, cut in thin diagonal slices

8 to 10 leaves Napa cabbage, rinsed, cut in 2-inch squares

12 fresh shiitaki mushroom caps, rinsed, or 6 dried shiitaki mushrooms, softened in hot water, stems trimmed, cut in half

1 bunch enokitaké mushrooms, root ends trimmed

2 to 2¼ pounds prime, thick sirloin or rib eye beef, partially frozen, cut into paper-thin slices (see Thinly Sliced Meats, page 93)

1 (5 × 4-inch) piece konbu, lightly wiped

Cooked noodles or rice (optional)

Prepare the Sesame Sauce, Citrus Dip and Grilled Tofu. Arrange all the ingredients attractively on 1 or 2 large platters. The meat slices should be neatly overlapping. If you prefer, divide the ingredients among 3 small platters, one for every two people.

Carry the platters to the table. Provide a bowl, a rice bowl, a small bowl of each sauce, a soup bowl, chopsticks and a fondue fork for each diner. Place the konbu and about 5 cups water in a Japanese metal hot pot (*hokonabé*) or alternate pot. Carry to the table and place over a lit portable tabletop burner. Slowly bring the water to a simmer. Remove the konbu and discard.

Add a few pieces of leek to the pot. With chopsticks or a fondue fork, each diner should dip a slice of meat into the stock and swish it back and forth 3 or 4 times just until it loses its pink color. The cooked meat can be dipped into either of the sauces. Add the vegetables to the pot as the meat is being cooked. Each diner can remove the foods he wants and place them in the individual bowl. Enokitaké mushrooms and tofu cook quickly so add them last. Skim the pot occasionally if necessary. Replenish the pot as the foods are eaten; add more warm konbu stock (konbu simmered in water) if needed. After the meat and vegetables are eaten, serve the broth in the soup bowls. Cooked noodles or rice can be added to the pot if desired.

VARIATIONS

Pork Shabu Shabu Substitute paper-thin slices of pork tenderloin for the beef and substitute the Peppered Peanut Sauce (page 151) for the Sesame Sauce if desired.

Mongolian Lamb Shabu Shabu Substitute thinly sliced lamb loin for the beef and serve with the Sesame Sauce or the Peppered Peanut Sauce (page 151). The Fresh Mint Sauce (page 155) can be substituted for the Citrus Sauce.

Country Chicken Hot Pot
Tori Nabé

In this flavorful hot pot, gingery chicken meatballs can be shaped and added to the simmering broth right at the table. While the chicken cooks, pass a bowl filled with the delicious Edamamé Appetizer (page 94). Your guests will be entertained as they place the pods in their mouths to pop out the tasty green soybeans. Edamamé are a favorite summer snack with beer at the *izakaya*, or Japanese pub. Serve this hot pot with Cooked Medium-Grain Rice (page 117).

Makes 4 servings

Citrus Dip (page 147)

Hot-Pot Condiments (page 148)

Spinach and Cabbage Rolls (page 134) or ½ small head Napa cabbage cut into 2-inch squares

1 large egg

1 tablespoon mirin

1 slice bread, crusts trimmed, torn into shreds

½ pound ground chicken or turkey

2 green onions, minced

2 teaspoons grated fresh ginger (page 108)

Freshly ground black pepper, to taste

4 boned chicken thighs, cut into 1-inch cubes (about 1¼ pounds)

1 (¾-pound) onion, peeled, cut in half, cut in slices

1 carrot, peeled, cut in thin flower shapes or slices

1 bunch enokitaké mushrooms, root ends trimmed

3 to 4 ounces oyster (*shimeji*) mushrooms, separated into pieces

1 (4- to 5-inch) piece konbu, lightly wiped

4 cups water or 5 cups Quick Asian Chicken Broth (page 183)

⅓ cup Japanese soy sauce (*shoyu*), or to taste

2 tablespoons mirin (Japanese rice wine)

1 to 2 tablespoons sugar, or to taste

Prepare the Citrus Dip, Hot-Pot Condiments, Spinach and Cabbage Rolls.

In a medium bowl, mix the egg, mirin and bread into a paste. Mix in the ground chicken until smooth. Stir in the green onions, ginger and black pepper. With a measuring tablespoon or large spoon, scoop up ½ tablespoon of the ground chicken mixture and shape the mixture into balls. Arrange the chicken balls, cubed chicken, and vegetables on 1 or 2 platters.

Carry the platter and condiments to the table. Provide a bowl, a rice bowl, a bowl of dipping sauce, chopsticks and a fondue fork for each diner. In the kitchen, heat the konbu and 4 cups water or broth in a large Japanese casserole (*don-abé*) or alternate pot over medium-low heat. When the water begins to simmer, discard the konbu. Stir in the soy sauce, mirin and sugar.

Transfer the casserole of hot stock to the table and place it over a lit portable tabletop burner. Adjust burner to keep the broth at a steady simmer.

Add some of the chicken cubes, onion and carrot to the pot. Add one-third of the chicken balls and some of each of the remaining ingredients until the pot is about three-fourths full. Simmer until chicken is cooked, 3 or 4 minutes. Each diner can remove the foods he wants and place them in the individual bowl. Dip each bite into the sauce seasoned with condiments, as desired. Replenish the pot as the foods are eaten; add more warm water or broth, if needed. Skim the pot occasionally if necessary.

Neri Seihin Long ago, ingenious Japanese fishermen found a way to preserve fish by turning it into a homogeneous gel or fish paste call *surimi*. From basic surimi they developed a number of food products collectively known as *neri seihin*, written with characters meaning, "knead" and "product."

The most representative type is *kamaboko*, the solid white or pink-coated fish-cake loaf mounted on a rectangular board. *Sasa-kamaboko* from Miyagi Prefecture is made from local flounder and shaped like a large oval leaf.

Narutomaki (or *sumaki*) has a bright spiral of color through the middle that creates a decorative pattern when sliced. *Naruto* means whirlpool.

Hanpen has a spongy marshmallowlike texture because air is incorporated during the grinding process.

Chikuwa is representative of the broiled surimi category and shaped into a roll on metal rods.

Oden Nabé

Oden is a unique fish-cake stew with origins that trace back to the days of Edo, old Tokyo, from 1603 to 1868. The ingredients are characteristically cut into large, interesting shapes. In *Kansai*-style oden, the ingredients are cooked separately in a light broth. Oden fans appreciate the dish's subtle flavors and chewy, resilient textures. Some specialty restaurants keep huge oden pots simmering day and night, year after year. Long, slow cooking in a large slow cooker is an easy way to prepare this dish with no danger of overcooking. If you have a smaller slow cooker, adjust the ingredient amounts to fit. Oden is served with *nerigarashi*, a hot, pleasantly bitter mustard paste. The stew tastes even better the next day. For a complete meal, include Hearty Miso Soup (page 185), Cooked Medium-Grain Rice (page 117), *oshinko* (vegetable pickles) and several rounds of saké or beer.

Makes 6 to 8 servings

Dashi (page 184) or Quick and Easy Chicken Broth (page 177) 6 to 7 cups broth)

3/4 pounds daikon radish, peeled, cut into 1 1/2-inch slices, cut in half

2 medium carrots, sliced diagonally in 1-inch pieces

8 small new potatoes, peeled, cut in half

2 pounds chicken thighs, skinned, boned, rinsed, quartered, or 2 or 3 pounds beef shank

1/2 cup Japanese soy sauce (*shoyu*), or to taste

1/4 cup saké (optional)

1 to 2 tablespoons sugar

1 (9- to 10-ounce) piece konnyaku (see page 221), blanched 1 minute, cut in 3/4-inch-thick slices

Boru dango are delicious fried fish-cake balls.

Ten-pura is deep-fried *kamaboko* in western Japan.

Ika-maki is a fish-cake roll with a baby squid inside. Besides these, there are many more regional varieties.

Neri seihin should not be considered a substitute for fresh seafood but a nutritious, delicious Japanese food that can stand on its own in any kitchen. Purchase the fish cakes in Japanese markets in the refrigerator or freezer sections. *Neri seihin* is the main ingredient in the Japanese stew, Oden. Add them to nabémono dishes, hot pots, stir-fry dishes, soups or serve with spicy mustard as an appetizer. If *neri seihin* products are unavailable, substitute the American-style surimi products found in the refrigerator section of every grocery store. Don't overcook these products since they are already cooked.

Fried Tofu Wedges (page 67)

1 (6-ounce) package fried gobo ten-pura (fishcake with gobo), cut into triangles, if available

1 large roll of chikuwa, 1 block of kamaboko, sliced ¾-inch thick, or other fish cake, as desired

6 to 8 hard-cooked eggs, peeled

Mustard paste, made by mixing equal parts of dry, hot Japanese mustard (*wagarashi*) and lukewarm water, or a prepared, grainy German mustard, as desired

Seven-Spice Powder (page 149)

Prepare the Dashi; pour 5 cups into a large (6-quart) slow cooker. Set the heat on high. In a large pot of boiling, salted water, boil the daikon and carrots 2 minutes, or until hot yet still firm; drain well. Add the daikon, carrots and potatoes to the slow cooker. The stock should just cover the vegetables; add more if necessary. Cover and cook on high 1½ hours.

In a large bowl, combine the chicken, soy sauce, saké and sugar. Add to the slow cooker with the konnyaku, tofu, fish cakes and eggs. Cook for 3 hours.

The stew can be eaten when the vegetables are tender. (If using beef shank, remove and cut meat from bone and return to cooker.) If desired, add more soy sauce to taste. If your slower cooker has a removable ceramic insert, it can be placed directly on the table for serving. I like to arrange the ingredients separately in a Japanese casserole (*donabé*) or a medium enameled cast-iron casserole. Add some of the broth. The casserole can be placed on a lit portable tabletop burner at the table, adjusted to keep the foods warm. Each diner can select the foods he wants and place them into an individual bowl. Replenish the broth and ingredients as they are eaten. Serve with the mustard and Seven-Spice Powder.

Oden

- Ingredients should be cut into large pieces so they do not disintegrate during the long simmering.
- Extra (nontraditional) seasonings might include sliced ginger, scallions, black pepper, a few drops of rice vinegar or lemon juice. Add a 3-inch square of konbu if you use chicken stock.
- Use any type Japanese fish cake from Asian markets (see pages 98–99).
- Substitute ingredients might include large shrimp, chicken legs, shiitaki mushrooms, small sausages, narrow strips of softened konbu rolled up and tied with gourd string, tied bundles of shirataki noodles (page 223), cubes of pumpkin or winter squash, deep-fried or blanched chicken or pork meatballs, blanched rolled cabbage rolls or skewered cooked quail eggs, squid or octopus bites.
- Oden can be simmered in a large saucepan on the stove for 3 to 4 hours on low heat. It can also be made in an electric skillet. Watch the broth level carefully; add more, as needed.
- Don't be afraid to make substitutions or vary the ingredient amounts as desired.

Salmon Hot Pot
Ishikari Nabé

The miso paste coating on the marinated salmon adds a rich flavor to the fish and makes a delicious broth. This type of salmon hot pot is popular in Hokkaido, the northernmost of Japan's four main islands. Salmon roe is often added to this dish. Salmon has been highly prized in Japan since ancient times. Even the skin is useful and has been fashioned into clothing and shoes. In the Kanto area (Tokyo), salted salmon is a traditional New Year's gift that originated during the Edo period (1603–1868). Serve this dish with plain rice or the Edamamé Rice (page 118).

Makes 4 or 5 servings

2 pounds salmon fillets, skinned, cut 1½- to 2-inch cubes

½ cup miso paste (white, golden or red)

5 cups Dashi (page 184)

2 paper-thin slices fresh ginger

⅓ cup Japanese soy sauce (*shoyu*)

¼ cup mirin

1 tablespoon sugar

8 to 10 green onions, cut in 1½-inch pieces

2 carrots, cut into ⅛-inch-thin diagonal slices

10 to 12 Napa cabbage leaves, rinsed in cold water, cut in 2-inch squares

⅓ pound fresh snow peas, strings removed

1 lemon, cut into wedges

Cooked rice

A day ahead, coat the salmon cubes with miso paste in a large bowl. Cover and refrigerate overnight.

At serving time, prepare the Dashi; add the ginger, soy sauce, mirin and sugar. Arrange the miso-coated salmon, vegetables and lemon wedges on a large platter. Place on the table along with a bowl, a rice bowl, a soup bowl, chopsticks and a fondue fork for each diner.

In the kitchen, heat 4 cups of the Dashi mixture in a Japanese casserole (*donabé*) or alternate pot over medium-low heat. Transfer the casserole of hot stock to the table and place it over a lit portable tabletop burner. Adjust burner to keep the stock at a steady simmer.

Add a portion of the green onions and other vegetables. After 1 to 2 minutes, begin adding the salmon. Simmer until the fish is cooked, 2 to 3 minutes. Each diner can select the foods he wants and place them in the individual bowl. Season the foods with the lemon. Replenish the pot as the foods are eaten; add more warm stock mixture if needed. The flavorful broth can be served as a soup course. Cooked rice can be added to the pot for a hearty soup if desired.

Skewered Seafood and Vegetable Bites

These skewered bites make great "pick-ups" for parties or casual meals. The origin of the recipe is *dengaku*, a medieval dish of grilled, skewered foods flavored with miso paste. A later Tokyo version featured skewered, small fish balls simmered in miso-flavored broth. The name, *dengaku*, became *den*, preceded with an honorific *O*. In this popular version, skewered foods are simmered in a mild stock and served with a fruity orange-flavored miso sauce. Where suggested, parboil the vegetables until hot and partially tender yet still firm, 2 to 3 minutes. In Japan, this type of food is part of the moveable feast served by street vendors. Serve with a bowl of Dry-Roasted Sesame Seeds (page 132) or Seven-Spice Powder (page 149) on the side for seasoning each bite.

Select seven or eight of the seafood and vegetables and prepare them as instructed.

Makes 6 to 8 servings

Peanut-Orange Miso Sauce (page 147)

4 cups Dashi (page 184) or Kelp Stock (page 184)

2 tablespoons thin Japanese soy sauce (*usukuchi shoyu*)

2 tablespoons mirin

1 tablespoon sugar

Fried Tofu (page 67)

1 or 2 small sweet potatoes, peeled, cut into 1-inch slices, cut in half, parboiled

2 or 3 (5-inch) small turnips, peeled, cut into ¾-inch slices, cut in half, parboiled

Small, fresh shiitaki mushroom caps, rinsed

½ pound large shrimp, peeled, deveined

Whole, small button mushrooms, rinsed, dried

1 (6-ounce) package fried gobo ten-pura, (fish cake with gobo), cut into small triangles, or fried fish cake balls

1 (9- to 10-ounce) piece konnyaku (see page 221), blanched 1 minute, cut in ¾-inch squares

Spinach and Cabbage Rolls (page 134)

Wedges of red, yellow or green bell pepper

12 hard-cooked quail eggs, peeled

5 small rolls chikuwa (broiled surimi), cut into ½-inch rings

12 tiny whole new potatoes, or larger potatoes, cut in half, parboiled

½ head cauliflower florets, blanched in salted, boiling water 1 minute, rinsed in ice water, drained

1 loaf kamaboko (steamed fish loaf), cut into ½-inch slices

1 or 2 thin Chinese eggplants, cut in ¾-inch slices

Prepare the Peanut-Orange Miso Sauce. Spoon the sauce into a small, heavy, heatproof bowl and place it into the middle of a large Japanese casserole dish (donabé) or other deep casserole.

In a large saucepan, heat the Dashi, soy sauce, mirin and sugar on low heat until warm. Place 1 piece of the selected seafood or vegetable on a separate 6-inch bamboo skewer or a 2-prong pine-needle skewer (bamboo fork). Place the skewered foods in the pot around the bowl of sauce.

Pour 3 cups warm Dashi mixture into the casserole or just enough to cover the foods. Place the casserole on a lit portable tabletop burner. Adjust the burner to keep the stock at a low simmer. Place small appetizer-size plates on the side. After 4 or 5 minutes, the skewered foods can be removed and dipped into the sauce just before eating. Season as desired.

VARIATION

Omit Dashi; substitute 1 (5 × 4-inch) piece konbu and 4 cups warm water. Place the konbu in the bottom of the casserole. Put the bowl of sauce on top. Add the skewered ingredients to the pot; pour in the warm water. Continue the recipe, as directed.

Riverbank Hot Pot Dote Nabé

A *doté* is a "riverbank" in Japan. In this dish, a riverbank of miso paste smeared around the inside rim of the cooking pot gradually melds into the hot stock, much the way the earth erodes into the river. This dish is traditionally made with oysters, a specialty of Hiroshima, but you could substitute a variety of other types of seafood. Begin with a weak stock since it will become enriched as the oysters and vegetables are added to the pot. Japanese cooks like to mix raw oysters with salt or finely grated daikon radish to refresh the flavor before they are cooked. Serve a pot of Cooked Medium-Grain Rice (page 117) on the side. The oysters taste good dipped into Mizore-zu (page 148) or the untraditional Mignonette Sauce (page 165).

Makes 4 or 5 servings

2¹/₂ cups Dashi (page 184), mixed with 2¹/₂ cups water

1 quart fresh-shucked oysters

1 tablespoon sea salt

1 leek, slit lengthwise, leaves separated, well rinsed, trimmed, cut in 2-inch pieces

¹/₄ head Napa cabbage, cut in 2-inch squares

1 medium carrot, peeled, cut in thin diagonal slices

6 medium fresh shiitaki mushroom caps, rinsed, cut in half

¹/₈ pound fresh chrysanthemum leaves (*shingiku*), or 1 (6-ounce) bag baby spinach leaves

Fried Tofu Wedges (page 67) or 1 (10- to 16-ounce) plain, firm tofu, cut into cubes

¹/₃ cup yellow or red miso paste or a blend

2 tablespoons mirin (Japanese rice wine)

1 tablespoon sugar

1 slice fresh ginger, diagonally sliced about ¹/₄-inch thick, smashed

1 (2- to 3-inch) square konbu, lightly wiped

In a medium saucepan over medium heat, heat the Dashi and water; keep warm.

Place the oysters into a large bowl of cold water with the salt; with your hands, swish oysters through the water. Drain, then rinse in cool water. Drain well then place into a medium bowl. Place the bowl of oysters in the middle of a large platter. Surround with the vegetables and tofu. Place on the table along with any side dishes. Provide a bowl, a rice bowl, chopsticks and a fondue fork for each diner.

Combine the miso paste, mirin and sugar in a small bowl. Spread the mixture in a band around the upper-middle inner rim of a Japanese casserole (*donabé*) or alternate pot.

Pour 4 cups warm Dashi into the casserole or enough to slightly cover the rim of miso. Add the ginger and konbu. Carry the casserole to the table and place over a lit portable tabletop burner. Adjust the burner to keep the stock at a steady simmer. If using an electric skillet, mound the miso on the square of konbu. Place it in the bottom of the pan; pour in the Dashi. Add a portion of each of the vegetables to the simmering stock. After 2 or 3 minutes, add some of the tofu and oysters. Cook 1 to 2 minutes. Each diner can select the foods he wants while scraping off a little miso from the pot. Eventually, the miso and broth will become blended. Replenish the pot as the foods are eaten. Add more warm stock if necessary.

Yose Nabé

Yose Nabé is a hodgepodge of ingredients simmered together in a flavorful seafood stock. The name, *Yose Nabé* means "thrown-together" pot, which means anything goes as long as the ingredients are extremely fresh. Part of the appeal of hot-pot cooking is the beautiful display of fresh ingredients that will be simmered in the pot. Feel free to substitute your favorite types of seafood, Japanese fish cakes or vegetables. Serve with an appetizer of fresh cucumber and carrot sticks with the Peanut-Orange Miso Sauce (page 147) and bowls of Cooked-Medium-Grain Rice (page 117).

Makes 4 servings

12 live cherrystone clams

5 cups Dashi (page 184)

1/3 cup Japanese soy sauce (*shoyu*)

1/3 cup mirin (Japanese rice wine)

Spinach and Cabbage Rolls (page 134)

Hot-Pot Condiments (page 148)

1 pound large shrimp, shelled, tails intact, deveined

1 pound salmon filet, cut on the diagonal in 2 × 1-inch pieces

1 pound sea bream, yellowtail, red snapper or cod, cut in 2 × 1-inch pieces

1/2 pound large scallops, cut in half crosswise

1 pound chicken thighs or boneless, skinless breasts, cut in 1-inch cubes

1 (10- to 16-ounce) block firm tofu, cut in 1 1/2-inch cubes

6 medium fresh shiitaki mushroom caps, rinsed, cut in half

2 bunches green onions, trimmed, cut in 2-inch lengths

1/4 pound fresh snow peas, blanched in salted, boiling water 1 minute, rinsed in ice water, strings removed

1 bunch watercress, rinsed, stems trimmed

2 ounces mung bean harusame, soaked in boiling-hot water 10 minutes, drained

To clean the clams, place on a small rack in a large bowl of cool water and add 2 teaspoons salt. Refrigerate for 1 to 2 hours. Drain and scrub the shells in cool water. Discard any that are not tightly shut.

Prepare the Dashi. Combine 4 cups Dashi with the soy sauce and mirin; set aside. Prepare the Spinach and Cabbage Rolls and Hot-Pot Condiments.

Arrange the seafood, chicken, vegetables and noodles on 1 or 2 platters. Carry the platters and Hot Pot Condiments to the table. Provide a bowl, a rice bowl, chopsticks and a fondue fork for each diner.

In the kitchen, heat the Dashi mixture in a large Japanese casserole (*donabé*) or alternate pot over medium-low heat. Transfer the casserole of hot Dashi to the table and place it over a lit portable tabletop burner. Adjust burner to keep the broth at a steady simmer. Add some of the chicken, vegetables and noodles. Simmer 2 or 3 minutes then add some seafood. Each diner can select the foods he wants and place them in the individual bowl with some of the broth. Season with the condiments to taste. Skim the pot occasionally, if necessary. Replenish the pot as the foods are eaten. Add more warm broth, if needed.

Teppan Yaki Party

In this style of cooking, meat or seafood and vegetables are quickly cooked on a *teppan* or "iron sheet." This version, called *bata yaki*, offers a mixed grill of beef, shrimp and vegetables cooked in butter and garlic. Restaurant teppan yaki is cooked on a large tabletop grill surrounded by the diners. The chef cooks each course while entertaining the diners, Western style, with a display of pyrotechnics and fancy knife skills. At home, dining on teppan yaki is a participatory experience, because everyone at the table can help cook. In top Japanese restaurants, the meat choice is cubed or sliced beef tenderloin or sirloin from the well-marbled Kobé or Matsusaka beef. The meat becomes meltingly delicious when quickly seared on a hot grill and served

rare. If you've heard the story that these pampered cattle are hand-fed beer, its true! They guzzle a bottle of beer daily because the yeast helps stimulate their appetites. Regular massages relieve stress and muscle stiffness. A soft, well-groomed hair coat is thought to reflect the meat's quality so the cattle are brushed with saké or beer. A variation of Teppan Yaki is stone cooking; the beef is seared at the table on a large flat rock or stone. If desired, include servings of plain cooked rice or fried rice on the side.

Makes 6 servings

Citrus Dip (page 147), omitting the daikon radish

Sesame Sauce (page 146)

Red Maple Radish (page 149)

Seven-Spice Powder (page 149), Curry Salt (page 160) or Sichuan Pepper Salt (page 160)

3 large potatoes, peeled, cut in ¾-inch cubes, parboiled, cooled

½ pound fresh shiitaki mushroom caps, rinsed, thickly sliced

½ pound fresh snow peas, blanched in salted, boiling water 30 seconds, rinsed in ice water, strings removed

1 sweet onion, cut in thin wedges

2 pounds top-quality beef tenderloin or sirloin, sliced ¼-inch thick (See Thinly Sliced Meats, page 93)

1 pound large shrimp, peeled and deveined, or scallops

4 or 5 finely minced garlic, or to taste

¼ cup unsalted butter

¼ cup canola oil

Prepare the Citrus Dip, Sesame Sauce, Red Maple Radish and Seven-Spice Powder. Arrange the vegetables, beef and shrimp attractively on 2 platters.

Carry the platters, small bowls of garlic, butter and oil, Red Maple Radish and Seven-Spice Powder to the table. Provide a plate, rice bowl, a serving of each sauce and chopsticks for each diner.

At the table, heat a large tabletop grill or electric skillet on high heat. Add a small amount of both the oil and butter. When hot, add some of the onion and a small amount of garlic. Add the potatoes, a portion of the meat, and six shrimp, keeping the foods in separate piles. Add a portion of each of the remaining ingredients, turning them as they cook. The beef cooks quickly and tastes best cooked just until no longer pink on the outside. Cook the shrimp until pink and barely firm, 2 to 3 minutes. The diners can help themselves to the foods. Replenish the grill as the foods are eaten. Each diner should season the Citrus Dipping Sauce with Red Maple Radish, to taste. Dip the meat into either sauce; season the foods with Seven-Spice Powder, to taste.

VARIATIONS

Buta Teppan Yaki Top Tokyo restaurants feature meat from the famous black pigs (Kagoshima *kuro buta*) of Kagoshima Prefecture. They are descendants of pigs from Okinawa, famous for its pork dishes. Restaurateurs say the meat fibers are finer than regular pork so the prepared meat is extremely tender. They also say the meat is high in Vitamins B_1 and E, which helps prevent fat oxidization so the body may absorb less fat when eaten. To make Buta Teppan Yaki, substitute very thinly sliced pork tenderloin or loin for the beef. Grill only until no longer pink. The meat is delicious with the Peanut-Orange Miso Sauce (page 147), the Peppered Peanut Sauce (page 151) and the Shoyu and Ginger Steak Sauce (page 152).

Additional Ingredients These might include: bean sprouts, Napa cabbage, small ears of corn, red or green bell pepper strips, thinly sliced blanched carrots, chicken cubes, lobster meat, sliced Japanese eggplant, sliced zucchini, thinly sliced lamb, sliced green onions, sliced cultivated mushrooms, cleaned squid and clams in the shell. Additional sauces might include the Bull's-eye Sauce (page 159), Chile-Sesame Sauce (page 152) or the Sesame Miso Sauce (page 166).

Udon Suki

Udon is the favorite noodle in the Kansai region of Osaka and Kyoto. Made from wheat flour, the noodle is softer and thicker than spaghetti and has a pleasant chewy texture. Scholars believe it came from China during the Nara period (710–794) and was first served in the form of a rustic stuffed dumpling. Udon has nearly achieved cult status on the island of Shikoku in the region of Sanuki, the historical name for present-day Kanagawa Prefecture. For one thousand years, *sanuki udon* has reigned supreme; thousands of udon restaurants thrive in the area. Local habitués eat udon during the day as frequently as other people drink cups of coffee or tea. *Te-uchi udon* is the favored noodle, made by hand. Udon Suki (*udon sukiyaki*) is the ultimate noodle dish. The pristine noodles may be the final ingredient into the pot, but clearly for the Japanese they are the star attraction. Udon is favored in hot pot dishes partly because it is so sturdy and can simmer longer without destructing.

Makes 4 servings

Cooking Noodles The Japanese refer to overcooked noodles as "stretched noodles." When cooking Asian noodles, always refer to the cooking times on the package. Japanese cooks use a method called *sashimizu* to avoid overcooking. When the noodles and water come to a full boil, pour 1 cup cold water into the pot. Repeat the process two or three more times. Be sure your pot is large enough to hold the extra water. Cook the noodles 1 to 4 minutes after the last addition of water, depending on the thickness of the noodle. After 1 minute, remove a noodle for tasting. The inside of the noodle should be even-colored and cooked through, just al dente or slightly past. Drain cooked noodles; place into a large bowl of cold water with some ice to stop further cooking. Drain and rinse under cool water, swishing with your hands, to remove excess starch. This step is especially important for fresh noodles. Drain well.

If not served for 1 hour or longer, toss the noodles with 1 tablespoon sesame oil or safflower oil to prevent sticking. If the noodles are to be added to a hot pot, cook slightly less. Boil until a pinhead size core of uncooked dough remains in the center. Noodles will soften further in the broth. Noodles to be cooked and served immediately in a warm broth can be drained and rinsed in tepid or lukewarm water just to remove the starch. Drain again and use at once.

7 cups Dashi (page 184)

1/3 cup soy sauce

2 tablespoons mirin (Japanese rice wine)

1 to 2 tablespoons sugar, or to taste

Spinach and Cabbage Rolls (page 134)

6 abura-agé (fried tofu puffs), blanched in boiling water 1 minute, rinsed in ice water, pressed to remove excess water and oil

4 or 5 mochi (glutinous rice cakes), cut in halves or thirds

1 pound dried udon

Hot-Pot Condiments (page 148)

1 pound shrimp, peeled, deveined

1 pound snow crab legs, cut in pieces

1/2 pound sea scallops, *dengaku* crosswise

1/2 loaf kamaboko (fish-cake loaf) or narutomaki (pink-swirled fish-cake loaf), sliced 1/2-inch thick or 1/2 pound surimi crab chunks

4 medium fresh shiitaki mushroom caps, rinsed, star-design cut in the top, if desired

1/8 pound fresh snow peas, blanched in salted, boiling water 1 minute, rinsed in ice water, strings removed

4 green onions, white parts cut diagonally into 1 1/2-inch lengths (mince the green parts for the condiments)

Make the Dashi. Combine 5 cups of the Dashi with the soy sauce, mirin and sugar; set aside.

Prepare the Spinach and Cabbage Rolls. Cut the abura-agé in half. Gently open up each piece and stuff with a slice of mochi.

Bring at least 4 quarts unsalted water to boil in a large pot. Cook the udon until just al dente, 6 to 8 minutes. Drain and rinse in cool water. (See Cooking Noodles, page 106.)

Prepare the Hot-Pot Condiments. Place the udon on a large platter; arrange seafood, vegetables and stuffed abura-agé around and on top of the noodles. Carry the platter and Hot Pot Condiments to the table. Provide each diner with a bowl, a soup bowl, chopsticks and a fondue fork.

In the kitchen, heat the Dashi mixture in a large Japanese casserole (*donabé*) or alternate pot over medium-low heat.

Transfer the casserole of hot broth to the table and place it over a lit, portable tabletop burner. Adjust the burner to keep the broth at a steady simmer. Add some green onions to the broth mixture. Begin adding the vegetables and seafood; cook 2 to 3 minutes. Each diner can select the foods he wants and place them in the individual bowl. Add the stuffed abura-agé; simmer until the mochi has softened. Replenish the pot as the foods are eaten. Add more warm broth, if needed.

VARIATIONS

You can make Udon Suki with thinly sliced chicken or other types of fresh seafood. Try lobster tail meat, clams in the shell or small pieces of fish like sea bream, red snapper, monkfish, salmon or cod. The seafood is also delicious dipped into Mizore-zu (page 148) or Mignonette Sauce (page 165).

Hot-Pot Noodles

At the end of a nabémono meal, you can add cooked noodles to the rich broth left in the pot after the foods are eaten. Or serve noodles for lunch or as a quick snack in bowls of Japanese noodle broth or in a stock or broth from the chapter on stocks. Season to taste with any of the Hot-Pot Condiments (page 148). Kishimen noodles are similar to udon except they are flat instead of round. They are a specialty in the city of Nagoya in Aichi Prefecture. Kishimen is often served with a sprinkling of katsuobushi filaments (dried bonito) on top.

Makes 5 or 6 servings

1 pound dried kishimen noodles or udon or soba noodles

Bring at least 4 quarts unsalted water to a boil in a large pot over high heat. Slowly add the noodles; stir with chopsticks to prevent sticking. Refer to the package for cooking instructions. Test noodles after 4 minutes; if not ready, cook 2 to 3 minutes more. Remove a noodle from the pot to taste. If noodles are to be added to a hot pot, cook until almost al dente. Don't overcook; the noodles continue softening in the hot pot broth. Drain and rinse. If the noodles won't be eaten for 1 hour or longer, prevent sticking by tossing them with 1 tablespoon sesame oil or safflower oil. Place noodles in a bowl to carry to the table with the hot-pot dishes. If you prefer, leave noodles in the colander in the sink and just before serving, douse with a large pot of boiling water. Shake dry and serve at once.

Noodle Etiquette Slurping noodles, Japanese-style, is considered proper etiquette. Noodle slurping has been practiced in Japan for a thousand years and is considered essential to the good taste of the noodles. The technique requires a little practice and involves sucking in the noodles with some air to cool them rapidly. It is also proper to lift the bowl to your chest while eating the noodles with chopsticks. The noodle broth should be sipped directly from the bowl.

Fresh Ginger Juice Use a Japanese flat metal grater (*oroshi gané*) with closely set ridges to grate peeled fresh ginger to obtain the pulp and juice. Hold the grater on a plate at a 45-degree angle; grate the ginger in a circular motion. Squeeze the pulp with your fingers or wrap it in damp cheesecloth then twist the top to squeeze out the juice. Three tablespoons pulp equal about 1 tablespoon ginger juice. Grind large amounts of chopped ginger in a food processor; squeeze pulp in cheesecloth over a bowl or freeze for later use. When thawed, frozen ginger becomes soft and spongy and it is easy to squeeze out the juice. Check with Asian markets in your area to buy a Japanese grater or refer to the Mail-Order Resources (page 225). Ask for a ginger or wasabi grater. A similar type has larger grating teeth and is used for larger vegetables such as daikon or lotus root.

CHANKO NABÉ

Chanko nabé is famous for being a mainstay in the diet of the sumo wrestler (*sumotori*). It is the grand champion of all nabémono created to keep the athletes nourished and robust. Sumotori enjoy all nabémono but chanko nabé is the deluxe version with many variations. It is prepared in Herculean portions and may contain twenty or more ingredients. You can prepare this dish using any of your favorite ingredients from the nabémono recipes in this chapter. Use the same cooking techniques. Include a few rib-sticking foods like potato chunks, whole baby squid, pieces of chicken on the bone, meatballs, chunks of tuna or daikon radish. The stock is often made with Dashi (page 184), and sometimes seasoned with miso paste.

A Tokyo restaurant specializing in chanko nabé makes the stew with a seasoned pot of homemade snapping-turtle broth. Okinawan versions are heavily influenced by the Chinese cuisine and may include just about any part of the pig including the trotters and ears.

Some *sumotori* decide to become a *chanko-cho* or sumo chef and eventually open a chanko-nabé restaurant upon retirement.

To make a pot at home, prepare Dashi (page 184) or Asian Chicken Stock (page 182). Simmer two pounds of cut-up chicken pieces, two potatoes, two carrots and any other firm vegetables until tender. Now add your favorite tender vegetables and about three pounds of seafood. Cooked noodles can go into the pot when all the other ingredients are eaten. Serve with the Hot-Pot Condiments (page 148), or any seasoning or dipping sauce in this chapter.

RICE POTAGE

Rice potage is a hearty, nourishing soup that is popular throughout Asia. Once served as a frugal one-dish meal, it can be served as a light lunch or late night supper. It makes an ideal meal for someone who hasn't been feeling well. *Zosui* is the Japanese name for rice potage.

A quick version can be made at the table at the end of a nabémono meal. Add cooked medium-grain rice to the leftover Dashi or chicken broth in the pot. Traditionally bland, this potage is enriched with the flavors of all the foods simmered in the broth along with small bits of seafood and vegetables. The amount of leftover stock and rice will vary with each nabémono dish. Generally, zosui is made with three cups leftover cooked rice and four cups broth. Add the rice to the broth; simmer for five to six minutes. Drizzle in two or three beaten eggs, stirring constantly with chopsticks. For seasoning, add salt and pepper, chili-flavored sesame oil and minced green onion, to taste. Each portion can be topped with colorful shreds of pickled ginger and pickled vegetables.

A similar rice gruel or congee can be made after a Chinese hot pot meal. Simmer cooked long-grain rice in the leftover hot-pot broth at least ten minutes; add any of the seasonings mentioned above. Garnish each portion with toppings such as chopped peanuts, preserved vegetables, salted fish or fermented bean curd.

Side Dishes for Fondues

THE RICE BOWL

Just as a refreshing salad is the perfect side dish for a cheese fondue, a bowl of white rice is the logical choice for any one of the Asian hot-pot recipes in this book. When rice is served in Asia, it is usually the most important food in the meal. You can examine the language of a culture to discover clues that reveal its culinary values and traditions. Throughout Asia, the common greeting for hello is synonymous with "have you eaten rice today?" The Japanese word *gohan*, refers to "cooked rice" as well as the meal. In China when people lose their jobs, it is said they have "broken their rice bowl." An abundance of rice equates with prosperity and well-being.

A bowl of unadorned white rice is the link that unites the elements of an Asian meal. Cooked Medium-Grain Rice is the perfect accompaniment for Japanese and Korean dishes. Cooked Long-Grain Rice is the preferred rice in China and much of Southeast Asia. Plain rice can neutralize chili heat, cut the richness of foods and add substance to lighter dishes. The diverse assortment of Asian one-pot dishes and Asian-influenced fondues in this book add flavor, character and balance to a bowl of rice.

Confucius wrote about the value of eating pol-ished white rice almost 2,500 years ago. But plain white rice is the jumping-off point for an endless variety of rice dishes. Coconut Rice, made with coconut milk, has a lovely taste and can used as a side dish or as a base for Coconut-Cilantro Rice Salad (page 117). Pieces of vegetables, chicken and seafood can be stirred into a pot of rice as it cooks, adding flavor and texture. Seasonings like soy sauce, kaffir lime leaves, lemongrass, fresh ginger, salt, mirin (Japanese rice wine) and minced green onion round out the taste.

Rice from around the world is available in a rainbow of colors. Red short-grain rice from the Himalayas has recently come into vogue. Forbidden Rice, once grown for China's Tang Dynasty emperors, has a tiny purple/black grain and a chewy texture reminiscent of wild rice. A small portion cooked with a pot of Long-Grain Rice gives the rice a pretty lavender hue. Soak about two tablespoons Forbidden Rice in water overnight; drain and rinse. Stir the grains into a pot of long-grain jasmine rice before cooking. For a stunning color contrast, toss the cooked lavender rice with stir-fried purple Chinese eggplant slices, red bell pepper squares and cilantro. Season, as desired. Use the lavender rice as a base for an attractive rice salad. Any of these rice dishes make an unusual, delicious side dish for

Asian hot pots and many hot-oil and broth fondues.

RINSING ASIAN RICE

The Asian ritual of rinsing rice probably stems from a time when milled rice was inadvertently stored with rice hulls, dust or insects. Rice from overseas may still be coated with talc, glucose or cornstarch to inhibit rancidity and enhance its whiteness. Asian cooks believe rinsing raw rice makes a perceptible difference in cooked rice, giving it a fresh, clean taste. Rinsed medium- and short-grain rice will still be cohesive or sticky, but not gummy. Rice is soaked to whiten the color, shorten the cooking time and keep the cooked rice grains separate. Newly harvested Japanese rice (*shinmai*) can be rinsed then drained in a fine strainer for 1 hour instead of being soaked. Especially white and tender, this seasonal treat is preferred over older rice. Place the rice in a large bowl; fill with cool tap water. Gently swish your fingers through the water to loosen any dust or coating. Pour the milky water and rice into a fine-mesh strainer or tip the bowl to drain the water into the sink. Add more water; repeat the sequence of steps. Continue rinsing until the water is almost clear. The rice will soften slightly in the water; handle it gently. Tap the strainer of rinsed rice in the sink to remove all the excess water. If you prefer, lower the strainer of rice into a large bowl of water for rinsing; lift the strainer to discard the water. The milky water from the first rinse can be used to cook bamboo shoots and root vegetables. Plain white rice is always cooked without salt or fat. Domestic long-grain rice is vitamin-enriched to replace nutrients lost during polishing; it isn't necessary to rinse this rice.

CAN RICE BE COOKED IN ADVANCE?

In Asia, fresh rice is cooked daily. As a timesaver, American rice growers suggest that rice can be cooked several days before it is needed; I prefer no more than one or two days. Cool the hot rice and wrap it tightly; store in the refrigerator. Cold, day-old rice is preferable for making fried rice. To reheat the rice, break up any large lumps and place it in a heatproof bowl; sprinkle with a few drops of water. Cover with a clean dish towel and place in a steamer over boiling water. Cover and steam for several minutes until hot. Check the rice as it heats, stir gently one or two times. Or place the covered bowl in a microwave; cook on high power two to three minutes or until soft and steamy. Some rice cookers will keep the rice warm for several hours.

SEMI-POLISHED AND UNPOLISHED (BROWN) RICE

Japan's cultural preference is for polished white rice (*seihakumai*), but semi-polished rice (*haigamai*) and brown rice (*genmai*) are available as well. Semi-polished rice can be categorized between brown rice and polished white rice. It retains a portion of the bran coat and some of the rice germ. Cook without rinsing to retain the nutrients. Semi-polished rice has an earthy, nutty flavor and a slightly chewy texture without the resilience of brown rice. Brown rice is milled to remove the husks but the bran and germ remain. It is high in fiber, vitamin E and magnesium. Cook one cup of medium- or short-grain brown rice in $2^{1}/_{2}$ cups water for 25 to 30 minutes. Like the Japanese *haigamai* rice, Bhutanese red rice is semi-polished and cooks up into a miniature, pinkish, tender grain. It is a staple rice in the far-away Kingdom of Bhutan in the Himalayas. (See the Mail-Order Resources, page 225.) Increase the cooking times for semi-polished rice by 5 to 10 minutes over polished rice.

STARCHY SIDE DISHES

Rice isn't the only starchy side dish that can be served with fondue. A hearty serving of Lowcountry Grits is a natural side dish for a topping of shrimp or chicken cooked in a savory broth fondue. Surprise your guests with a big bowl of garlicky mashed potatoes with tender beef cooked in a hot-oil fondue. Roasted Potatoes with Fresh Herbs is an exceptional side dish with the Swiss Râclette, a meal of melted cheese. Rösti is a crusty potato pancake that is a popular Swiss farmhouse breakfast. It makes a wonderful side for râclette and cheese or meat fondues.

To make rösti, cook unpeeled, waxy boiling potatoes (one per person) in boiling, salted water until they can be pierced yet feel slightly firm inside. Cool for several hours. Some Swiss don't chill the potatoes; others do. Peel and shred the potatoes on a coarse grater. Sprinkle evenly with salt. Fry in a heavy skillet with butter until crisp and golden brown. Press with a turner to make the potatoes stick together; sprinkle with black pepper. Invert onto a plate. Add more butter to the pan; slide the potato cake back in. Cook until crisp and brown on the second side; continue pressing. Turn out of the pan and cut into wedges. Chopped onions or bacon can be partially fried in the pan before the potatoes are added. Herbs, sautéed mushrooms and cumin or caraway seeds are popular additions. The potato cake is delicious topped with fried eggs and leftover cheese fondue. An equally delicious rösti can be made with sweet potatoes.

Vegetables and noodles are often served as a side dish for meats and seafood. In an Asian hot pot, all of these ingredients are cooked together. They are carefully blended to create a colorful balance of textures and flavors. Noodles are especially favored in areas remote from rice growing regions. Thin bean thread noodles and rice noodles are especially unique. They have a better taste and texture if soaked and rinsed before being briefly cooked, usually 1 to 2 minutes. Soaked noodles can be held in a sealed plastic bag in the refrigerator overnight. The noodles have no flavor of their own, but soak up the marvelous flavor of the hot-pot broth.

Lowcountry Grits

A bowl of creamy grits is the quintessential southern comfort food. In the old Charleston "receipts," grits were called hominy, a name you will still hear in parts of the Carolina Lowcountry. Grits are versatile and can be cooked in chicken stock or flavored with sharp cheese, crisp bacon bits, country ham, jalapeños or sautéed wild mushrooms. Stone-ground grits contain speckles of the nutritious bran and bits of the kernel. They taste best but quick-cooking grits will work fine too. Do avoid the instant variety. White grits or yellow grits? It's up to you because they are interchangeable. A bowl of creamy hot grits makes a filling and satisfying side dish for seafood fondues.

Makes 6 servings

4 cups water, more if needed

1 cup heavy cream

1/2 cup (1 stick) butter

2 cups quick-cooking grits

Salt and white pepper, to taste

Bring the water and cream to a boil in a heavy saucepan. Add the butter. Slowly pour in the grits, whisking as you pour. Reduce the heat to low and cook, stirring occasionally to prevent scorching, for 20 minutes. If the grits are quite thick, stir in extra water, as needed. Grits should be soft and creamy. Season with salt and black pepper. Serve at once or set aside, covered to keep warm. Stir before serving. Serve in wide-rim soup bowls with seafood toppings.

Pecan Rice with Sausage and Sage

Wild Pecan® aromatic rice from Louisiana has a rich, nutty flavor and aroma that is reminiscent of pecans. Serve this richly flavored rice dish with beef, pork, turkey, chicken, duck and venison fondues. The rice can be made ahead and reheated in the microwave or in a 325F (165C) oven until hot.

Makes 5 or 6 servings

2 tablespoons unsalted butter

1 cup Wild Pecan® aromatic rice or other long-grain rice

2 cups Basic Chicken Stock (page 176), Quick and Easy Chicken Broth (page 177) or canned chicken stock

1/4 pound spicy bulk sausage

1/2 teaspoon fennel seeds

4 green onions, thinly sliced

1/2 cup diced red bell pepper

1 medium yellow crookneck squash, cut in quarters, sliced 1/4-inch thick

1 small zucchini, cut in quarters, sliced 1/4-inch thick

1 tablespoon minced fresh sage leaves or 1 teaspoon dried sage, crumbled

2 tablespoons minced fresh parsley

1/3 cup chopped pecans, toasted see Toasting Nuts, page 196)

Salt and black pepper, to taste

In a heavy saucepan, melt the butter over medium heat. Add the rice; sauté for 30 seconds. Stir in the stock; bring to a boil. Cover tightly and reduce heat to low. Simmer for 20 minutes.

While the rice cooks, sauté the sausage and fennel seeds in a medium skillet, stirring until crumbly. Add the onions, bell pepper, crookneck squash and zucchini; cook until crisp-tender, 1 minute. Stir in the herbs. Remove pan from the heat. Gently mix in the rice and pecans. Season with salt and pepper.

Garlic Mashed Potatoes

This dish is the ultimate indulgence for mashed potato lovers and wonderful company fare, especially since it can be prepared in advance! The garlic taste is subtle; for a stronger taste, add minced garlic instead of whole cloves. Serve as a side dish or base with fondue toppings. The dish reminds me of a luxurious mashed potato bar at a supper-party at the Bellagio Hotel in Las Vegas. Mashed potatoes were served in martini glasses with an assortment of toppings to pick from including fried chicken bites with gravy and beef with wild mushroom sauce. For a delicious lower-calorie version, substitute a healthier vegetable spread like Benecol® spread, chicken stock, Neufchatel cheese and low-fat sour cream.

Makes 6 servings

4 large (3 pounds total) Idaho potatoes, peeled, sliced no thicker than $1/2$ inch

3 tablespoons unsalted butter

1 to 2 garlic cloves, peeled, flattened with a large knife

$2/3$ cup whipping cream, milk or chicken stock, more if desired

$1^{1}/_2$ teaspoons salt, or to taste

$1/2$ (3-ounce) package cream cheese, at room temperature, cut into small cubes

$1/4$ cup sour cream

White pepper, to taste

Bring a large pot of water to a boil over medium-high heat. Add the potatoes. Bring the water back to a boil and reduce heat to low. Simmer the potatoes, covered, until tender, 15 to 20 minutes. Melt the butter with the garlic in a small saucepan over medium-low heat. Cook the garlic 1 to 2 minutes then add the cream and salt; keep warm.

Drain the potatoes. Return to the saucepan and dry over low heat 1 minute to evaporate all the water. Discard the garlic from the cream mixture. Mash potatoes with a potato masher, or push through a ricer into a large bowl then put back into the saucepan. Blend in the cream cheese and sour cream. Gradually add the hot cream mixture, stirring until the potatoes are smooth. Season with white pepper. Serve at once or cover and set aside for 1 hour. Rewarm over low heat, adding a little more cream, if necessary. (If made a day ahead, remove from the refrigerator 1 hour before serving.

Place in a 350F (175C) oven for 12 to 15 minutes, or until hot. Or cover lightly and microwave 3 to 5

minutes on 100 percent power. (Give potatoes a good stir before serving.)

VARIATIONS

Horseradish Mashed Potatoes Omit the garlic; stir 2 tablespoons prepared horseradish into the warm mashed potatoes.

Chive Mashed Potatoes Omit the garlic; stir 2 to 3 tablespoons minced fresh chives into the warm mashed potatoes.

Wild Mushroom Mashed Potatoes Sauté 4 to 6 ounces sliced wild mushrooms in 1 tablespoon butter then stir into the warm mashed potatoes.

Roasted Potatoes with Fresh Herbs

The traditional side dish for Râclette (page 37) is a bowl filled with small new potatoes boiled in their jackets. For a change of pace, I like to roast the potatoes with fresh herbs. With a meal of râclette, serve the small potatoes whole. For fondue, cut them in half. Larger potatoes can be cut into bite-size chunks. Jazz up this dish with one of the trendy potatoes now available in many markets. Yellow-fleshed potatoes are popular in Europe; try buttery Yellow Finns or Yukon Golds. For fun, look for the small violet-skinned Caribe or Peruvian Blues. Russian Banana Fingerlings are immature potatoes that resemble Tom Thumb–size bananas; they need about 10 minutes less cooking time.

Makes 6 servings

2½ pounds petite new potatoes (about 30 new potatoes or 40 fingerlings), 1½ to 1¾ inches in diameter, lightly scrubbed, or use large potatoes, cut in pieces

2 tablespoons extra-virgin olive oil

Salt and freshly ground black pepper, to taste

1 to 2 tablespoons fresh, chopped herbs (rosemary, basil, thyme)

Knorr's Aromat® seasoning (optional), to taste

Preheat the oven to 375F (190C). Put the potatoes into a large shallow casserole; coat with the olive oil. Roast for 20 minutes, turning the potatoes 1 or 2 times to prevent sticking. Sprinkle lightly with salt, black pepper, herbs and seasoning if using. Stir the potatoes; cook 10 minutes more or until tender when pierced with a knife.

VARIATION

For a nice luncheon or supper dish, top the potatoes with Cheddar Melt with Smoked Trout (page 26).

Cooked Long-Grain Rice

Rice came to South Carolina from Madagascar in the 1690s. Rice cultivation shaped the landscape, economics and politics of the Lowcountry for more than 150 years. The Civil War, competition from Louisiana growers and violent hurricanes brought it all to an end. Carolina Gold rice was king during the heyday of Carolina's rice culture. The most remarkable feature of the high-quality rice was its delicate, snow-white grain. Ambassador Thomas Jefferson wrote from France that the "white rice" was in great demand in France and England. It was sought after in China, as well.

Even though rice isn't grown in large amounts in

South Carolina now, the name Carolina is still synonymous with high-quality rice that cooks up into dry, individual grains. Long-grain rice is also the table rice of China and most of Southeast Asia. Perfumed jasmine rice from Thailand has a seductive floral smell and a pleasant, nutty taste. It cooks up softer than American long-grain rice; presoaking isn't necessary. Jasmati® is an American strain of jasmine rice from Texas. It has an appetizing aroma and soft texture. Both are ideal as side dishes for Chinese, Southeast Asian and Western fondues. For more information, see Long-Grain Rice in the Glossary (page 221).

Makes 5 or 6 servings

2 cups jasmine rice, Carolina-style rice or other long-grain rice

3 cups bottled spring water or tap water

If using Asian rice, rinse 3 or 4 times in cool water and drain well (see Rinsing Rice, page 111). Combine the rice and water in a heavy 3-quart saucepan with a tight-fitting lid. Bring to a rolling boil. Cover the pan tightly; reduce heat to the lowest setting. Simmer just until the water is absorbed, 12 to 15 minutes.

Remove the pan from the heat, leaving the lid securely in place. Let the rice stand, undisturbed, for 15 minutes. Fluff the rice with a large damp, wooden spoon. (If covered and put into a warm place, rice will stay warm about 30 minutes. You can place a thin dish towel over the rice before you add the lid to absorb condensation.) Scoop the rice into a serving bowl or individual bowls. If using for fried rice, cool and refrigerate the rice overnight.

COOK'S NOTES

Water Measurements for Long-Grain Rice
For Carolina-style rice and jasmine rice, use 2 cups

water for the first cup of rice. For each additional cup of rice, add 1 cup water.

1 cup rice: 2 cups water

2 cups rice: 3 cups water

3 cups rice: 4 cups water

COOK'S NOTE

Rice Cookers Good cooks throughout Asia now rely on electric rice cookers. They are an excellent investment if you enjoy cooking and eating rice. Once the ingredients are added to the pot, simply push a button to start cooking. Rice cookers are designed to cook each batch of rice the correct amount of time then turn off automatically. Some models keep the rice warm up to 12 hours. A rice cooker will free up the stovetop for other cooking chores.

Advanced models can be programmed to preset the finish time. They can cook perfect brown rice, sushi rice or rice porridge. Many double as a slow cooker or a steamer with a steaming tray to hold the foods. Rice cookers come with recipes, a rice paddle and a special measuring cup for the rice (it holds about 80 percent of the volume of the U.S. dry measuring cup). The insert pot has markings inside to show exactly how much water is needed. Rice cookers that have nonstick insert pans are a breeze to clean.

Fragrant Coconut Rice

Tired of the same, plain old rice? Try this lovely coconut-scented rice, which tastes wonderful plain or embellished with a fruity condiment like the Mango, Cucumber and Cashew Relish (page 163). The light coconut milk has almost 50 percent less fat than regular coconut milk. If available, add 2 pairs or 4 fragrant kaffir lime leaves or a small piece of nutty-flavored pandan leaf to the pot. Look for these seasonings in the freezer section of Asian markets.

Makes 5 to 6 servings

> **2 cups jasmine rice or Carolina-style long-grain rice**
>
> **1 (13.5-ounce) can unsweetened, light coconut milk**
>
> **1¼ cups water**
>
> **1 teaspoon salt**
>
> **½ teaspoon sugar**

Rinse and drain the rice 3 or 4 times in cool water; drain well (see Rinsing Rice, page 111). Combine the rice, coconut milk, water, salt and sugar in a 3-quart saucepan. Bring to a boil. Cover the pan tightly; reduce the heat to low. Simmer until the liquid is absorbed, 15 minutes. Remove the pan from the heat, leaving the lid securely in place. Allow the rice to stand, undisturbed, for 15 minutes. With a large spoon, gently scrape rice into a serving container or individual serving bowls. Serve at once.

VARIATIONS

Coconut Rice Pilaf Prepare Coconut Rice; cool to room temperature. Heat 2 tablespoons butter and 2 tablespoons safflower oil in a large skillet over medium heat. Sauté 1 large diced onion, 2 large cloves garlic and 1 teaspoon fresh ginger until soft but not brown. Reduce the heat to low; blend in the rice. Toss in ½ cup torn fresh cilantro leaves. Add salt to taste. Makes 5 or 6 servings.

Coconut-Cilantro Rice Salad Prepare Coconut Rice; cool to room temperature. In a large bowl, combine the rice with 4 minced scallions, 1/2 cup packed chopped cilantro leaves, 1/3 cup sliced, toasted almonds, 1/2 cup golden raisins and 1 medium tart, green Granny Smith apple, cut into 1/4-inch dice. Toss with a blend of 1/2 cup safflower oil and 1/4 cup fresh lemon juice. Add salt and black pepper to taste. Serve at room temperature within 3 or 4 hours; the texture is best if not refrigerated. Makes 6 servings

Baked Sweet Potatoes with Honey-Spice Butter

Sweet potatoes are rich in vitamins A and C. They are a nutritious side dish for pork, turkey and chicken cooked in fondue. Buy sweet potatoes with darker skins and colorful orange flesh; when baked, they will be moister and have a sweeter taste.

Makes 4 servings

4 medium sweet potatoes

About 2 tablespoons vegetable oil

Honey-Spice Butter (page 172)

Preheat the oven to 400F (205C). Rinse and dry sweet potatoes; coat with the oil. Place the sweet potatoes on a baking sheet lined with foil. Bake for 1 hour, or until soft when pressed.

While the sweet potatoes bake, prepare the Honey-Spice Butter. Slit open each sweet potato and top with a small scoop of Honey-Spice Butter. Serve at once. (Potatoes can be baked 1 day ahead and reheated in the microwave.)

Cooked Medium-Grain Rice

California medium-grain and short-grain rice are best-suited for Japanese and Korean dishes and can be used for risotto, paella and puddings. Medium-grain Japanese rice is also popular with many Taiwanese. The plump, slightly elongated grains become sticky when cooked, ideal for using chopsticks. Short-grain rice is often labeled as sushi rice. Premium grades of these types of rice remain glossy after cooking and offer subtle, pleasing differences in aroma, taste and texture. Newly harvested rice, or *shinmai* in Japan, is available from October to January. *Shinmai* is moister and needs less water; use equal portions of rice and water. As rice ages, it dries and loses moisture. End-of-the-year rice will need about 2 tablespoons more water than the amount below. For older rice, double the amount of soaking time. In Japan, a bowl of well-cooked, plain white rice has an aura of simplicity that equates with elegance. But embellishments can be added like the nutritious green soybeans in the variation, Edamamé Rice. For more information on similar types of rice, see Medium-Grain Rice in the Glossary (page 222). The rice can be prepared in a rice cooker.

Makes 5 1/2 to 6 cups rice

2 cups California premium, medium-or short-grain rice

2 1/3 cups bottled spring water or tap water

Rinse and drain rice 3 or 4 times in cool water (see Rinsing Asian Rice, page 111). Combine the rice and water in a heavy 3-quart saucepan with a tight-fitting lid. Soak for 30 minutes to 1 hour.

Bring the water to a rolling boil. Reduce the heat to the lowest setting; cover the pan with the lid. Simmer until water is absorbed, 15 minutes. Remove the pan from the heat, leaving the lid securely in place. Let the rice stand, undisturbed, for 12 to 15 minutes.

Remove lid; gently fluff the rice with a damp rice paddle (*shamoji*) or spatula. If covered and put into a warm place, rice will stay warm for about 30 minutes. Place a thin, clean dish towel over the rice then put the lid back in place to absorb condensation. Scoop rice into a serving bowl or individual bowls.

<hr>

VARIATION

Edamamé Rice When rice is cooked, just before the 15-minute resting period, remove the lid and quickly add a mixture of ³/₄ cup blanched, shelled green soybeans and 1 thinly sliced green onion over the top. Cover tightly and allow the rice to stand for 20 minutes. To serve, carefully toss the ingredients with a dampened rice paddle. Garnish servings with Black-Sesame Salt (page 149).

Cook's Notes Water Measurements for Short-Grain Rice

> **1 cup medium-or short-grain rice: 1 cup plus 3 tablespoons water**
>
> **1¹/₂ cups medium- or short-grain rice: 1³/₄ cups water**
>
> **3 cups medium- or short-grain rice: 3¹/₂ cups water**

Plum Blossom Sherbet

This refreshing low-fat plum sherbet is the perfect ending for a hot-pot meal. Choose plums with purple skins to create the prettiest pink hue. Drizzle each serving with a small amount of plum wine and decorate with a plum blossom or organic viola when in season. For a seasonal treat, stir 2 to 3 tablespoons shredded plum blossoms into the ice cream halfway through the freezing process.

Makes 6 servings

> **1 pound firm, ripe plums (5 or 6), pitted, cut into chunks**
>
> **¹/₂ cup sugar**
>
> **¹/₄ cup water**
>
> **8 ounces soft tofu (*kinogoshi*)**
>
> **¹/₂ cup freshly squeezed tart orange juice**
>
> **¹/₂ cup corn syrup**
>
> **Grated zest of 1 orange**
>
> **1 to 2 teaspoons fresh lemon juice**
>
> **Pinch salt**
>
> **2 tablespoons good-quality plum wine**
>
> **1 teaspoon pure vanilla extract**

Simmer the plums, sugar and water in a small covered saucepan over medium-low heat until plums are soft, 12 to 15 minutes. Cool slightly. Puree the plum mixture in a food processor fitted with the steel blade. Add all the remaining ingredients and process briefly until smooth. Refrigerate the mixture until chilled, 2 to 3 hours.

Freeze in an ice cream machine according to the manufacturer's directions. Store in the freezer for several hours to ripen. If you do not have an ice cream machine, freeze in ice cube trays until slushy. Stir mixture, scraping it away from the sides of the pans. Freeze again until firm. Beat in an electric mixer to incorporate air and lighten the texture. Freeze until firm. Serve within 1 to 2 days for the best texture.

Salads

A refreshing salad is the perfect counterpart for a hearty fondue. As a first course, its purpose is to awaken all the senses for the meal to come. Served alongside the fondue, it provides a welcome contrast in flavor, temperature, texture and color. If you prefer to serve your salad European-style after the main course, its fresh, lively taste will help refresh and cleanse the palate.

It seems that everything old is eventually new again. Fondue has never been more popular and salads have never been more tantalizing. In fourteenth-century England, King Richard's household salad recipes called for two dozen ingredients including fennel, garlic, parsley, cresses, rosemary, mint, olive oil and vinegar. An astonishing variety of lettuces were grown. Many trendy "new" salad ingredients we now enjoy have been grown in American gardens since the 1600s. Thanks to creative chefs, a culinary gardening renaissance, specialty seed companies and committed farmers, we are reclaiming many of these neglected heirloom treasures.

The twenty-first century American salad bowl has expanded to include a world of possibilities beyond iceberg lettuce, once the foundation upon which salads were built. Mixed Greens with Pear and Ginger Vinaigrette calls for a blend of fresh, young greens called mesclun. Its origins began in France. After a long winter of preserved foods, people foraged the fields for a spring tonic of fresh greens. Mesclun might include: chervil, arugula, mâche, sorrel, purslane, oak leaf lettuce or frisée. Similar Asian blends include Asian herbs and greens. Today's chef considers these innovative salad blends, the "iceberg" lettuce of the new millennium. Other choices include spinach, watercress, butterhead lettuces, escarole, leaf lettuces, romaine (cos lettuce) and the Italian chicory, *puntarelle*.

Use convenient preblended bags of greens or even better, select the ingredients and combine your own. To create a perfect balance, select leaves of various textures with flavors ranging from spicy and tart to nutty and sweet. Slightly bitter greens, like frisée or mizuna, add an accent flavor; a touch of bitterness adds depth and rounds out other flavors. Delicate greens should be dressed with lighter dressing such as vinaigrettes. Mesclun is the perfect canvas for colorful, edible flowers. Cooking with flowers reflects an early Roman influence and is an easy route to salad sophistication.

Marinated vegetable salads add instant appeal to a fondue meal. Hot and Spicy Thai Coleslaw brings home the Asian flavors that have fast become an American favorite. The intense flavors and brilliant colors of fresh fruit are a stunning enhancement. Sugar Pea and Shrimp Salad with Creamy Strawberry Vinaigrette is a lovely accompaniment for a simple cheese or broth-based fondue.

Many components of these salads can be prepared well in advance. Many can be assembled entirely ahead; others need a little attention in the final minutes before serving.

TIPS FOR GREAT SALADS

1. Select high-quality, seasonal salad ingredients that are dazzling-fresh. Lettuce leaves should be crisp and shiny, never limp. If a recipe calls for a type of lettuce and it is past its prime at the market or unavailable, choose something else. Create a good balance of flavors, colors and textures in your salad bowl.

2. Cheese should not have the starring role in a salad partnered with cheese fondue. Likewise, avoid cheese-rich dressings. A salad of crisp, mixed greens with a light vinaigrette is a better choice. Cheese-enriched salads harmonize better with vegetarian and broth-based meat, seafood and poultry fondues.

3. Baby greens are delicate; dress them lightly. Tear slightly larger "teenage" greens and lettuce leaves into pieces. Don't make the pieces too small; it detracts from the character of the salad. Smaller leaves can be left whole or torn in half, following the European fashion. Mature, large lettuce leaves and greens are best left for cooking.

4. The classic ratio for French vinaigrette is three parts oil to one part acid. You can lighten the classic formula to half oil and half vinegar with a pinch of sugar to temper the tartness. Or, use naturally sweet balsamic vinegar.

5. Create low-fat salads by sprinkling a few drops of balsamic vinegar over tender lettuce or fresh fruit; no oil is necessary. A few drops also enhance the flavor of not-quite-ripe strawberries, cherries, vegetables and grilled steaks. Cut fat calories in vinaigrettes by substituting a small portion of concentrated, unsalted chicken stock for the oil. Fruity, darker oils deliver more flavor so less can be used.

5. Choose cider vinegar, balsamic vinegar, unseasoned rice vinegar, citrus juices, fruit and herbal vinegars. Red wine vinegar or sherry wine vinegar goes well with chicories and bold-tasting greens. *Verjus*, a centuries-old byproduct of winemaking with a tangy-sweet taste without the acetic acid of vinegar, can be used instead of vinegar.

6. French cooks use shallots to help cut the vinegar's acid. Dijon mustard adds flavor and helps emulsify the oil and vinegar. Fruit purees add body. Garlic, fresh herbs, curry powder and citrus zest are additional winning flavor additions.

7. Light-bodied, extra-virgin olive oil from the first gentle pressing is a superior oil for salads. Olive oil is monounsaturated, Vitamin-E rich and contains disease-fighting antioxidants, which are heart-protective. Deep-colored olive oil has more flavor than lighter oils; if too strong, dilute to taste with a neutral-flavored oil like canola, safflower or sunflower oil. These are all healthy choices, as well. Nutty-tasting sesame oil, hazelnut oil, walnut oil and

macadamia oil add depth and flavor; use in smaller amounts. Vitamin E–rich grapeseed oil can also be used.

8. A pinch of salt in vinaigrette and salad dressing balances flavors, enhances the sweet taste of the salad greens and heightens the flavor of produce or fruits, especially when not perfectly ripe. Don't forget to add a touch of black pepper, preferably freshly ground.

9. The pure pleasure of snipping fresh garden herbs for salad activates all the senses: visual, olfactory and gustatory. Different herbs create a variety of subtle tastes, which can bring perpetual delight.

RINSING SALAD GREENS

Rinse lettuce and salad greens in a large bowl of cool water in the sink. Drain off water. Dry thoroughly with a salad spinner. Spin-dry in one or two portions then blot with paper towels to remove all moisture. Mesclun mixtures can bruise easily in the lettuce spinner; spin gently or carefully blot dry. Wrap lettuce loosely in paper towels; slide into a zip-top plastic bag and press out the air. Lettuce will hold nicely for two to three days in the salad spinner. Use cleaned lettuce within three to four days. Baby greens deteriorate if not completely dried; they are best used within one to two days. Wash tender microgreens as you use them. Certain types of salad material like spinach, arugula and cilantro need several rinsings in cool water to remove the grit. (No salad spinner? Drain the rinsed lettuce; thoroughly dry leaves with paper towels or gently roll up in a thick, clean towel. When dry, wrap in paper towels; store in a plastic bag.)

The onion is the poetic soul of the salad bowl.

—English Proverb

Herbal Sushi Splash

Use this scented vinegar blend to make herb-flavored sushi rice that can be used for sushi-style salads to accompany meat, poultry and seafood fondues. The fresh herbs are untraditional but give the rice a unique, refreshing taste. If you prefer, omit the herbal seasonings to make a pot of traditional-flavored sushi rice.

To use the sushi splash, prepare Cooked Medium-Grain Rice. Put the hot rice into a damp wooden or glass bowl then sprinkle in 5 to 6 tablespoons of the dressing while gently cutting and turning the rice with a damp rice paddle or large spoon. At the same time, fan the rice to cool it rapidly, creating a nice sheen. If you don't have a partner to help with the fanning, use a small electric fan. Cover the rice with a damp dish towel; do not refrigerate. Use within 1 day. See Sushi Salads, below.

Makes about 1 cup

> 2 or 3 green shiso leaves, 5 or 6 mint leaves or lemon verbena leaves, 2-inch piece of the tender inner portion of lemongrass, mashed or 1 pair fragrant kaffir lime leaves (optional)
>
> ¾ cup unseasoned rice vinegar
>
> ¼ cup sugar (for a sweeter taste, add 1 more tablespoon sugar)
>
> 4 teaspoons sea salt
>
> 3 tablespoons mirin (Japanese rice wine)

If using, select one of the herbs. Rinse and dry. Tear the leaves slightly then place them in a steril-

---

ized pint jar with a lid. In a medium saucepan, heat the vinegar, sugar and salt over low heat, stirring constantly, until sugar and salt dissolve. Remove from the heat and stir in the mirin. Pour into the jar covering the herbs. Cover lightly and steep at room temperature for 2 hours or longer for a stronger herbal taste. Strain the dressing and pour back into the jar. Store in the refrigerator for up to 10 days. Pour out the amount needed and bring to room temperature or heat until barely warm.

Sushi Salads A light, refreshing sushi salad makes a delightful side dish for meat and seafood fondues. It also pairs well with Asian or western vegetarian fondues. Make a pot of herb-flavored or plain sushi rice following the instructions in the recipe, Herbal Sushi Splash, above. For complete information on making sushi rice and all types of creative sushi, refer to my cookbook, *Japanese Cooking for the American Table.*

Select one of the following quick recipes:

Miyabizushi (elegant sushi) To 1 batch sushi rice, add 1½-inch strips julienne vegetables such as carrots, cucumber, yellow bell pepper, soaked, dried, seasoned shiitaki mushrooms. Add chopped, cooked shrimp and shredded shiso, if desired. Spoon into attractive bowls and top with shredded egg pancake and red pickled ginger (*ben-ishoga*). For a special presentation I place the bowls in beautiful folded origami bowl covers made from gold-flecked washi paper. You can use elegant gift-wraps or small boxes lined with waxed paper that open up into a fancy fold at the top.

Harvest Sushi Salad To 1 batch sushi rice, add small diced cubes or pieces of blanched vegetables such as broccoli, pumpkin or squash, red bell pepper, asparagus tips, thawed frozen corn, red onion, small cooked black beans. Spoon into Jack-Be-Little Pumpkin Bowls (page 207).

Tropical Sushi Salad To 1 batch sushi rice, add cooked seafood (lobster, crab chunks or shrimp), shelled, fresh green soybeans, diced fresh pineapple, minced green onion, chopped macadamia nuts and shredded shiso leaves. Serve in fresh pineapple shells.

Carolina Sushi Salad To 1 batch sushi rice, toss in sliced pickled okra, diced ham, diced green onion, diced green bell pepper, grape tomatoes (cut in half and drained), minced fresh parsley. Garnish with dry-roasted benne (sesame) seeds.

Alpine Mushroom Salad

The creamy green dressing has a vibrant color and lively flavor, which you will find addictive. Hearts of palm add an elegant touch but thin wedges of ripe avocado or baby artichoke hearts would be delightful as well. When in season, toss in a few fresh herbs such as fresh lovage, lemon balm or mint. Serve this salad with Râclette (page 37), or a cheese fondue.

Makes 6 servings

GREEN ONION DRESSING

1 clove garlic, peeled, cut in half

3 small green onions, with green stems, cut in 2-inch lengths

¼ cup cider vinegar

2 tablespoons sugar

½ teaspoon salt, or to taste

1¼ cups safflower oil, sunflower oil or canola oil

1 tablespoon fresh lemon juice

Freshly ground black pepper, to taste

5 or 6 large cultivated mushrooms, wiped clean

10 to 12 cups torn mixed lettuce leaves (Boston lettuce, Bibb lettuce and red leaf lettuce)

1 (16-ounce) can hearts of palm, drained, tough outer portion removed, cut in ½-inch slices

About 24 red or yellow teardrop or cherry tomatoes, cut in half

⅓ cup toasted pine nuts (see Toasted Nuts, page 196)

To prepare the Green Onion Dressing: Put the garlic, green onions and vinegar into a blender. Process until onions are pureed. Add the sugar and salt. With the machine running, pour in the oil in a steady stream. When blended, mix in the lemon juice and black pepper. Taste dressing; add more salt and pepper, if desired. Use at once or cover and refrigerate. Use within 2 days. Makes about 1¾ cups.

Trim off the mushroom stems level with the caps. Place the mushrooms, stem sides down, on a cutting board. Cut into very thin slices. Arrange the lettuce on 6 salad plates. Arrange a portion of the hearts of palm, sliced mushrooms and tomatoes over each portion of lettuce. Drizzle each salad with Green Onion Dressing; sprinkle with the pine nuts. Serve at once.

Edible Art Tête de Moine or "head of the monk" is a delicious cow's milk cheese made for at least 800 years in the Jura region of Switzerland in the Bellelay monastery. It is cut in a special way with a Swiss cutter called a *girolle*. The top of the cheese is skillfully shaved into a continuous ruffled spiral that resembles a beautiful flower-like rosette. Only when cut in such a manner is the aromatic, rich spicy flavor of the cheese revealed. For a breathtaking presentation, arrange one beautiful Tête de Moine flower on a salad of baby greens arranged on a luncheon-size plate. The *girolle* can be used to shave a flower rosette of marbled chocolate for embellishing the top of a cake. (See Mail-Order Resources, page 225.)

Cucumbers with Fresh Dill

There is a recipe for marinated cucumbers in the national recipe box of almost every culture. The textures and flavors in this version go well with cheese fondue or Swiss Râclette (page 38). European cucumbers are not waxed and do not require peeling. You should peel thick-skinned American cucumbers then cut in half lengthwise and scrape out the seeds. Cut crosswise into thin half-rings. The fennel variation has a delicate anise taste.

Makes 6 servings

2 European cucumbers, unpeeled, ends trimmed (about 1½ pounds)

⅔ cup white wine vinegar

2 heaping tablespoons sugar

½ teaspoon sea salt, or more to taste

3 tablespoons minced fresh dill or shredded fresh mint leaves

Freshly ground black pepper, to taste

Fresh dill sprigs, for garnish

To create a decorative edge, use the tines of a fork to score the skin of each cucumber along its length. With a sharp knife, cut each cucumber into ¼-inch-thick diagonal slices. Place into a large bowl. In a small saucepan, heat the vinegar, sugar and salt over low heat, stirring until sugar dissolves. Cool; pour over cucumbers. Stir in the dill. Cover; chill for 1 to 2 hours, stirring once or twice. Pour into a serving dish. Season with black pepper; garnish with dill sprigs.

VARIATIONS

Cucumbers with Fennel Prepare recipe as directed, except use 1 cucumber and omit the dill. Stir in 2 cups thinly sliced fennel (1 small, quartered bulb). Substitute fennel leaves for the dill and dill garnish. Just before serving, drain off the marinade and transfer to a serving dish. Drizzle with 1 to 2 tablespoons extra-virgin olive oil; season with black pepper.

Cucumbers in Cream Prepare recipe as directed, except reduce vinegar to ¹/₂ cup; stir in ³/₄ cup Crème Fraîche (page 161) or sour cream and 1 finely minced small clove garlic.

Vietnamese Table Salad

The centerpiece of a Vietnamese meal is an artfully arranged platter of tender lettuce, aromatic herbs and fresh, sliced vegetables. The platter might also include garlic chives, fresh shiso leaves (perilla), fine shreds of fresh ginger, lifelike vegetable flowers or sliced tropical fruits. Small stainless steel cutters for sculpting flowers, animals, birds and butterflies are available from The Wok Shop in San Francisco (see Mail-Order Resources, page 225). Add these ingredients to Southeast Asian noodle soups or pick-up salads made by rolling fondue-cooked meats and

seafood in damp 6-inch rice papers lined with Boston (butter) lettuce leaves. Dip the rolls into Indochine Sauce (page 170) or Peppered Peanut Sauce (page 151). Rice papers can be softened by dipping each one quickly into hot tap water; drain on cloth towels. Grilled seafood and meats can be rolled in the packets, as well.

Makes 6 servings

1 large bunch cilantro leaves, torn into small sprigs

1 cup packed small basil leaves, torn if large

1 bunch fresh small mint, stems removed

³/₄ pound fresh bean sprouts, dipped into boiling water 10 seconds, chilled in iced water, drained, tails and tips removed, if desired

2 limes, cut into wedges

1 small European cucumber, ends trimmed, seeded, cut in julienne strips

4 small red Thai chilies, chopped, or Siracha hot chili sauce, to taste

Arrange all the ingredients on 1 or 2 plates for passing at the table. The platters can be tightly covered and refrigerated for up to 3 hours before serving.

FROM MY RECIPE BOX

Butterfly Crisps Unwrap a 1-pound package of wonton skins. Rewrap half and store for later use. Cut the remaining skins in half, forming rectangular pieces. Make a 1-inch slit in the center of each rectangle. Turn one end through the center cut of each piece. Shape the remaining rectangles. Make double butterflies by stacking 2 rectangular shapes. Deep-fry in canola oil at 360F (180C), turning 1 or 2 times, until golden brown and crisp. Drain on paper towels; sprinkle with Green-Tea

Salt (page 159) or other seasoning. Serve with dips and as a snack. Makes about 50 butterfly shapes.

Celery Root Rémoulade

Celery root, or celeriac, is a favorite European winter vegetable developed by Renaissance-period gardeners. Enriched with vitamin C, iron and calcium, it has a mellow celery-like flavor. Celery root is grown for its brown, globe-shaped root crown rather than the stalks and leaves. Enjoy the simplicity of this salad as a side dish with Fondue Chinoise (page 44). Cooked celery root can be sauced with Italian Fonduta (page 34). Select firm, hard, clean roots with no hint of softness. To prevent discoloration as you peel the roots, drop them into 1 quart of water mixed with 3 tablespoons vinegar.

Makes 6 servings

1³/₄ to 2 pounds celery root, cut in half

1¹/₂ teaspoons sea salt

4 tablespoons fresh lemon juice

About ¹/₂ cup Fresh Mayonnaise (page 157) or good-quality, prepared mayonnaise

1 tablespoon Dijon mustard

1 tablespoon capers, rinsed, chopped

2 or 3 cornichon pickles, minced

1 green onion, chopped

1 tablespoon chopped fresh Italian parsley, tarragon or chervil

Salt and freshly ground black pepper, to taste

Red leaf lettuce

With a sharp, sturdy knife, peel the celery root halves. Cut each half into 3 slices then into pieces that will fit into the food processor's feed tube.

Push through the feed tube of a food processor fitted with the shredding blade. Or, cut by hand, into ¹/₈-inch-thick slices, then in matchstick strips (see Matchstick Strips, page 133). Toss the celery root in a large bowl with the salt and 2 tablespoons of the lemon juice and let stand for 1 hour.

In a large bowl, combine the remaining lemon juice, mayonnaise, mustard, capers, cornichons, green onion and parsley. Mix the celery root into the dressing. Cover and refrigerate for several hours or overnight. (Celery root tenderizes after several hours of marinating.) Before serving, season with salt and black pepper. Serve on lettuce-lined plates.

VARIATION

Celery Root Rémoulade with Dried Blueberries and Hazelnuts Omit the pickles and capers. Stir in ¹/₃ cup finely chopped dried blueberries, cherries or cranberries and ¹/₃ cup finely chopped toasted hazelnuts or walnuts.

Field Greens with Radicchio Ribbons

Se lo mangi, é un paradiso. "If you eat it, you are in paradise." This Italian sentiment pays tribute to Red Verona radicchio, the claret-colored chicory found in *misticanza*, a Northern Italian salad mix similar to mesclun. Radicchio provides a pleasing touch of astringency, a taste appreciated by the Italian palate. Select two or more field greens or substitute a blend of other wild greens, lettuce or herbs, as desired. This salad goes well with cheese fondue or Râclette (page 37). If served with a broth-based fondue, sprinkle with 2 ounces crumbled blue cheese, or add paper-thin curls of mellow Swiss mountain cheese or garnish the salad with an exquisite, ruffled Tête ee Moine cheese flower (see Edible Art, page 123).

Makes 5 or 6 servings

THYME VINAIGRETTE

¼ cup red wine vinegar

1 small shallot, minced

1 large clove garlic, finely minced

1 teaspoon Dijon mustard

1 teaspoon sugar

6 tablespoons extra-virgin olive oil

6 tablespoons safflower oil

1 teaspoon fresh thyme leaves or ¼ teaspoon dried herb

¼ teaspoon salt

Freshly grated black pepper, to taste

1 small head radicchio, separated, rinsed, dried

2 cups mixed baby field greens (sorrel, mâche, arugula, dandelion leaves, mizuna)

5 to 6 cups torn Bibb (Limestone) lettuce leaves (about ½ pound)

¼ wedge of a small to medium red onion, cut in paper-thin slices, separated

½ cup chopped hazelnuts or pine nuts, toasted (see Toasted Nuts, page 196)

To prepare the Thyme Vinaigrette: In a medium bowl, whisk together the vinegar, shallot, garlic, mustard and sugar. Add oils in a slow, steady stream, whisking until the mixture is blended. Stir in the thyme, salt and pepper. Let stand for 30 minutes for the best flavor. Makes 1 cup.

Cut the radicchio leaves into ½-inch ribbons. Toss the radicchio, field greens, lettuce and red onion in a large bowl. Dress the salad with enough vinaigrette to coat the leaves; divide among 5 or 6

chilled salad plates. Garnish with hazelnuts. Serve at once.

FROM MY RECIPE BOX

Grilled Radicchio For a simple salad, brush split heads of radicchio with olive oil and grill briefly; drizzle with Thyme Vinaigrette or a few drops of good balsamic vinegar.

Arugula and Orange Salad with Blueberries and Lavender

Arugula, a peppery salad green from the mustard family, was enjoyed in early Rome. The marinated blueberries are addictive and good for you, too; you might be tempted to eat the entire bowl. Researchers at Tufts University discovered blueberries have one of the highest antioxidant levels, beneficial for improving eyesight and reducing age-related diseases. Lavender is thought to be good for aging skin and induces calmness by releasing serotonin in the brain. This dish makes an ambrosial side dish or light dessert for any savory fondue.

Makes 6 servings

BLUEBERRIES AND LAVENDER

1 pint plump, fresh blueberries

¼ cup packed light brown sugar

2 tablespoons good-quality balsamic vinegar

1 tablespoon finely minced fresh lavender leaves

2 tablespoons finely minced red onion

Pinch of Kosher salt

½ pound small arugula leaves, thick stems removed, rinsed, dried (about 6 cups)

2 cups mâche, frisée, watercress or mesclun, rinsed, dried

5 or 6 navel oranges

3 or 4 tablespoons extra-virgin olive oil

Coarsely ground black pepper, to taste

⅓ cup toasted walnuts, chopped

To prepare the Blueberries and Lavender: Rinse and drain the blueberries; remove any stems. In a large bowl, whisk together the sugar, vinegar, lavender, onion and salt. Gently mix in blueberries. Cover and refrigerate for 30 minutes or up to 2 days. Makes about 2 cups.

Spread the arugula and mâche evenly over a large platter. Peel the oranges, removing as much of the white membrane as possible. Cut into thin slices. Place in a wide circle on the bed of greens, slightly overlapping. With a slotted spoon, scoop the Blueberries and Lavender inside the ring of orange slices. Spoon the blueberry marinade over the salad; drizzle with the olive oil. Season with pepper. Scatter the walnuts over the oranges. Serve at once. (The salad can be covered and chilled for up to 1 hour; add the marinade when served.)

Orange-Caraway Beets with Spinach

If your guests are ho-hum about beets, they might change their minds when they taste them in this warm, colorful salad. The dynamic flavors complement a hearty cheese fondue. Admittedly, beets are a high-maintenance vegetable and it takes a lot of cleaning to get rid of the psychedelic pink stains they leave behind. Minimize the color loss and preserve flavor by wrapping and baking the beets. If you don't tear the skins or cut off the root or stem-ends, the pigments will stay locked inside. The beets can be cooked and diced a day in advance; chill until needed. Try this salad with beautiful golden beets; they are sweeter and don't lose as much color.

Sauté tender, young beet greens in olive oil then dress with a few drops of balsamic vinegar for a delicious side dish.

Makes 5 or 6 servings

5 medium red beets, tops removed (2½ cup diced)

8 slices lean bacon, cut in 1-inch pieces

½ teaspoon freshly grated orange zest

⅓ cup freshly squeezed tart orange juice

2 tablespoons sherry vinegar

1½ teaspoons sugar

½ teaspoon salt

¼ cup plus 1 tablespoon extra-virgin olive oil

6 to 8 cups baby spinach leaves, rinsed, dried, stems trimmed

1 large shallot, minced

1 large clove garlic, minced

1½ teaspoons caraway seeds

Freshly ground black pepper, to taste

½ cup coarsely chopped walnuts, toasted (see Toasted Nuts, page 196)

Preheat the oven to 375F (190C). Wrap the beets in foil. Place in a heavy baking pan; bake for 45 minutes, or just until tender when pierced with a knife. Remove the foil; cool beets completely. Scrub off the skins; cut the beets in ½-inch dice.

In a medium nonstick skillet, fry the bacon until crisp. As the bacon cooks, blend the orange zest, juice, vinegar, sugar, salt and the ¼ cup olive oil in a small bowl.

Arrange beds of spinach leaves on 5 or 6 salad plates. Remove bacon from the pan; set aside. Discard all but 1 tablespoon of the bacon fat in the skillet; add the 1 tablespoon olive oil. Place the skillet over medium heat; sauté the shallot and garlic for 1 minute. Add the caraway seeds; cook for 30 seconds. Stir in the orange juice mixture then mix in the beets. Season with pepper. Heat for about 30 seconds; spoon a portion of hot beet mixture on each spinach-lined plate. Scatter a portion of bacon and walnuts over each salad. Serve at once. (The hot, dressed beets can be covered and set aside for 30 minutes. Warm the beets briefly just before serving.)

Cucumber Salad with Fresh Mint and Red Chili Vinaigrette

This spicy, minty-fresh Southeast Asian cucumber salad is a perfect partner for Asian hot pots. For a heartier version, include ¼ pound seafood such as thin rings of cooked small squid or cooked chopped shrimp.

Makes 6 small servings

½ teaspoon freshly grated lime zest

¼ cup fresh lime juice

¼ cup unseasoned rice vinegar

2 tablespoons light brown sugar

1 clove garlic, mashed to a paste

1 small Thai chili, thinly sliced

½ teaspoon sea salt

2 teaspoons Southeast Asian fish sauce (*nuoc mam or nam pla*)

2 tablespoons shredded fresh mint leaves or fresh cilantro

1 European cucumber (about 1 pound), ends trimmed, halved lengthwise

½ small red onion, cut in half, then cut in paper-thin slices

2 tablespoons finely chopped dry-roasted peanuts

In a medium bowl, whisk together the lime zest, lime juice, rice vinegar, brown sugar, garlic, chili, salt and fish sauce. Stir in the mint; set aside.

With a small spoon, scrape the seeds from the cucumber halves. Using a sharp knife cut each half crosswise into ¼-inch-thick slices. Slice the onion. Add the cucumber and onion to the dressing; mix well. Chill for 30 minutes or up to 2 hours. Spoon the cucumber mixture into 6 small bowls. Garnish with the peanuts; serve at once.

Hot and Spicy Thai Coleslaw

Lillian Johnson and I share a passion for collecting Asian dishes, an addiction we freely indulged while living in Japan as military spouses. An expert cook and entertainer, Lillian served this fantastic coleslaw in the most exquisite Japanese tulip bowls at a luncheon at her Florida home. She says this coleslaw adds lots of zing to Western fondues. In the early twentieth century in California's Monterey Peninsula, Lillian's grandfather invented an important machine for compressing and bailing dried squid for export to China. Yee Won and his shop,

now a landmark, are immortalized in John Stein-
beck's *Cannery Row*.

Makes 6 to 8 servings

½ **pound cucumbers, peeled, quartered
lengthwise, seeded**

1 **pound tender green cabbage, cored and
finely shredded**

4 **thin green onions, trimmed, chopped**

½ **cup dry-roasted peanuts, coarsely chopped**

2 **cloves garlic, finely minced**

1 **or 2 Serrano chilies, stems, seeds removed,
finely minced**

¼ **cup unseasoned rice vinegar**

2 **tablespoons sugar**

½ **teaspoon curry powder**

½ **cup canola or safflower oil**

1 **to 2 tablespoons chopped fresh cilantro**

1 **tablespoon chopped parsley**

Using a sharp knife, cut each cucumber quarter
crosswise into ⅛-inch-thick slices. Place into a
large bowl. Add the cabbage, green onions,
peanuts, garlic and chilies to the bowl. Toss the
ingredients together.

In a small bowl, whisk together the rice vinegar,
sugar, curry powder and oil. Pour over the vegetable mixture; toss to combine. Mix in the
cilantro and parsley. Serve at once or cover and
chill for several hours before serving.

VARIATION

To cut preparation time, Lillian uses a food
processor fitted with the steel blade to chop the
peanuts then the combined garlic and chilies. She
switches to the shredding blade to cut the cabbage. Cut the cucumbers and onions by hand.

Mixed Greens with Pear
and Ginger Vinaigrette

Mesclun is a Provençal mixture of young, tender
greens harvested before their flavors become
strong. A large, crisp Asian pear adds a fresh, clean
taste and complements the flavor of the delicate
vinaigrette. This salad pairs up nicely with a cheese
fondue made with Fendant, a Swiss dry white wine
with hints of pear. For a garnish that echoes the
theme, make pear fans by following the instructions
below. For an equally suitable garnish, try the Lotus
Crisps (page 64). If the salad is to accompany a
broth-based fondue, you could include a small
wedge of ultra-creamy, triple-cream blue cheese.

Makes 6 servings

PEAR AND GINGER VINAIGRETTE

1 **(11.5-ounce) can pear nectar**

3 **tablespoons unseasoned rice vinegar**

½ **teaspoon grated fresh ginger (see Fresh
Ginger Juice, page 108)**

⅛ **teaspoon sea salt**

½ **teaspoon sugar**

1 **tablespoon light olive or safflower oil**

10 **to 12 chive blossoms or other small edible
blossoms (optional)**

8 **cups mesclun (mixed baby greens)**

1 **crisp Asian pear, peeled, sliced, cut into
matchstick strips**

3 **tablespoons chopped hazelnuts or walnuts,
toasted (see Toasted Nuts, page 196)**

To prepare the Pear and Ginger Vinaigrette: Pour
the nectar into a 2-quart saucepan. Bring to a boil;
reduce heat to medium-low and simmer until mixture reduces to slightly more than ⅓ cup, 10 to 12
minutes. Watch carefully; the nectar tends to bub-

ble up. Pour the reduced nectar into a 1-pint jar with a screw-top lid. Cool completely. Add remaining ingredients; shake well. Chill for at least 1 hour or overnight for the best flavor. Makes about ⅔ cup.

Separate the tiny lavender flowers that make up each chive blossom, if using. Place the mesclun in a large bowl. Add the vinaigrette and gently toss to coat. Divide the salad among 6 chilled salad plates. Scatter a portion of the pear strips over each salad; garnish with chive blossoms and hazelnuts. Serve at once.

FROM MY RECIPE BOX

Pear Fans Cut 2 ripe pears, preferably with red skin, if in season, from stem to blossom end into 4 quarters. Trim out the cores. Starting ½ inch from the stem of each quarter, make 3 or 4 parallel slices the length of the pear. Press gently on the slices to spread open each pear into a fan. Place 1 quarter on each plate, skin side up.

Fried Green Tomato and Goat Cheese Stacks

Southerners will walk a mile for fried green tomatoes. The fresh water-ground cornmeal creates a crunchy coating on the tomatoes that contrasts beautifully with the creamy goat cheese topping. Of course, I always fry the tomatoes in a cast-iron skillet, seasoned years ago by my East Tennessee grandmother. The traditional fat for frying tomatoes is bacon drippings. It gives them a sweet, smoky taste. Southerners love bacon fat as much as the Chinese love soy sauce, but I prefer to use healthier

olive oil. Occasionally I will indulge and add 1 or 2 tablespoons of bacon fat to the olive oil for flavor. Select firm green tomatoes without the slightest trace of pink to produce the authentic crisp texture and tart flavor of the fried green tomatoes that were such a hit at the renowned Whistle Stop Cafe!

Makes 6 servings

HERB VINAIGRETTE

¼ cup white wine vinegar

1 shallot, peeled

¾ cup extra-virgin olive oil

1 tablespoon each chopped fresh chives, parsley and basil or thyme

⅛ teaspoon salt

8 to 10 ounces fresh, young, mild-tasting goat cheese, chilled

2 (8-ounce) firm, solid-green tomatoes, each cut in 3 (½- to ¾-inch-thick) slices

⅓ cup buttermilk or milk

About ⅔ cup stone-ground cornmeal

Salt and freshly ground black pepper, to taste

6 to 8 tablespoons extra-virgin olive oil

8 to 10 cups torn mixed greens (red leaf lettuce, Boston lettuce, arugula, watercress)

½ cup coarsely chopped, toasted pecans

To prepare the Herb Vinaigrette: Add the vinegar to a food processor fitted with the steel blade. With the machine running, drop the shallot through the feed tube. When minced, slowly pour in the oil. Pour the vinaigrette into a bowl; stir in the herbs and salt. Let stand for 30 minutes for the best flavor. Makes about 1 cup.

Divide the cheese into 6 portions; pat into flat rounds slightly less wide than the tomato slices. Place into a dish; drizzle each with 1 tablespoon of the vinaigrette.

Preheat the oven to 350F (175C). Put the buttermilk and cornmeal in separate shallow bowls; place a baking sheet nearby. Dip both sides of the tomato slices in buttermilk. Coat slices completely with cornmeal. Place the slices on the baking sheet; lightly season with salt and pepper.

Heat 2 tablespoons of the oil in a heavy medium skillet over medium heat. Fry half of the tomato slices until crisp and nicely browned on each side, about 2 minutes. Add another 1 tablespoon oil, as needed. Place fried tomatoes on the baking sheet. Fry the second batch in the remaining oil.

With a small spatula, place a round of goat cheese on each tomato slice. Bake for 3 minutes, or until the cheese is warm. (Goat cheese softens but will not melt.) Divide the greens among 6 salad plates. Place a tomato-cheese stack in the center of each salad. Sprinkle pecans over the goat cheese; drizzle salads with remaining vinaigrette. Serve at once.

Sugar Pea and Shrimp Salad with Creamy Strawberry Vinaigrette

This recipe provides all the qualities of a splendid salad; eye appeal, freshness, crisp textures and intriguing flavors to stimulate the taste buds. Plump sugar snap peas contain fat little peas; snow peas are flatter. The pods of both types are entirely edible. Two hints for preparing sugar peas: Don't overcook them and remove the strings from both sides of each pod. All the components of this dish can be prepared a day ahead and refrigerated until assembled. The berry vinaigrette tastes delightful on a salad of baby spinach leaves with sliced strawberries, diced Bel Paese or Gouda cheese and toasted pecans. Or use the vinaigrette as a dip for fresh fruit and vegetables.

Makes 5 to 6 servings

CREAMY STRAWBERRY VINAIGRETTE

1/2 cup chopped strawberries (5 to 6 medium)

1 small shallot, cut in quarters

2 tablespoons raspberry or red wine vinegar

1 tablespoon sugar

1/2 teaspoon salt

1/2 cup safflower or canola oil

3/4 pound medium shrimp, cooked 2 to 3 minutes, shells removed, deveined

1/2 pound small, crisp sugar snap peas or snow peas

8 to 10 medium strawberries, tops removed

1 tablespoon sesame seeds, dry-roasted (see below), lightly crushed

Fresh pea blossoms or herb blossoms, if available

To prepare the vinaigrette: In a food processor fitted with the steel blade, mince the strawberries and shallot. Add the vinegar, sugar and salt; process briefly. With the motor running, slowly pour in all of the oil. The vinaigrette will become thick and creamy. Scrape into a small jar with a tight-fitting lid. Serve at once or refrigerate overnight. Shake the dressing just before serving. Makes 1/2 cup.

Chill the shrimp until needed. Bring a medium pot of water to a boil; add the peas. When the water comes back to a rolling boil, drain peas. Rinse with cold water, drain well and pat dry. Remove the stem ends, strings and tails.

Slice the strawberries. In a medium bowl, gently combine the shrimp, peas and strawberries.

Divide the mixture among 5 or 6 salad plates. Spoon some of the vinaigrette over each salad. Garnish with sesame seeds and pea blossoms if using. Serve at once.

COOK'S NOTES

Dry-Roasted Sesame Seeds To dry-roast sesame seeds, place them in a small heavy skillet over medium-high heat. Stir seeds until they turn golden and smell fragrant; do not burn. Crush or chop lightly to release the aromatic flavored oils. Black sesame seeds can quickly burn; watch carefully. Dry, whole spices can be dry-roasted the same way then ground in a small electric coffee or spice mill.

Kayoko's Spring-Rain Salad

Kayoko Tazoe of Fukuoka, Japan, was often asked to serve this noodle salad at her famous parties when she lived in South Carolina. Coated with mayonnaise dressing, translucent bean threads turn alabaster white, absorbing the tasty flavors around them. They look pretty tossed with colorful egg, ham and vegetable shreds. Kayoko's recipe uses Chinese bean threads; delicate Japanese harusame noodles made from potato starch are called "spring rain." Both noodles have similar uses. Kayoko uses Kewpee mayonnaise, a popular Japanese brand with a bright flavor (look for a cupid on the label). Ginger juice is my contribution; sometimes I add 6 or 8 shredded shiso leaves, a minced green onion or a few drops of tangy rice vinegar. Serve this salad with hot-pot meals that don't call for noodles and with chicken, seafood or pork fondues.

Makes 6 to 8 servings

> 2 (2-ounce) skeins Chinese bean threads (see Bean Threads, page 219)
>
> 1 large egg beaten with 1 teaspoon mirin
>
> 6 ounces baked ham, cut in ⅛-inch-thick slices, cut in 2-inch matchstick strips (see Matchstick Strips below)
>
> 1 medium carrot, peeled, cut in ⅛-inch diagonal slices, then in matchstick strips
>
> ½ European cucumber, cut into ⅛-inch diagonal slices, then in matchstick strips
>
> ⅔ cup Japanese mayonnaise or good-quality prepared mayonnaise
>
> 1 teaspoon sugar
>
> 1 to 2 tablespoons fresh ginger juice (see Fresh Ginger Juice, page 108), or to taste
>
> ½ teaspoon sea salt, or to taste
>
> 2 tablespoons white sesame seeds, dry-roasted, slightly crushed (see Dry-Roasted Sesame Seeds, page 132)

Place the noodles in a medium bowl; cover with hot tap water. Soak for 15 minutes; drain. Drop into a large pot of boiling water; simmer for 1 minute. Drain and rinse in a fine sieve, pressing out all the water. Place into a large bowl; cut into shorter lengths.

To make egg shreds, heat a lightly oiled nonstick 9-inch skillet over medium heat. Add the beaten egg; roll the pan to spread the egg over the bottom into a thin sheet. Cook, watching constantly, until the edges of the egg sheet begin to dry and it can be lifted from the pan, about 1 minute. Turn out; trim off dry edges. Fold over twice like a letter. With a large sharp knife, cut into ⅛-inch shreds. Add to the noodles. Mix the ham, carrot and cucumber into the noodles.

In a small bowl, combine the mayonnaise and sugar; season with ginger juice and salt. Blend into the noodle mixture. Adjust seasonings to taste, if desired. Serve at once or cover and chill for several hours. Spoon noodles onto 6 to 8 small serving plates; sprinkle with the sesame seeds.

COOK'S NOTES

Matchstick Strips These are often used in Asian cooking for vegetables, meats and tofu. This precision cut creates smaller strips than the usual julienne cut. It is essential to the final taste and appearance of many dishes. For vegetables like large carrots or daikon, use a chef's knife to square off the sides and cut it into 2-inch sections. Cut the sections into $1/8$-inch-thick slices. Stack a few slices; cut vertically into $1/8$-inch-thick matchstick strips. For larger strips, just make thicker cuts. Another way to make carrot matchsticks is to cut a whole carrot diagonally into thin slices; stack and shred the slices. Prepare large amounts of matchsticks a day ahead; refrigerate in plastic bags. Add a little water and salt to carrots to preserve the color and slightly soften the texture.

Orange-Flavored Carrot and Pear Salad Rolls

Orange-flavored carrots, Asian pears and cilantro are rolled up with lettuce leaves in soft rice paper wrappers. Juicy Asian pears lend a delicate crispness not found in regular pears. The final flavor burst comes from the spirited dipping sauce made with the hauntingly flavorful Vietnamese fish sauce called *nuoc mam*. You can add chunks of crab or 1 extra-large cooked shrimp, cut in half horizontally, to each roll. Serve on a platter lined with lettuce or cabbage leaves. For information on precision Asian cutting, refer to Matchstick Strips (opposite). A mandolin or Benriner slicer can help make the job easier. In a pinch, look for bags of precut julienned carrots at the grocery store. The carrots should be moist and fresh and have a bright color.

Makes 6 to 8 servings

Indochine Sauce (page 170)

1 cup unseasoned rice vinegar

$1/4$ cup water

$1/2$ cup sugar

$3/4$ teaspoon salt

Thin outer peel of 1 orange removed in large strips with a vegetable peeler, white pith scraped off

4 tender carrots (1 pound), peeled, cut in 2-inch matchstick julienne strips

1 large or 2 small Asian pears, peeled, cut in matchstick julienne strips

18 (8-inch) round rice papers, dipped quickly into hot water, placed on a dish towel for 2 or 3 minutes

Boston lettuce leaves, rinsed, dried, torn in 5- or 6-inch pieces

About $1/2$ bunch fresh cilantro sprigs, well rinsed

$1/3$ cup roasted chopped peanuts or toasted sesame seeds

Blanched thin strips of leek or green onion (optional)

Prepare Indochine Sauce and refrigerate. In a large bowl, whisk together vinegar, water, sugar, salt and orange rind until sugar dissolves. Mix in carrots; cover and chill 2 hours or overnight.

One hour before serving, stir in Asian pear; chill. Dip each rice paper quickly into hot tap water; place on clean tea towels. To form salad rolls, place 1 piece of lettuce in the middle of each rice paper. Add a spoon of well-drained carrot and pear salad. Add 2 cilantro sprigs and a sprinkle of peanuts. Fold up the bottom of the rice paper wrapper to enclose the filling then fold in the sides. Carefully roll the bundle into a neat package. If desired, tie the middle of each roll with a strip of leek. Keep rolls covered as they are formed. Place on a platter; serve at once with Indochine Sauce for dipping. (Salad rolls can be tightly wrapped with plastic wrap and held at room temperature 1 hour. If refrigerated, the rice papers harden.)

VARIATION

To create a popular French-style sandwich found in Vietnam, substitute julienne strips of daikon radish for the pear. Marinate the vegetables together several hours or overnight. Drain and serve the slaw on hard French rolls spread with mayonnaise and thin slices of Chinese Roast Pork Tenderloin (page 87) or plain roast pork.

Romaine Salad with Lemon-Basil Fromage Blanc

Creamy goat cheese fondue can be chilled and used as a delicious dressing for salad greens. Six trimmed radishes cut into paper-thin slices can be substituted for the grape tomatoes. This salad is good with meat fondues.

Makes 4 to 6 servings

Fondue au Fromage Blanc with Lemon and Basil (page 31)

Half and half, as needed

1½ heads of romaine hearts, ribs trimmed off, torn into smaller pieces

18 to 24 red or yellow teardrop or cherry tomatoes, cut in half

¼ cup toasted sunflower seeds (see Toasting Nuts, page 196)

Prepare Fondue au Fromage Blanc with Lemon and Basil; do not heat. Use at once or cover and chill until needed. If the chilled dressing seems too thick, thin with half and half to a desired consistency.

To serve, divide the romaine among 4 to 6 chilled salad plates. Spoon some of the dressing over each salad. Garnish with the tomato halves and sunflower seeds. Serve at once.

Spinach and Cabbage Rolls

When sliced, these cabbage rolls have a pretty dark green center. They can be added to any seafood or chicken hot pot. Cabbage rolls made without the spinach centers can also be added to hot pot dishes or bowls of soup. To serve as a tasty salad course, set 2 pieces upright on each small serving plate. Drizzle with a blend of ¾ cup Dashi (page 184), 1 tablespoon Japanese soy sauce (*shoyu*), 1 tablespoon mirin and 1 teaspoon rice vinegar. Sprinkle with ¼ cup Dry-Roasted Sesame Seeds (page 132). For a cross-cultural taste experience, sprinkle with a little aged balsamic vinegar or the Spicy Creole Vinegar (page 157).

Makes 6 servings

2 (8-ounce) bunches fresh spinach, with roots

2 tablespoons salt

4 large Napa cabbage leaves

Working with 1 bunch at a time, untie spinach; carefully rinse the leaves. Gather all the roots and form the leaves back into the original shape. Tie with the spinach ties or kitchen string. Prepare the second bunch.

In a large saucepan, bring 8 cups water and the salt to a boil. Holding the stems, lower 1 spinach bunch into the water. Release stems; boil until wilted and bright green, 1 minute. Remove from the boiling water; drop into a pot of iced water. Repeat with the second bunch. Rinse the spinach in iced water until chilled, 1 or 2 minutes. Squeeze the water from each bunch. Trim off the tip end of the spinach stems and roots. Each spinach bunch can be divided and rearranged with stems on each end for even-shaped rolls. One at a time, place each spinach bunch on a bamboo sushi mat; roll up. Press gently to remove excess water and form cylinder shapes. Set aside.

Cook whole cabbage leaves in boiling water until pliable, 2 minutes. Rinse in cool water; drain well and pat dry. Trim off any tough parts.

Place 2 cabbage leaves horizontally on a bamboo sushi mat, with the tender ends overlapping in the middle. Lay a spinach roll horizontally on top. Starting at the side nearest you, roll up the spinach log tightly inside the cabbage leaves. Press gently but firmly with the mat to set the shape. Prepare the second roll. Trim the ends. Cut each roll into 6 pieces.

Breads and
Beverages

THE BREAD BASKET

Swiss restaurants serve cubes of French bread with cheese fondues. Many home cooks like to choose from a variety of earthy, rustic farmhouse breads. Choose an unsliced loaf with plenty of crust. Cut the bread roughly into 1-inch cubes, making sure each piece gets some crust so the cubes stay securely on the fondue forks and don't disintegrate in the pot. Use plain bread cubes or toast them lightly in the oven. For bread cubes with an interesting flavor and texture, try the crispy Herb Croutons. Serve the bread cubes in baskets lined with colorful cloth or paper napkins.

The term fondue also applies to plain melted cheese. Use any rustic bread to make Crostini, thin little Italian toast. Topped with cheese and broiled, Crostini can be served as an appetizer or snack. Bruschetta is thick-sliced Italian toast rubbed with garlic and drizzled with fine olive oil. It is delicious topped with melted cheese. Plain Bruschetta makes a substantial base for "knife and fork" fondues like Welsh Cheddar Rabbit (page 26). If the bread slices are really large, cut them in half. Melba Crisps can be served with fondues, dips and spreads.

Try your hand at making two superb home-made breads for fondue. Cowboy Flat Bread is made with the curious ingredient refried beans. The beans add color, flavor, moistness and protein. Tear into pieces for dipping into fondue or heat with a topping of melted cheese. Potato Focaccio is moist and delicious; use it for fondue or sandwich squares. It is especially good dipped into the Parmesan and Garlic Dipping Oil or Olive Oil and Balsamic Vinegar Dip. The breads are not complicated to make; they just require a little attention and time.

Below is a list of breads that make excellent fondue dippers; most can be used for the toasts mentioned above. Choose those that are available and taste good to you. Rustic farmhouse breads can be mail-ordered from shops such as Zingerman's Delicatessen in Michigan (see the Mail-Order Resources, page 225).

BREAD DIPPERS FOR FONDUE

Bâtarde (fat loaf)

Black-olive bread

Challah

Ciabatta

Crumpets

English muffins

French baguette

Onion rye bread

Pain de campagne

Pita bread (warmed or toasted wedges)

Pumpernickel

Rye bread

Sliced bagels

Sourdough bread

Sun-dried tomato bread

Warmed rice cakes

Whole-wheat bread

Herb Croutons

Crusty, garlicky herb croutons complement the creamy-smoothness of cheese fondue. The croutons should be crunchy yet slightly chewy to skewer easily with fondue forks. To make cheese-flavored croutons, toss in 3 tablespoons of freshly grated Parmigiano-Reggiano, Pecorino Romano, Asiago or California Dry Jack. The croutons are great with soups and green salads.

Makes 6 to 8 cups

1 (12-ounce) sourdough or plain French baguette or other crusty bread, sliced 1 inch thick

2 tablespoons finely minced fresh herbs (rosemary, thyme, basil or dill) or 2 teaspoons dried herbs

½ cup (1 stick) unsalted butter

¼ cup virgin olive oil

2 cloves garlic, crushed

Fine sea salt, to taste

Knorr's Aromat® seasoning (optional), to taste

Preheat the oven to 350F (175C). Cut the bread slices in half, then each piece into thirds. Place into a large bowl; sprinkle with the herbs.

In a small saucepan over medium-low heat, melt the butter with the oil. Add the garlic; cook until butter mixture sizzles and garlic begins to brown, 1 to 2 minutes. Watch carefully; do not brown butter. Discard the garlic.

Pour the butter mixture over the bread cubes in small amounts, mixing after each addition. Sprinkle lightly with salt and seasoning if using. Spread bread cubes over an ungreased baking sheet.

Bake for 10 minutes; turn with a spatula 1 or 2 times. Bake for 4 to 5 minutes, or until slightly crisp and golden brown. Use at once or cool and store in a tightly covered container. Good served warm.

VARIATION

To make larger croutons for hand dipping, cut the 1-inch-thick bread slices in half instead of into thirds.

Melba Crisps

Dame Nellie Melba from Australia was considered the "toast of the town." The diva sang and ate her way around three continents. Chefs vied for the privilege of creating new dishes for her at lavish late-night suppers. Auguste Escoffier created thin, dry Melba toast in her honor. (Perhaps Nellie was on a diet!) Melba Crisps are perfect for soft, melted cheese spreads, for dipping or accompanying soups and salads.

Makes about 7 dozen

1 (10-ounce) loaf day-old French baguette or other rustic loaf

Bruschetta and Crostini

Bruschetta and Crostini Italian-style garlic bread is as popular today as it was two thousand years ago when the Romans grilled thick slices of rustic bread over wood fires.

To make bruschetta, cut ¾- to 1-inch-thick slices from a loaf of crusty, chewy Italian or French peasant-style bread. Grill lightly on both sides on an outdoor barbecue or under the broiler. Rub one side of each piece with a crushed clove of garlic; brush lightly with extra-virgin olive oil. Large bread slices can be cut into smaller pieces or wide strips for dipping into fondues and melted cheese dishes. Bruschetta can become part of the meal. They make a great base for knife-and-fork fondues such as Welsh Cheddar Rabbit (page 26).

Crostini is thinner and more delicate than bruschetta, the name crostini means "a little crust." These delicious toasts can be purchased in specialty food shops but they are simple to make and far more delicious.

To make crostini, cut a day-old French or Italian baguette into ¼-inch-thick slices. Dark crusty loaves can be used but cut the pieces small enough to be eaten in two or three bites. Brush lightly with extra-virgin olive oil. If you wish, infuse the olive oil with garlic. Toast on a baking sheet in a 325F (125C) oven, turning once, for 15 minutes, or until crisp all the way through. Toasts can be rubbed with a crushed clove of garlic. Use with many types of toppings including cheese spreads, leftover spreadable cheese fondues and pieces of cheese melted under the broiler.

Crostini can be broken into large pieces and used as dippers.

Preheat the oven to 275F (135C). Using a serrated knife, cut the bread into ¼-inch-thick slices. Arrange slices on a ungreased baking sheet. Bake, turning once or twice, for 20 minutes, or until the slices become crisp, dry and golden brown. Cool completely and store in an airtight container.

VARIATIONS

Seeded Melba Crisps Brush 1 side of each slice with Clarified Butter (page 160) or extra-virgin olive oil. Sprinkle with raw sesame seeds, celery seeds or poppy seeds. Bake as directed above.

Herbed Melba Crisps Brush 1 side of each slice with Clarified Butter (page 160) or extra-virgin olive oil. Sprinkle with minced fresh herbs or dried herbs.

Cowboy Flat Bread

I developed this delicious flatbread recipe for the National Cheese Institute. Refried beans add color, protein and moistness. Tear the bread into pieces for dipping into the Smoke 'n' Jack Fondue Fiesta (page 32), or scooping up cheese in the Border Melt (page 27). You can top and bake the dough with cheese, salsa, green onions and sliced olives to make a Southwestern-style pizza. I like to blend queso asadero and queso anejo or use Monterey Jack, sharp Provolone or manchego.

Makes 1 (15 × 12-inch) flatbread

1 (¼-ounce) package active dry yeast (about 1 tablespoon)

1 teaspoon sugar

¾ cup warm water (110–115F; 45C)

½ cup vegetarian refried beans, stirred

1 tablespoon extra-virgin olive oil

1 teaspoon salt

½ teaspoon ground cumin

2½ cups unbleached all-purpose flour

In a 2-quart mixing bowl, dissolve the yeast and sugar in water. Let stand until foamy, 5 minutes. Add the beans, olive oil, salt, cumin and 1 cup of the flour. With a wooden spoon, stir mixture until well blended. Stir in enough remaining flour to make a soft dough.

Turn out the dough on a lightly floured surface; knead until smooth and elastic, 6 to 8 minutes. Shape into a ball.

Place the dough in a lightly oiled 2- to 3-quart bowl; turn to coat the surface. Cover with plastic wrap and let rise in a warm place until doubled in size, about 1 hour. Punch down dough. (Dough can be refrigerated covered in a big bowl overnight. Bring back to room temperature and proceed.)

Carefully pull and stretch the dough over an ungreased 15 × 12-inch jelly-roll pan. Press the dough into the edges of the pan. Brush lightly with olive oil. Cover with a clean dish towel; let the dough rise in a warm place for 10 minutes.

Preheat the oven to 400F (205C). Bake for 15 minutes, or until lightly browned. If pizza toppings are added (see above), bake for 15 to 20 minutes.

Potato Focaccia

This rustic hearth bread can be dipped into cheese fondue or served with meat and seafood fondues. To make wonderful *panini* or Italian-style sandwiches, cut the bread into 4-inch squares. Spread with Sun-Dried Tomato and Rosemary Mayonnaise (page 159). Stuff with thin-sliced salami, prosciutto, shaved ham or smoked turkey. Add some thin-sliced sharp provolone and fresh arugula. For a wonderful luncheon include the White-Bean Fondue with Kasseri and Feta, chilled or at room temperature. Serve with vegetable dippers.

Makes 1 (17 × 11-inch) loaf

1 (¼-ounce) package active dry yeast (1 tablespoon)

½ teaspoon sugar

1 cup warm water (110F; 45C)

1 cup warm potato water, reserved from mashed potato

1 cup unseasoned mashed potato

2 teaspoons salt

½ cup plain or herb-flavored olive oil, plus extra for topping

6½ to 7 cups unbleached all-purpose flour

Dissolve the yeast and sugar in the warm water in a large mixing bowl. Let stand until foamy, 5 minutes. Add the potato water, potato, salt and oil. With a heavy-duty mixer, slowly beat in enough flour to form a soft, sticky dough. With the mixer, knead until smooth and elastic, 1 to 2 minutes.

Turn out the dough on a lightly floured surface; knead for 30 seconds. Shape into a ball. Place the dough in a lightly oiled large bowl; turn to coat the surface. Cover with plastic wrap; let rise in a warm place until doubled in size, about 2 hours.

Gently pull and stretch dough to fit a 17 × 11-inch ungreased baking sheet. (Dough can also be baked in 2 jelly-roll pans.) Work it to the edges. Cover and let rise for 30 minutes. With your fingers, press deep indentations over the dough. Brush with oil. Cover lightly with a dish towel; let rise for 1 hour.

Preheat the oven to 400F (205C). Bake for 20 minutes, or until golden brown. Brush lightly with oil; cool partially. Remove bread from the pan to cool on a rack. When cool, cut in strips or squares.

VARIATIONS

Fondue Bread Sticks Make the bread dough. After it rises, punch down and divide into 4 portions. Cover 3 portions with plastic wrap. Cut the remaining portion into 8 pieces. Roll out each piece into a bread stick 10- to 12-inches long. Place on an ungreased baking sheet. Brush lightly with olive oil; sprinkle with Kosher salt. Shape remaining dough. Let rise for 30 minutes. Bake in a preheated 400F (205C) oven for 10 to 12 minutes, or until lightly browned. Cool and serve or store for up to 2 days. Rewarm bread sticks before serving. Minced herbs or sun-dried tomatoes, sautéed onions, chopped olives or grated cheese can be added to the dough with the flour.

Sesame-Peanut Pockets
Shao-bing

Shao-bing (baked roll or cake) is the basic bread in Northern China, popular at breakfast and throughout the day. One popular method calls for unleavened dough to be rolled like puff pastry with an oil and flour roux. In this version, I roll a leavened dough, jelly-roll style, with a nutty filling of sesame paste and peanut paste; both quite popular in China. Traditional Chinese dough doesn't call for salt; I add some to improve the flavor. *Shao-bing* can be split open into fragrant pockets and stuffed with hot-pot lamb, Mongolian-style barbecue meats or stir-fried meat mixtures.

Makes 12 pockets

- 2 teaspoons active dry yeast
- ¾ cup warm water (110–115F; 45C)
- 1 tablespoon sugar
- 2 teaspoons safflower or peanut oil, plus extra for cooking
- 1 teaspoon salt
- 2½ cups unbleached all-purpose flour
- 1½ tablespoons fresh creamy peanut butter
- 1½ tablespoons Japanese sesame paste or peanut butter
- ¼ teaspoon salt
- 1 teaspoon Asian sesame oil
- 2 tablespoons light corn syrup, honey or golden syrup mixed with 1 teaspoon water
- ½ teaspoon soy sauce
- ½ cup sesame seeds in a pie plate

Sprinkle the yeast into a 2-quart mixing bowl. Add the warm water then sprinkle in sugar. Let stand until foamy, 5 minutes. With a wooden spoon, stir in the oil, salt and 1 cup of the flour until well blended. Gradually stir in enough remaining flour to make a moderately soft dough. If dough seems too sticky, knead in a few tablespoons flour.

Turn out dough on a lightly floured surface; knead until smooth and elastic, 4 to 5 minutes. (Dough can be made in a heavy-duty electric mixer; knead in the machine 1 minute then by hand 1 to 2 minutes.) Shape into a smooth ball. Place dough in a lightly oiled 2- to 3-quart bowl; turn to coat the surface.

Cover loosely with plastic wrap and let rise until doubled, 1 hour. In a small bowl, combine the peanut butter, sesame paste, salt and sesame oil until smooth; set aside. Remove dough from bowl.

Place the dough on a lightly floured surface and cut in half. Roll out one half into a 13 × 7-inch rectangle. Spread half the peanut mixture over the dough to within 1 inch of the edge. Beginning on the long side, roll dough tightly like a jelly roll. Pinch the edges to seal. Cut into 6 equal pieces. Tightly pinch the sides of each piece to seal. Place pinched sides down, and press to flatten. Fill and shape remaining half of dough. Roll each flattened piece of dough into about 4$\frac{1}{2}$ × 2$\frac{1}{2}$-inch ovals.

Combine diluted corn syrup and soy sauce; lightly dip 1 side of each flattened bun into the mixture. Shake off excess syrup then press into the sesame seeds to coat. Place, seeded sides up, on a baking sheet. Let rise about 20 minutes.

Heat 2 large skillets or a large griddle over medium-low heat. Brush with oil. Place several buns in each skillet, sesame seeds up. Cover and cook until the bottoms are medium golden-brown, 4 minutes. Turn breads and cook the other sides in the covered pan until bread is a bit puffy, slightly crisp and no longer doughy inside, 3 minutes. Watch carefully; do not allow sesame seeds to burn. If the burner is too hot, cover with a heat-diffusing pad. The buns can be baked in a 400F (205C) oven for 8 to 10 minutes; the crust will be thicker than if pan-grilled.

Serve the bread at once or cover lightly for up to 3 or 4 hours. Heat briefly in a warm skillet or in the microwave before serving. Bread will be softer when heated in the microwave but still delicious. A warming drawer set on crisp will hold the breads, as well.

VARIATION

Ham and Onion Buns Omit the peanut butter mixture. Substitute $\frac{1}{2}$ cup finely minced cooked country-style ham or bacon mixed with 3 minced green onions. Coat the top of each half of the rolled-out dough with 1 teaspoon sesame oil. Sprinkle half the ham mixture over each portion of the dough. Roll up dough and continue with the recipe, as directed above.

Olive Oil and Balsamic Vinegar Dip

This saucy blend can be used sparingly as a dip for bread and raw vegetables, as a dressing for salads or as a marinade.

Makes about $\frac{2}{3}$ cup

$\frac{1}{2}$ **cup extra-virgin olive oil**

2 tablespoons balsamic vinegar

1 small clove garlic, mashed

2 to 3 teaspoons chopped fresh basil, thyme or sage

$\frac{1}{8}$ **teaspoon salt**

$\frac{1}{2}$ **teaspoon chili pepper flakes**

Combine all the ingredients in a small bowl. Cover lightly and let stand at room temperature for 2 hours. Refrigerate leftovers; use within 2 to 3 days.

Asparagus Toasts

These attractive asparagus toasts resemble pieces of rolled sushi when cut and presented. Add your favorite aged, hard grating cheese as a flavor accent inside the rolls. For a tasty variation, sprinkle grated cheese outside the butter-coated asparagus rolls before baking. Serve with Fonduta (page 34) or your favorite cheese fondue or dip.

Makes 24 pieces

12 square slices of soft, white bread, crusts trimmed

12 fresh asparagus spears, rinsed, patted dry

½ cup (1 stick) unsalted butter, melted

1 ounce (¼ cup) freshly grated imported Parmigiano-Reggiano cheese or Pecorino Romano

Preheat the oven to 350F (175C). With a rolling pin, slightly flatten each slice of bread. Trim each asparagus spear to 4½ inches long or the width of each slice of trimmed bread. Brush 1 side of each bread slice lightly with butter; sprinkle each with 1 teaspoon of the cheese. Place 1 asparagus spear at the bottom of each slice; roll up, enclosing asparagus.

Place the rolls, seam side down, on an ungreased baking sheet. Brush all over with the remaining butter. (Bake at once or cover with plastic wrap and leave at room temperature for up to 2 hours before baking.) Bake for 8 to 10 minutes, or until

crisp and golden brown. With a sharp knife, slice each roll in the middle, using a diagonal cut. Trim the ends slightly so that each piece stands upright for serving. Serve at once.

Thyme in a Bottle

Serve a bowl of oil and a crusty, rustic loaf of bread while waiting for dinner to be served. Invite your guests to "take a dip" and enjoy one of life's simple pleasures.

Makes 1 cup

1 cup extra-virgin olive oil

4 or 5 sprigs of thyme, rosemary, sage or oregano

1 or 2 small, dried hot chilies

Heat the olive oil, thyme and chilies in a small saucepan over low heat just until the oil becomes hot. Cool the oil to room temperature. Pour into an attractive bottle and cover tightly. Steep for 1 to 2 days before opening. Use as a bread dipping sauce, on pasta, in salad dressings or to flavor homemade mayonnaise.

Parmesan and Garlic Dipping Oil

In Europe, good olive oil is often served in a small bowl for dipping crusty bread at the table. The oil might be plain or seasoned with herbs, spices or hot peppers. This version includes freshly grated

Parmigiano-Reggiano cheese. Bread-dipping oil is versatile and can be drizzled on cooked vegetables, salad greens or mixed into pasta. Use it for homemade croutons. Select a good-quality oil that pleases your taste, whether it be a heavy, robust northern Italian olive oil or a gentle, light-bodied French oil labeled *douce* or sweet.

Makes about 1 cup

1 cup extra-virgin olive oil

2 cloves garlic, crushed

1 tablespoon chopped fresh rosemary, thyme or sage

Pinch salt

1 ounce (¼ cup) freshly grated Parmigiano-Reggiano, Pecorino Romano or Asiago cheese

Combine all the ingredients in a small bowl. Let the mixture stand for 30 minutes before serving.

Hot Ginger Tea

Fresh ginger is valued throughout Asia for its medicinal and digestive qualities as well as its pungent, addictive flavor. Ginger is thought to heat the blood and benefit people with anemia. Few beverages are more soothing than a cup of aromatic hot ginger tea. The addition of toasted pine nuts is a distinctive Korean touch and adds a wonderful flavor and textural contrast. The tea is refreshing between courses or after a rich, spicy meal.

Makes 6 servings

1 quart water

⅓ pound fresh ginger, peeled, thinly sliced, smashed

1 cup packed dark brown sugar

Pinch salt

¼ cup pine nuts, toasted (see Toasting Nuts, page 196)

Canton ginger liqueur, almond liqueur or brandy, to taste (optional)

In a medium saucepan, combine water, ginger, sugar and salt. Simmer, partially covered, on low heat about 25 minutes or longer for a stronger infusion. Strain and pour into 6 Asian-size teacups. Add 2 teaspoons pine nuts to each cup. Stir in liqueur, to taste.

Iced Lemongrass Tea

I grow huge lemongrass plants in my garden just to make this refreshing lemon-scented tea. For sweetened tea, provide a pitcher of sugar syrup or honey on the side. A stainless tea ball will allow the leaves to be easily removed after brewing. The tender inner portion of a stalk of lemongrass can be chopped and brewed in a pot of hot tea.

Makes 5 to 6 servings

6 cups bottled spring water

2 (10- to 12-inch) stalks fresh lemongrass, outer leaves removed, smashed, chopped in 2-inch pieces

2 (⅛-inch) diagonal slices fresh ginger

1½ tablespoons loose tea, preferably Ceylon, Darjeeling or Broken Orange Pekoe, or 3 tea bags

Leafy end portions of 5 or 6 stalks fresh lemongrass (about 7 inches long) or thin lemon slices, for garnish

Put 2 cups of the water in a 1-quart heatproof measuring cup. Add lemongrass and sliced ginger. Heat in the microwave, on 100% power, for 3 minutes or until the water begins to bubble. Steep the lemongrass until the water cools or for several hours for a stronger infusion. Strain and discard lemongrass. Place 4 cups water in a large heatproof measuring cup. Heat in the microwave 4 to 5 minutes until very hot. Steep tea leaves 5 minutes or to desired strength. Strain tea; blend with the lemongrass infusion. Refrigerate until cold. Pour into 16-ounce glasses filled with ice. Garnish each serving with a lemongrass stalk. Sweeten to taste, if desired.

VARIATION

For a mint version, substitute 1 cup fresh mint leaves for the lemongrass.

Condiments

Mayonnaise . . . one of the sauces, which serve the French in place of a state religion.
—**Ambrose Bierce,** *The Devil's Dictionary*

Fondues are experiencing a rebirth with exciting new ingredients and a polished presentation. Mild-tasting meats, seafood and vegetables cooked in a savory broth or pot of bubbling oil, gain instant panache when paired with zesty condiments. Condiments come in the form of dipping sauces, spice blends, seasoning salts and relishes. Each member of this lively team serves as a flavor counterpoint, contributing to the overall quality of a fondue meal with a mélange of multi-dimensional flavors, colors and textures. The condiments can be served in small bowls on the side, allowing each person to control the seasoning to his own taste!

Within this chapter you will find dozens of recipes for useful, delicious condiments. They can be creatively interchanged with most of the fondue and hot-pot recipes.

Flavor-infused dipping sauces like the Lemon-Parsley Sauce offer a cool, refreshing contrast to the taste of lamb, chicken, seafood, veal or turkey cooked in a fondue. If you prefer hot and spicy condiments, dip right into the Hot Pepper Jelly Sauce. For aficionados of chunky, fruit sauces and relishes, try the unusual Apple-Raisin Sauce, the Zucchini and Mango Relish with Ginger or the Mango, Cucumber and Cashew Relish. For a creamy dipping sauce try the Horseradish and Tarragon Cream Sauce or one of the terrific variations of the homemade mayonnaise recipe.

IT'S ALL ABOUT TASTE!

Variety may be the hallmark of an Asian hot pot, but flavor always rules! Many regional Asian cuisines have a strong flavor profile derived from the generous use of spices and seasonings. The Korean Chili-Sesame Sauce is a delicious rich-tasting condiment that features *kochu jang*, a fermented bean paste from Korea. It can be used as a dipping sauce, in marinades or on cooked vegetables or noodles. Brandied Hoisin Sauce is a versatile Chinese condiment based on hoisin sauce and a flavorful salty-hot fermented broad bean paste known as *toban djan* (*jiang*), also popular in the Japanese kitchen. Brandy is added to fortify and enhance the flavor. This wonderful condiment can be used as a dipping sauce, a spread for Chinese meat-stuffed buns, as an ingredient in marinades or in other sauces.

Fresh Mayonnaise is a creamy, emulsified sauce in which egg yolks play a leading role. Egg yolks contain lecithin, a protein that combines with oil and water. Lecithin causes the oil and vinegar in mayonnaise to come together and hold in suspension. Salt, dry mustard, cayenne and lemon juice also play a vital supporting role. Mayonnaise is a versatile sauce and can be used for dozens of flavor variations. The Basil Dijon Aïoli is a garlic-laced mayonnaise that is popular in Provence. My version also contains Dijon mustard. Garlic is said to be the poor man's spice in Southern France. It is reputed to have antiseptic properties and contain antioxidants. The variation, Sauce Rémoulade, is a classic French sauce that pairs deliciously with poached seafood and cold sliced meats. Tartar Sauce is also a natural accompaniment for seafood. You can experiment with the basic recipe and come up with many more varieties. For an Asian variation, good with seafood, add some quality oyster sauce, hot chili sauce and green onion. Or try a sesame variation with toasted sesame seeds and Asian (toasted) sesame oil. Lemon peel and lemon juice make a refreshing version, as well.

A HARMONY OF FLAVORS

Compared to other herb- and spice-infused cuisines throughout Asia, Japanese foods are seasoned with a gentle hand. Japanese cooks follow the ancient Chinese principle of yin and yang, enhancing food tastes through the balance of five flavors: sour, sweet, salty, spicy-hot and bitter.

Sour flavors are provided by rice vinegar (*komezu*) and by citrus like the citron *yuzu*. Sweetness comes from the Japanese rice wine called mirin; the salty taste comes from soy sauce; spicy-hot flavors come from ingredients like wasabi, long green onions (*naganegi*), ginger and dry Japanese mustard (*wagarashi*). A touch of bitter-

ness is found in foods like edible chrysanthemum leaves, dry Japanese mustard or yuzu citron. Bitterness provides flavor-depth in foods and rounds out the other four tastes.

The Japanese have identified an additional flavor component called *umami*. It is sometimes referred to as "tastiness" or "deliciousness." It is a savory taste found in a variety of foods including dried seaweed, soy sauce, dried bonito and dried mushrooms. The real beauty of a dish lies in its flavor. Soy sauce used in tandem with mirin, saké and Dashi (dried bonito and seaweed stock) produces *umami*, that special flavor that is the cornerstone of Japanese taste. Without the subtle and skillful blending of these seasonings and foods, Japanese cuisine would be *umami no nai* (without *umami*) and rendered flat and insipid, no matter how beautiful.

Sesame Sauce
Gomadaré

Japanese sesame paste comes in a can and is made from ground white sesame seeds. In Japan, homemade sesame paste is made by hand in a *suribachi*, or mortar with ridged walls. It is difficult to grind the seeds completely smooth; canned sesame paste is a convenient, tasty alternative. You can also substitute Middle Eastern tahini made from toasted sesame seeds. Do not use the darker, stronger Chinese kind. Refrigerated sesame paste will keep for 2 to 3 months. The consistency becomes very stiff but it softens again at room temperature. Stir to blend the paste and top layer of oil back together. Mash out any lumps with a spoon. Serve this sauce with hot-pot meats, fried tofu or grilled meats. It can be used as a dressing for cooked vegetables or mix it into a batch of cooked noodles with a little hot chili sauce, to taste.

Makes about 1 1/2 cups

1/2 cup Japanese sesame paste

2 tablespoons sweet white miso paste (*saikyo miso*) or other white or yellow miso paste

1/2 cup Dashi (page 184)

1/3 cup Japanese soy sauce (*shoyu*)

1/4 cup mirin (Japanese rice wine)

1 tablespoon fresh lemon juice or rice vinegar

1 generous teaspoon finely minced fresh ginger

1 clove garlic, minced

1/2 cup minced green onions

In a medium bowl, whisk together the sesame paste, miso paste, Dashi, soy sauce and mirin until mixture is smooth. Stir in the lemon juice, ginger and garlic. Let the mixture stand, at room temperature, for 1 hour. Spoon into small bowls for serving. Serve the green onions on the side for the diners to mix into the sauce, as desired.

Citrus Dip/Ponzu

In Japan, Citrus Dip is made from the slightly bitter juice of a type of citron called *yuzu*. It resembles a green lime during the summer and ripens to yellow in the winter. The thick peel can be grated and used like lemon zest or even candied in long strips. *Yuzu* is hard to find in this country so substitute another citrus juice or use a blend of juices. You can include a small amount of grapefruit juice for a hint of the

astringency of *yuzu*. This dipping sauce is delicious with hot-pot beef, pork and seafood. It is also delicious with grilled steak.

Makes about 1 1/4 cups

1/2 cup Japanese soy sauce (*shoyu*)

1/3 cup water

1/4 cup unseasoned rice vinegar

2 tablespoons fresh *yuzu* juice, lime juice, lemon juice or tart orange juice

2 tablespoons mirin (Japanese rice wine)

1 tablespoon dried bonito threads (*ito-kezuri-katsuo*)

3/4 cup grated, peeled daikon radish

Combine all the ingredients, except the daikon radish, in a small bowl. Cover and steep for 2 hours or longer, if desired. Strain before using, discarding the bonito threads. Pour into small bowls for serving. Serve the grated daikon radish on the side for the diners to mix into the sauce, as desired.

Peanut-Orange Miso Sauce

This orange-kissed dipping sauce is also good with grilled meats and can be used as a dressing for cooked vegetables. Stir in some hot chili paste and you will have a spicy sauce for cooked pasta. Try it as a marinade for chicken before roasting. Use sweet white miso (*saikyo miso*) or yellow miso paste for this dip. Red miso paste is delicious too but slightly saltier.

Makes about 1 1/3 cups

1/4 cup fresh peanut butter

1 cup miso paste

2 tablespoons mirin (Japanese rice wine)

Grated zest of 1 small orange

2 tablespoons fresh tart orange juice

2 tablespoons light brown sugar

1 thin green onion, finely minced

1/3 to 1/2 cup Dashi (page 184), or as needed

In a medium bowl, blend together the peanut butter, miso paste, mirin, orange zest, orange juice, brown sugar and green onion. Stir in up to 1/2 cup Dashi to thin the sauce to a dipping consistency. Use at once or store in the refrigerator for up to 2 days. Bring back to room temperature before using.

Mizore-zu

Mizore refers to the appearance of the sauce; the large amount of grated daikon resembles fallen snow. Daikon contains a large amount of the digestive enzyme, diastase. It helps aid the digestion of fats and helps absorb excess starch. Serve this dipping sauce with any hot pot recipe except Sukiyaki Nabé (page 94). It is good with seafood, especially oysters.

Makes about 1 1/2 cups

1/2 cup unseasoned rice vinegar

1/2 cup Dashi (page 184)

2 tablespoons thin Japanese soy sauce (*usukuchi shoyu*)

1/2 cup finely grated, peeled daikon radish

Combine all the ingredients in a medium bowl. Divide among small sauce bowls to be carried to the table. Serve at once.

Hot-Pot Condiments

Seasonings and condiments are added to Japanese dishes to enhance natural food flavors, never to disguise or diminish them. Stir 1 or more of these condiments into hot-pot dipping sauces or mix into bowls of hot-pot foods with broth. They add a wonderful contrasting flavor to a bowl of noodles in noodle broth. Additional condiments might include fine strips of *yuzu* (see page 147) or lemon peel, ground sansho pepper, dried red chilies (*togarashi*), mustard paste (*nerigarashi*), mitsuba leaves (herb from the parsley family), chopped sansho leaves (*kinomé*) and *myoga* buds or mountain ginger.

Use a Japanese flat metal grater (*oroshi gané*) to prepare the daikon radish and ginger.

Makes enough for 6 hot-pot servings

3/4 cup thinly sliced thin green onions

3/4 cup grated daikon radish

2 tablespoons grated fresh ginger (see Fresh Ginger Juice, page 108)

2 lemons, cut in wedges

If the green onions taste too strong, place in a fine strainer and rinse under cold water. Wrap in 2 layers of cheesecloth and gently press out the water. Place each ingredient into a small bowl or into a special condiment dish with separate compartments. (When using with a hot-pot recipe, omit any ingredient that is already called for in the recipe or sauce.) Condiments can be prepared up to 1 hour in advance, covered and refrigerated until needed.

Red Maple Radish/
Momiji Oroshi

Momiji refers to the red color of the leaves in the fall. *Oroshi* means peeled and grated daikon. When grated with dried red chilies, daikon becomes the same hue of those familiar autumn colors. Stir this sassy condiment into the Tempura Dipping Sauce (page 168) or the Citrus Dip (page 147). It goes well with any of the *nabé ryori* dishes except Sukiyaki Nabé (page 94).

Makes 6 servings

3- to 4-inch piece peeled daikon radish, cut from the root end of the radish

3 or 4 tiny, dried Japanese red chili peppers (*aka-togarashi*)

1 tablespoon finely grated fresh ginger (see Fresh Ginger Juice, page 108)

With a chopstick, push 2 or 3 deep holes into the piece of daikon. Push a chili pepper into each hole. Use at once or wrap and chill until needed. Grate in a circular motion using a Japanese flat metal grater (*oroshi gané*). Place mounds of the grated radish and ginger in a shallow bowl to carry to the table.

Seven-Spice Powder/
Shichimi Togarashi

The recipe for this popular Japanese spice blend is from my cookbook, *Japanese Cooking for the American Table*. I learned to make it from a Japanese friend during a visit to Kyoto. At festivals and open-air markets, vendors will blend the spices according to the customer's taste. Serve the condiment with noodle dishes, one-pot dishes, stir-fried dishes or on salad.

Makes about ¼ cup

1½ tablespoons grated tangerine peel or navel orange peel

½ teaspoon dried *sansho* pepper pods

1 ounce (½ cup) dried, whole red chilies, about 1½ inches long, with most of the seeds removed

1 teaspoon sesame seeds, toasted (page 196)

1 teaspoon flax seeds, toasted (page 196)

1 teaspoon poppy seeds, toasted (page 196)

¼ teaspoon powdered green seaweed (*ao-noriko*)

Preheat the oven to 200F (95C). Spread the tangerine peel over a pie plate. Dry in the oven for 30 minutes. Place in a small bowl. Place the pepper pods in a Japanese grinding bowl, mortar or small electric coffee mill; grind to a powder. Add to the tangerine peel. Grind the red chilies to a powder. Add the ground chilies and sesame seeds to the sansho and tangerine peel. Pound mixture lightly to bruise the seeds and blend the mixture together. Stir in the remaining ingredients. Store in a cool dry place in a small jar with a tight-fitting lid. To serve, place in a spice shaker or a small bowl to carry to the table. Use within 6 weeks. The recipe can be doubled.

Black-Sesame Salt/Goma-shio

This nutty blend is delicious sprinkled on rice, vegetables, noodles and salads. Untoasted sesame seeds are preferable but if the package says toasted sesame seeds, go ahead and toast them again at home. Store this seasoning in the refrigerator or freezer to keep it fresh. Sesame seeds are high in calcium, iron, protein and vitamins.

Makes about 1/3 cup

1/3 cup black or unhulled white sesame seeds

1 tablespoon sea salt

To dry-roast sesame seeds, place in a small heavy skillet over medium-high heat. Shake or stir seeds 1 minute or until they become hot and fragrant. Watch carefully; black sesame seeds can quickly burn. Add the salt; stir 30 seconds. Crush the mixture in a Japanese grinding bowl (*suribachi*) just enough to release some of the flavor-rich oils from the sesame seeds. Do not destroy the texture. Or place mixture in a small heavy plastic bag, press the air out and seal. Pound the mixture a few times with the end of a rolling pin. Store in a small jar with a tight-fitting lid. To serve, place in a spice shaker or a small bowl to carry to the table. Use within 6 weeks.

Hot-Pot Dipping Sauce and Condiments

Well-seasoned sauces are an integral part of Asian hot pots and fire-grilled dishes, adding spicy, sweet, tart and pungent flavors. Choose from the condiments below to create your own unique blend of sauce. The Chinese diner might beat in a raw egg or pour it from a saucer into the hot pot broth for poaching. If you serve raw eggs for the sauce, be sure they are pasteurized (see page 158). Light-col-

ored soy sauce is often used in dipping sauces. It is thinner, saltier and not as strongly flavored as regular soy sauce.

Makes 6 servings

HOT-POT DIPPING SAUCE

1 cup dark or light soy sauce

1/2 cup Chinese rice wine (*shaohsing*) or dry sherry

1 or 2 teaspoons Asian sesame oil, or to taste

CONDIMENTS

1 bunch green onions, trimmed

1 bunch cilantro, large stems removed

4 large cloves garlic, minced, mixed with 1 teaspoon peanut oil

2 tablespoons minced fresh ginger

Firepot Oil (page 153), to taste

1/2 cup Brandied Hoisin Sauce (page 151)

1/2 cup fresh peanut butter

1/2 cup Japanese sesame paste

Hot, garlicky pepper paste (Lan Chi or Kim Lan brand) or chili paste with fermented soybeans

1/2 cup rice wine vinegar

1/2 cup Chinese black vinegar or good-quality balsamic vinegar

1 large pasteurized egg, per diner (see Egg Safety, page 158)

1/4 cup packed light brown sugar

Pickled garlic, to taste

Shrimp paste, to taste

Oyster sauce, to taste

To prepare the dipping sauce, combine the soy sauce, wine and sesame oil; pour into a small pitcher.

For the condiments: To arrange a "create-your-own" sauce tray, select at least the first 10 condiments. Finely chop the green onion stems for dipping sauces; cut the white parts into 2¹/₂-inch slivers for garnishing Chinese-style sandwiches. Chop part of the cilantro for dipping sauces; tear the rest into sprigs to garnish meat and vegetable platters and Chinese-style sandwiches. Mince the garlic and ginger; prepare the Firepot Oil and Brandied Hoisin Sauce. Thin the peanut butter and sesame paste with 2 or 3 tablespoons boiling water or stock to blend smoothly into the dipping sauce. Place each condiment into separate small bowls. Provide small spoons on the side.

At the table, pour 2 to 3 tablespoons dipping sauce in each sauce bowl; diners can add the condiments of their choice.

Peppered Peanut Sauce

This is the easy version of an addictive Indonesian sauce for *satay*. It is quite delicious and can be served with lamb, beef, pork, chicken and seafood cooked in an oil or broth fondue or hot pot. Serve it with Fried Tofu Wedges (page 67) or the Genghis Khan Fire-Grill (page 82). Use it as a dressing for steamed fresh vegetables or noodles. Additional traditional ingredients might include fish paste, dried shrimp, ground coriander and five-spice powder.

Makes 1³/₄ cups

1 tablespoon canola oil

4 shallots or 1 small onion, finely chopped

1 large clove garlic, minced

2 teaspoons finely minced tender, inner portion of lemongrass or grated zest of 1 large lemon

¹/₂ teaspoon ground cumin

1 (13.5-ounce) can unsweetened, light coconut milk

¹/₂ cup fresh peanut butter

2 tablespoons light brown sugar

2 tablespoons fresh lime juice

2 or 3 dashes ground Sichuan peppercorns or regular black pepper

1 tablespoon hot chili paste (*sambal oelek*), or to taste

Heat the oil in a medium saucepan over medium-low heat. Sauté the shallots and garlic, stirring constantly, until very soft, 5 minutes. Add the lemongrass and cumin; cook, stirring often, for 2 to 3 minutes more. Pour in the coconut milk. Whisk in the peanut butter until smooth. Stir in the brown sugar, lime juice, ground pepper and chili paste. Cook over low heat 2 to 3 minutes. Spoon the sauce into small serving bowls. Sauce can be made 3 days ahead and stored in the refrigerator. Serve warm or at room temperature.

Brandied Hoisin Sauce

This sweet-spicy bean jam is made with hoisin sauce, a smooth, sweet Cantonese soybean paste often used as a condiment. In this recipe, it is enriched with chunky Sichuan-style chili bean sauce (*toban djan or jiang*) for extra flavor, texture and heat. The mixture is briefly cooked and enhanced with a soupçon of brandy. Both seasonings are produced by Lee Kum Kee and available at Asian markets. Use in Chinese barbecue sauce, stir-fries, marinades, dipping sauces, hot pot broths, on noodles or on Asian-style wrapped sandwiches.

Makes about 1¹/₂ cups

1 tablespoon light olive oil or canola oil

1 large shallot, finely minced

1 large clove garlic, finely minced

1¼ cups hoisin sauce

2 tablespoons chili bean sauce

1 tablespoon balsamic vinegar or unseasoned rice vinegar

1 to 2 tablespoons brandy

Heat the oil in a small saucepan over medium-low heat. Sauté the shallot and garlic until softened, 2 minutes. Do not brown or the sauce will taste bitter. Stir in the hoisin sauce, chili bean sauce and vinegar. When hot, stir in the brandy. Remove from heat and cool to room temperature. Store in an airtight jar in the refrigerator for up to 3 or 4 months.

Shoyu and Ginger Steak Sauce

Serve this rich, tangy Asian-style steak sauce with meats cooked in oil and broth fondues. It is also delicious with tabletop grilled meats or a steak cooked on the barbecue grill.

Makes 1½ cups

1 cup ketchup

3 tablespoons Japanese soy sauce (*shoyu*)

2 tablespoons sugar

2 tablespoons dry sherry

1 tablespoon Worcestershire sauce

1 teaspoon finely minced fresh ginger

2 cloves garlic, finely minced

Combine all the ingredients in a small bowl. Cover and let stand at room temperature at least 30 minutes or refrigerate overnight. If refrigerated, bring back to room temperature and spoon into small bowls for serving.

VARIATION

Creamy Shoyu and Ginger Sauce Stir ½ to ¾ cup Fresh Mayonnaise (page 157) or good-quality prepared mayonnaise into the Shoyu and Ginger Steak Sauce. Makes 2 to 2¼ cups

---

COOK'S NOTES

Garlic The best way to peel garlic is to give each clove a forceful whack with the broad side of a cleaver or chef's knife. The skins loosen and can be easily removed. Smashed garlic is easier to mince; the released juices add more flavor. Garlic pounded with a mortar and pestle blends smoothly with other ingredients and has a mellow taste. Use the flat side of a large knife to press the minced garlic into paste; a pinch of salt helps break down the fibers. A garlic press can be used to push an unpeeled clove through fine holes to extract the pulp and juice. Commercial garlic salt, garlic powder and garlic juice are not good substitutes for whole garlic.

Chili-Sesame Sauce

This delicious Korean dipping sauce is the same color of ripe, orange-gold persimmons. It has a creamy consistency and tastes spicy, sweet and salty all at once. It pairs well with meats and noodles in Asian-style fondues or Korean grilled meats. Spread it on Asian wrapped sandwiches. The star ingredient is *kochu jang*, a rich, russet paste made of soybeans, ground chilies and rice flour. The paste can be refrigerated in an airtight jar for several months.

Makes 1¼ cups

1 large clove garlic, peeled

1 (⅛-inch-thick) slices fresh ginger

3 tablespoons red wine vinegar

1 tablespoon Japanese soy sauce (*shoyu*)

2 teaspoons sesame oil

2 generous tablespoons Korean bean paste (*kochu jang*)

½ teaspoon salt

Several dashes black pepper

1 cup safflower or canola oil

1 generous tablespoon dry-roasted sesame seeds, lightly crushed

Drop the garlic and ginger through the feed tube of a food processor or blender with the motor running. Process until finely chopped. Stop the machine; add the vinegar, soy sauce, sesame oil, bean paste, salt and black pepper. With motor running, pour the oil through the feed tube in a steady stream until thickened and combined. Stir in the sesame seeds by hand. Use at once or store in a pint jar in the refrigerator for up to 4 weeks. Shake well before using. Pour sauce into small bowls for dipping.

Firepot Oil

A few drops of this aromatic chili oil will add flavor-depth and pizzazz to hot pot broths, dipping sauces, marinades, noodles and stir-fries. Be sure the oil and sesame seeds are fresh and the chili bits are bright red and pungent. Wash your hands carefully after working with chilies to remove any trace of volatile oils. To vary the flavor, omit the sesame seeds and include one of the following: 3 mashed slices of fresh ginger, 4 sliced green onions, 2 finely chopped dried black mushrooms or 2 tablespoons unrinsed salted Chinese black beans. The oils flavored with ginger and green onions are perishable and should be used within 1 week.

Makes about 1 cup

1 tablespoon unroasted Sichuan peppercorns

2 tablespoons chopped dried red chilies or dried chili flakes

2 tablespoons unhulled sesame seeds, slightly crushed

1 cup peanut or canola oil

Place the peppercorns, chilies and sesame seeds into a heatproof bowl. Heat the oil in a small saucepan to 250F (120C). Pour the hot oil over the seasonings in the bowl. Cool completely. Pour the mixture into a jar and steep for up to 2 days. Strain the oil, discarding the solids; pour the oil into a clean jar. Keep in a cool place or in the refrigerator. For the best flavor, use within 5 or 6 months.

Apple-Raisin Sauce

McIntosh apples are tart yet sweet and available from late September through March. When out of season, try this recipe with crisp, juicy Granny Smith apples, available year round. This fruity sauce is especially good with pork, turkey and chicken fondues.

Makes about 2 cups

2 large McIntosh apples (about 1 pound), peeled, cored, diced

2 cups apple cider or apple juice, more if needed

2 tablespoons unsalted butter

½ cup sugar

½ cup dark and golden raisins, mixed

Pinch of salt

Place all the ingredients into a medium saucepan. Bring to a boil over medium-high heat. Reduce the heat to low and cook, stirring occasionally, until the apples are soft, 10 to 12 minutes. For a softer consistency, mash the apples slightly with a potato masher. To thin the sauce, stir in a little more cider if needed.

Hot Chinese Mustard

Hot Chinese-style mustard can be used as a spicy-hot dipping sauce or blended into other sauces.

Makes about ¼ cup

¼ cup good-quality dry mustard, such as McCormick's

2 tablespoons water

1 teaspoon unseasoned rice vinegar

⅛ teaspoon salt

1 teaspoon extra-virgin olive oil or canola oil

In a small bowl, combine the mustard and water until smooth. Stir in the vinegar, salt and oil. Let stand for 10 minutes to develop the flavor. Use at once or seal in a small container and refrigerate until needed.

Hot Pepper Jelly Sauce

Serve this spicy-hot red sauce with poultry, pork and turkey cooked in a fondue. It can also be served with fried wontons, spring rolls or fried shrimp. Use it as a glaze for roast pork or barbecue pork ribs.

Makes about 1 cup

1 (10-ounce) jar red-hot pepper jelly

¼ cup ketchup

2 tablespoons unseasoned rice vinegar

Grated zest of 1 small orange

2 tablespoons fresh orange juice

¼ teaspoon ground cumin

½ teaspoon soy sauce

Melt the pepper jelly in a small saucepan over medium-low heat. Add all the remaining ingredients. Simmer the mixture for 3 to 4 minutes. The mixture will be thin but thickens upon standing. Spoon into small bowls for serving.

Spicy Black Bean Sauce

Spoon a dollop of sour cream on each serving of this hearty dipping sauce to complement the flavor and add a contrast in color. Serve with meats and seafood for dipping.

Makes about 1½ cups

1 large clove garlic, peeled

1 (16-ounce) can black beans, undrained

½ cup tart orange juice

2 tablespoons balsamic vinegar

½ teaspoon Asian hot chili sauce

¼ teaspoon salt

Black pepper, to taste

Drop the garlic through the feed tube of a food processor with the motor running. Process until finely chopped. Add all the remaining ingredients to the food processor. Process until the mixture is smooth. Scrape the mixture into a small saucepan. Simmer over medium heat for 10 minutes, stirring occasionally. Spoon the warm sauce into small bowls for dipping.

Smoky Tomato Salsa

This salsa has a slightly smoky flavor from the grill. For a more intense flavor, cut the tomatoes in half and place them in a smoker for one hour.

Makes about 2 cups

4 medium ripe fresh tomatoes, blistered over an outdoor grill or under the broiler, or plain tomatoes

1 large clove garlic, finely minced

1 jalapeño chili pepper, seeded, minced

½ small red onion, finely minced

2 tablespoons minced fresh cilantro leaves

2 tablespoons fresh squeezed lime juice or lemon juice

¼ teaspoon ground cumin

½ teaspoon salt, or to taste

Cool the tomatoes. Cut each tomato in half; squeeze gently over a bowl to remove the seeds and juice. Strain the juice into a medium bowl; discard the seeds. Finely chop the tomato pulp; add with all the remaining ingredients to the bowl of juice. Let the salsa sit at room temperature for 1 hour for the best flavor. Spoon into small bowls for serving.

Fresh Mint Sauce

Serve this minty fresh sauce with lamb fondue.

Makes about 2 cups

1 cup packed fresh mint leaves (1½ to 2 ounces), finely minced

1 cup unseasoned rice vinegar

⅔ cup water

2 tablespoons sugar

Large pinch salt

Combine all the ingredients in a medium bowl. Serve at once or refrigerate for several hours. Pour into small bowls for serving.

Daikon Dipping Sauce

This flavorful sauce can be served with fried foods. Chilled, it makes a fine dipping sauce for cold soba noodles. Daikon radish helps aid the digestion of fatty foods. You can add additional condiments such as grated fresh ginger, minced green onion or a squeeze of fresh lemon juice. The sauce can be slightly thickened with potato starch or cornstarch and served over pieces of fried tofu.

Makes about 2 cups

2 cups Dashi (page 184)

¼ cup thin Japanese soy sauce (*usukuchi shoyu*)

2 tablespoons mirin (Japanese rice wine)

½ cup dried bonito shavings (*katsuobushi*)

2 tablespoons grated daikon radish

In a small saucepan, heat the Dashi, soy sauce and mirin over medium-low heat. When warm, add the bonito shavings. Remove pan from heat and steep 5 minutes. Pour the mixture through a fine mesh strainer into a bowl; discard the bonito shavings. Pour the liquid into small bowls for serving. Season each portion with a small amount of the grated radish. The sauce can be refrigerated overnight. Warm before using.

Raspberry Cabernet Sauce

This tangy raspberry wine sauce is so delicious, you will want to keep some on hand at all times for dozens of uses. Try it as a dip for skewered fruits or Rose Meringues (page 202), or stir a few table-spoons into your favorite chocolate fondue.

Makes 2 cups

2½ cups California Cabernet Sauvignon

1 (16-ounce) package frozen raspberries or frozen mixed berries, thawed

1 cup sugar

3 strips of lemon zest

1 to 2 tablespoons fresh lemon juice, to taste

Pinch salt

In a medium saucepan, combine the wine, rasp-berries, sugar and lemon zest. Bring mixture to a boil over medium heat. Reduce the heat; simmer until the mixture is reduced by half, 25 minutes. Remove from the heat. To strain, pour half the sauce at a time into a fine mesh sieve placed over a bowl. With a large spoon, press the fruit through the strainer until only the seeds remain. Wipe the spoon; scrape pulp from the bottom of the strainer into the bowl. Discard the seeds. Stir the salt into the sauce. Chill the sauce before serving.

VARIATION

Blackberry Cabernet Sauce: Substitute frozen blackberries for the raspberries.

Stilton and Roasted Red Pepper Dip

Blue cheese lovers will appreciate this dip. It tastes like blue cheese but has a pretty rosy hue; not the usual drab melted blue cheese color. Serve as a warm dipping sauce for beef fondue or as a dip with crisp, fresh vegetable sticks.

Makes 5 or 6 servings

1 teaspoon cornstarch

½ cup whipping cream

8 ounces Stilton or other blue cheese, crumbled (2 cups)

1 large red bell pepper, roasted, peeled, seeded, chopped (see Roasted Chilies, page 28)

1 to 2 teaspoons fresh lemon juice

1 teaspoon fresh rosemary leaves, chopped

In a medium saucepan, blend cornstarch and cream. Stir over medium heat until the mixture begins to bubble. Add large spoonfuls of the cheese; stir gently after each addition until the cheese is melted. Do not boil; remove pan from the stove if the sauce gets too hot. When melted, stir in the bell pepper. Puree the mixture in a blender until smooth. Stir in the lemon juice and rosemary. Pour the warm sauce into small bowls for dipping. Sauce can be made ahead and refrigerated; reheat before serving.

Spicy Creole Vinegar

Use this zesty vinegar in dipping sauces, vinaigrettes or for marinating sliced cucumbers and onions.

Makes 1 cup

- 1 cup cider vinegar
- 1 heaping tablespoon Zatarin's seafood seasoning mix
- 1 or 2 red hot chili peppers, seeds removed
- 1 clove garlic, mashed

Put all the ingredients into a small bowl. Steep at room temperature for at least 6 hours or longer for a stronger flavor. Pour through a fine strainer into a bowl. Refrigerate the vinegar in a pint jar with a tight-fitting lid.

FROM MY RECIPE BOX

Creole Cucumber Salad Lightly score 1 European cucumber; cut into ¼-inch-thick slices. Place in a bowl and add ½ cup Spicy Creole Vinegar, 2 tablespoons sugar and a pinch of salt. Optional ingredients include 1 small red bell pepper, cut in 1-inch squares, or 1 small sweet onion, cut in half and thinly sliced into half-moons. Chill for 1 hour, stirring once.

Fresh Mayonnaise

Using this basic mayonnaise, you can create a rainbow of colorful mayonnaise sauces for fondue. For the best-tasting mayonnaise, use a mild flavored oil like safflower or canola oil. Some vegetable oils have subtle off-flavors and odors that can be detected in homemade mayonnaise. All the ingredients must be at room temperature. The food processor is a wonderful tool for making mayonnaise. The blender works well too, but may clog up when more than 1 cup of oil is added. All the sauces in the Variations (see below) taste best if prepared 1 to 2 days in advance.

Makes about 1½ cups

- 1 large egg, at room temperature (see Egg Safety below)
- ½ teaspoon salt
- ½ teaspoon dry mustard or 1 teaspoon Dijon or Creole mustard
- ⅛ teaspoon red (cayenne) pepper
- ¼ teaspoon sugar
- 2 dashes white pepper
- 1 tablespoon fresh lemon juice
- 1¼ cups safflower oil or 1 cup safflower oil and ¼ cup pure olive oil
- 1 tablespoon unseasoned rice vinegar or herb vinegar such as tarragon or basil

Put the egg, salt, mustard, cayenne, sugar, white pepper and lemon juice in the bowl of a food processor fitted with a steel blade. Process about 10 seconds to blend. With the motor running, slowly begin dripping in about 1 teaspoon of oil at a time. When the mixture begins to thicken and half of the oil is incorporated, drizzle in the vinegar. Now you can increase the oil flow to a thin but steady stream. When all the oil is added, scrape the thickened mayonnaise from the bowl and put it into a small container with a tight-fitting lid. Cover and store in the refrigerator; use within 1 week.

Cook's Notes Repairing Broken Mayonnaise: If you add the oil too fast and the mayonnaise breaks before all the oil is added, scrape the curdled mixture into a small bowl and wash the food processor. Process 1 egg yolk and 1 teaspoon Dijon mustard. Add the remaining oil, a few drops at a time. Then add the broken sauce, 1 teaspoon at a time until completely added and the mixture is emulsified.

Egg Safety Recent concerns about salmonella have prompted us to re-evaluate methods of food preparation and kitchen sanitation. In recent years, *salmonella enteritidis* has been found in some of the nation's chicken flocks, contaminating an estimated 1 in every 20,000 eggs. Salmonella is rare but can cause serious illness, especially for the elderly, the young, pregnant women and those with impaired immune systems. In May of 2000, Davidson's Pasteurized Eggs™ introduced salmonella-free, pasteurized shell eggs, which are heat-treated to destroy any bacteria. These eggs can safely be eaten raw in foods like eggnog and Caesar salad dressing or cookie dough before it is baked. The pasteurized eggs cook like unpasteurized eggs and look like unpasteurized eggs except for a slightly enlarged yolk. The slightly cloudy egg whites take about four times as long to beat into meringue and they will not reach quite the same volume as unpasteurized eggs. Store the eggs up to 30 days in the refrigerator. For more information on pasteurized eggs, go to www.davidsoneggs.com.

MAYONNAISE-BASED SAUCES

Basil Dijon Aïoli Pulse 3 or 4 large cloves garlic with the egg mixture until smooth, 20 seconds. Scrape down the side of the bowl. Continue making mayonnaise, as directed, using the safflower and olive oil blend. Process in 3 to 4 tablespoons chopped fresh basil leaves and 2 tablespoons Dijon mustard. Serve with meat and seafood fondues. Makes 1¹/₂ cups

Herb Mayonnaise Pulse 1 to 2 cloves garlic with the egg mixture until smooth, 10 seconds. Scrape down side of the bowl. Continue making mayonnaise, as directed. When the mayonnaise has thickened, add ¹/₂ cup of 1 or more stemmed fresh herbs (flat-leaf parsley, basil, marjoram, cilantro and dill). Pulse a few times to chop the herb and blend it into the mayonnaise. Add salt to taste. This is good with pork, chicken, beef and seafood fondues. Makes about 1¹/₂ cups

Chipotle-Orange Sauce Pulse 1 large garlic clove with the egg mixture until smooth, 10 seconds. Scrape down side of the bowl. Continue making mayonnaise, as directed. Pulse in 2 chipotles en adobo until smooth. In a small bowl, combine the mayonnaise with ¹/₂ cup sour cream, 2 teaspoons grated orange zest, 2 tablespoons fresh orange juice and 2 small minced green onions. Serve with pork, chicken and beef fondues. Makes 2 cups

Apple and Curry Cream To 1 cup Fresh Mayonnaise, stir in ¹/₂ cup sour cream, 1 minced green onion, 1 minced garlic clove, ½ cup finely chopped tart green apple, and 1 teaspoon hot chili paste. In a custard cup, heat 1 rounded teaspoon curry powder with 1 tablespoon unsalted butter in the microwave on 80 percent power for 1 minute or until fragrant and hot; cool and stir into sauce. Serve with pork, chicken, turkey and seafood fondues; use as a dressing for chicken salad or rice salad. Makes 1¾ cups

Sauce Rémoulade To 1 recipe Fresh Mayonnaise, stir in 1 tablespoon chopped capers, 2 tablespoons minced fresh parsley, 1 tablespoon Creole mustard, 2 small minced green onions, ½ rib celery finely minced, 1 minced garlic clove, 1 teaspoon Hungarian paprika and black pepper and hot pepper sauce to taste. Serve with seafood fondues. Makes about 1¾ cups

Tartar Sauce To 1 recipe Fresh Mayonnaise, stir in ¼ cup sweet pickle relish, 2 tablespoons minced sweet onion, 1 large minced garlic clove, 1 tablespoon Dijon mustard, 2 tablespoons minced fresh dill or parsley, 1 tablespoon lemon juice, black pepper and hot pepper sauce, to taste. Serve with seafood fondues. Makes about 1¾ cups

Sun-Dried Tomato and Rosemary Mayonnaise To 1 recipe Fresh Mayonnaise, add ½ cup chopped, rehydrated sun-dried tomato halves (well-drained), 1 shallot and 1 garlic clove. Process until pureed. Scrape into a bowl and stir in 2 to 3 teaspoons minced fresh rosemary, thyme or cilantro. Makes about 1¾ cups

Parsley and Cognac Mayonnaise Prepare 1 recipe Herb Mayonnaise. Stir in 2 to 3 tablespoons Cognac or brandy, or to taste. Makes about 1¾ cups.

Bull's-eye Sauce Prepare 1 recipe Herb Mayonnaise (page 158), or quality, prepared mayonnaise. Stir in ½ cup Bull's-eye Sauce and hot pepper sauce, to taste. Makes about 2 cups

Zesty Tomato Sauce Prepare 1 recipe Herb Mayonnaise (p. 158). Stir in ½ cup ketchup, 1 teaspoon Hungarian paprika and 1 teaspoon hot pepper sauce, or to taste. Makes 2 cups

Lemon-Parsley Sauce

Light-tasting and tangy, serve with seafood, chicken, veal and turkey fondues.

Makes about 1 cup

1 cup Fresh Mayonnaise (page 157) or good-quality, prepared mayonnaise

½ cup plain yogurt

2 tablespoons minced fresh flat-leaf parsley

1 large clove garlic, finely minced

Grated zest of 1 large lemon

2 tablespoons fresh lemon juice

½ teaspoon sugar

Combine all the ingredients in a small bowl. Spoon the sauce into small bowls for dipping.

Green-Tea Salt

Flavored salts are popular in Japan for sprinkling on fried foods. Serve each diner a tiny bowl of Green-Tea Salt or a small plate with mounds of two or three flavors. *Matcha* is the special powdered green tea used for the tea ceremony, *Chanoyu*. It is made from *gyokuro*; the top grade of tender tea leaves.

The protected young leaves are taken from the tops of the bushes during the first spring picking. Matcha can be ordered from several sources; refer to the Mail-Order Resources (page 225). For optimum freshness, store the tea in the freezer.

Makes ¼ cup

¼ **cup sea salt**

2 slightly rounded teaspoons matcha

Place the salt and matcha into a small jar with a tight-fitting lid. Shake until blended. Store in a cool dry place.

VARIATIONS

Red-Pepper Salt Omit the matcha; substitute 2 teaspoons cayenne pepper and ¹/₂ teaspoon Hungarian paprika.

Curry Salt Omit the matcha; substitute 2 teaspoons curry powder and ¹/₂ teaspoon tumeric.

Sichuan Pepper Salt Omit the matcha; substitute 1 tablespoon lightly toasted, ground Sichuan peppercorns.

Three-Spice Salt Omit the matcha. Lightly toast a 1-inch piece of cinnamon stick, 3 star anise and 1 teaspoon cumin seed until aromatic. Grind to a powder in an electric spice grinder. Combine with the salt.

Clarified Butter

If water and milk solids are removed from butter, it can be used to sauté foods without fear of burning. In India, clarified butter or *ghee*, is a popular cooking fat. It is simmered long enough to develop a deep, nutty warm flavor. Clarified butter can be served as drawn butter with seafood. It can be infused with herbs and spices. It won't become rancid; nevertheless, I store it in the refrigerator.

Makes about 1¹/₂ cups

1 pound good-quality unsalted butter

In a heavy, medium saucepan, melt butter over the lowest possible heat. Use a flame tamer if the burner is still too hot. Heat 30 minutes. Butterfat will separate from the milk solids that will turn golden brown. Watch carefully to prevent burning. Pour the top layer of clear butterfat into a bowl through a strainer lined with a large coffee filter. Try to hold back most of the milk solids. If necessary, strain again with a clean coffee filter. Store in a covered container; refrigerate and warm as needed. Spoon warm butter into small bowls for dipping.

VARIATIONS

Dill Butter Heat clarified butter with 2 to 3 tablespoons minced fresh dill weed. Serve with seafood.

Oven-Clarified Butter Put butter in a large glass bowl. Place into an oven heated to 140F (60C) for one hour. The butter will separate; the milk solids will sink to the bottom. Remove from the oven and cool slightly; cover and refrigerate until cold. Beware of refrigerator odors; the butter will quickly absorb them. Lift the solid disc of butterfat from the bowl. Scrape off moist milk solids; pat dry. Store in an airtight container.

Cocktail Sauce

Here's the traditional cocktail sauce with a flavor twist!

Makes about 1½ cups

1½ cups ketchup

2 to 3 tablespoons prepared horseradish, or to taste

2 tablespoons fresh lemon juice

½ teaspoon ground cumin

Combine all the ingredients in a medium bowl. Spoon the sauce into small bowls for dipping.

VARIATION

Stir in 2 tablespoons fresh tart orange juice.

Southern Comfort Barbecue Sauce

This spunky barbecue sauce is a specialty of chef and restaurateur Steve Kish at his restaurant, 82 Queen, in Charleston, South Carolina. He spoons the sauce over a dish of creamy Carolina grits and sautéed shrimp. It is equally delicious as a dipping sauce for meat and seafood fondues.

Makes about 1½ cups

¼ pound good-quality, hickory-smoked bacon, diced

1 cup diced red onion

1 cup diced red bell pepper

1 cup diced green bell pepper

3 to 4 tablespoons Southern Comfort

1 (14-ounce) bottle ketchup

½ cup packed light brown sugar

Salt and freshly ground black pepper, to taste

In a medium saucepan, cook the bacon until almost crisp. Add the onion and bell peppers. Sauté until the onion is translucent, 3 to 4 minutes. Add the Southern Comfort to the pan and carefully ignite the liquor with a long-stemmed match. When the flames die down, stir in the ketchup and brown sugar. Season with salt and pepper. Simmer the sauce over low heat for 10 minutes. Use at once or cool and refrigerate (warm sauce before serving). Spoon sauce into small bowls for dipping. Use as a dipping sauce with meats cooked in hot oil or broth fondue.

Crème Fraîche

This luxurious crème has a texture like sour cream but tastes more like the thick, rich cream that is a specialty in France. Use in place of sour cream in any of the dipping sauces in this book or as a topping for desserts and soups. Crème Fraîche is a luscious dip for fresh strawberries. Unlike sour cream, Crème Fraîche resists curdling when boiled. The buttermilk makes a slightly tangier version. For a heavenly thick spread for scones, drain the Crème Fraîche through a coffee filter placed in a strainer set into a bowl overnight in the refrigerator.

Makes about 1 to 1½ cups

1 cup heavy whipping cream

2 tablespoons buttermilk or ½ cup sour cream

Pour the cream and buttermilk into a small saucepan. Using an instant thermometer, heat the mixture to 90F (30C) over low heat. Do not warm any higher or the cream will not thicken. (Slightly warm crème thickens faster.) Pour into a sterilized jar and cover lightly. Let the mixture stand at room temperature until the cream ripens and becomes thick, at least 12 hours or up to 24 hours. Refrigerate for 6 hours before using. The cream continues to thicken in the refrigerator.

Tomato and Red Onion Chutney

The chutney can double as an easy appetizer when poured over a block of cream cheese and served with crackers. It tastes best if refrigerated overnight before serving.

Makes about 2 cups

1 tablespoon olive oil

1 tablespoon unsalted butter

1 medium red onion, chopped

1 tablespoon minced fresh ginger

1 large clove garlic, minced

1/4 rounded teaspoon caraway seeds

1 (10-ounce) jar Smucker's tomato preserves

1/2 cup ketchup

1/3 cup red wine vinegar

2 tablespoons coarsely chopped golden raisins

2 tablespoons sugar

1 to 3 teaspoons Asian hot chili paste or other hot sauce, to taste

In a medium saucepan, heat the oil and butter over medium-low heat. Add the onion; cook slowly until soft, 5 to 6 minutes. Add the ginger, garlic and caraway seeds. Cook for 2 minutes more. Add the tomato preserves, ketchup, vinegar, raisins, sugar and chili paste. Simmer the mixture, stirring often, until well blended and slightly thickened, about 5 minutes. Serve warm or at room temperature in small bowls.

Mustard and Tarragon Sauce

This luxurious mustard dipping sauce is equally delicious with beef, pork, chicken, veal or seafood.

Makes about 1 1/4 cups

2 cups whipping cream

2 minced shallots

1 tablespoon fresh tarragon leaves or 1 teaspoon dried tarragon

2 generous tablespoons grainy Dijon or German-style mustard

1/4 teaspoon salt

Black pepper, to taste

Put the cream, shallots and tarragon into a medium saucepan. Simmer over medium heat just until the cream reduces to 1 1/4 cups, 10 to 12 minutes. Pour the cream through a fine strainer into a bowl, discarding the solids. Stir in the mustard, salt and black pepper. Spoon the sauce into small bowls for dipping.

Horseradish and Tarragon Cream Sauce

Horseradish sauce is a classic accompaniment for beef. This airy version almost melts in your mouth. Seasoned with tarragon, the sauce is excellent with beef fondue; substitute fresh dill for seafood fondues. If you plan to make the sauce a day in advance, light sour cream will help keep the sauce stable.

Makes about 1½ cups

1 cup Fresh Mayonnaise (page 157) or good-quality prepared mayonnaise

½ cup sour cream

2 tablespoons prepared horseradish

2 tablespoons fresh lemon juice

2 tablespoons minced fresh tarragon or dill or 2 teaspoons dried

1 cup heavy whipping cream

Salt and freshly ground black pepper, to taste

In a medium bowl, blend the mayonnaise, sour cream, horseradish, lemon juice and tarragon until smooth. In a mixing bowl, beat the whipping cream until stiff. Fold into the horseradish mixture just until blended. Use at once or cover and refrigerate overnight. Spoon sauce into small bowls for dipping.

Mango, Cucumber and Cashew Relish

The flavors in this Southeast Asian condiment transcend cultural barriers to enliven a variety of table-top dishes. It goes well with many dishes from Latin America. For the best taste and appearance, dice the cucumber and mango into tiny uniform cubes. The relish can be spooned over rice dishes and makes a nice salad served on tender baby lettuce leaves.

Makes 3 cups

2 medium cucumbers, seeded, diced in small cubes

2 ripe mangoes, peeled, seeded, diced in small cubes

¼ cup unseasoned rice vinegar

3 tablespoons sugar

2 tablespoons minced fresh mint or cilantro

¼ teaspoon salt, or to taste

1 small green chili, seeded, finely minced, or to taste

3 to 4 tablespoons finely chopped unsalted cashews or peanuts

In a medium bowl, mix together all the ingredients. Serve at once. (To make ahead, do not stir in the cashews, cover and refrigerate for 2 to 3 hours. Stir in the cashews just before serving.) Serve in a shallow bowl.

Zucchini and Mango Relish with Ginger

Spicy, sweet and tangy! This relish is really good as a dipping sauce for smoked sausage bites cooked in a hot oil fondue. Serve it plain or mix into sour cream with a touch of hot pepper sauce. It's a good refrigerator keeper and great for gift giving!

Makes 4 pints

10 cups grated zucchini

4 cups chopped sweet onion

3 rounded tablespoons salt

5 cups sugar

2 mangoes, peeled, seeded, chopped

2¼ cups white vinegar

1 tablespoon turmeric powder

1 teaspoon celery seeds

2 tablespoons minced fresh ginger

2 teaspoons freshly ground black pepper

½ teaspoon mustard seeds

In a large bowl, combine the zucchini, onion and salt. Cover and refrigerate overnight. Squeeze the juice from the vegetable mixture. Place the pulp and remaining ingredients in a large saucepan. Bring the mixture to a boil over high heat. Reduce the heat to medium and simmer for 30 minutes, stirring often. Pack the mixture into hot sterilized jars. Seal with the lids. Cool completely then store in the refrigerator for up to 2 months. The relish can be processed in a water bath for 15 minutes, if desired.

Wasabi Crème

This lively sauce is a natural accompaniment for seafood fondues. It can be used as a dressing over sliced tomatoes, sliced cold beef and cold poached salmon. This sauce should be eaten soon after it is made because the wasabi will soon lose its flavor after it is reconstituted. Fresh wasabi tastes even better than the dried blend.

Makes 1 cup

2 tablespoons wasabi powder

2 tablespoons water

½ cup Fresh Mayonnaise (page 157) or good-quality, prepared mayonnaise

½ cup Crème Fraîche (page 161) or sour cream

1 tablespoon dry-roasted sesame seeds, lightly crushed

Place the wasabi powder in a small custard cup; stir in the water to form a paste. Turn the cup upside down on a saucer for 10 minutes so the flavor can fully develop. In a medium bowl, blend the mayonnaise, Crème Fraîche, vinegar and prepared wasabi. Stir in the sesame seeds. Spoon into small bowls for serving. Serve at once.

VARIATION

Substitute 1 tablespoon or to taste fresh wasabi for the dried wasabi paste.

Dried Cherry and Port Sauce

If you don't have stock on hand, use one quality bouillon cube and 2 cups of water. Adjust the salt in the recipe, to taste. This rich-tasting, fruity sauce goes especially well with veal, venison and duck fondues.

Makes about 1½ cups

2 cups rich chicken or beef stock

3 tablespoons red port wine

⅓ cup dried cherries or cranberries

1 large shallot, chopped

1 garlic clove, minced

2 sprigs fresh thyme

2 tablespoons red wine vinegar

2 teaspoons cornstarch dissolved in
1 tablespoon beef stock

$^1/_8$ teaspoon salt, or to taste

Freshly ground black pepper, to taste

4 tablespoons butter, cut in 4 pieces

In a medium saucepan, combine stock, port, cherries, shallot, garlic and thyme sprigs. Simmer over medium heat 5 minutes. Remove and discard thyme. Pour mixture into a blender; add vinegar. Process until smooth. Return mixture to the saucepan and place over medium-high heat. Bring to a boil; stir in cornstarch mixture and stir until thickened. Remove from the heat. Add salt and pepper, to taste. Stir in the butter until melted. Pour warm sauce into small bowls for dipping.

Mignonette Sauce

The east-west version of this classic sauce is an ideal accompaniment for seafood cooked in fondues and hot pots, especially oysters.

Makes about $^2/_3$ cup

$^1/_2$ cup unseasoned rice vinegar

1 tablespoon red wine vinegar

1 tablespoon finely minced shallot

1 teaspoon finely minced fresh ginger

2 tablespoons minced fresh cilantro

$^1/_2$ teaspoon minced hot chili, or to taste

Combine all the ingredients in a small bowl. Spoon the sauce into small serving bowls.

Guacamole Sauce

Unlike traditional guacamole, this sauce contains Crème Fraîche which gives it a creamy texture and softer consistency for dipping. It is delicious with pork, poultry and seafood fondues.

The sauce is best made just before serving but if made 1 to 2 hours ahead, squeeze extra lime juice on top and cover directly with a layer of plastic wrap to seal out the air.

Makes about 1$^1/_4$ cups

1 ripe Hass avocado, cut in half, pit removed

1 to 2 tablespoons fresh lime or lemon juice, or to taste

$^1/_2$ cup Crème Fraîche (page 161) or sour cream

1 green onion, minced

1 small, ripe plum tomato, seeded, minced

1 small clove garlic, finely minced

$^1/_2$ jalapeño chili pepper, seeded, finely minced, or to taste

2 tablespoons cilantro leaves, chopped

Salt, to taste

With a fork, mash the avocado with the lime juice in a medium bowl. Stir in the remaining ingredients until blended. For a smooth sauce, process in the blender for a few seconds. Stir before serving.

Red Bell Pepper Sauce

Roasted red bell peppers and mascarpone are blended to make a dipping sauce so delicious it can be used as a dressing for cooked pasta. It is the ultimate pimiento cheese!

Makes 6 servings

> **2 cups chopped, roasted red bell peppers (see Roasted Chilies, page 28)**
>
> **1 large clove garlic, minced**
>
> **1 cup mascarpone or 1 (8-ounce) package cream cheese, softened**
>
> **1 to 2 tablespoons raspberry vinegar or red wine vinegar, or to taste**
>
> **Salt and ground white pepper, to taste**

In a food processor fitted with the steel blade, process the peppers and garlic until smooth. Scrape the mixture into a large bowl. Blend in the mascarpone until smooth. Stir in the vinegar, salt and pepper. Spoon the sauce into small bowls for dipping.

Soy Sauce and Sesame Dip

Serve this Korean dipping sauce with meatballs, fried dumplings and squares of fried tofu.

Makes about ³/₄ cup

> **¹/₂ cup Japanese soy sauce (shoyu)**
>
> **1 cup water**
>
> **2 teaspoons sugar**
>
> **2 tablespoons unseasoned rice vinegar**
>
> **1 green onion, finely minced**

> **1 large clove garlic, finely minced**
>
> **1 teaspoon toasted sesame oil**
>
> **1 tablespoon dry-roasted sesame seeds, lightly crushed**
>
> **1 teaspoon Korean red pepper powder, chili paste with garlic or hot pepper sauce, or to taste**

Combine all the ingredients in a medium bowl. Spoon into small bowls for serving.

Sesame-Miso Sauce

The flavors in this East-West sauce will complement the taste of seafood in a fondue or hot pot dish. It can also be served as a dip with Butterfly Crisps (page 124) or crisp fresh vegetable sticks.

Makes about 1¹/₃ cups

> **2 tablespoons red miso paste (akamiso)**
>
> **¹/₂ cup sour cream**
>
> **2 green onions, finely minced**
>
> **¹/₂ cup Fresh Mayonnaise (page 157) or good-quality prepared mayonnaise**
>
> **2 tablespoons unseasoned rice vinegar**
>
> **2 teaspoons grated ginger (see Fresh Ginger Juice, page 108)**
>
> **2 tablespoons dry-roasted sesame seeds, lightly crushed**

In a small bowl, combine all the ingredients. Spoon the sauce into small bowls for dipping.

Five-Spice Orange Sauce

The citrus flavor of this spicy orange dipping sauce accents the taste of seafood, chicken or pork in a fondue, crispy fried seafood dumplings and spring rolls.

Makes about 1½ cups

1 (12-ounce) jar sweet orange marmalade or apricot preserves

¼ cup prepared horseradish

2 tablespoons fresh lemon juice

1 generous teaspoon finely minced ginger

½ teaspoon five-spice powder

Combine all the ingredients in a medium bowl. Serve at once or refrigerate until needed. Serve the sauce warm or at room temperature. Spoon into small bowls for dipping.

Creamy Artichoke and Parmesan Sauce

This hearty artichoke sauce has a rustic, chunky texture before it is puréed. Best when warm, serve it as a warm spread with Bruschetta or Crostini (page 138).

Makes about 3 cups

1 (9-ounce) package frozen artichoke hearts, thawed

1 tablespoon fresh lemon juice

1 cup Fresh Mayonnaise (page 157) or good-quality prepared mayonnaise

½ cup sour cream

2 cloves garlic, minced

1 minced shallot or 2 tablespoons minced green onion

2 tablespoons minced fresh parsley

2 tablespoons freshly grated Parmigiano-Reggiano or Romano cheese

¼ cup whipping cream or light cream

Dash hot pepper sauce

1 teaspoon whole-grain mustard, preferably Maille brand

1 teaspoon salt

Several dashes freshly ground black pepper

Put the artichoke hearts in a glass pie plate and cover with plastic wrap. Microwave for 5 minutes on high (100 percent) power; leave covered for 10 minutes. With a large sharp knife, mince the artichoke hearts. Combine all the remaining ingredients in a large bowl. Taste; adjust seasonings, if desired. For a silky-smooth dipping sauce, put the mixture into a blender and process until pale green, creamy and smooth. Serve warm. (The sauce can be covered and refrigerated up to 2 days. Warm the sauce over low heat before serving.)

Zestful Blue Cheese Dressing

This creamy blue cheese dressing was created by Chef Tom Brocaglia, when he was executive chef for Clemson University in Clemson, South Carolina. Tom constantly created innovative dishes using blue cheese produced by Clemson's dairy. This dressing is a staple at Seasons by the Lake, a restaurant for fine dining located on campus. As a tasty variation, Tom suggests stirring in 3 tablespoons chopped pimiento.

Makes about 1½ cups

2 ounces Clemson Blue Cheese Crumbles (½ cup) or other crumbled blue cheese

2 tablespoons cider vinegar or fresh lemon juice

1 cup good-quality mayonnaise

½ clove garlic, crushed

¼ cup thick sour cream

1 tablespoon sugar

Pinch salt

In a medium bowl, combine all the ingredients. Blend well until the mixture is smooth and creamy. Serve at once or cover and store in the refrigerator for up to 3 days.

Tempura Dipping Sauce/ Tentsuyu

The traditional accompaniment for Tempura (page 65), dip each morsel of fried food briefly into the warm sauce before taking a bite.

Makes about 2⅔ cups

2 cups Dashi (page 184)

⅓ cup light Japanese soy sauce (*usukuchi shoyu*)

⅓ cup mirin (Japanese rice wine)

1 tablespoon sugar

½ cup grated daikon radish

2 tablespoons grated fresh ginger (see Fresh Ginger Juice, page 108)

3 or 4 pencil-thin green onions, cut in paper-thin slices (mostly the green portion)

In a medium saucepan, combine the Dashi, soy sauce, mirin and sugar. Simmer, stirring, over low

heat until the sugar is dissolved, 2 to 3 minutes. Pour into 5 or 6 small bowls for serving. Arrange a small amount of daikon, ginger and green onion on each of 4 small saucers. At the table, each diner can stir condiments into the warm dipping sauce, as desired.

Banana and Cilantro Sauce

For a taste of the tropics, try this creamy, smooth banana sauce. The flavor is mellow but not too sweet. It is especially good with shrimp, scallops and fish cubes fried in hot oil fondues.

Makes about 2 cups

4 firm, ripe medium bananas

½ cup sour cream or low-fat sour cream

¼ cup Fresh Mayonnaise (page 157) or good-quality prepared mayonnaise

1 heaping tablespoon Creole mustard

1 tablespoon fresh lime or lemon juice

½ to 1 teaspoon Asian hot sauce (*sambal oelek* or pepper *saté* sauce), or to taste

Pinch of salt and ground white pepper

2 tablespoons minced fresh cilantro or mint

Put all the ingredients, except the cilantro, into the bowl of a food processor fitted with the steel blade. Process just until smooth. Pour the sauce into a medium bowl; stir in the cilantro. Serve at once or cover and refrigerate for up to 2 hours. Spoon the sauce into small bowls for dipping.

Cucumber-Dill Sauce

Kathy McCorkle recommends serving the cucumber sauce with fish or as a dip for vegetables. She says, "With a little horseradish stirred in, it is spectacular with filet mignon!"

Makes about 2 cups

1 large cucumber, peeled, seeded, cut in small dice

1 cup sour cream

Juice of $\frac{1}{2}$ lemon

1 to 2 tablespoons fresh minced dill

Salt and freshly ground black pepper, to taste

Put the diced cucumber into a blender or food processor fitted with a steel blade. Process the cucumber until reduced to a pulp. Scrape the pulp into a fine strainer. Press all the liquid out. Put the pulp into a medium bowl. Stir in the sour cream, lemon juice and dill. Season with salt and black pepper.

Jalapeño-Cranberry Port Sauce

A lively sauce bursting with flavor, it is especially good with pork, chicken, turkey and venison.

Makes about 2 cups

1 (12-ounce bag) fresh cranberries, rinsed, picked over

1 cup port

$\frac{1}{2}$ cup sugar

Grated zest of 1 medium orange

2 to 3 tablespoons fresh orange juice

1 teaspoon finely minced fresh ginger

$\frac{1}{4}$ teaspoon ground allspice

$\frac{1}{8}$ teaspoon ground cinnamon

$\frac{1}{8}$ teaspoon salt

$\frac{1}{2}$ jalapeño chili pepper, seeded, finely minced, or $\frac{1}{8}$ teaspoon cayenne pepper

Put the cranberries, port and sugar in a medium saucepan. Simmer over medium-low heat until cranberries begin to pop, 8 to 10 minutes. Cook, stirring, 1 to 2 minutes more. Pour the mixture into a food processor fitted with the steel blade. Process until smooth. Scrape the sauce into a medium bowl; stir in the remaining ingredients. Serve at once or cover and refrigerate for up to 1 week. Serve warm or at room temperature. Thin the sauce with more orange juice or port, if necessary.

Buffalo Wing Sauce

Frank's Hot Sauce was used in the original recipe for Buffalo chicken wings in 1964 at the Anchor Bar in Buffalo, New York. Here, it is used in a similar sauce that is good for dipping chicken strips fried in a fondue.

Makes about 1 cup

$\frac{3}{4}$ cup Clarified Butter (page 160)

3 tablespoons Frank's hot sauce or other hot sauce

1 to 2 tablespoons fresh lemon juice, or to taste

$\frac{1}{2}$ teaspoon cayenne pepper, or to taste

1 tablespoon finely minced parsley

In a small saucepan, combine all the ingredients in a small saucepan. Warm over low heat, and then pour into small bowls for dipping.

Inca-Gold Sauce

Ground achiote seeds, also called *annatto*, are used to add a yellow color to commercial butter and cheese. Achiote can give foods a musky, earthy flavor. Buy it in markets that sell Latino foods. For the best flavor, dry-toast cumin seeds and grind them in a spice mill.

Makes 1½ cups

1 cup Fresh Mayonnaise (page 157) or good-quality prepared mayonnaise

½ cup sour cream or plain yogurt

1 rounded teaspoon ground cumin

1 to 3 teaspoons hot pepper sauce or chili paste, or to taste

½ teaspoon Japanese soy sauce (*shoyu*)

½ teaspoon annatto powder

¼ teaspoon salt, or to taste

2 green onions, finely minced

1 clove garlic, finely minced

In a medium bowl, combine all the ingredients. Spoon into small bowls for serving.

Indochine Sauce

Nuoc mam is a thin, salty Vietnamese fish sauce made from salting and fermenting anchovies and other small fish. It is rich in amino acids, iodine and B Vitamins. Fish sauce is used as a seasoning and dipping sauce in Southeast Asian cuisine the same as soy sauce is used in Japan. It is highly concentrated and should be diluted before use. A Vietnamese restaurant owner remarked to me that *nuoc mam* is so extraordinary, it would make Chanel No. 5 taste good! The finest brands have a delicate taste and ever-so-subtly enhance the flavor of many foods. Some top Vietnamese brands are made on the island of Phu Quoc; look for these words on the bottle. Premium Three Crabs Brand fish sauce is another good choice. Golden Boy, Squid or Tiparos brands from Thailand can be substituted.

Indochine Sauce is similar to *nuoc cham*, the everyday table sauce of Vietnam.

Makes 1 cup

¼ cup *nuoc mam* or *nam pla* (fish sauce)

½ cup water

¼ cup freshly squeezed tangy orange juice

2 tablespoons unseasoned rice vinegar

2 tablespoons fresh lime juice

2 tablespoons sugar

1 or 2 cloves garlic, finely minced

1 small fresh whole red chili pepper, stemmed, seeded, minced, or Siracha hot chili sauce, to taste

Combine all the ingredients in a medium bowl. Let the sauce stand at room temperature at least 30 minutes or for several hours in the refrigerator. Refrigerate leftover sauce.

Chimichurri Sauce

Chimichurri, the ubiquitous sidekick for steak in Argentina is a zesty green herb sauce and is as popular as ketchup or barbecue sauce in America. Serve it with beef, pork, chicken and lamb fondues. For the best flavor, make this sauce at least 1 or 2 days in advance and refrigerate.

Makes about 1½ cups

¼ packed cup cilantro leaves

¼ cup fresh parsley

1 tablespoon fresh oregano leaves or 1 teaspoon dried oregano

3 green onions, chopped

2 garlic cloves

2 tablespoons fresh lime or lemon juice

3 tablespoons white wine vinegar

¼ teaspoon sugar

1 teaspoon salt

Freshly ground black pepper, to taste

½ cup pure olive oil

½ cup safflower or canola oil

Place all the ingredients, except the oil, into a food processor fitted with the steel blade. Process until the mixture is chopped. With the machine running, pour in the oils in a steady stream. Process until mixture becomes fairly smooth. Serve at once or refrigerate in an airtight container for up to 2 weeks. Pour the sauce into small bowls for serving.

Kiwi-Mango Salsa

A refreshing foil for meat and seafood fondues, this colorful blend of fruits and flavors creates a taste of traditional island fare. For an attractive appearance, make sure all the fruits and vegetables are uniformly chopped into small pieces.

Makes 2½ cups

4 firm, ripe kiwifruit, peeled, cut into ¼-inch dice

1 mango or red papaya, peeled, seeded, cut into ¼-inch dice

½ cup finely chopped red bell pepper

2 tablespoons minced red onion

3 tablespoons fresh lime juice

1 tablespoon light brown sugar

1 tablespoon minced fresh parsley

1 tablespoon minced cilantro leaves

Pinch of salt

2 tablespoons finely chopped macadamia nuts

Combine all the ingredients, except the macadamia nuts, in a medium bowl. Serve within 2 hours for the best taste. If refrigerated, bring to room temperature; stir in macadamia nuts just before serving.

Creole Honey-Mustard Sauce

A fantastic dipping sauce that blends two flavorful mustards, serve it with your favorite fondue meats and seafood or with fried foods.

Makes about 1 cup

¼ cup honey mustard, such as Honeycup Mustard

¼ cup Creole mustard

½ cup Fresh Mayonnaise (page 157) or good-quality prepared mayonnaise

1 teaspoon Japanese soy sauce (*shoyu*)

1 tablespoon fresh minced herb or 1 teaspoon dried herb (tarragon, parsley, dill, thyme, oregano)

Plenty of hot pepper sauce, to taste

Combine all the ingredients in a medium bowl. Serve at once or refrigerate until needed. Spoon the sauce into small bowls for serving. The recipe can be doubled.

Beef and Wine Dipping Broth

Richly flavored, this herb dipping sauce is exceptional with beef, veal and venison fondues.

Makes about 1 cup

½ cup red wine, such as Cabernet Sauvignon

1 large shallot, minced

1 garlic clove, mashed

2 cups Basic Beef Stock (page 178) or canned beef broth

1 tablespoon minced fresh thyme, mint, rosemary or sage

1 tablespoon unsalted butter

Put the wine, shallot and garlic in a small saucepan over medium-high heat. Boil until wine reduces by half. Add the stock and thyme; boil until the mixture reduces by half. Pour sauce through a mesh strainer; add back to the saucepan. Heat sauce; whisk in the butter. Serve warm.

Honey-Spice Butter

This spice-scented butter can be used on baked sweet potatoes, baked squash, tea breads, scones or biscuits. The recipe can be made with 1 (8-ounce) carton cholesterol-lowering vegetable spread like Benecol®. When measuring honey, grease the measuring cup and the honey will slide out easily.

Makes 1 cup

1 cup (2 sticks) salted butter, at room temperature

½ cup honey

1 teaspoon ground cinnamon

½ teaspoon ground nutmeg

¼ teaspoon ground allspice

In a medium bowl, beat all the ingredients together until creamy. Use at once or cover and refrigerate for up to 1 week. Remove from the refrigerator 30 minutes before using.

VARIATIONS

Honey-Spice Butter with Pecans Stir 2 tablespoons finely chopped toasted pecans into Honey-Spice Butter.

Maple-Spice Butter Substitute ¹/₃ cup pure maple syrup for the honey. If you wish, add ¼ teaspoon pure maple extract to enhance the maple flavor.

Stocks
and Soups

Stock is the rich, flavorful liquid left from simmering bones, vegetables and seasonings in water for a long period over low heat. Stocks are used for soups, sauces and as braising liquids. In this book, they become the foundation for broth-based fondues and Chinese hot pot meals.

In France, stock is called a *fond* or the "foundation." A well-made stock or broth is the key to making a tasty broth-based fondue. There are many stock options; brown veal stock or beef stock, chicken stock, fish stock, vegetable stock and court bouillon. The ingredients for the stocks in this chapter are not expensive; the cooking techniques are not difficult. The major investment will be your time. Even so, when the stock begins to barely simmer, you can attend to other duties or pleasures, leaving it alone. A classic French stock might simmer on the backburner for eight to twelve hours to extract every bit of flavor. A stock this rich and concentrated isn't necessary for a fondue or hot pot. The cooking liquids for these one-pot meals continually become enriched from the essence of the meats, seafood and vegetables the diners dip into the pot.

Basic Beef Stock is a brown stock made with meaty bones and vegetables. The ingredients are slowly browned to intensify the final flavor. Many beef stocks are made only with bones. I use meaty

bones for extra flavor since the stock only simmers about four hours. Neck, back and shank bones provide collagen, a protein found in connective tissues that dissolves while simmering in the stock. Long simmering converts the collagen into gelatin. When a stock is boiled down and concentrated, it will have a jellylike consistency when cool. Gelatin is valued for the richness and body it adds to stock. Veal bones are favored for their rich collagen supply. Shank bones are filled with marrow, which also provides richness and flavor.

Basic Beef Stock is a flavorful liquid base for broth-based fondues or soups. You don't have to use the finest grade of ingredients for this stock but they should be very fresh. If you like, include 1/2 cup or so red wine in the stockpot. A narrow stockpot helps reduce excess evaporation. Always pour cold water over the ingredients in the stockpot to extract the most flavor. To concentrate the finished stock's flavor, strain it well then simmer until reduced, as desired. Never add salt until the reduction is finished or the salty taste will be concentrated, as well.

Basic Beef Stock can be used for cooking a variety of foods in the fondue pot including paper-thin slices and cubes of beef, veal, game, meatballs, dumplings and vegetables. Once the stock is made, the hardest part of a fondue meal is finished. The stock can be divided into convenient portions and refrigerated or frozen for later use.

Broth is a stock's close culinary cousin. Have you ever wondered about the difference between a broth and a stock? Broth is the richly flavored liquid that is a by-product of poaching a large piece of meat, a whole chicken or chicken parts; vegetables and herbs are included in the pot. Taken one step further, it is the richly flavored liquid resulting from a variety of simmered one-pot meals such as the New England boiled dinner, the French *pot-au-feu*, the German *rinderbrust*, the Belgian *hochepot* or the Italian *bollito misto*. The savory liquid from these dishes is often served as a first course; the meat is sliced and served as the main course. The broth can be saved and used for soups, broth fondues and similar dishes. Chill the broth and skim off the fat before using. The French word for broth is *bouillon*. Although broths are common in home cooking, we most often associate the word bouillon with concentrated salty flavoring cubes that are diluted in water. Bouillon cube broths do not produce the same fine flavor as a homemade stock or broth.

A rich, golden chicken stock is easier and quicker to make than beef stock. The flavor is lighter and more delicate. The recipe for Basic Chicken Stock calls for chicken parts such as backs and necks. It is possible to make a richer stock but it isn't necessary. Leftover chicken broth from poached chicken can be added to the fondue pot; if you like, add a little dry white wine for extra flavor. The Saffron Chicken Broth is a golden, saffron-scented broth that is ideal for cooking all types of seafood and poultry in a fondue.

All the flavor needed for a fish stock can be extracted from the ingredients within twenty-five to thirty minutes. Overcooking will make a fish stock bitter. Sauté the onions or shallots in butter to enhance the stock and give it a mellow flavor. Don't add too much carrot or the stock will end up too sweet. If you don't use the stock at once, cool it rapidly and refrigerate; use within one to two days. Freeze for about one week.

A court bouillon is an aromatic vegetable infusion used for poaching a variety of foods. Its basic ingredients are wine, aromatic vegetables and herbs. Choose a wine that is crisp and acidic, as you would for a fish stock. A court bouillon is quickly prepared, usually within thirty minutes. Although it doesn't usually become part of the finished dish, a court bouillon is an excellent cooking liquid for the fondue pot. Use it for simmering vegetables, seafood, fish and meats. It is delicious, light and fat free.

Choose your own creative flavor touches for fondue stocks by adding different wines, herbs and vegetables. To make a vegetarian mushroom stock, slowly simmer 1/2 pound richly flavored dried porcini or shiitaki mushrooms (or a blend) in about five quarts of water for two hours. Include a mixture of onions, celery and carrots and garlic, peppercorns and herbs. Make a wine broth by simmering a favorite dry red wine with peppercorns, spices and herbs to make a unique cooking liquid for beef fondue.

Consommé is made from an extra-rich stock featuring beef, chicken, seafood or even venison. The stock is clarified until it is crystal clear and completely fat free. Consommé has a special flavor that is meaty-rich yet quite delicate. Although I include a brief explanation in this chapter on how to clarify stock, it isn't necessary to complete this additional step when using stock for fondue. A carefully prepared stock that is skimmed regularly and barely allowed to simmer will have good clarity and flavor after it is strained.

If your freezer is bare and you don't have time to make a homemade stock or broth for fondue, prepare a quick substitute using a commercial product. Straight out of the can, beef consommé, bouillon and broth are not as tasty as the homemade kind. To improve their flavor, simmer them briefly with chopped vegetables, herbs and seasonings.

To make the Enriched Beef Consommé, start with Campbell's Beef Consommé, canned beef bouillon or canned beef broth. Most of these products are very concentrated; some brands more so than others. Don't be tempted to use them undiluted; they taste far too strong. The canned products are often too strong diluted according to the manufacturer's instructions. Use $3^1/_2$ to 4 times the amount of water to broth for a strength equivalent to homemade. The flavor, of course, will not be the same. Taste as you add the water; if you are not sure, it is better to over-dilute canned stock than to use one too strong.

For a fresher beefy flavor, include $^1/_4$- to $^1/_2$-pound of lean ground or chopped beef. Triple the simmering time over low heat, adding additional water, if necessary to maintain the volume. Strain the broth well before use. Do not use larger pieces of meat; the cooking time is short and the flavor cannot be fully extracted.

Homemade consommé is often fortified with a fine wine or sherry just before it is served. A dry, slightly acidic wine can be simmered with the canned product to enhance its flavor. Remember when choosing a wine, that its flavor characteristics become more pronounced as the wine is reduced.

A few brands of canned chicken broth taste fairly good, but they will taste more like homemade if briefly simmered with a few chopped chicken parts, vegetables and herbs. To make the Quick and Easy Chicken Broth or the Quick Asian Chicken Broth, choose a highly rated national brand like Swanson's chicken broth or Campbell's chicken broth. In the recipes, I suggest a low-sodium brand like Swanson's Natural Goodness chicken broth. I also like the pleasant chicken taste found in Swanson's broth in the 32-ounce aseptic packages. If you like, substitute one (32-ounce) box and one (14.5 ounce) can of Swanson's chicken broth for the three (14.5 ounce) cans called for in the quick chicken broth recipes. The extra three ounces of broth won't make a difference.

If you are completely out of time, but still want to improve the flavor of a plain, diluted canned stock or broth, boil it in a large pot and add some of the fresh cut vegetables that will be served with the fondue. Vegetables like carrots, potatoes, cauliflower and broccoli benefit from a brief blanching and the broth will taste much better. After the veggies are blanched, reduce the heat to a simmer; if you have any on hand, add two or three chopped green onions, garlic cloves and some decent wine.

ASIAN STOCKS

Asian stocks are made with the same care as their western counterparts but usually taste lighter and have a variety of different flavor notes. The aromatic Asian Beef Stock sings with the flavors of lemongrass, cilantro, cinnamon and star anise. The stock's wonderful fragrance will perfume your entire house as it cooks. It can be used in endless variations of Southeast Asian hot pot dishes including the Vietnamese Beef and Rice Noodle Hot Pot. By adjusting the distinctive Southeast Asian seasonings, you can adapt this stock for use in any Asian cuisine.

The light, aromatic Asian Chicken Stock is useful for preparing many types of Asian one-pot dishes. A clarified stock that is crystal-clear is not a priority in every part of Asia, but Chinese cooks might clear up a cloudy stock by simmering tough cabbage leaves until they are tender. Discard the leaves before straining the stock. Some Chinese cooks enrich their chicken stocks with a small portion of pork knuckles or ribs. For a delicate seafood flavor, simmer a chicken stock with 1/2 pound or so of freshly peeled shrimp shells.

No time to fortify canned chicken broth for a Chinese hot pot meal? Use plain, diluted canned chicken stock or even water as many Asian cooks do. At the table, throw chopped green onions, a slice of ginger, two dried mushrooms, some cabbage and carrot into the pot with the broth. When the water bubbles, invite the guests to start cooking the seafood and meats. As the fire-breathing dragon pot is fed, the water will magically be transformed into an enchanted broth.

BOUQUET GARNI

A little bundle of herbs called a *bouquet garni* works its flavor magic on broths, soups and sauces. When the cooking is done, the herbs are easy to retrieve. For each bundle, use several sprigs of fresh parsley, a bay leaf and two or three sprigs of fresh thyme. Wrap in a 4-inch cheesecloth square; tie with kitchen string.

Basic Chicken Stock

A good stock is the foundation for a great dish. This stock is light yet intense enough to add real flavor to foods cooked in a broth-based fondue. Chicken bones add richness, color and flavor. Backs and necks are often hard to come by unless you bone them out of whole chickens and stash them in the freezer. If necessary, supplement the bones with chicken legs and thighs for a full-flavored stock. Chicken wings add a rich, gelatinous quality. Never boil stock or it will become cloudy.

Makes about 3 1/2 quarts

4 to 5 pounds chicken bones (backs, wings, and necks) trimmed of fat, chopped into smaller pieces

4 quarts water

2 large onions, quartered

2 ribs celery with leaves, cut in pieces

1 carrot, cut in pieces

2 cloves garlic, smashed

1 teaspoon peppercorns

1 bay leaf

6 sprigs parsley

4 sprigs thyme

Rinse the chicken parts under cool water; drain well. Place into a stockpot with the water, onions, celery, carrot and garlic. Bring to a boil; reduce the heat to the lowest setting. Skim the foam from the top. Barely simmer, uncovered, for 1 hour. Add the peppercorns and all the herbs; simmer for 2 hours more. Skim stock, as necessary. Add a little more hot water, only if necessary, to keep the stock level just above the ingredients. Use a large slotted spoon to discard the bones. Pour the stock through a strainer into a large bowl. Press the ingredients to extract the liquid.

Quickly cool to room temperature, uncovered. Refrigerate for up to 3 days. Before using, scrape off the top layer of fat. Bring to a boil and season to taste. Stock can be frozen; boil briefly after thawing.

VARIATION

Rich Chicken Stock For a richer stock for soups and casseroles, sauté a whole chicken, cut into small pieces, in 2 tablespoons canola oil. When lightly browned, add the vegetables and cook over the lowest heat setting for about 20 minutes, turning ingredients several times. Pour in 4 quarts water and the seasonings; continue the recipe as directed above.

COOK'S NOTES

Cooling Stock It is important to cool a stock quickly to prevent the formation of bacteria. The fastest way to accomplish this is to set a metal pot holding the strained stock into a sink filled with water and ice. Stir the stock occasionally, to promote cooling. Stock should be uncovered while cooling, to prevent souring. To save space and containers, pour stock in 3- to 4-cup increments into sturdy plastic storage bags with flat bottoms that stand on end. Place the bag inside a tall narrow pot for filling; seal before removing from the pot.

Quick and Easy Chicken Broth

Prepare this broth when you don't have time to make a long-simmered chicken stock. Starting with canned broth, you can produce an excellent broth in about one hour. Use it in any recipe that calls for chicken stock.

Makes about 6¹/₂ cups

3 (14¹/₂-ounce) cans low-sodium chicken broth

3 cups water

1 pound chicken wings or backs, chopped into pieces, or chicken drumettes

¹/₂ leek, slit lengthwise, leaves separated, well rinsed, chopped

1 rib celery, chopped

¹/₂ carrot, chopped

1 small bay leaf

2 sprigs parsley

2 sprigs thyme or ¹/₂ teaspoon dried herb

Pour the broth and water into a 4-quart saucepan. Rinse the chicken parts under cool water; drain well. Place into the saucepan along with the leek, celery, carrot and herbs. Bring to a boil; reduce heat to low. Skim off any foam from the top. Gently simmer, uncovered, for 45 minutes. Pour broth through a strainer into a large bowl. Press ingredients to extract the liquid.

Use the broth at once, or quickly cool to room temperature, uncovered. Refrigerate for up to 3 days. Before using, scrape off the top layer of fat. Bring to a boil and season to taste. The broth can be frozen. Boil briefly after thawing in the refrigerator.

Saffron Chicken Broth

This golden, saffron-scented broth can be used for simmering chicken, seafood and veal in fondue. If saffron isn't available, substitute about 1/4 teaspoon ground turmeric. The broth will have a golden hue and although the flavor won't exactly be the same, it will taste delicious. Saffron is produced from the three yellow-orange stigmas found inside each purple crocus. Because they are so labor-intensive to harvest, saffron is the most expensive spice in the world. Use this flavorful broth for making golden rice pilaf using long-grain rice.

Makes about 6 cups

1 tablespoon olive oil

3 shallots, coarsely chopped

3 large cloves garlic, coarsely minced

1 fennel stalk with fronds, cut in small pieces (about 1 cup)

6 1/2 cups Basic Chicken Stock (page 176) or 1 recipe Quick and Easy Chicken Broth (page 177)

1/2 to 1 cup dry white wine, to taste

3 sprigs fresh oregano or 1/2 teaspoon dried

3 sprigs fresh thyme or 1/2 teaspoon dried

Between 1/16 and 1/8 teaspoon saffron

1 teaspoon salt, or to taste

Freshly ground black pepper, to taste

Heat oil in a large saucepan over medium heat. Sauté the shallots, garlic and fennel until vegetables are soft, 3 to 4 minutes. Add the stock, wine, oregano, thyme and saffron. Simmer the broth, partially covered, for 15 minutes. Pour the broth through a mesh strainer into a large bowl. Season with salt and black pepper. Use at once or quickly cool to room temperature and refrigerate overnight.

Mirepoix A *mirepoix* is a mixture of onions, celery and carrots used to enhance the flavor of home-made stock. For long-cooking stocks, the *mirepoix* can be cut into large pieces. For quick-cooking stocks, chop the *mirepoix* into small pieces to extract more flavor. When making stock, it isn't necessary to peel the carrots, remove strings from the celery, remove skins from tomatoes or peel the onions and garlic. Onion skins can add color to a brown stock.

Basic Beef Stock

The underpinning of a delicious broth-based fondue is the *fond de cuisine*, or "base" stock. Bones from younger animals contain ample collagen that converts into gelatin, adding richness and body to stock. Shank, neck and backbones are especially good. This brown stock takes time, but the technique isn't difficult. The ingredients are caramelized or roasted in the oven to brown the sugars found on their surface. This creates a richly flavored stock. To prevent cloudiness, cook the stock on low heat and never allow it to boil. Ask the butcher to saw large bones in smaller pieces to extract more flavor.

Makes about 4 quarts

2 tablespoons canola oil

4 1/2 to 5 pounds meaty beef or veal bones (or a blend) sawed into pieces

2 large onions, cut in half

2 cups hot water

4 quarts cold water

2 ribs celery with leaves, cut in pieces

1 small carrot, cut in pieces

2 large cloves garlic, mashed

1 leek, slit lengthwise, leaves separated, well rinsed, cut in pieces

2 tablespoons tomato paste or 2 chopped tomatoes

8 to 10 mixed, fresh herb sprigs (parsley, thyme and dill)

Freshly ground black pepper, as desired

2 bay leaves

Preheat the oven to 400F (205C). Put the oil in a heavy roasting pan. Add the bones and onions. Cook for 1 to 1¹/₂ hours, turning occasionally, or until well-browned but not burned. Spoon the mixture into a large stockpot.

Pour off the fat in the roasting pan. Add the hot water and heat over low heat, stirring, to loosen the caramelized juices; pour into the stockpot.

Add the cold water and all the remaining ingredients to the stockpot. Bring to a boil; reduce the heat to low. Skim the foam from the top. Simmer gently, uncovered, for 3¹/₂ to 4 hours. Skim stock, as necessary. Add a little more hot water, only if necessary, to keep the stock level just above the ingredients. Use a large slotted spoon to remove and discard bones. Pour stock through a strainer into a large bowl. Press ingredients to extract stock. Quickly cool to room temperature, uncovered.

Refrigerate up to 3 days. Before using, scrape off the top layer of fat. Bring to a boil and season to taste. The stock can be frozen; boil briefly after thawing in the refrigerator.

VARIATION

Add 2 cups dry red wine to the stock.

COOK'S NOTES

Clarifying Stock Professional chefs clarify stock to make a crystal-clear consommé. The process involves simmering the stock with a number of ingredients: raw egg, eggshells, chopped meat and vegetables. I don't feel the extra step is necessary when making a fondue broth, but it pays off if you want to serve an elegant, clear broth. The simplest method is to add 1 slightly beaten egg white and 1 crushed eggshell to every quart of stock. Whisk the stock continually as it slowly comes to a boil. Otherwise, the egg will sink to the bottom and burn. Stop whisking when the stock boils. Simmer on the lowest-heat setting for 10 minutes. The egg and eggshell will attach themselves to the impurities floating through the soup. Carefully remove them with a skimmer. Strain the stock through several layers of dampened cheesecloth. For extra clarity, you can strain the stock once again.

Skimming Fat If you make stock and need to use it right away, there is a quick way to remove most of the fat from the top. If the stock is in a large bowl, place a paper towel on top and immediately lift it off, effectively removing some of the top layer of fat. Repeat the process one or two more times, as needed. Tear the paper towel, if necessary, to fit smaller containers.

Asian Beef Stock

Beef shank and oxtails are meaty, flavorful additions to a stock. Use this stock for Southeast Asian-influenced fondues, casserole dishes and hot pots. To make a delicious noodle soup, simmer 1 quart of the

---

stock for 5 minutes to concentrate the flavor; ladle into 3 or 4 large bowls filled with cooked rice noodles. Season with salt, lime juice, hot chili paste, fish sauce and cilantro, to taste. Leftover tender meat that simmered in the stockpot is a tasty addition, as well

Makes about 4 quarts

2 tablespoons light olive oil

3½ to 4 pounds beef shanks or oxtails, sawed into pieces

1 leek, slit lengthwise, leaves separated, well rinsed, cut in pieces

3 large diagonal slices fresh ginger, mashed

1 cinnamon stick

2 star anise

2 large cloves garlic, mashed

Tender inner portion of 1 (14-inch) piece lemongrass, chopped, or strips of zest from 1 medium lemon

4 quarts water

6 to 8 sprigs fresh cilantro

1 teaspoon Sichuan peppercorns or other peppercorns

In a stockpot, heat the oil over medium heat. Add the beef shanks; cook until well browned. Pour off the excess fat. Add the leek, ginger, cinnamon, star anise, garlic and lemongrass. Stir and cook until aromatic, 2 or 3 minutes. Add the water, cilantro and peppercorns. Bring to a boil; reduce the heat to low. Skim the foam from the top. Simmer gently, uncovered, for 3 hours. Skim stock, as necessary. Add a little more hot water, only if necessary, to keep the stock level just above the ingredients.

Use a large slotted spoon to remove and discard the bones. Pour the stock through a strainer into a large bowl. Press ingredients to extract the liquid.

Quickly cool to room temperature, uncovered. Refrigerate for up to 3 days. Before using, scrape off the top layer of fat. Bring to a boil and season to taste. The stock can be frozen; boil briefly after thawing in the refrigerator.

Enriched Beef Consommé

Canned beef consommé can be quickly enriched and will add a good hearty flavor to beef and vegetable fondues. Sip the flavorful, leftover broth in small teacups. This recipe can also be made with low-sodium canned beef broth.

Makes about 2 quarts

3 (10½-ounce) cans beef consommé or beef broth

4 cups water

1½ cups dry red wine or white wine

1 medium onion, coarsely chopped

1 large garlic clove, mashed

1 rib celery, cut in 1-inch pieces

½ carrot, cut in pieces

1 bay leaf

2 sprigs parsley

2 sprigs thyme or ½ teaspoon dried

2 cloves

¼ teaspoon coarsely ground black pepper

1 tablespoon tomato paste

Put all the ingredients into a 2-quart saucepan; bring to a boil. Reduce the heat to the lowest setting and simmer for 15 minutes. Pour the consommé through a strainer into a large bowl. Use at once or quickly cool to room temperature and refrigerate for several hours before using. Season to taste.

COOK'S NOTES

Bouillon cubes Their flavor cannot compare in flavor with a rich homemade stock, but if you are in a pinch for time, try Knorr's bouillon cubes. They were recommended by Swiss-German friends, who use them successfully when lacking time to make a stock for fondue. I tried the beef bouillon and it has a pleasant, meaty taste that keeps getting better as it simmers in the pot. Prepare the broth a couple of hours ahead then strain off the layer of fat that congeals on top. Blend each bouillon cube into 2 cups boiling water then stir until dissolved. The broth will be slightly salty and can be diluted further, if desired. This brand of bouillon cubes is available in beef, chicken, vegetarian vegetable, ham and fish flavors.

Court Bouillon

Court bouillon means, "short broth" in French. It isn't a stock but a vegetable-enriched liquid that is good for poaching fish and seafood. It can be successfully used as a fondue broth. Other ingredients that will add enrichment to a court bouillon include fennel stems, shallots, the white parts of a leek, mushrooms, lemon slices and a pat of butter. When you plan to make shrimp fondue in a court bouillon, add the shrimp shells to the broth and simmer 10 minutes to enrich the flavor.

Makes about 1½ quarts

1½ quarts water

2 cups dry white wine

1 large onion, chopped

2 ribs celery, chopped

2 carrots, chopped

3 parsley sprigs

2 or 3 sprigs fresh thyme

1 bay leaf

½ teaspoon black peppercorns

Put all the ingredients into a large saucepan. Bring to a boil; reduce the heat and barely simmer for 30 minutes. Remove from the heat and let the vegetables cool in the broth for up to 2 hours. Strain, season and use at once or refrigerate until needed.

FROM MY RECIPE BOX

Quick Clam Broth Make a quick clam broth by simmering 4 cups bottled clam juice with 3 cups water, 2 cups dry white wine, 1 large, thinly sliced, peeled onion, 1 chopped rib celery, 2 sprigs parsley, 2 sprigs thyme and ½ teaspoon black peppercorns for 30 minutes on low heat. Dilute the broth slightly if it is too salty. Strain and use immediately or refrigerate overnight. This amount makes about 1½ quarts.

Fish Stock

A specialty fish market is a good place to begin your search for fish bones and fish heads for stock. Select bones from mild, lean fish like flounder, red snapper, porgy, cod, sole or whiting. Avoid stronger, high-fat fish with a distinctive flavor like mackerel, tuna and salmon. Don't skip the initial step of carefully rinsing the bones to remove blood, scales and other impurities. If the fish bones are well rinsed, the stock will not become murky.

Makes about 6 cups

2 pounds fresh fish bones and trimmings

2 tablespoons butter

1 large onion, thinly sliced

2 cloves garlic, smashed

6 cups water

1 cup dry white vermouth

1 tomato, chopped

1 carrot, chopped

1 bay leaf

1 rib celery with leaves, chopped

2 sprigs fresh thyme

6 to 8 peppercorns

4 sprigs parsley

Salt, to taste

Rinse the fish bones thoroughly in cool water several times until the water is clear. In a large saucepan, melt the butter over medium heat. Add the onion and garlic. Sauté gently until vegetables are slightly softened, 1 to 2 minutes. Do not brown. Add the fish bones and trimmings. Cook, stirring, over low heat for about 5 minutes. Add the water and all the remaining ingredients except parsley and salt. Bring to a boil; reduce the heat to low and simmer for 20 minutes. Add the parsley and simmer for 5 minutes more.

Pour the broth through a fine strainer into a large bowl. Season with salt. Use at once or cool to room temperature and refrigerate overnight.

Asian Chicken Stock

The ingredients and degree of richness in chicken stocks can vary throughout Asia, but this stock can be used in any Asian-influenced fondue or hot pot recipe in this book. The delicate ginger-flavored stock is delicious when enriched further with poultry, seafood and vegetables. Asian cooks prefer light, clear stocks for everyday use. Many Japanese and Chinese cooks will blanch the chicken quickly in boiling water to remove impurities before using it to make stock.

Makes about 3½ quarts

About 4 pounds chicken parts (backs, wings, thighs and legs), cut in smaller pieces

4 quarts cold water

4 green onions, cut in pieces

4 (2 × ¼-inch) slices fresh ginger, mashed

Rinse the chicken parts under cool water; drain well. Place into a stockpot with the water, green onions and ginger. Bring to a boil; reduce the heat to the lowest setting. Skim the foam from the top. Gently simmer, uncovered, for 2 hours. Add a little hot water, if needed, to keep the stock level just above the ingredients. Pour stock through a strainer into a large bowl. Press ingredients to extract the liquid.

Quickly cool the stock to room temperature, uncovered. Refrigerate for up to 3 days. Before using, scrape off the top layer of fat. Bring to a boil and season to taste. The stock can be frozen; boil briefly after thawing in the refrigerator.

Quick Asian Chicken Broth

If you need a quick, tasty Asian broth in a hurry, you can make this recipe in less than an hour. To make mugs of savory hot broth for sipping, season the broth with a few drops of light soy sauce and saké or dry white wine. Add salt to taste and a garnish of finely minced green onion. Add a small amount of cooked rice for a more substantial broth.

Makes about 2 quarts

3 (14½-ounce) cans low-sodium chicken broth

3 cups water

¾ to 1 pound chicken wings or backs, cut into pieces, or drumettes

2 (2 × ¼-inch) slices fresh ginger, smashed

2 green onions, chopped

Pour the broth and water into a 4-quart saucepan. Rinse the chicken parts under cool water; drain well. Add the chicken, ginger and green onion to the saucepan. Bring to a boil; reduce heat to low. Remove any foam from top. Gently simmer, uncovered, 30 minutes.

Pour broth through a strainer into a large bowl. Press ingredients to extract stock. Broth can be used at once. Or, quickly cool to room temperature, uncovered. Refrigerate up to 3 days. Before using, scrape off the top layer of fat. Bring to a boil and season to taste. Broth can be frozen. Boil briefly after thawing.

VARIATION

Southeast Asian Chicken Broth Prepare 1 recipe Quick Asian Chicken Broth, as directed. Include the rinsed, cut-up stems from 1 bunch cilantro, the tender inner portion of 1 (14-inch) piece lemongrass, chopped, or strips of zest from 1 medium lemon and 3 pairs or 6 fragrant kaffir lime leaves or strips of peel from 1 lime, and 1 small, hot red chili with the seeds removed.

Thai Coconut Broth with Lemongrass

The flavor and aroma of this fragrant coconut milk broth is almost intoxicating when simmered in a hot pot with chicken, seafood, pork and beef. After a fondue meal, serve the rich herbal broth in small bowls with cooked rice noodles as a soup course.

Makes about 5 cups

3 cups Asian Chicken Stock (page 182) or Quick Asian Chicken Broth (page 183)

Tender inner portion of 1 (14-inch) piece lemongrass, chopped, or strips of zest from 1 medium lemon

4 pairs or 8 kaffir lime leaves, torn, or strips of zest from 1 lime

1 slice fresh ginger, mashed

1 (13.5-ounce) can unsweetened, light coconut milk

2 tablespoons light brown sugar

2 to 3 tablespoons fresh lime or lemon juice

2 tablespoons Thai fish sauce (nam pla)

1 to 3 teaspoons Asian hot chili paste, or to taste

Place the chicken stock in a medium saucepan. Add the lemongrass, fragrant lime leaves and ginger. Simmer on medium-low heat about 10 minutes. Stir in coconut milk, brown sugar, lime juice, fish sauce and chili paste, to taste. Simmer over low heat for 5 minutes.

Strain the broth and use in hot pot recipes, as desired. If the broth is not to be used at once, you can cool and refrigerate it with all the seasonings; strain and use within 2 days. The flavor will be greatly enhanced.

Dashi/Japanese Soup Stock

Ichiban dashi is Japan's "number one" soup stock. The finest quality stock is reserved for making *suimono*, a clear, elegant consommé. Well-made *suimono* is the hallmark of a good chef. Dashi is used for *miso shiru*, a nutritious soup that is thickened naturally with miso paste. Dashi is made from dried bonito and dried kelp or konbu. Other shellfish and fish such as dried baby sardines are used for stock, as well.

Makes 6 cups

2 (5 × 4-inch) pieces dashi konbu, lightly wiped

2 quarts water, preferably bottled spring water

1 cup thin bonito shavings (*katsuobushi* or *hana katsuo*)

With scissors, slash the konbu 2 or 3 times but do not cut through. Place in a 3- or 3½-quart saucepan with the water. Heat over low heat, until the water slowly comes to the simmering point, 8 to 10 minutes. Remove the konbu just as the water begins to simmer around the edges. With chopsticks, stir in the bonito shavings; remove the pan from the heat. After 2 or 3 minutes, the shavings will begin sinking to the bottom.

Strain the stock through a fine mesh sieve into a large bowl. For a clear stock, pour through a mesh strainer lined with a large, dampened coffee filter or 4 dampened layers of cheesecloth. Stock is best if used at once or can be refrigerated for up to 3 days; freeze for longer storage.

VARIATIONS

Niban Dashi After you have made Dashi, immediately use the leftover fish shavings and kelp to make a second-quality, weaker stock; simmer on low heat with 7 cups of water for 8 to 10 minutes. Strain and use at once, refrigerate or freeze. Niban Dashi is good for cooking vegetables, hot pots, miso soups and simmered dishes.

Mushroom Dashi Soak konbu in the water with 3 or 4 dried shiitaki mushrooms for 3 hours or to the preferred strength. Omit the bonito shavings. Heat stock just to the simmering point and strain, as directed. The mushrooms can be sliced and added to the soup or one-pot dishes. For additional flavor, simmer the stock with vegetable pieces: sliced carrots, chopped cabbage, sliced green onion, leeks or fresh ginger. Serve as a clear broth or add miso paste if desired.

Kelp Stock For a subtle-tasting, quick sea vegetable stock, soak the konbu in the water for 15 minutes or longer for a stronger flavor. Heat and strain, as directed. Use as desired.

Instant Dashi Instant Dashi soup stock can be made with granular *hondashi*, *katsuo dashi* liquid concentrate or powdered *dashi-no-moto*. Use about ¼ teaspoon *hondashi* to 1 cup boiling water. Use ½ teaspoon *katsuo dashi* to 1 cup boiling water. Add 1 envelope *dashi-no-moto* powder to 4 cups boiling water; simmer for 2 minutes. Use at once.

Unlike most instant products in the West, these have a pleasant taste and can be used for miso soup or other dishes. In Okinawa, I watched chefs cautiously sprinkle *dashi-no-moto* into Chinese-style stir-fry dishes. Instant Dashi does not have the refined, delicate taste of homemade stock, but it blends in well with the other ingredients and is convenient to use in a pinch.

Suimono To make *suimono*, heat 4 cups Dashi with 2 teaspoons light soy sauce and about 1 teaspoon salt. Into each soup bowl place a protein garnish such as a cooked, cleaned shrimp or small cooked clam in a shell. Add a vegetable garnish; perhaps a small mushroom, carrot flower, cucumber ring or tender slice of okra. Add an appropriate seasonal garnish; in the spring you might add a strip of lemon zest, thin green onion rings or a tiny herb sprig. Light-colored soups equate with elegance; darker soups are more country-style.

Cook's Note Leftover konbu from stock can be wrapped tightly and refrigerated and added to the rice pot or to simmered dishes for extra flavor. Cooks often roll up the soft konbu and tie it several times with soaked kampyo, a gourd string. The konbu is cut in short sections; each tied securely with gourd string. Add to long-simmering stews like Oden (page 91) or simmer in seasoned dashi until tender then serve as a side.

Hearty Miso Soup/Miso Shiru

Japan's favorite breakfast soup is a nutritional powerhouse. Miso soup is made with miso paste, a richly flavored, fermented soybean paste high in protein, vitamins and minerals. It is often served at every meal of the day. Miso is classified into three groups: mild *komé miso* fermented with rice, reddish *mugi-miso* fermented with barley and dark, rich *mamé miso* made from pure soybeans. There are many varieties within these groups. Select one type for this soup, or blend 2 or 3 for a more delicious, complex flavor. If sodium is a problem, try the low-sodium miso pastes. *Tatsoi*, a member of the kale family, is a tiny Asian green with a big peppery-lemon taste. You can substitute baby spinach leaves or *wakamé*, a naturally sweet, calcium-rich sea vegetable. Its dried form expands several times its size when re-hydrated. In Japan, miso soup is served in small lacquer bowls. Besides keeping the soup hot, the accompanying lid heightens the anticipation of discovering the aroma and flavors hidden within.

Makes 6 servings

> **5 cups Dashi (page 184) or Quick Asian Chicken Broth (page 183)**
>
> **1 block silken tofu, cut in 1/2-inch cubes**
>
> **2 tablespoons salty, red miso paste (*aka miso*)**
>
> **3 tablespoons mellow white Hawaiian miso paste or other mild white or yellow miso paste**
>
> **1 cup *tatsoi or* baby spinach**
>
> **2 pencil-thin green onions, cut into paper-thin rings (mostly the green part)**

Prepare the Dashi. Divide the tofu cubes among 6 Japanese soup bowls or other small bowls. Slice green onions; set aside. In a small bowl, whisk the miso pastes with about 1/2 cup of the Dashi until smooth. Pour the remaining Dashi into a large saucepan and place over medium-high heat. When the stock is hot, whisk in the dissolved miso pastes until smooth. Heat the soup just to the simmering point; do not allow it to boil. Stir in tatsoi. Use a 1/2 cup ladle to pour hot soup over the tofu in the bowls. Sprinkle each serving with a little of the green onions. Top with the lids. Serve at once.

Setsuko's Kyoto-Style Miso Substitute 6 to 8 tablespoons *saikyo miso* (sweet white miso from Kyoto) for the red and white miso pastes in the recipe. Add 1 to 2 tablespoons mirin to the soup. Omit the *tatsoi* and add the green onions and pieces of *mochi* grilled on both sides until puffed and lightly browned. Stir about $^1/_2$ teaspoon prepared dried mustard into each serving.

Mushroom and Fried Tofu Chowder Heat 1 tablespoon light olive oil in a 2-quart saucepan over medium-high heat. Sauté 2 thinly sliced shallots for 1 minute. Add 4 sliced, fresh medium shiitaki mushroom caps. Sauté for 2 to 3 minutes until soft. Add 5 cups Dashi; simmer for 2 to 3 minutes. Broth can be thickened with 1 scant tablespoon potato starch or cornstarch mixed with 2 tablespoons Dashi if desired. Add 1 cup 1-inch squares Napa cabbage and 1 recipe Fried Tofu Wedges (page 67), cut into bite-size pieces. Reduce the heat; whisk in $^1/_3$ cup reddish, seasoned miso paste (*dashi iri miso*), or other miso paste. Add 2 sliced green onions. Do not boil; serve hot. Add a pinch of Seven-Spice Powder (page 149) to each serving. Makes 4 or 5 servings.

Mix-and-Match Soups A variety of garnishes can enrich a pot of basic miso soup. For each pot, select a cooked protein garnish, 1 or 2 vegetable garnishes and a seasoning. For starters, pick from: shrimp, salmon cubes, crabmeat, lobster, scallops, littleneck clams, slices of fish cake, chicken, baby spinach leaves, cubes of cooked taro or new potato, simmered shreds of gobo, cubes of cooked squash (winter or summer), sliced mushrooms, fresh herbs, cooked noodles, cooked cubes of carrot or daikon radish, fried cubes of tofu, shredded shiso leaves, fresh herbs, prepared mustard or strips of lemon.

Dessert Fondues

Food fads may come and go but dessert fondues will always be synonymous with celebration! They are a wonderful conversational centerpiece and the "life of the party." When families and friends participate in the dipping process, the instant fun and laughter brings lots of big smiles from the kids. Besides tasting undeniably delicious, fondues are among the most convenient desserts to prepare. Many can be made in advance then rewarmed; others require only minutes of last minute assembly. Fondue is inherently rich, so always include a platter of fresh seasonal fruits for dipping. Cookies and cake dippers can be baked days in advance. In the rare instance you have leftovers, gently reheat the fondue in the microwave at 75 percent power in 20 to 30 second increments. Stir the fondue gently after each pause to check its progress.

CHOCOLATE FONDUE: A TASTE OF PLEASURE AND PASSION

Unlike the other courses of a meal, a good dessert should offer more than substance. It should create a sense of homey comfort, lend an air of rich indulgence and seduce with a touch of romance. Few desserts achieve this ideal as effortlessly as a pot of warm, luscious chocolate fondue. Swiss Chocolate Fondue is made with the famous Toblerone chocolate, which is enriched with nougat and almonds. The chocolate is subtly perfumed and melts smoothly in your mouth. Toblerone bars have a unique triangular contour that represents the Swiss Alps. This decadent fondue quickly captured America's heart during the '60s when it was first served in New York City. Soon after, the popularity of chocolate fondue spread to Switzerland and Germany.

Around 1520, Spanish explorer Hernando Cortez traveled to the New World and learned about cacao (chocolate) from the Aztecs. He carried the cacao beans to Spain, where the first chocolate processing plant was set up in 1580. Eventually, chocolate spread through Europe. It came to Switzerland late; the first factory opened around 1819. But the Swiss perfected chocolate technology, becoming a major producer of chocolate confectionery. We can thank them for many chocolate innovations, including the invention of milk chocolate. It seems appropriate that America should be the first to use Swiss chocolate in a fondue since chocolate's origin is firmly rooted in the New World's prehistory.

German Chocolate Fondue is the sweetest fondue of all and will please those who adore German chocolate cake. Double Chocolate Pudding Fondue falls into the category of pure comfort food and will delight your children as well as your own inner child! If you are looking for a more intense chocolate experience, try the light and airy Cinnamon Mocha Fondue made with bittersweet chocolate, hot coffee and marshmallows.

Fondue is perfect for holiday entertaining. For an open house or after a festive meal, serve the Belgian Chocolate Fondue with holiday dippers such as the Meringue Peppermint Sticks or cubes of fruitcake, stollen or panettone, a fruited, holiday yeast bread. Surprise a bride-to-be with a spring bridal shower and a centerpiece of White Chocolate and Mascarpone Fondue. Serve with Rose Meringues, dried apricot halves, plump strawberries and cubes of Almond Dipping Cake. Decorate the tray with scattered rose petals.

WHICH CHOCOLATES FOR FONDUE?

Establish your reputation as a fondue chef by using quality ingredients. European bittersweet chocolates offer some of the finest flavors and textures. Slightly less sweet, they can be interchanged with American semisweet chocolate. Quality bittersweet or dark chocolate has 60 to 70 percent or more cocoa solids (including cocoa butter) and enough sugar to enhance the taste. Quality milk chocolate is harder to find; it will contain about 40 percent cocoa solids, a milk product and additional sugar. Quality chocolates for fondue include Swiss Toblerone, Swiss Lindt, French Valrhona and Callebaut from Belgium. American Ghirardelli produces a range of quality chocolate bars; Hershey's produces popular dark and milk chocolate.

The quality rule also applies to white chocolate; stick with the best. White chocolate fondue will taste only as good as the white chocolate. In the United States, white chocolate isn't considered real chocolate because it contains no cacao solids, or what we call cacao liquor. Quality European white chocolate, made from cocoa butter, sugar, milk and flavorings, is sweet, rich and smooth. It is valued most for its contrasting color and novelty. White chocolate should be melted with extra care since it does not withstand heat well. Quality brands of white chocolate include Lindt, Tobler Narcisse, Callebaut, Valrhona or Suchard. Cocoa butter will be listed as the primary fat. Taste several to decide which you like best. Do not use confectionery coatings made with vegetable fat; the texture and flavor won't be the same.

Melting straight chocolate can be tricky; overheating or contamination by a single drop of water can cause it to seize and turn into a grainy lump. Milk chocolate and white chocolate burn even more rapidly over direct heat than semisweet or bittersweet chocolate. Fortunately, chocolate for fondue is melted in enough liquid to eliminate seizing and protect it from burning. Heat the liquid to a simmer then remove the pan from the heat and add the chopped chocolate to soften. No real cooking is needed but the mixture can be warmed, if necessary, by placing it back on a low burner and stirring for a few seconds. A heat diffuser can deflect too much heat from an electric or professional-style stove. Be aware that chocolate can retain its shape when melted in the microwave. Check by touching it with your finger or a spoon. If almost melted, allow the residual heat to finish the job. Microwave chocolate in 30-second intervals, checking after each time.

FONDUE FLAVORS AND FANTASIES

Which is your favorite fruit flavor: raspberry, orange, apricot or cherry? Part of the fun in making fondue is adding a final flavor note from a dazzling array of flavor accents. Stir in one or two tablespoons of your favorite liqueur; if you prefer abstinence, add a few drops of concentrated extract imitating the flavor of a fine liqueur. Other creative options include: French steam-distilled fruit and floral essences, spices, citrus zest, German flavor pastes, flavor syrups, concentrated fruit purees, pure flavor extracts and instant espresso powder. For the greatest flavor boost, use pure extracts; artificially flavored extracts taste sharp and can throw off the flavor of fine chocolate.

A fondue dessert can turn an ordinary meal into a memorable one. Hot Buttered Rum Fondue is an appropriate indulgence after a light meal. Follow a rich, extravagant meal or a seafood extravaganza with a refreshing finale like the sun-kissed Tropical Lime Fondue with Coconut Logs. People can't seem to get enough! The melt-in-your-mouth coconut meringues are light and delicious; I've included five tasty variations. Green Tea-ramisu is simply tea-licious! It is Asia's Zen-like contribution to the fondue/dipping genre. Not overly sweet, it is the perfect "pick-me-up" for afternoon tea or serves equally well as dessert after an Asian-style broth fondue or hot pot meal.

In Victorian Britain, small cheese-based savories were presented at the end of a meal as a digestive while the gentlemen finished off their wine before dessert. Cheese straws, Welsh Cheddar Rabbit (page 26) and Cheese Fritters were typical offerings. For the most part, the cheese tray supplanted the savory course and often appears as a dessert. If, on occasion, you would like to partake in this tradition and end the meal on a savory note, surprise your guests with a pot of the Creamy Brie and Pear Fondue.

FONDUE DIPPERS

Marshmallows

Graham crackers

Rolled cookie sticks

Animal cookies

Shortbread strips

Potato chips

Large pretzel sticks

Fruitcake squares

Coconut macaroons

Homemade candied lemon slices

Peanut butter cookies

Biscotti

Stollen

Panettone

Panforté

Crepes spread with ice cream, rolled and frozen, cut in 1½-inch pieces

Deep-fried tortilla wedges, dusted with sugar and cinnamon

SEASONAL FRUITS FOR FONDUE

Whatever the season, you will find a selection of fresh fruits and quality dried fruits for dunking into fondues and creamy dips. To make a dessert platter, select 2 or 3 fruits from each group; add other foods like cookies or cake cubes to round out your platter.

WINTER FRUIT PLATTER

Mandarin orange segments (clementine, tangerine, satsuma) blood oranges, Hachiya persimmon wedges, crisp apple and pear slices, black dates, kumquats, dried apricot halves, wedges of dried peaches and pears, homemade candied fruit peels, strips of crystallized ginger, pitted Medjool dates stuffed with almond paste flavored with orange flower water or rose water, plump pitted prunes stuffed with walnut pieces or almond paste, dried figs stuffed with toasted blanched almonds and 5-minute, oven-baked, sugared cranberries

---

SUMMER FRUIT PLATTER

Strawberries, sliced apricots, blueberries, sliced peaches, kiwi half-slices, raspberries, blackberries, sliced nectarines, cherries with stems, sliced red Cuban bananas, pineapple wedges, mango and summer melons

---

SPRING FRUIT PLATTER

Navel oranges, blood oranges, strawberries, white peaches, olallieberries and flame grapes

---

FALL FRUIT PLATTER

Sliced red-skinned Bartlett pears, sliced crisp apples (Granny Smith, Fuji, Gravenstein, Winesap, Red Delicious), quartered ripe figs, Concord grapes, Asian pears, lychee fruits, fresh dates, carambola (star fruit)

FROM MY RECIPE BOX

Cheese Fritters Recycle a large, leftover party Brie or Camembert to make cheese fritters. Shape the cold cheese into 1-inch balls, including a little topping such as nuts, chutney, minced mushrooms or sun-dried tomato mixture. Coat the cheese balls with beaten egg and fine bread crumbs; deep-fry in hot oil until crisp. Drain and serve with a dipping sauce.

Camper's Fondue

My husband, an avid hiker and camper in the Smoky Mountains, wanted an easy fondue to share with friends over the campfire at the end of the day. Two chocolate bars, marshmallows and hot coffee are all you need. Chocolate and marshmallows are easily packed; coffee is often a camp staple. Sometimes we use a "spirited" coffee from Pigeon Forge, made with Tennessee whiskey–infused coffee beans. Select a flavor-packed chocolate like the orange-filled bars recommended here. If you are partial to dark chocolate, add 2 (3- to 4-ounce) bittersweet chocolate bars or chocolate chips in place of two of the milk chocolate bars. The lovely orange flavor in the Swiss chocolate still comes shining through.

Makes 6 to 8 servings

> **1 cup hot strong coffee, orange-flavored or plain**
>
> **1 cup packed small marshmallows**
>
> **4 (3.5-ounce) bars Swiss milk chocolate with orange or raspberry filling, broken into pieces**

FOODS FOR DIPPING

> **Fresh fruits (bananas slices, crisp apple slices, orange segments)**
>
> **Brownies, cut in cubes**
>
> **Toasted marshmallows**
>
> **Cinnamon grahams**
>
> **Dried fruits (orange or lemon-flavored pitted prunes, apricots, pears, figs)**

Heat the coffee in a medium saucepan over the campfire or on a portable stove burner. Add the marshmallows; stir until almost melted. Add the chocolate pieces; stir until completely blended and smooth. Do not allow the fondue to become too hot. Dip from the pot or spoon into individual disposable bowls. Serve with Foods for Dipping. The recipe can be cut in half.

Mulled Apple Cider Fondue

When the pretty autumn leaves start falling and the harvest moon appears, it's time to stir up a pot of this spicy cider fondue. The tangy fondue conjures up memories of my Tennessee childhood and fall activities like apple-picking in the mountains and stirring apple butter in giant cauldrons over crackling wood fires. Try this fondue as a sauce over pumpkin pancakes, baked apples, poached pears or bread pudding. For a grown-up version, stir in 1 to 2 tablespoons of dark rum or apple brandy. Two tablespoons toasted, chopped pecans are a nice addition, as well.

Makes 6 servings

2 cups plus 2 tablespoons apple cider

1/2 cup sugar

1/2 cup corn syrup

1/4 teaspoon *each* ground ginger, cinnamon, nutmeg and allspice

1/4 teaspoon salt

2 tablespoons cornstarch

2 tablespoons unsalted butter

2 teaspoons fresh lemon juice

1/2 teaspoon pure vanilla extract

FOODS FOR DIPPING

Cubes of bread pudding (especially with apple, pumpkin, or cranberry)

Small profiteroles filled with butter pecan or rum raisin ice cream (miniature stuffed cream puffs)

Pull-apart bubble loaf of sweet bread

Apple chips

Cubes of quick bread (date, pumpkin, apple)

Fig Newtons (or other fruit-filled bars such as cranberry or apple)

Cubes of firm gingerbread

Sausage balls and waffle bites for brunch

Soft, chewy oatmeal cookies

Apple and pear wedges

Cubes of apple or vanilla pound cake

In a medium saucepan, whisk together the 2 cups apple cider, sugar, corn syrup, the spices and salt. Simmer over medium heat until the mixture is blended and the sugar is dissolved, 2 to 3 minutes. In a small bowl, blend the cornstarch with the 2 tablespoons apple cider. Slowly add to the cider mixture, and cook, whisking constantly, until thickened. Add the butter, lemon juice and vanilla; stir until the butter melts. Pour the hot fondue into a chocolate or cheese fondue pot. Place over a tea light to keep the fondue warm. If the fondue is too hot, let it cool slightly for dipping. Serve with some of the Foods for Dipping.

Hurry-up Chocolate Fondue

This is the easiest of all fondues, just the ticket when you are in a hurry! The entire family, especially the kids, will love this satiny-smooth fondue made with mildly sweet, dark chocolate candy bars. If just for grownups, stir in 2 or 3 tablespoons of your favorite liqueur. At room temperature, the fondue firms up into *ganache*; a rich chocolate frosting that can be used on the Cheesecake Brownie Bites (page 205), cupcakes or spread between cake layers. Chilled fondue (without the almonds) can be shaped into truffles and rolled in nuts, unsweetened Dutched cocoa or confectioners' sugar. Don't overlook the Chocolate S'Mores Fondue in the Variation for a nostalgic taste of a popular childhood treat.

Makes 6 to 8 servings

1 cup whipping cream

2 (7-ounce) bars Hershey's Special Dark, Mildly Sweet Chocolate, broken in small pieces

¼ cup finely chopped, toasted almonds (optional)

FOODS FOR DIPPING

Cheesecake Brownie Bites (page 205) or Peppermint Patty Cakes (page 205)

Meringue Peppermint Sticks (page 202)

Fresh fruits (strawberries and sliced bananas)

Small profiteroles filled with peanut butter ice cream or other flavor (miniature cream puffs)

Large potato chips, preferably unsalted

Heat the cream in a medium saucepan over medium-low heat until it begins to simmer. Remove from the heat and add the chocolate. After 2 or 3 minutes, blend the melted chocolate and cream until smooth. Stir in the almonds, if using. Pour the fondue into a warmed chocolate pot. Place over a tea light to keep the fondue warm. Serve at once with any of the Foods for Dipping.

VARIATION

Chocolate S'Mores Fondue Prepare Hurry-up Chocolate Fondue, substituting milk chocolate bars, if desired. Spread 9 full cracker sheets of cinnamon-flavored grahams with 1 (7-ounce) jar marshmallow creme; using 1 heaping tablespoon per sheet. Cover each cracker completely. Place on a baking sheet; run under a preheated broiler for 1 to 2 minutes, or until the marshmallow creme sets and turns light brown. Remove from oven. With a large sharp knife, cut each cracker into 4 strips. Serve at once with the warm fondue.

Marshmallow Tea Cakes (page 205) and Girl Scout cookies are also nice for dipping.

Cinnamon Mocha Fondue

Strong black coffee gives this very intense chocolate fondue a subtle mocha essence; marshmallow creme creates a soft, airy texture.

Makes 2½ cups; 4 or 5 servings

½ cup strong black coffee, hazelnut, pecan-flavored or plain

1 (7 ounce) jar marshmallow creme

3 (3- to 4-ounce) bars of quality bittersweet chocolate, such as Lindt or Toblerone, broken into small pieces

1 to 2 teaspoons fresh lemon juice, or to taste

⅛ teaspoon ground cinnamon

½ teaspoon pure vanilla extract

FOODS FOR DIPPING

Fresh fruits (strawberries, pineapple wedges and clementine segments)

Rolled cookie sticks

Toffee Meringue Puffs (page 202)

Biscotti

Heat the coffee in a medium saucepan over medium-low heat until it begins to simmer. Add the marshmallow creme; reduce the heat to low. Stir until the marshmallow creme has almost dissolved. Add the chocolate pieces to the marshmallow mixture; stir until smooth. Do not allow the mixture to become too hot. Blend in the lemon juice, cinnamon and vanilla. Pour into a warmed chocolate fondue pot. Place over a tea light to keep the fondue warm. Serve with some of the Foods for Dipping.

Green Tea-Ramisu

New green leaves. Cool moss. Soft, billowing clouds. This verdant, tea-flavored dipping cream offers the delicate aroma, subtle taste and visual appeal of all these soothing elements. Matcha is the powdered, jade-green tea served during the Japanese tea ceremony. Of the highest quality, this wholesome tea is super-packed with vitamin C; use it to flavor ice tea, ice cream, cookies, candy or sponge cake. To preserve freshness, store matcha in the freezer.

Green Tea-Ramisu has many uses: use as a filling for crepes, roulades or layer cakes, or put spoonfuls on sponge cake squares. To make a delectable Green Tea Mousse, reduce the cream to ¹/₂ cup; whip and fold into mixture. Pipe or spoon the mousse into small dishes.

Makes 6 servings

¹/₂ cup sugar

¹/₄ cup water

2 teaspoons fresh lemon juice

Tiny pinch salt

1 teaspoon matcha (Japanese powdered green tea) or pure almond or vanilla extract

¹/₂ cup mascarpone or 4 ounces cream cheese

1 (3-ounce) package cream cheese, softened

1 cup heavy cream

2 tablespoons Midori melon liqueur (optional)

FOODS FOR DIPPING

Fresh fruits (small wedges of ripe persimmon, honeydew, cantaloupe or Asian pear, kiwifruit slices, lychee fruits, clementine segments)

Italian pizzelles

French gaufrettes

Vanilla Moravian cookies

Almond Dipping Cake (page 204), cut into cubes

Rose Meringues (page 202)

Combine the sugar and water in a small saucepan. Bring the mixture to a boil. Reduce the heat and cook just until sugar dissolves, 1 minute. Cool slightly.

Measure ¹/₄ cup of the sugar-water mixture; pour into a small bowl. Whisk in the lemon juice, salt and green tea until blended. With a large spoon, blend the mascarpone and cream cheese in a medium bowl until smooth. Blend in the green-tea syrup, 1 tablespoon at a time. With an electric mixer, whip the cream until soft peaks form. Lightly fold into green-tea mixture with melon liqueur. For a sweeter flavor, add 1 to 2 tablespoons of the remaining sugar syrup.

Spoon the tea-ramisu into a scalloped melon half or pretty glass bowl. Place on a platter surrounded by fresh fruits and cookies for dipping. If desired, drizzle additional melon liqueur on top. Recipe can be doubled.

If powdered green tea is unavailable, substitute about $^1/_8$ teaspoon tropical banana essence, jasmine essence or nutty-tasting pandan leaf essence from Thailand. Equally nice are the sweet crème liqueurs, French flavor essences (try passion fruit or violet) or German flavor pastes that come in a variety of fruit flavors. Pure vanilla or almond extract can be used, as well. (See the Glossary, page 209 and Mail-Order Resources, page 225.)

Cinnamon Plum-Tea Dip

Serve this spicy plum dip with an assortment of skewered, mixed fresh fruits such as melon balls, strawberries, banana cubes, lychee fruits, flame grapes, pineapple cubes and papaya cubes. Thread 3 or 4 pieces on each bamboo skewer.

Makes 6 servings

1 tablespoon spiced-plum tea leaves or Raspberry Zinger tea

1 cup boiling water

$^1/_2$ cup sugar

1 pound ripe plums, unpeeled, pitted and quartered

Pinch salt

$^1/_8$ teaspoon ground cinnamon

$^1/_4$ cup good-quality Japanese plum wine

Place the tea in a small, heatproof bowl; cover with boiling water. Steep for 2 to 3 minutes. Strain the tea through a fine sieve into a medium saucepan. Add the sugar and plums. Bring the mixture to the boiling point; reduce heat to low. Simmer until plums are tender, 10 minutes. Strain the liquid into a medium bowl; reserve. Put the plum pulp into a food processor fitted with a steel blade; process until smooth. Scrape the pulp into the bowl of reserved liquid. Stir in the salt, cinnamon and plum wine. Cover and refrigerate for 2 hours or overnight. Serve with skewered fresh fruit for dipping.

Double-Chocolate Pudding Fondue

When chocolate pudding is on the menu, sometimes a little kid just can't wait! Those last warm bites in the pan are positively finger-dipping good! Indulge your pudding fantasies with this deep, dark, delicious chocolate fondue. Cocoa alone will provide a satisfying chocolate taste, but the bittersweet chocolate bar melted in at the end delivers a knockout punch of luxurious richness and intensified flavor.

Makes 6 servings

$^1/_3$ cup unsweetened cocoa powder

$^3/_4$ cup sugar

3 tablespoons cornstarch

$^1/_4$ teaspoon salt

$3^1/_2$ cups whole milk

2 large eggs

1 (4-ounce) bar top-quality bittersweet or semisweet chocolate, broken into small pieces

2 teaspoons pure vanilla extract

Bite-size or regular Oreo cookies

Cinnamon Crisps

Animal cookies

Fresh strawberries

Tiny clean fingers

In a medium bowl, whisk together the cocoa powder, $1/2$ cup of the sugar, cornstarch and salt. Whisk in $1/2$ cup milk until smooth; set aside. Beat the eggs slightly in a medium bowl.

Combine the remaining 3 cups milk and $1/4$ cup sugar in a heavy medium saucepan over medium heat. Heat until bubbles form around the edges of the pan. Slowly pour about half of the hot milk into the eggs, whisking vigorously. Pour the egg mixture back into the remaining hot milk. Cook 1 to 2 minutes, stirring constantly. Scrape the cocoa mixture into the milk. Cook, stirring, just until the mixture simmers and becomes thick.

Remove from the heat; add the chocolate pieces and stir until melted. Blend in the vanilla. Pour into a warmed chocolate fondue pot. Place over a tea light to keep the fondue warm. Or, divide mixture among 6 small bowls. Serve warm with Foods for Dipping.

VARIATION

Served chilled and top with lightly sweetened, whipped cream.

Cannoli Dipping Cream

Sweetness is the Italian flavor of passion and delight. This luscious cream reminds me of the filling for Sicilian cannoli, deep-fried pastry horns filled with sweetened ricotta cheese, orange peel, chopped chocolate and nuts. The microwave is a handy tool for melting small amounts of chocolate but watch it closely to prevent burning.

Makes 6 servings

1 (4-ounce) bar quality bittersweet chocolate, finely chopped (Tobler or Lindt)

1 cup whole milk ricotta cheese, drained in a lined strainer if too moist

8 ounces cream cheese

4 ounces fresh chèvre

1 cup confectioners' sugar

2 teaspoons grated orange zest

1 to 2 tablespoons orange liqueur, preferably Grand Marnier

1 cup heavy cream (2 cups whipped cream)

$1/3$ cup finely chopped hazelnuts or almonds, toasted (page 196)

Biscotti

Strawberries

Amaretti di Saronno

Anise or almond toast cookies

Almond Dipping Cake (page 204)

Savoiardi ladyfingers

Almond Meringue Puffs (page 202)

Hazelnut-Spice Dipping Cookies (page 206)

Sift the chopped chocolate to separate the pieces from the fine chocolate powder. Reserve both, separately.

With a large wooden spoon or hand mixer, cream the ricotta, cream cheese, chèvre, confectioners' sugar and orange zest until smooth. Blend in the liqueur.

In a medium mixing bowl, beat the cream until soft peaks form. Fold into the cheese mixture. By hand, fold in chocolate pieces and hazelnuts.

Transfer the mixture to an attractive glass bowl. Sprinkle reserved chocolate powder on top. Serve at once with any of the Foods for Dipping.

COOK'S NOTES

Toasting Nuts Toasting pecans, almonds, walnuts, pine nuts and hazelnuts intensifies their rich flavors, enabling you to use far less. Freshness is essential; store them in the freezer. Spread the nuts in a shallow baking dish or jelly-roll pan. Place in a 325F (165C) oven for 10 to 12 minutes, stirring 1 or 2 times, or until fragrant and lightly browned. Toast hazelnuts just until the papery skins begin to crack. Wrap small amounts of the warm hazelnuts in a clean, dry towel; rub firmly to remove most of the skins, which can taste bitter. Watch pine nuts carefully; they burn easily. Coconut can be toasted in a similar way but must be stirred often and watched carefully for even browning.

Swiss Chocolate Fondue

A savvy marketing ploy to promote Swiss products in the United States was the impetus for creating chocolate fondue. It was first served on July 4, 1964 by Chef Konrad Egli at New York's defunct Chalet Swiss restaurant. Here is my rendition of the classic dessert, using Toblerone, the original chocolate. I prefer to blend the bittersweet and milk chocolate bars for a taste that everyone loves. Almond liqueur enhances the chocolate's honey-almond nugget, made with choice California almonds. This fondue is so good you won't know whether to dip something into it or just start eating it with a spoon! Be sure and try the Belgian variation using Callebaut, another superb fondue chocolate.

Makes 4 or 5 servings

¾ cup heavy cream

2 (3.52-ounce) bars Toblerone Swiss Milk Chocolate with Honey and Almond Nougat, chopped

2 (3.52 ounce) bars Toblerone Swiss Bittersweet Chocolate with Honey and Almond Nougat, chopped

2 tablespoons almond liqueur, preferably amaretto, or Cognac

FOODS FOR DIPPING:

Fresh fruits (strawberries, blueberries, clementine segments, pineapple wedges)

Coconut Logs (page 201)

Almond Dipping Cake (page 204), cut into cubes

Small profiteroles filled with ice cream or pastry cream (miniature cream puffs)

Almond Meringue Puffs (page 202) or other variation

Heat the cream in a medium saucepan over medium-low heat until it begins to simmer. Remove the pan from the heat and add the chocolate. Let stand for 3 to 4 minutes; stir melted chocolate and cream until smooth and blend in the almond liqueur. Pour the fondue into a warm chocolate fondue pot. Place over a tea light to keep the fondue warm. Serve at once with any of the Foods for Dipping.

VARIATION

Belgian Chocolate Fondue Omit the Swiss chocolates; substitute 12 ounces of the bitter-sweet Belgian chocolate, Callebaut, chopped. Stir in 1 to 2 tablespoons of liqueur, if desired (Cognac, Kahlúa, Grand Marnier or Canton Ginger liqueur).

Camembert with Sour Cherries and Almonds

A small wheel of Camembert, decorated with glazed, dried red cherries and sliced almonds, resembles a small, fancy jewel box. Serve this when you want a bite of something special for dessert, but nothing too complicated. Spread the warm cheese on water crackers or sliced French bread.

Makes 3 to 4 small servings

2 tablespoons dried sour cherries or dried cranberries

3 tablespoons kirsch or amaretto

1 (8-ounce) wheel ripe Camembert, chilled

1/3 cup sliced almonds, lightly toasted (see page 196)

2 or 3 tablespoons strained, warmed cherry preserves

Crackers, to serve

Put the cherries and 2 tablespoons of the kirsch in a small bowl. Cover tightly; set aside to soak for 6 hours or overnight.

Preheat oven to 350F (175C). Use a small knife to scrape off the bloomy white rind from the top of the cheese. Or, to remove, use a small knife to outline a circle, 1/2 inch from the edge. Trim directly under the circle. Lift off; remove any cheese from the lid and spread back on the wheel. Discard the top. Brush the top and sides of the cheese with the remaining 1 tablespoon kirsch.

Place the soaked cherries in a 2 1/2-inch circle in the center of the cheese. Arrange the almond slices around the cherries. Place the cheese on a baking sheet lined with foil. Bake for 4 to 5 minutes, or until the cheese is soft and warm. Brush with the preserves. Place on a serving plate; surround with crackers. Serve at once. (If made 1 day ahead, leave off the almonds; wrap and refrigerate. Remove from refrigerator 1 hour before heating; add almonds.)

VARIATION

Camembert with Plums Trim cheese as directed. Brush with plum wine. Cut 1 firm, ripe red plum in 1/4-inch slices. Overlap slices around the top of the cheese. Brush with warm plum preserves or Raspberry Coulis (page 199). Bake as directed.

Creamy Brie and Pear Fondue

In Normandy, pear and apple blossoms are a lovely sight in the springtime. Local products include pear and apple ciders, Calvados (apple brandy) and Camembert cheese. Camembert cheeses are often soaked in the cider and apple brandy. This smooth fondue has a lovely, buttery flavor and can be served as an indulgent cheese course or novel dessert. Swedish Pear Sparkler is a bubbly pear and apple beverage with a fresh, crisp taste. It is available in specialty food stores.

Makes 6 to 8 servings

1 cup Swedish Pear Sparkler (sparkling pear-apple beverage) or perry (pear cider)

1 pound Camembert cheese, chilled, rind trimmed, cut into cubes (about 2 cups)

8 ounces fontina or Emmentaler cheese, shredded (about 2½ cups)

1 slightly rounded tablespoon cornstarch

2 to 3 tablespoons pear liqueur such as William's (Poire William), Cognac or pear apple beverage, as desired

FOODS FOR DIPPING

Crusty French bread slices

Fresh fruits (crisp pear or apple slices)

Heat the pear-apple beverage in a heavy medium saucepan over medium heat. Add the cheeses in 3 or 4 handfuls. Stir gently after each addition until the cheese melts. In a small bowl, blend the cornstarch with 1 tablespoon of the pear liqueur; stir into the fondue. Cook, stirring, until the fondue bubbles gently, becoming smooth and well-blended, 2 to 3 minutes. Stir in remaining pear liqueur, as desired. Pour into a warmed cheese fondue pot. Place over a lighted burner adjusted to keep the fondue barely bubbling. Serve with any of the Foods for Dipping.

VARIATION

Creamy Brie and Apple Fondue Prepare fondue as directed except omit Swedish Pear Sparkler and substitute sparkling apple juice or apple cider. Omit pear liqueur and substitute an apple brandy such as Calvados.

German Chocolate Fondue

Are you a fan of German chocolate cake? If so, this fondue is for you! Dip bite-size pieces of homemade chocolate angel food cake or chocolate pound cake. Plump, juicy strawberries add a delightful taste contrast and help cut the overall sweetness. Double-dipping is permitted here; dunk the cake and fruits into the chocolate fondue then into the toasted coconut and pecan mixture for an over-the-top finish.

Makes 4 servings

¾ cup coconut

¾ cup finely chopped pecans

1 cup whipping cream

3 (4-ounce) packages German Sweet Chocolate bars, broken into pieces

1 tablespoon orange-flavored liqueur, such as Grand Marnier

1½ teaspoons grated fresh orange peel

FOODS FOR DIPPING

Chocolate angel food cake or white angel food cake

Chocolate pound cake, preferably homemade, cut into bite-size pieces

Fresh fruits (strawberries and pineapple wedges)

Coconut Logs (page 201)

Preheat the oven to 350F (175C). Combine the coconut and pecans; spread over a small baking sheet. Bake for 3 minutes then stir the mixture.

Bake for 2 minutes more or until the coconut is golden. Remove from the oven; cool completely. Divide among 4 small serving bowls.

Heat the cream in a medium saucepan over medium-low heat until it begins to simmer. Remove the pan from the heat and add chocolate. Let stand for 3 to 4 minutes; stir melted chocolate and cream until smooth then blend in the orange liqueur. Pour the fondue into a warm chocolate fondue pot. Place over a tea light to keep the fondue warm. Serve with the bowls of coconut mixture and any other Foods for Dipping.

FROM MY RECIPE BOX

Yin-and-Yang Fondue To create a Yin and Yang Fondue, place a foil-covered cardboard divider in the middle of a chocolate fondue pot. Pour dark chocolate fondue on one side and white chocolate fondue on the other side. Lift out the divider, swirling slightly as it is removed.

A Box of Chocolate Fondues A fondue tastes like a piece of candy from a box of fancy chocolates when combined with sauces and other fondues.

Turtle Fondue Pour 1 recipe warm Swiss Chocolate Fondue (page 196) into a chocolate fondue pot; swirl in 1/2 cup Hot Buttered Rum Fondue (page 203), at room temperature. Do not blend. Dip broken pieces of pretzel rods into the fondue then into finely chopped toasted pecans.

Chocolate Raspberry Bon Bon Fondue Pour warm Swiss Chocolate Fondue (page 196) into a chocolate fondue pot; swirl in 3 or 4 tablespoons Raspberry Cabernet Sauce (page 156) or Raspberry Coulis (page 199).

White-Chocolate and Lemon-Cream Fondue Pour 1 recipe warm White-Chocolate and Mascarpone Fondue (page 201) into a chocolate fondue pot; swirl in about 1/4 cup Luscious Lemon Fondue (page 200) or homemade lemon curd.

White-Chocolate and Lime-Cream Fondue Pour 1 recipe warm White Chocolate and Mascarpone Fondue (page 201) into a chocolate fondue pot; swirl in about 1/4 cup Tropical Lime Fondue (page 200) or homemade lime curd.

Tennessee Candy Bar Fondue Pour 1 recipe slightly warm Hot Buttered Rum Fondue (page 203) into a chocolate fondue pot; swirl in chopped Goo Goo Clusters coated with dark chocolate. This fondue features the famous candy bar of the Grand Old Opry.

Raspberry Coulis

The simplest ingredients can come together to create a symphony of flavor. A sweet-sour balance of sugar and lemon juice intensifies the overall taste of this fruity sauce. Kirsch enhances the fruity taste; a pinch of salt wakes up the flavor. Stir 2 or 3 spoonfuls of Raspberry Coulis into your favorite fondue or dessert dip or use as a dipping sauce.

Makes about 1 cup

1 (10-ounce) package frozen raspberries in syrup, thawed

1 tablespoon sugar

1 tablespoon fresh lemon juice

Pinch salt

1 tablespoon kirsch (optional)

Put the raspberries into a food processor fitted with the steel blade. Puree until smooth. With a spatula, push the puree through a fine strainer into a medium bowl. Wipe the seeds from the spatula; scrape the pulp from the bottom of the strainer into the bowl. Discard the seeds in the strainer. Stir the sugar, lemon juice, salt and kirsch, if using, into the puree. Store in the refrigerator in an airtight container for up to 3 days.

I will make an end to my dinner,
there's pippins and cheese to come.
—Shakespeare, *The Merry Wives of Windsor*

Tropical Lime Fondue

This tangy fondue captures the essence of fresh limes, one of Florida's most esteemed fruits. Lime juice is pale yellow; stir in 2 or 3 drops of green food coloring if you want the fondue to match the pretty green zest. Warm lime fondue is sensational spooned over slices of coconut pound cake, home-made angel food cake or ice cream.

Makes 6 servings

2 large egg yolks

2 cups water

¾ cup sugar

3 tablespoons cornstarch

¼ teaspoon salt

½ cup plus 1 tablespoon fresh lime juice (4 or 5 small limes)

1 rounded teaspoon grated lime zest

2 tablespoons unsalted butter

FOODS FOR DIPPING

Coconut Logs (page 201)

Coconut or plain shortbread

Almond Dipping Cake (page 204)

Thin chocolate wafer cookies

Beat the eggs slightly in a small bowl; set aside. In a nonreactive medium saucepan, combine the water, sugar, cornstarch and salt. Cook over medium-high heat, whisking constantly, until mixture thickens. Set off the heat briefly.

Blend the lime juice and zest into the egg yolks. To temper egg yolks, slowly pour 1 cup of the hot cornstarch mixture into the egg yolk mixture, beating constantly until blended. Whisk blended mixture back into the pan. Cook over medium-low heat, whisking, until mixture thickens a little more, 1 to 2 minutes. Remove from the heat. Stir in the butter, 1 tablespoon at a time. Pour the fondue through a mesh strainer into a warmed cheese fondue pot. Place over a lighted burner adjusted to keep the fondue slightly warm. Serve at once with the Foods for Dipping.

VARIATION

Luscious Lemon Fondue Substitute fresh lemon juice and lemon zest for the lime juice and lime zest.

The kitchen is a country in which there are always discoveries to be made.
—Grimad de la Reynierè, 1804

White-Chocolate and Mascarpone Fondue

Desserts made with white chocolate have undeniable cachét. I have toned down the inate sweetness of white-chocolate fondue with mascarpone, a luscious, ultrarich, ivory-colored cow's milk cream cheese of Italian origin. With a texture similar to sour cream, the mascarpone gives the fondue a sumptuous quality not unlike that of a fine pastry cream.

Makes 6 to 8 servings

⅔ cup mascarpone

½ cup whipping cream

4 (3-ounce) good-quality white-chocolate bars, such as Tobler Narcisse or Lindt, broken in small pieces

2 tablespoons Godiva liqueur or coffee-flavored liqueur

1 to 2 tablespoons Cognac or brandy

FOODS FOR DIPPING

Chilled chocolate brownie cubes

Fresh fruits (strawberries, fresh pitted cherries, plump raspberries)

Coconut Logs (page 201) or Rose Meringues (page 202)

Frozen cheesecake bites

Good-quality dried apricot halves

Stir the mascarpone in a small bowl; set aside. Pour the cream into a heavy, medium saucepan; place over low heat. When the cream begins to simmer, remove the pan from the heat and add the chocolate pieces. Let the chocolate soften in the hot cream for 5 minutes; stir until smooth.

With a whisk, blend in the mascarpone in 3 portions. Place over a low burner for about 30 sec-

onds to warm the fondue, stirring constantly. Pour into a warmed chocolate pot. Place over a tea light to keep the fondue warm. Serve with Foods for Dipping.

VARIATION

White-Chocolate and Apricot Fondue Blend in ¼ cup good-quality apricot preserves and 2 or 3 drops French apricot essence. (See Mail-Order Resources, page 225.)

Coconut Logs

With this recipe, you get six types of crisp meringue cookies to dip into fondue. Eggs are easier to separate when cold, but produce more volume at room temperature. Place the bowl of cold egg whites into a larger bowl of warm tap water to remove the chill. Be sure the mixing bowl is fat-free; a single drop will prevent egg whites from beating up properly. If available, use superfine sugar for lighter meringues. Coconut Logs are heavenly dipped into the Tropical Lime Fondue (page 200).

Makes about 5 dozen strips or 3 dozen drop cookies

3 large egg whites, at room temperature

¼ teaspoon cream of tartar

½ cup granulated sugar

¾ teaspoon coconut or pure almond extract

¼ cup confectioners' sugar

½ packed cup flaked, sweetened coconut

Preheat the oven to 200F (95C). Line 2 baking sheets with parchment paper or foil. With an electric mixer, beat the egg whites on medium speed until foamy. Add the cream of tartar and 1 tablespoon of the sugar. Beat until soft peaks begin to form. Add the coconut extract. Beat on high speed and sprinkle in sugar, 1 tablespoon at a time. Continue beating until stiff and glossy. Remove bowl from mixer.

Sift the confectioners' sugar over the egg whites and sprinkle in the coconut; with a whisk or spatula, fold in just to blend. Spoon the meringue into a large pastry bag fitted with a number 6, $1/2$-inch-diameter star or plain decorating tube. Pipe the meringue onto baking sheets in 3-inch logs or into tight "S" shapes, holding the tube just above the baking sheet. Or, drop rounded tablespoons of meringue onto baking sheets, $3/4$-inch apart.

Bake for 1 hour. If both baking sheets are in the oven at once, rotate after 45 minutes. Meringues should feel crisp and dry but not change color. Turn off the oven; leave meringues in the oven for 1 hour more. Cool; remove from parchment. Store in an airtight tin. Properly dried and stored, meringues stay crisp for weeks. Serve with fondues.

VARIATIONS

Meringue Peppermint Sticks Prepare the recipe as directed, except omit flaked coconut and coconut extract. Add $3/4$ teaspoon peppermint extract. With a small artist's brush, paint 6 red stripes of food color around the inside of a large pastry bag; fill with peppermint meringue mixture. Pipe into 3-inch sticks. Bake as directed.

Toffee Meringue Puffs Prepare the recipe as directed, except omit flaked coconut and coconut extract. Add 1 teaspoon pure vanilla extract. Fold

$3/4$ cup finely chopped milk chocolate–covered butter toffee candy with almonds (such as Skor candy) and $1/4$ cup gingersnap crumbs into beaten egg whites. Drop tablespoons of meringue onto prepared baking sheets. Bake as directed.

Cocoa-Cinnamon Meringue Logs Prepare the recipe as directed, except omit flaked coconut and coconut extract. Add 1 teaspoon pure vanilla extract. Sift a blend of 2 tablespoons unsweetened cocoa powder (preferably Dutch processed) and $1/2$ teaspoon ground cinnamon over the beaten egg whites; gently fold in. Pipe meringue into logs or "S" shapes or drop tablespoons onto prepared baking sheets. Bake as directed.

Almond Meringue Puffs Prepare the recipe as directed, except omit flaked coconut and coconut extract. Add $3/4$ teaspoon pure almond extract. Fold in $1/2$ cup finely chopped, toasted, blanched, sliced almonds. Drop tablespoons onto prepared baking sheets. Bake as directed.

Rose Meringues Prepare the recipe as directed, except omit flaked coconut and coconut extract. Add $1/8$ teaspoon rose essence or rose extract (20 drops) and a few drops of red food color to create a soft pink shade. If available, stir in 1 heaping tablespoon edible, crushed, dried rose petals. Pipe meringue into logs or "S" shapes or drop tablespoons onto prepared baking sheets. Bake as directed.

Meringue Sandwich Cookies Sandwich pairs of meringue cookies filled with chilled, spreadable chocolate fondue and dip into the Raspberry Cabernet Sauce (page 156) for a delectable treat. Or sandwich them with red berry jam then dust with plain or chocolate-flavored confectioners' sugar. Serve as soon as possible to enjoy the crisp texture.

Makeshift Pastry Bag Don't have a pastry bag? Substitute a sturdy, gallon-size, plastic freezer bag. With scissors, cut off a tiny corner then insert the large pastry tube. Fill the bag with meringue then close the top. Twist the top to grasp it securely then begin piping.

Hot Buttered-Rum Fondue

It's hard not to love the warm, rich flavor of butterscotch; a caramel sauce enriched with lots of butter, brown sugar and cream. I like to offset the sweetness by including tangy grilled fruits for dipping. Be aware that hot bubbling sugar can cause burns. Use the correct-size pot made from a sturdy material like enameled cast iron and don't taste the sauce until it cools down. For a special treat, serve a chocolate fondue on the side for a bit of legal double-dipping; finish with a final dip into chopped macadamia nuts or toffee crunch.

Makes 6 to 8 servings

4 tablespoons unsalted butter

1 packed cup light brown sugar

1/2 cup granulated sugar

2/3 cup corn syrup

1/3 cup water

1/2 teaspoon salt

1 cup heavy cream

1 teaspoon fresh lemon juice

1 teaspoon pure vanilla extract

1 tablespoon dark rum, preferably Meyers

FOODS FOR DIPPING

> **Fresh fruits (bites of grilled fresh pineapple and peaches, sliced sautéed bananas, tiny lady apples skewered on wooden sticks, crisp apple or pear slices)**
>
> **Bread pudding, cut in bite-size pieces**
>
> **Small profiteroles filled with ice cream or pastry cream (miniature cream puffs)**
>
> **Cocoa-Cinnamon Meringue Logs (page 202)**
>
> **Brioche sandwiches filled with chocolate spread and orange marmalade, sautéed in butter, cut in bite-size pieces**

Add the butter, sugars, corn syrup, water and salt to a heavy 3-quart saucepan over medium-high heat. Bring the mixture to a boil. Use a long wooden spoon to stir often to help dissolve the sugars. Cook until large bubbles form over the surface, 5 minutes.

Remove pan from the heat and slowly whisk in the cream. Mixture may bubble up; watch for splatters. Mixture will be thin but thickens as it cools. Cool for 10 minutes; stir in the lemon juice, vanilla and rum. Cool mixture to around 115F (45C). Pour into a warmed chocolate fondue pot. Place over a tea light to keep the fondue warm. Serve with Foods for Dipping. (Fondue can be made up to 1 week ahead; store in the refrigerator. Fondue can be warmed in the microwave.)

Drizzle Hot Buttered-Rum Fondue over homemade apple tarts, baked apples or pears, Häagen-Dazs Coconut Gelato or other signature ice cream blends, fresh popped popcorn, squares of gingerbread, prune cake or apple cake.

Hazelnut Fondue

Here is an easy, delicious fondue made with *gianduja*; a delicious Italian hazelnut spread. The type I use in this recipe is available in most supermarkets under the name of Nutella. Made with cocoa from the African coast and hazelnuts from Langa, Italy, the creamy spread melts beautifully into a rich, dark fondue. In Italy in the 1940s, this "Supercrema" *gianduja* was so popular, local food stores offered a service known as "the smearing." For five *lira*, children could bring in a slice of bread to be coated with the delicious spread.

Makes about 1 1/2 cups; 4 or 5 servings

1 (13-ounce) jar Nutella hazelnut spread with skim milk and cocoa

1/2 cup whipping cream

1 to 2 tablespoons hazelnut liqueur or other liqueur (optional)

FOODS FOR DIPPING

Fresh fruits (crisp apple slices and strawberries)

Fruit and nut bread, cut in cubes

Chocolate-cherry bread, cut in cubes

Banana bread, cut in cubes

Cocoa-Cinnamon Meringue Logs (page 202)

Pound cake, cut in cubes

Scrape the hazelnut spread from the jar into a small saucepan. Add the cream to the jar and shake hard to remove some of the remaining spread. Pour into the pan. Place the pan over the lowest heat and whisk constantly just until the mixture starts to become smooth. Do not overheat or simmer. Remove from the heat; stir in the hazelnut liqueur if using. Pour into a warmed chocolate pot. Place over a tea light to keep the fondue warm. Serve with Foods For Dipping.

Almond Dipping Cake

Cut this exquisite, moist pound cake into cubes for dunking into your favorite fondue. It is impossible to resist dipped into the Swiss-Chocolate Fondue (page 196). Spend a pleasurable afternoon with friends and a cup of tea. Serve slices of almond cake topped with the cloud-like Green Tea-ramisu (page 193) and slices of fresh honeydew melon. Or top with rose-flavored whipped cream and a handful of fresh raspberries.

Makes 1 loaf cake

1 cup soft-wheat flour, such as White Lily (see Mail-Order Resources, page 225)

1/4 teaspoon baking soda

1/4 teaspoon baking powder

1/4 teaspoon salt

1/2 cup almond paste, crumbled

1/2 cup unsalted butter, at room temperature

1 cup sugar

3 large eggs, at room temperature

1/2 cup sour cream

Preheat the oven to 325F (165C). Grease and flour a 9 × 5-inch nonstick loaf pan. Sift the flour, soda, baking powder and salt into a small bowl; set aside.

In a medium bowl, beat the almond paste and butter until smooth. Gradually beat in the sugar. Add the eggs, 1 at a time, beating well after each addition. Beat until the batter is thick and creamy, 1 minute more. Add half of the sour cream and half the flour mixture. Beat on medium-low speed until the flour mixture is incorporated. Add the remaining sour cream and flour mixture. Beat just until flour mixture disappears and batter is blended.

Spoon batter into prepared pan. Bake for 20 minutes; reduce heat to 300F (150C). Bake for 20 minutes, or until a wooden pick inserted in center comes out clean. Cool completely before removing from pan. Cake can be wrapped and refrigerated for up to 2 weeks. Cut into 1-inch squares for dipping into fondue.

Cheesecake Brownie Bites

Half brownie, half cheesecake and every bite moist, chocolate and delicious. Make the cakes a day in advance; they can be served chilled for dipping. Wrap well for freezing; thaw as needed. In the Variation, freshly baked Peppermint Patty Cakes have soft, creamy centers, which firm up as they cool. Either way, they taste heavenly dipped into rich chocolate fondue.

Makes 36 brownie bites

2 ounces unsweetened chocolate

1/2 cup (1 stick) unsalted butter, chilled

1 cup plus 1 rounded tablespoon sugar

1 teaspoon pure vanilla extract

2 large eggs

1/2 cup all-purpose flour

4 ounces mascarpone or cream cheese, at room temperature

1 teaspoon pure vanilla or almond extract

Preheat the oven to 350F (175C). Place the chocolate in a medium glass bowl; top with the butter. Microwave on high (100 percent power) for 1 minute. Butter will melt, softening the chocolate. Let stand for 1 or 2 minutes; stir to blend. If chocolate chunks remain, microwave for 10 to 20 seconds more; stir until smooth. (Butter and chocolate can also be melted in a small saucepan over low heat.)

With a large spoon, stir the 1 cup sugar and vanilla then the eggs, 1 at a time, into the chocolate mixture. Blend in the flour. For the filling, blend the mascarpone, 1 tablespoon sugar and vanilla in a small bowl until smooth; set aside.

Line 3 (12-cup) miniature muffin pans with small paper cups. Coat with vegetable spray. Put 1 teaspoon batter into the bottom of each paper cup. Top each with a scant teaspoonful cheese filling then add a final teaspoonful of chocolate batter on top. Smooth the tops. Bake for 10 minutes, or until brownie tops are rounded. Cool 10 minutes; remove from pans. When completely cool, tear off the paper cups.

VARIATION

Peppermint Patty Cakes Prepare batter as instructed; omit cheese filling. Unwrap 36, (1½-inch) foil-wrapped chocolate-covered Peppermint Patties. Place 1 tablespoon batter into each paper cup. Place 1 peppermint patty in each cup on top of the batter. Spoon remaining batter on the top. Bake about 10 minutes, or until the tops are puffed and peppermint cream begins to seep through. Cool for 10 minutes, remove from the pans and tear off the paper cups. For the best texture, serve within 2 or 3 hours. Makes 36

FROM MY RECIPE BOX

Marshmallow Tea Cakes On a baking sheet, place good-quality, wafer-thin chocolate, ginger, black walnut or lemon cookies such as Mrs. Hanes Moravian cookies. Top each cookie with a large, soft marshmallow. Place another cookie on top. Preheat the oven to 350F (175C). Bake the tea cakes 3 minutes or just until the marshmallows soften and begin to sag. Remove from the baking sheet; cool 3 minutes. Serve with the Chocolate S'Mores Fondue (page 192), or any fondue in this chapter.

Hazelnut-Spice Dipping Cookies

Crisp, dry Italian biscotti are the ultimate dipping cookies, designed to be dunked into a small glass of sweet red wine while eaten. You can dip biscotti into steaming hot cups of cappuccino, coffee, hot tea or milk, as well. These biscotti-like cookies are usually baked twice to create their unique, crisp, dry texture. To prevent them from becoming too hard, I prefer to dry the cookies in the oven after it is turned off for a delicate crispness. When cooled, the cookies can be drizzled with melted bittersweet chocolate.

Makes about 2¹/₂ dozen cookies

2 large eggs, plus 1 egg separated (3 eggs)

¹/₃ cup hazelnut oil or light olive oil

1¹/₂ cups sugar

Grated zest of 1 large orange

1 teaspoon ground cinnamon

¹/₂ teaspoon each ground cloves, nutmeg and ginger

1 tablespoon brandy, dark rum or coffee liqueur

2 teaspoons baking powder

2¹/₂ cups hazelnuts with skins removed, walnuts or whole almonds, lightly toasted (see Toasting Nuts, page 196)

3 cups all-purpose soft-wheat flour, lightly spooned into a measuring cup.

Preheat oven to 350F (175C). With a wooden spoon, beat 2 eggs plus 1 yolk with the oil and sugar in a large bowl. Stir in orange rind, spices, brandy, baking powder and nuts. Add flour; stir until dough forms.

Divide in half and place on a 17-inch × 11-inch oiled baking sheet. Shape dough into 2 thin loaves, 2-inches wide, 16-inches long. Loaves must be at least 2 inches apart. Brush lightly with egg white.

Bake 25 minutes; remove from the oven and cool 5 minutes. Turn off the oven. Carefully cut warm loaves into 1-inch-thick slices. Gently lift and place cookies on 2 baking sheets. Place in the oven to dry for 1 hour. The flavor tastes best after 24 hours. Cookies keep in an airtight tin 2 to 3 weeks.

VARIATIONS

Macadamia-Spice Dipping Cookies Substitute macadamia nuts and macadamia oil for the hazelnuts and hazelnut oil. Substitute 1 teaspoon 5-spice powder for the ground cinnamon, if desired.

Walnut-Spice Dipping Cookies Substitute walnut pieces and walnut oil for the hazelnuts and hazelnut oil.

FROM MY RECIPE BOX

Perfumed Oranges Serve this quick, refreshing dessert after a fondue or hot pot meal. Peel 10 naval oranges, trimming off the white pith. Cut in thin slices. Spread over the bottom of a large, shallow pan. In a small saucepan, combine $1/2$ cup fresh-squeezed, tangy orange juice, $1/2$ cup honey, $1/4$ teaspoon cinnamon and a tiny pinch salt. Warm over low heat, stirring constantly, until honey melts. Remove from the heat and stir in $1/4$ cup Cognac or brandy. Pour over orange slices. Cover with plastic wrap. Refrigerate at least 2 hours. Serve in shallow plates with spoonfuls of whipped cream flavored with a few drops of rose essence or a tablespoon of rosewater.

Jack-Be-Little Pumpkin Bowls

Use these adorable miniature pumpkin bowls as individual fondue containers. For a special harvest treat, fill them with Hot-Buttered-Rum Fondue (page 203). If you prefer a little chocolate with your pumpkin, fill them with your favorite chocolate fondue.

Jack-Be-Little miniature pumpkins or squash, (8 ounces or less), as needed

Preheat the oven to 350F (175C). With a metal cake tester or a fork, lightly pierce the top of each pumpkin several times. Place the pumpkins in a baking pan. Bake for 20 minutes, or just until the pumpkins are tender; do not overcook.

Cool slightly. Slice off the top third from each pumpkin to form a lid. Carefully scrape out and discard the seeds and strings from each pumpkin; pat dry. Do not remove too much pulp from the bottom to avoid tears and leaks. Fill the pumpkin

shells with warm fondue. Place lids on top of the filled pumpkins or prop them up on the sides. Pumpkin bowls can be made ahead, wrapped airtight and refrigerated. Remove from, refrigerator and let stand at room temperature for 1 hour before filling.

MENUS

Alfresco Lunch

White-Bean Fondue with Kasseri and Feta
(page 22)

Crostini (page 138) and Herb Croutons (page 137)

Cold platter with thinly sliced cured meats

Platter of crudités and marinated olives

Wine or beer

Perfumed Oranges (page 206)

Holiday Fireside Tea

Savory Camembert with Wild Mushrooms
(page 21)

Asparagus Toasts (page 142)

Swiss Chocolate Fondue (page 196)

Winter Fruit Platter (page 190)

Meringue Peppermint Sticks (page 202)

Hot tea

Fondue Shower for the Bride

Chocolate Raspberry Bon Bon Fondue
(page 199)

White-Chocolate and Mascarpone Fondue
(page 201)

Spring Fruit Platter (page 190)

Rose Meringues (page 202)

Almond Dipping Cake (page 204)

Champagne

End-of-Summer Patio Party

South Carolina Beaufort Stew (page 45)

Hot and Spicy Thai Coleslaw (page 128)

Crusty French bread

Iced Lemongrass Tea (page 143)

*Tropical Lime Fondue (page 200)
with Coconut Logs (page 201)*

Celebrate Cinco de Mayo

Cheese Scorpions and Bugs (page 30)

Border Melt (page 27)

Cowboy Flat Bread (page 138)

Pork Fondue With Guacamole Sauce (page 51)

Smoky Tomato Salsa (page 155)

Spicy Black Bean Sauce (page 154)

*Jicama strips and navel orange segments with lime
juice and chili powder*

*Vanilla ice cream topped with Hot-Buttered Rum
Fondue (page 203, made with Kahlúa)*

Fireworks and Asian Sizzle for the Fourth

Genghis Khan Fire-Grill (page 82)

Sesame-Peanut Pockets (page 140)

Iced Lemongrass Tea (page 143)

*Cinnamon Plum-Tea Dip (page 194) with skewered,
grilled fresh fruit bites*

Storybook Supper

*Welsh Cheddar Rabbit (page 26)
with accompaniments*

*Double-Chocolate Pudding Fondue
(page 194)*

Fresh sliced fruits

911 Supper

Steak Fondue Hoedown (page 59)

Horseradish Mashed Potatoes (page 114)

Cucumbers with Fresh Dill (page 123)

Hurry-up Chocolate Fondue (page 191)

Fresh fruit platter

Cheesecake Brownie Bites (page 205)

Eight Precious Friends Hot Pot Party

*Butterfly Crisps (page 124) with Tofu Dill Dip
(page 22)*

Eight Precious Hot Pot (page 84)

Sliced Marinated Lotus Root (page 74)

Plum Blossom Sherbet (page 118)

Hearts and Chopsticks: Valentine's Day

Edamamé Appetizer (page 94)

Obi-Wrapped Tuna Fondue (page 61)

Miyabizushi (page 122)

Kayoko's Spring-Rain Salad (page 132)

Green Tea-Ramisu (page 193)

CHEESES

Each sort of cheese reveals a pasture of a different green, under a different sky.

—Italo Calvino

Appenzeller Mature, part-skim cow's milk cheese from the Swiss Canton of Appenzell. In the Gruyère family, dates back seven-hundred years. Sharper than Gruyère, tangy Appenzeller is bathed in spirits, herbs and black pepper during the curing process. Available in Classic and Extra (aged), both wonderful accent cheeses for fondue.

Asiago (ah-zee-AH-go) Straw-colored, cow's milk cheese from the Veneto area of northern Italy. Fresh, semisoft Asiago is mild and sweet; use as a table cheese. Aged two years, Asiago has a sharp, intense flavor, excellent for grating and cooking. Italians refer to Asiago as the "poor man's Parmesan." It is a wonderful accent cheese for fondue. Imported and good quality domestic Asiago is available.

Baby Swiss cheese A creamy American cow's milk cheese with a sweeter, milder taste than Swiss Emmentaler. Unlike Swiss cheese, the cream is left in. It has a pale color and smaller holes. It's a smooth melter.

Beaufort Known since Roman times, this soft, luscious Gruyère is made from cow's milk in the Haute-Savoie region of France near Switzerland. Desirable, pale-yellow Beaufort d'Alpage is a rich summer cheese made high in the Alps. Huge wheels are toted down the mountain on mules. Beaufort has a slightly sweet, fruity taste. A superb melter for fondue and sandwiches, it is exquisite with ripe, red berries, apples, cider. Slice or cube for cooking. Substitute Swiss Gruyère or Italian fontina. Available in Specialty Cheese Stores (see page 227).

Bel Paese An Italian cow's milk cheese with a sweet flavor and buttery texture. The wrapper for the authentic cheese displays the map of Italy. Bel Paese is a good melting cheese and can be substituted for mozzarella.

Blue cheese (Bleu in French) Generic term for a variety of semi-soft cheeses in North America and Europe. Unpressed white cheese is inoculated with blue mold that spreads into the interior. Most blues have a sharp, tangy flavor and a crumbly texture. Blue cheese melts well and will add a piquant taste to fondue, salad dressings, dips and gratins. Minnesota Treasure Cave is the oldest commercially made blue in this country. British blues include Blue Wensleydale, Blue Cheshire,

Shropshire Blue and creamy Irish Cashel Blue. Three triple-cream blues with an extra-creamy texture and subtle taste are Danish Saga, Danish Blue Castello and German Cambozola. See Clemson Blue, Maytag Blue, Gorgonzola and Stilton.

Brick Soft-ripened, German-style cow's milk cheese that ranges from mild to moderately sharp. Also called *Bierkäse* or "beer cheese." Usually found in a yellow loaf brick, it is great for sandwiches, snacks and melted in fondue.

Brie French cow's milk cheese with 50 to 60 percent butterfat. Underripe Brie has a hard, chalky core and tastes bland; if cut, all ripening ends. Ripe, pasteurized Brie should be plump, creamy, glossy and bulge a bit. Overripe Brie oozes and has the pronounced smell and taste of ammonia. Pasteurized American Brie has a bloomy white rind from being sprayed with *Penicillum* spores; unpasteurized Brie in France has a reddish rind, indicating healthy bacterial activity. Eat or trim off the rind; true Brie lovers devour it like "icing on a cake." Brie melts beautifully in fondue. Not all Brie is created equal; look for Brie de Meaux imported by Rouzaire of France. French Coulommiers (koo-LOAM-yay), related to Brie and Camembert is also imported by Rouzaire. Quality, pasteurized French Brie is made by Vitelloise, Ermitage and Henri Hutin. Bresse and Reny Picot are French-owned American companies that produce good Brie. These brands are available in upscale markets and Specialty Cheese Stores (see page 227).

Brillat-Savarin Triple-crème cheese named after the French gastronome Brillat-Savarin. Enriched with hot cream to raise the butterfat content to 75 percent. Available in Specialty Cheese Stores (see page 227).

Caerphilly (caer-FILLY) First made circa 1830, this semi-soft, white cow's milk cheese is Wale's only surviving traditional cheese. Called the "miner's cheese" because it stays fresh underground and provides salt lost during hard labor. Crumbly and moist with a lemony twang, it tends to dry out quickly; wrap well and keep refrigerated. A classic for Welsh Rabbit and good with bread, fruit and chutney. Substitute English Cheddar, Double Gloucester or Cheshire. Available in Specialty Cheese Stores (see page 227).

Camembert Soft-ripened cow's milk cheese with a flavor and texture almost identical to Brie but with slightly less butterfat. A specialty of Normandy and one of France's best known cheeses. Ripe, domestic Camembert is covered with an edible white, bloomy rind. Like Brie, ripening takes place from the outside to the inside. As it ripens, the cheese becomes stronger and runnier. The aroma should be fresh with no trace of ammonia. Usually sold in eight-ounce rounds.

Cheddar Cow's milk cheese first produced in the sixteenth century in England. It is named after the famous Cheddar Gorge in the Somerset area. Created through a unique process called "cheddaring," or stacking and turning the curds to press out the whey. Cheddar is rindless and can be naturally white or dyed orange. Flavors range from mild and smooth to sharp and crumbly, depending on the age. It has about 45 to 50 percent butterfat. Cheddar can be made with pasteurized milk or raw milk. The United States requires raw-milk cheese be aged at least 60 days. An aged cheddar has the most flavor and adds the most flavor to fondue. Look for cheddar aged at least six months, a year is better. Outstanding aged domestic cheddar comes from Vermont and New York

State. New York cheddar is some of the longest-aged and tends to be more crumbly; Vermont cheddar is moister. Wisconsin produces excellent cheddar, most of it the milder type. Tillamook is an excellent raw milk cheddar from Oregon. Cheddar may be smoked or embellished with herbs, aromatics, fruit and spices. Canada produces excellent white cheddar. For a fine British cheese look for John and Ruth Kirkham's Farmhouse Cheddar from Beesley Farm in Lancashire in specialty stores (see page 227).

Cheshire (Chester) Cantaloupe-colored, cheddarlike cheese from rich, raw cow's milk. First made by the Celts; dates back to pre-Roman Britain. It was a favorite of Dr. Sammuel Johnson. Blue Cheshire is also available. It is mild when young; sharp when aged. Best eaten within three months of production. The distinctive, slightly salty, tangy flavor is said to come from salt springs running under pasturelands. Good for melted dishes, especially Welsh Rabbit. Look for the Cheshire made by the Appleby family at their Shropshire family dairy. Huntsman (Stilchester) is layered Cheshire and Stilton. Substitute Double Gloucester, Red Leicester, Lancashire or cheddar. Available in Specialty Cheese Stores (page 227).

Chèvre (SHEHV) Generic French term for goat cheese. Soft, unripened, mild, domestic fromage blanc, or "white cheese" is only days old. Use like cream cheese. (*Fromage frais* is the French counterpart.) Mild French Montrachet is shaped in logs; it may be wrapped in grape leaves or coated with ash. Spread it on bread or use for cooking. Chabis comes in five-ounce cylinders; it has more zing than fromage blanc. It is good for eating and cooking. Crottins are small and compact; they are good breaded and sautéed in oil. Grate when hard and dry. As goat cheese ages, it becomes firmer, saltier and sharper. Soften the taste with yogurt or cream cheese. The appearance of goat cheese can be illusory when heated; it doesn't spread like cow's milk cheese. The appearance stays basically the same yet the interior becomes meltingly soft and warm. Goat cheese is heat sensitive and can become grainy if overheated. It has fewer fat grams and cholesterol per ounce than regular cream cheese and it is higher in protein, calcium, phosphorus, vitamins A and B than cow's milk. It is a good substitute for people with a sensitivity to cow's milk. Excellent chèvre is made in America.

Clemson blue cheese Handmade from cow's milk, it has a unique, mild flavor. The texture is softer, creamier than other blues with less of a sharp bite. It is made on the campus of Clemson University in Clemson, South Carolina. One of America's tastiest blue cheeses, Clemson Blue Cheese is becoming the hottest blue cheese around; the producers can't keep up with the demand. Use in sauces, fondue, dips, salads, cheesecake and ice cream. Available from Clemson University (see page 167).

Cream cheese Soft, white, unripened, cow's milk cheese with around 35 percent fat. It is available in three-ounce or eight-ounce packages. Use in baking, dips, dressings and spreads.

Crowley cheese It is an unique Vermont cheese similar to, but not exactly cheddar. It is made in small batches by hand from premium milk that is growth-hormone free. It has a robust sharpness and unmatchable creaminess when melted.

Double Gloucester (GLOSS-ter) This close cousin of cheddar is made from the yield of two milkings of cow's milk and cream. Dense, golden, richly flavored with a silky texture, it is one of

Britain's finest. It is superb for melting. Cotswold (Sturminster) is a favorite version with onions and chives. Substitute Red Leicester, Lancashire, Cheshire or cheddar. Available in Specialty Cheese Stores (see page 227).

Dry Jack Hard grating cheese made from cow's milk, it is reminiscent of Parmigiano-Reggiano. It was created by accident when a supply of Monterey Jack was stored and forgotten during the food rationing days of the 1940s. The cheese lost considerable moisture during the long storage, intensifying the flavor. It became a favorite of Italian immigrants, deprived of their native Parmesan. The dark exterior is from a coating of cocoa and pepper. It is one of America's finest cheeses. Available in Specialty Cheese Stores or order from Vella Cheese (see page 232).

Edam (EE-duhm) This round, mellow-tasting Dutch cow's milk cheese has a bright red wax coating. In 1841, the British-led Argentine Navy lost a sea battle with the Uruguayan fleet when under American command. Rock-hard aged Edam balls were substituted when the cannonballs ran out. Edam is a popular breakfast cheese in Holland. It is good in fondue, especially blended with sharper cheeses. Substitute Gouda, fontina or Leyden, which is seasoned with caraway seeds.

Emmentaler (EM-en-TA-ler) The "authentic" Swiss cheese. One of Switzerland's premier cheeses, it can be traced back to the thirteenth century in the Emme Valley. It is made in small village dairies from farm-fresh milk delivered twice daily. Pale and golden, it has characteristic large eyes or holes, caused by expanding gas from bacterial activity. Even though low in salt and made with part-skim milk, Emmentaler has a full, rich nutty flavor, reminiscent of hazelnuts. Aged a

minimum of one-hundred days. Cave-aged Emmentaler is aged up to twelve months in the mineralized air of Emmi sandstone caves; it has a dark, thin rind and mature full flavor. Several countries make shorter-aged, less flavorful copies. French Emmental is similar, but longer-aged. See Baby Swiss Cheese and Swiss Cheese.

Explorateur Exquisite French, soft-ripened, triple crème cheese with a mild, buttery flavor. It is made of cow's milk with cream added to bring the butterfat up to 75 percent. Avoid overripe, runny cheeses with a mottled brownish rind. Look for the space rocket on the cheese wrapping. A cheese created for Champagne, it is the ultimate luxury cheese for fondue. Available in Specialty Cheese Stores (see page 227).

Feta Crumbly, salty, tangy sheep's milk cheese made in Greece, Bulgaria and Denmark. Fresh feta is preserved in brine; rinse before use. It is a great accent cheese for fondue and salads.

Fontina Val d' Aosta Straw-colored, Italian cow's milk cheese with a gold, crusty rind. Fontina d' Aosta is the original, authentic fontina, made exclusively in Val d'Aosta. Its earthy, nutty flavor is more intense than its imitators, some of which are coated with a bright red rind. Fontina d'Aosta is used in the Italian dish, Fonduta. Substitute Vacherin, Gruyère, Beaufort or Bel Paese. Available in Specialty Cheese Stores (see page 227).

Fromage Blanc Creamy soft, fresh cheese made from goat's milk. See Chèvre.

Gorgonzola (gohr-guhn-ZOH-lah) Italian blue cheese made from cow's milk. It is Italy's oldest cheese, made since the ninth century. It has a creamy, soft interior with bluish-green streaks. Gorgonzola Piccante is sharper than Stilton but not as sharp as Roquefort. Dolcelatte or Sweet

Gorgonzola is a mild, sweet, creamier version. Buy from a dependable source to avoid getting strong, over-aged cheese. It is wonderful with pears, apples, salads, melted in sauce and fondue. Substitute Maytag Blue, Clemson Blue or Saga Blue.

Gouda From the Netherlands, this creamy, straw-colored cow's milk cheese has a distinctive red, waxed coating. Historians say a similar cheese was a provision on the Mayflower when it set sail in 1620. It is a popular breakfast cheese in Europe, especially with fruit. Young Gouda has a mild, buttery taste and melts easily with other ingredients. Aged Gouda has a sharper, tangier taste. Both are good in fondue. Substitute Edam.

Grana Northern Italian hard grating cheese made from cow's milk, it is similar to Parmigiano-Reggiano but less expensive. Grana Padana is made in the Plain of Lombardy.

Gruyère Made in Western Switzerland in the Canton of Fribourg, near Lake Geneva since the twelfth century. Produced from rich cow's milk, Gruyère melts to a creamier consistency than Emmentaler and has a greater flavor intensity with hints of apples and pears. It is outstanding for fondue, grilled sandwiches, French onion soup and with eating with pears and apples. Use gentle heat when melting. Fribourg is a sharper version that is aged two to three years. Cave-aged Gruyère has an exquisite full flavor and crumbly texture; it excellent in fondue. French Gruyère, Emmentaler, French Beaufort are similar.

Gruyère du Comté (kohn-tay) Made in the mountainous southeast of France, Comté is a close relative of Swiss Gruyère. A French staple, this creamy, ivory-yellow cheese is made from rich cow's milk and has a slight fruity flavor. A good melter, it is great for fondue, soups, quiche or on the cheese tray. Substitute Swiss Gruyère, French Beaufort or Italian Fontina. Available in Specialty Cheese Stores (see page 227).

Havarti Danish version of the German cow's milk cheese, Tilsiter. This tangy, creamy cow's milk cheese is excellent melted in fondue. Some varieties have caraway seeds.

Jarlsberg (YARLS-berg) This mild, creamy cow's milk cheese is the Norwegian version of Swiss cheese. It has large holes and is popular in the United States. Substitute Baby Swiss, Emmentaler, Gruyère or Râclette.

Kasseri (kuh-SAIR-ee) Salty and tangy Greek cheese made from sheep's milk, it is wonderful in fondue or on pizza. Substitute sharp Provolone or other salty Greek cheese.

Lancashire (LANG-kuh-sheer) Rich cheddarlike British cow's milk cheese made with a single batch of curds. It is traditionally made in the farmhouse kitchen. It is one of the best toasting cheeses around. Look for Ruth Kirkham's cheese made at Beesley Farm in Lancashire. Substitute English Cheddar, Red Leicester or Double Gloucester. Available in Specialty Cheese Stores (page 227).

Leyden (LIE-dehn) Dutch cheese flavored with caraway seeds and cumin, it is good blended with milder cheese in fondue. Substitute Edam or Gouda; add a small amount of cararway seeds and cumin, lightly toasted.

Manchego Originally from the plains of La Mancha, Spain, this semi-firm, golden cheese has a mild, full flavor. It is good melted in Mexican dishes, on tortilla chips or in fondue. The aged version (*queso manchego viejo*) is for grating; use as an accent cheese in fondue. Substitute Monterey Jack, cheddar or *queso asadero*.

Maytag blue cheese An artisanal cow's milk blue cheese, it is made by the people in Iowa who created the dependable Maytag appliances. Aged in hillside cellars, it is creamy and peppery with a distinctive blue cheese flavor. One of America's finest cheeses, it is good in sauces, fondue, dips, salads. Available in fine cheese shops or order from Maytag Dairy Farms (see page 231).

Mimolette Made in Northern France, this colorful pumpkin-colored cheese has a lightly salty, spicy, distinctive taste. Use like Parmesan as an accent cheese for fondue, spaghetti and many other dishes. It was the favorite cheese of Charles de Gaulle. Substitute Parmesan, Asiago or extra-sharp cheddar. Available in Specialty Cheese Stores (see page 000).

Mascarpone (mas-car-POH-neh) Luxurious, soft, spreadable Italian cheese made from rich pasteurized cow's cream. Italians spread it on foods like we use butter and use it in desserts and savory dishes. American mascarpone is not as fluffy, but every "bite" as delicious. Handle lightly; don't beat or overmix to avoid making butter. Perishable, use soon after opening. Try it on toasted *ciabatta* (Italian bread), topped with seasonal fruits and drizzled with honey. BelGioioso Auricchio is a popular, delicious brand.

Monterey Jack An American original, it was first made by Spanish missionaries in California during the eigtheenth century. It is named after Scotsman David Jacks from Monterey County, who successfully produced it during the gold-rush era. Jack is made in several states Wisconsin, Illinois, Maine, and North Carolina. Exceptional California Jack is pale and mild with a creamy, softer texture. Jalapeño Jack is the most popular flavor variation. A superb melting cheese, great for Mex-

ican, Southwestern, Tex Mex and border cuisines. See Dry Jack.

Mountain cheese (Sbrinz) One of Switzerland's oldest dating back as far as 23 to 79 A.D. It is made in Switzerland's central region from fresh, part-skim cow's milk. Aged over twelve months, it is popular in Italy and often referred to as a "rich Parmesan." The flavor of hard mountain cheese is reminiscent of butterscotch. Swissparme® is a fancy shredded version. Excellent for grating, use in fondue, pasta sauces, soups. Shave and serve on salads. Available in Specialty Cheese Stores (page 231).

Mozzarella The pizza cheese. Perishable *mozzarella di bufala* is a high-moisture, fresh Italian cheese packed in a milky brine. Best sliced and served as a salad with dead-ripe tomato slices. *Fiore di latte* is fresh cow's milk mozzarella shaped like small balls and packed in brine. American supermarket mozzarella, made from whole or partly skimmed cow's milk, is a firmer product with a lower moisture content; it is best for melting in fondue. Melt with milk instead of wine. Handmade, high-moisture cow's milk mozzarella is made domestically; supplies of fresh Italian buffalo mozzarella are increasing. Scamorza is a similar dense-textured cheese smoked over pecan shells.

Muenster Alsatian Muenster, made from cow's milk, was first made in the Middle Ages in France near Germany. It has a spicy, powerful flavor. American Muenster is a milder version and good for melting.

Neufchâtel American Neufchâtel is a lower-fat cream cheese that melts a little more smoothly than regular cream cheese. French Neufchâtel is completely different. It is an unripened cow's milk cheese from Neufchâtel-en-Bray, France with about 48 percent fat content. Available in Specialty Cheese Stores (see page 227).

Parmigiano-Reggiano An artisanal, handmade cow's milk cheese from Northern Italy, it is one of a group of hard Italian grating cheeses known as *grana*. There are many Parmesans but only one Parmigiano-Reggiano. It has less moisture and lower milkfat than Romano. Aged a minimum of two years, the texture is slightly crumbly, the taste slightly salty and incomparably delicious. Look for the words Parmigiano-Reggiano etched on the circumference of the rind. Buy in chunks; grate just before use. Substitute Grana Padana, Romano, Asiago or California Dry Jack. Domestic, pack-aged grated Parmesan is not a good substitute.

Pecorino Romano (peh-koh-REE-noh) Hard, ripened Southern Italian grating cheese, it has a slightly salty, sharp flavor. Pecorino cheeses are made from sheep's milk; *pecora* means "ewe." Inported Romano is one of the most popular types with a unique, flavor not matched by domestic Romano. Small amounts of rich milk are produced in the countryside near Rome; cheese making is carefully regulated. Well-known brands are Fulvi Pecorino and Locatelli. Pecorino Sardo is a sharp grating cheese from Sardinia; Caprino Romano is even sharper. Substitute Parmigiano-Reggiano, Grana Padana, California Dry Jack or Asiago.

Pasteurized process cheese A pasteurized blend of fresh and aged natural cheeses, all ripening ends with pasteurization. It may contain added ingredients and may be smoked. It melts easily. Process American cheese, Swiss cheese and brick cheese are a few varieties available in slices and loaves.

Pasteurized process cheese food is a similar product but contains nonfat dry milk and less cheese. Cheese food is softer than pasteurized process cheese. It spreads more easily and melts faster than processed cheese; but it does not have as much cheese flavor.

Pasteurized process cheese spreads are even more moist and contain stabilizers. Available in small jars, they are spreadable.

Coldpack cheese is a blend of fresh sharp and aged natural cheeses that are packed, without heating, into jars, rolls and links. Coldpack cheese food is similar to coldpack cheese, but it includes dairy ingredients and sweeteners.

Provolone Cow's milk cheese from Italy with a natural tang, it is often found in Italian markets, tied up and hanging from the ceiling in a variety of shapes and sizes. Dolce Provolone is a young cheese with a sweet taste. After four months of aging, provolone tastes buttery; in six months, the flavor becomes much sharper. It is excellent in fondue. It is available in a domestic, smoked version. Try a blend of young and aged provolone in fondue. It blends well with Gruyère and mozzarella.

Queso Anejo Hard cow's milk cheese from Mexico; not as strong as aged cotija. Grate and use like Parmesan for seasoning.

Queso Asadero White, firm Mexican cheese sometimes called "Mexican Velveeta." Smooth texture with a bit more tang than milder Queso Quesadilla. Excellent for oven-melted cheese dishes because of the stronger flavor. Comes in balls, braids and rounds.

Queso Cotija (Queso Añejo) Sharp, salty, white cow's milk cheese from Mexico. Softens but doesn't melt when heated. A bit sharper than queso fresco with a taste similar to feta. It can be crumbled. A hard, strong-tasting, aged version can be grated and used like Parmesan. Use these cheeses to season many dishes including fondue. Substitute queso anejo, pecorino Romano or Asiago.

Queso Quesadilla White, smooth, slightly salty cow's milk cheese from Mexico. A great melting cheese, use for quesadillas, sandwiches, cheeseburgers and Southwestern-style fondues. It is also known as queso Chihuahua. Queso jalapeño is a zesty variation with jalapeño peppers.

Râclette A collective group of unique Swiss mountain cheeses made from cow's milk, they have a smooth, creamy texture and a delicious flavor that intensifies when heated. Râclette also refers to a melted cheese dish from the Canton of Valais. There are several râclette cheeses; four of the best are Gomser, Bagnes, Orsières and Conches. The names, actually the villages of production, can be found molded on the rinds. Versatile râclette can be used in cooking or sliced and eaten with crackers. French Râclette, made in the Savoie and Franche-Comté regions of France, is softer with a mild flavor resembling Jarlesberg. It is mainly used for melting. Tomme de Chèvre, a goat's milk cheese from Eastern France, is also melted and used like râclette. Available in upscale markets and Specialty Cheese Stores (see page 227).

Red Leicester (LES-ter) British cow's-milk cheese with an attractive russet-red color from annatto, a natural dye, it is similar to cheddar with a rich, nutty flavor and a hint of tanginess. Leicester is an excellent melting cheese and delicious for snacking, especially with fruits. Especially nice in tomato-based rabbits. Substitute Lancashire, Cheshire, Double Gloucester or cheddar. Available in Specialty Cheese Stores (see page 227).

Ricotta Soft, white, low-fat Italian cow's milk cheese made from milk whey separated from the curds, it has a mild taste with a consistency similar to cottage cheese, but with smaller curds.

Roquefort cheese Rich, strong blue-veined sheep's milk cheese aged in the caves in mountainous Comgalou overlooking the town of Roquefort, it has been made since the eleventh century. Slightly salty with a sharp, distinctive taste, it is good with a sweet dessert wine like Sauterne. Use as an accent cheese in cheese fondue.

Sapsago Small, hard, cone-shape seasoning cheese produced in the Canton of Glarus, Switzerland, as early as 1464. Made from skim cow's milk, the green cheese has an aromatic pungency from the addition of the sharp-tasting, dried clover, *melilotus coerulea*. Grate and add cautiously to fondues, soups, sauces, and pasta dishes. Available in Specialty Cheese Stores (see page 227).

Stilton The "King of English cheeses" has been immortalized in the works of great writers such as Jane Austin and Charles Lamb. Stilton has a distinctive, mellow flavor and cheddarlike texture, setting it apart from other blue cheeses, with an ivory interior streaked with greenish-blue veins. Made from rich cow's milk and cream, the rind is inedible. Creamy-white Stilton has no blue veining but might be flavored with ginger, pineapple, orange or apricots. England's only name-protected cheese is lovingly crafted. An English dairywoman once remarked, "Except that they make no noise, Stiltons are more trouble than babies." Good drizzled with honey and served with port or a robust red wine, it adds a special cachét to fondue and melted cheese dishes. Colston Basset, Long Clawson Dairy and Tuxford & Tebbutt produce top brands. Available in Specialty Cheese Stores (see page 227).

Swiss cheese Excellent Swiss cheese (Emmentaler) is produced in the United States, especially in Wisconsin and New York State. The taste is slightly milder than the authentic Swiss cheese or Emmentaler.

Teleme (Sonoma Teleme) An American original, this Northern California white cheese has a soft creamy texture resembling Brie or Stracchino. Superb for melting alone as a sauce or fondue. Good with crusty bread, salads and fruit. It can be eaten ten days after production and is soft and creamy at one month. The tasty traditional version is dusted with rice flour. The rind darkens with age as the center becomes ripe and soft. Refrigerated 3 to 4 months, the flavor becomes complex and can be eaten with a spoon like French Vacherin Mont d'Or. Freeze fresh cheese in small portions; the crumbly texture is still good for melting. Available in Specialty Cheese Stores or order from Peluso Cheese Inc. (see page 231).

Tilsiter (Tilsit) Semi-firm cow's milk cheese, it has irregular eyes or cracks and is pale yellow in color. The flavor is mild but becomes stronger with aging; 30 to 50 percent fat. It is great for fondue.

Tomme de Savoie From the mountainous French Savoy region near Switzerland and Italy; often made with rich alpine milk left over from the production of cheese like Beaufort. Only 20 percent butterfat, Tomme has a satisfying full flavor. Substitute Oka, a Canadian monastery cheese, or aromatic, semi-soft French Saint Nectaire. Good in fondue. Available in Specialty Cheese Stores (see page 227).

Vacherin Fribourgeois (Vacherin a Fondue) France and Switzerland produce a variety of cow's milk cheeses under the category of Vacherin. Swiss Vacherin Fribourgeois from Fribourg is a smooth, buttery, semi-firm cheese with a natural rind and mild flavor that becomes pronounced as it ages. It is best in the winter months during skiing season and often used in fondue. Vacherin Mont d'Or is a winter cheese, made in France and Switzerland. It is bound with a strip of birch, which adds to the flavor. Creamy and soft, it can be eaten as is or melted in the packing box and scooped up with bread or a spoon. Available in Specialty Cheese Stores (see page 227).

Vignerons Fresh, part-skim milk cheese from Switzerland. *Vignerons* meaning "winemakers," is marinated twice a week in a mixture of alpine herbs and red wine as it cures, creating a black rind. Vignerons has an unforgettable aroma and rich, creamy taste characterized by the natural wine flavor. Available in Specialty Cheese Stores (see page 227).

Wensleydale British cow's milk cheese made in the Yorkshire Dales for one thousand years, it has a mild flavor with a sour cream tang and honeyed aftertaste. It is often served with apple pie and fruitcake. Produced by the Cistercian Monks of Jervaulx Abbey who came to England with William the Conqueror, when Henry VIII destroyed their abbey, the fleeing monks abandoned their recipe to local farmers. It is sometimes available in a blue cheese or honey-laced version with cranberries or apricots. Available in Specialty Cheese Stores (see page 227).

Arugula (Rocket or Rugula) From the mustard family, assertive, peppery taste. A restaurant favorite, it is now gaining popularity at home. Rich in iron and vitamin C. Good cool weather crop.

Basil Herb from the mint family. Opal basil has beautiful purple leaves. Lemon basil is good in Asian and Italian cuisines. Sweet basil is excellent for pesto. Cinnamon basil has a pleasant spicy taste and aroma. Fresh basil is far superior to the dried herb. Easy to grow.

Butterhead Another head lettuce, with leaves softly folded on top of one another. Outer leaves are dark green to brownish with butter colored leaves inside. It has a buttery, tender texture. Includes Boston (butter) and Bibb (Limestone).

Chervil An herb from the parsley family; feathery leaves with a delicate anise flavor. It's a French favorite.

Chicory Curly leaf vegetable with a mildly bitter taste. A close cousin of the endives (Whitloof, escarole and Frisée), leaf chicory is a staple Italian table green. Red chicory, like radicchio, is preferred in the north. Good in salads or cooked.

Claytonia (miner's lettuce) This is an attractive tasty salad plant with heart-shaped leaves.

Cos (romaine) This lettuce grows upright, eight to nine inches tall. The flavor is sweeter than most other lettuces. The tightly folded leaves are greenish-white in the center and medium-green on the outside.

Crisphead (iceberg lettuce) A tight, firm, crisp head of leaves with a passing resemblance to a bowling ball. Out of vogue for the past few years, it has been referred to as the "polyester of lettuce." Stays crisp in the salad bowl. Use in lettuce salads, stir-fries, on tacos. For a classic steakhouse favorite, cut quarter wedges and top with the Zestful Blue Cheese Dressing (page 167). Sprinkle with blue cheese crumbles. Predictions say iceberg is poised for a big comeback.

Dandelion greens From the French, *"dent de lion."* A familiar garden weed, pick the leaves very young before the flowers appear. It has a spicy tonic taste. Good in salads or it can be cooked. It is grown commercially.

Endive (Whitloof) About six inches long with a slightly bitter taste, it has tightly packed leaves. Endive grows in the dark to keep it white; the bitterness intensifies when exposed to light. Good in salads and it can be cooked.

Escarole Endive with flat leaves, it has a lightly tonic taste, more delicate taste than endive. Good in salads and can be cooked.

Frisée (curly endive) From the chicory family, it has crisp, tender frilly, narrow-toothed green leaves, yellowish ribs and a pleasant bitter flavor. Good in salads and can be cooked.

Golden Purslane Crunchy, small, oval leaves with a nutty flavor, it grows wild.

Leaf-Loose Lettuce (Bunching lettuce) Good flavor with attractive, tender leaves that make a good base lettuce for salads.

Lollo Rossa Frilly red-leaf lettuce.

Mâche (corn salad, field salad or lamb's lettuce) Wild salad herb with tender, small leaves that resembles large sprouts, vitamin-rich with a rich, nutty flavor.

Mesclun A blend of "cut-and-come-again" salad greens, from France that are combined in set proportions of chervil, arugula, lettuce and endive. Mesclun grows easily in hanging pots, window boxes and kitchen gardens. The greens germinate in cold temperatures; begin sowing seeds two weeks before the last frost date. After one month, use large scissors to snip the top two to three inches of growth. Blends of Asian greens are also available in supermarkets.

Microgreens Mix of tiny, colorful baby greens, one-inch tall and more tender than baby lettuce. Microgreens taste similar to sprouts but have more character. They are packed with vitamins and nutrients. The mix might include tatsoi, mizuna, purple mustard, ruby chard, red Russian kale and red cabbage. Rinse well before eating. If you can't locate them in your market, ask your green grocer to make them available.

Mizuna Feathery mustard green from Japan, pleasant mustard flavor.

Oak Leaf Lettuce Delicate small leaves that resemble oak leaves.

New Zealand Spinach (Tetragonia) Bright green, small pointed leaves with a spinach-like taste. Use raw in salads or can be cooked.

Puntarelle Italian chicory that is popular in Rome and becoming popular in this country. Each head weighs 1 1/2 to 2 pounds and has long, thin hollow stalks with elongated leaves on the ends. When sliced, the stalks are hollow and vaguely resemble rings of squid.

Radicchio (Trévise) Magenta and white chicory, with cupped leaves on a tightly bunched head, it has a pleasant bitter flavor.

Savoy spinach Dark-green, small ruffled leaves with a spicy aftertaste.

Sorrel Light green spade-shaped leaves with a lemony taste. Good in salad or in cream of sorrel soup.

Tatsoi Asian green with a tiny leaf that is a member of the kale family, peppery-lemon taste

---

MISCELLANEOUS INGREDIENTS

Bean threads (cellophane noodles, vermicelli, pea starch noodles, transparent noodles, glass noodles and long rice) Wiry-thin, tough Chinese noodles made from mung beans. Use in cold, tossed noodle dishes, stir-fried dishes and one-pot dishes. One-pound packages hold eight (two-ounce) skeins wrapped in cellophane or bound with red rubber bands.

To use in cold dishes, soak noodles fifteen minutes in hot tap water; cook one minute in boiling water; drain and rinse in cold water.

To stir-fry or add to soups and hot pots, soak twenty minutes in hot tap water, drain and use as desired. Soak banded noodles intact; snip the loop ends into shorter lengths then remove rubber bands. With high drama, bean threads instantly expand in size and turn white when deep-fried in oil at 400F (205C). Cut the wiry strands inside a paper bag; snip with kitchen scissors. Deep-fry small amounts, drain and lightly salt. Use the crispy filaments in salads and as a nest for stir-fry dishes. Can fry three hours in advance. See Harusame.

Bindenfleisch Air-cured Swiss beef from selected cuts of leg meat. The meat is slowly dried, salted, pickled, cured with herbs and stored for several weeks at near-freezing temperatures. Finally, it is air-dried in a process that takes over three months. A traditional accompaniment for râclette.

Champagne grapes Seedless miniature currant grapes are seedless. Blue-black when mature. Each bunch is about the length and width of a hand. Available from California, July to October. Often used to drape over champagne and wine glasses.

Chipotle chilies Smoked, dried jalapeño chiles with a reddish-brown wrinkled skin. Of medium-heat, they add sweet-hot flavor to soups, fondues, sauces, beans and salsas. Available pickled or canned in red adobo sauce. Almost one-fifth of the Mexican jalapeño crop is produced to make the chipotle. To re-hydrate, remove stems and seeds. Cover with boiling-hot water. Soak thirty minutes; chop as desired. If chipotle sauce is unavailable, puree and strain a can of chipotles en adobo. Refrigerate leftovers.

Clementines A type of mandarin orange with a thin peel and delectible tangy-sweet flesh. The sections separate easily, usually seedless. A cross between a Mediterranean mandarin and a sour orange, it was named for Father Clement Rodier, who cultivated the fruit in Algeria. Harvested November through January. Use in cooking or simply peel and eat or dip into chocolate fondue to appreciate the special flavor. Available in specialty markets, Asian markets and some supermarkets.

Cream Whipping cream contains 30 to 36 percent fat. Heavy cream is richer with 36 to 40 percent fat. Cream must have at least 30 percent fat to whip. Whipping cream produces soft folds when whipped; perfect for spooning over desserts.

Heavy cream is denser with more body. It holds its shape better when piped or folded into other ingredients. One cup liquid cream makes 2 cups whipped cream.

Flavor essences Add a few drops of French steam-distilled essence to chocolate fondues, cream dips, custards, whipped cream, frostings and beverages. Available in a variety of fruit and floral flavors from La Cuisine in Alexandria, Virginia. They add flavor and enhance existing flavors. German flavor pastes can be used like essences. They are especially useful when you want to retain a food's consistency. Small one-ounce bottles of exotic Thai essences can be purchased in Thai and Southeast Asian markets. Look for pandan leaf or screwpine extract (*krin-bai-toey*); jasmine (Mali essence) and tropical banana. Long, slim pandan leaves are used in Thai desserts and rice dishes to impart a sweet, floral, nutty flavor.

Flavoring powders Dry herbs, vegetables and mushrooms in the microwave, in a low oven or in a special dryer to create instant flavoring powders. When dried, use an electric coffee mill or spice grinder to reduce herbs and vegetables to powder. Use sparingly to add flavor to fondues, stocks, soups and other dishes. Dried *dashi-no-moto* is a richly flavored powder of dried bonito fish and seaweed. I noticed that cooks in Okinawa like to sprinkle it into noodles, rice dishes and stir-fry dishes. *Kinako* is a delicious powder made of roasted soybeans and used for coating rice balls stuffed with bean paste. Indian cooks dry mangoes and ginger for seasoning powders. Dried chipotle chiles can be seeded and ground into a dynamic seasoning powder.

Fragrant lime leaves (kaffir lime) Highly aromatic tree with jade-green leaves that give food a unique citrus flavor. Brush against the leaves and the air becomes perfumed with an aroma the intensity of cologne. Only the zest of the fruit is used, not the juice. Use small, tender new leaves for mincing, preferably new growth. Mince very finely or cut into hairlike shreds. Use sparingly, the flavor is vivid. Check Asian markets for frozen lime leaves. Several California nurseries stock the trees if you want to grow your own.

Harusame Japanese noodles made from vegetable flours by the extrusion method. One major type is a Chinese-style wiry, coiled noodle made from mung beans. Soak these noodles in hot water five to ten minutes; simmer one to two minutes. Rinse in cold water; drain. Cut in shorter lengths. The second major type is a similar, slightly larger straight noodle made from potato starch. Also called Japanese *saifun* and used by some Vietnamese cooks in this country. Soak potato-starch harusame in boiling-hot water ten minutes; rinse in cold water, drain. Cut in shorter lengths. Good in salads and soups. Many Japanese prefer the mung bean noodles, which are less fragile. For shrimp noodle tempura, dip large cleaned shrimp in cornstarch then in egg white. Coat thoroughly with bean thread noodles snipped in $^1/_2$-inch pieces. Deep-fry in hot oil one minute until beautifully puffed and crisp. See Bean Threads.

Konnyaku Bars of jellied vegetable paste made from konnyaku, the "devil's tongue plant." Little taste; appreciated for texture. Use in simmered dishes. Available in dark or lighter refined forms. Rinse upon opening; blanch one minute to remove the milk of lime odor, used during processing.

Lemongrass (citronella) A tropical grass with a unique, rich lemon aroma and taste. Peel off and discard the outer stalks. Use only the lower, inner, tender white portion of the stalk. Slice into thin rings then mince finely. The woody, outer stalks can be used in stocks or placed in the barbecue grill for a citrusy aroma. Ja-San's lemongrass comes packed in jars of water. Nothing to trim; use as desired. Fresh lemongrass is readily available in Asian markets, fresh and frozen. Dried stalks and trimming provide no flavor. Lemongrass is easy to find and easier to grow.

Long-grain rice Indica-type rice from the species, *Oryza sativa*. Moderately high in starchy amylose, the slender grains are three or more times as long as wide. They cook up dry and fluffy and remain separate. Side dishes and salads made with long-grain rice go well with many hot oil and broth-based fondues and Chinese hot pots. Texmati is Texas-grown American basmati with the aroma of popcorn and a subtle, nutty taste. Royal Blend is a quick-cooking, nutty-tasting blend of Texmati White, Texmati Brown and wild rice. Jasmati is an American strain of jasmine rice from Texas. Kasmati is Indian-style rice with a delicious flavor and exotic aroma; great for curry. Fragrant, nutty Basmati from India is aged one year after harvest. It cooks best if presoaked thirty minutes. *Kalijira*, a miniature long-grain Basmati, cooks up fluffy in about ten minutes. Of ancient origin, it is reserved for religious festivals and special occasions in Bangladesh and Calcutta.

Mayonnaise Homemade mayonnaise is delicious and easy to make but if you prefer to use a store-bought brand, try Hellman's or Best Foods as it is known west of the Rockies. Any sauce recipe in this book that calls for mayonnaise can be successfully made with light mayonnaise, which has about 50 percent less fat. If you live in the South, try Duke's Mayonnaise, a southern institution and the only mayonnaise for many Southerners. Eugenia Duke first made it in 1917 in her South Carolina kitchen. It is now being made by C. F. Sauer Company in Richmond, Virginia, using Eugenia's recipe. I like it because of the slightly tart taste from the cider vinegar. It contains no sugar and uses only egg yolks. I prefer homemade mayonnaise with the same fresh tanginess.

Medium-grain rice California medium-grain rice is Japonica ("Japanese") rice from the species, *Oryza sativa*. About 95 percent of the crop comes from the Sacramento Valley, which has a warm Mediterranean climate. Also produced in the temperate climates of Japan, Korea, Italy and Spain. Less than 2 percent of the crop is short-grain rice; excellent for sushi. Waxy Japonica is high in amylopectin, a starch that causes cohesion. Medium- and short-grain rice requires a little less water than long-grain; soak to tenderize and shorten the cooking time. Japanese-Americans enjoy premium California grades including Koshihikari, which sets the standard for short-grain rice in Japan. Imported Koshihikari is now available in this country. (See Mail-Order Resource, page 225.) Other quality short-grain rices include Tamaki Gold and Tamanishiki. For premium medium-grain rice buy Kokuho Rose, Akita Otome and Nishiki. Himalayian Bhutanese red short-grain rice is semi-glutinous and cooks in about twenty minutes. Steam or use it in pilafs or risotto.

Miso paste Steamed soybeans mixed with salt and a fermenting agent of rice, barley or soybeans. Color, taste and aroma vary with each type. Protein-rich with essential amino acids needed for good nutrition. Pale *shiromiso* or "white miso," is

fermented with rice koji and has a mild, sweet taste. It is the least salty type with about 5 percent salt content. Primarily used in Kansai or Kyoto cuisine. Add to delicate-flavored dishes, salad dressings, soups, fish and vegetable dishes. (Look for *saikyo miso*, highly perishable and not easy to come by. Saltier, less sweet brands of *shiromiso* are available from other areas of Japan, ranging from yellow to light brown; look for *shinshu miso*. Use as a substitute for Kyoto miso, in smaller amounts and sweetened with about an equal amount of sugar or twice as much mirin. Or use Hawaiian sweet white miso mixed with a little sugar. *Akamiso* or "red miso" is fermented with rice or barley koji and comes in shades from reddish to brown. It is one of the most popular types in Japan. (Look for Sendai miso.) Good for meat stir-fries, marinades and soups. *Mamémiso* or "soybean miso" is fermented with soybean koji and often so dark, rich and intense, it may resemble fudge. It is used for hearty dishes and often blended with other kinds of miso; (look for Hatcho miso.)

Miso is also catagorized by ingredients. *Komémiso* is rice miso; *mamémiso* is pure soybean miso and *mugimiso* is barley miso. Taste many types; choose your favorites. *Shiro miso* and *akamiso* are good basics. Unpasteurized miso has good flavor; check natural food stores. Refrigerate in airtight containers. Properly sealed, miso provides maximum flavor three to four months. Tasty *shinshu-ichi miso* and *dashi iri miso* are seasoned with bonito stock flavor; a boon for inexperienced cooks.

Porcini mushrooms (French *Cèpes*) Fresh porcini season is short; dried porcini adds a rich, earthy flavor to many dishes, including fondue. Highly prized, they are expensive but a small amount delivers big flavor. Look for large, sliced caps of uniform color, with a rich, pleasant aroma. Examine carefully for bug infestation. Save the valuable soaking liquid to season foods; freeze leftover liquid for other uses. To make seasoning powder, grind the dried mushrooms with an electric spice grinder. Dust meats, poultry and seafood before cooking; add to vegetable dishes, soups, sauces and breads.

Salt Without salt, foods taste one-dimensional. Salt heightens flavors and acts as a preservative. A tiny pinch can lift the flavor of sweets and fondue. Common kitchen salt contains chemicals to keep it free-flowing and to prevent moisture absorption. Iodized salt is similar but contains iodine, an essential nutrient.

Kosher salt is purified rock salt with larger crystals. It has a pure, mild flavor favored in many world cuisines including Korea. Kosher salt is half as salty as table salt and sea salt.

Sea salt is made from purified crystals of evaporated seawater. It has no additives, contains more minerals than table salt and has a better flavor. *Fleur de sel* from Brittany is considered the "caviar" of sea salts. Of all the salts, table salt tastes the "saltiest" and has the least flavor, not the best choice for fine cooking.

Saké Japanese rice wine is often used in sauces, fish cookery to neutralize odors and improve textures, and in meat marinades to tenderize. Saké is perishable; store in the refrigerator and use as soon as possible. Two major saké types are *Jozo-shu* (with alcohol added) and *Junmai-shu* (without added alcohol.) *Futsu-shu* is the basic grade of *Jozo-shu*, good as an everyday table saké and for cooking purposes. To drink, serve warm at 105F (40C) to 125F (50C). *Honjozo-dai-ginjoshu* is the top grade of *Jozo-shu* with a delicate, refined,

slightly fruity taste. Drink chilled. Dry saké or *karakuchi* has a higher acid content and is preferred by saké drinkers. Read bottle labels to determine this information. Amakuchi is sweeter and often used for cooking. Extra cooked rice and less fermentation make saké taste sweeter.

Sesame Oil An aromatic oil with a strong nutty flavor. Pressed from dark, toasted sesame seeds. Add sparingly, like a fine perfume, to Japanese, Chinese and Korean dishes. Do not substitute untoasted sesame oil. To my taste, the Japanese brands have the best flavor.

Shallots From the onion family; essential in French and Thai cooking. In India, certain Buddhist sects use shallots exclusively in cooking. They create flavor subtleties in foods unmatched by ordinary onions. Can be roasted in foil like garlic. Select firm, dry bulbs with no green shoots or dark spots.

Shaohsing wine A popular Chinese wine, good for drinking and cooking. Produced for centuries in the coastal province of Chekiang in eastern China. The best brands have a deep golden color and taste like a rich, fine sherry. The Pagoda brand with a blue label is recommended. Don't use anything less than the best brand; many are not very good. If unavailable, you can successfully substitute a good dry sherry.

Shirataki (white waterfall) Gelatinous noodle-like strands used in Japanese one-pot dishes. Made from konnyaku, the "devil's tongue plant," by an extrusion method. Comes water-packed. Drain off the water and parboil for one minute. Drain and rinse in cool water.

Soy Sauce Soy sauce is the "secret" ingredient that enhances the flavor of Asian and western foods. Kikkoman International Inc. produces excellent light and dark soy sauces, both important to Japanese cuisine. They are naturally brewed and aged like fine wine to develop perfectly balanced flavors.

Light soy sauce (*usukuchi shoyu*) is saltier with a less strong flavor; use in dipping sauces and to preserve the natural, light colors of foods.

Dark soy sauce (*kokuchi shoyu*) has a rich, mellow flavor, excellent for Japanese, Chinese and Korean cooking. The two are usually interchangeable. Kikkoman makes a low-sodium soy sauce with 40 percent less salt. To preserve the flavor, add to foods in the last stage of cooking. Chinese Pearl River Bridge "Superior Soy" and mushroom soy sauce are excellent for Chinese dishes, especially stir-frying. Chinese soy sauce is much saltier than Japanese *shoyu*; the flavor is not compatible with Japanese dishes.

Star anise A wonderful aromatic dried spice with a flavor somewhat like licorice. I don't care for licorice but I do love star anise. Each star has eight points. Purchase a bag of whole stars in an Asian food market; store in an airtight jar in a cool place. Add to stocks, soups, Chinese barbecue marinades, poached fruits, braised pork, lamb and chicken dishes. Grind with a spice mill; use in small amounts in baking.

Vidalia onions Grown in Southern Georgia, available early May through December. Susceptible to bruising because of a higher water content than other onions. Keep cool and dry. Place onions in the legs of clean pantyhose with a knot tied above each onion; cut pantyhose above the knot. Chill whole in the refrigerator for one hour to bring out the sweetness or soak in iced water thirty minutes; drain on paper towels.

Vinegars Japanese rice vinegar is milder and sweeter than western vinegars. Excellent for salads and pickling. In a dipping sauce, it neutralizes the fatty flavors of fried foods. Select unseasoned rice vinegar, without salt and MSG. Look for naturally brewed brands and brown rice vinegar in natural food stores. *Umé su* is a tasty Japanese plum vinegar made from the *uméboshi* or pickled green plums. Chinese black vinegar has a rich, sweet, mild flavor; made from grain rather than rice. The best brands are well-aged and have the complexity of good balsamic vinegar. Use as an ingredient or condiment. Look for Chinkiang black vinegar under the Gold Plum label. Or substitute a good balsamic vinegar. Available in Asian markets and some supermarkets.

The Baker's Catalogue

P.O. Box 876

Norwich, Vermont 05005-0876

Telephone 800-827-6836

Catalog

http://www.kingarthurflour.com

Salter Electronic Aquatronic, the Baker's Dream, Model 3007 (scales), bakers' supplies

Le Creuset of America, Inc.

P.O. Box 67

Early Branch, South Carolina 29916

Telephone 877-CREUSET

Fax 803-943-4510

http://www.lecreuset.com

Porcelain enameled cast-iron cookware from France. Râclette cookers, woks, bouillabaisse pots, Traditionnelle Fondue with Burner and 6 forks; Contemporary Fondue with Burner and 6 forks; Compact Fondue with Burner and 6 forks; La Saucière is a ¾-quart white ceramic bowl with a stainless steel holder and tea light. Its petite size is just right for chocolate, delicate cheese fondues, sauces or drawn butter. Also, casseroles that are suitable for cooking Japanese nabémono dishes.

Fante's Kitchen Wares Shop

1006 S. Ninth Street,

Philadelphia, PA 19147-4798

Telephone 215-922-5557 or 800-44-FANTES

Online catalog

http://fantes.com

Numerous fondue pots, copper Asian hot pot from Italy, quality cooking equipment, Microplane Grater/Zester/Shaver: Stainless steel, razor-sharp Microplane® graters shave fresh ingredients instead of ripping and shredding. Good for citrus rinds, garlic, nutmeg, hard cheeses (Parmesan) and softer cheeses

Iwatani & Company (USA), Inc

60 E. 42nd St. Suite 1740

New York, New York 10165

Telephone 800-775-5506 (California)

Casset Feu grill, tabletop burner unit and gas canisters. State-of-the-art induction tabletop ranges cook faster and more efficiently. Useful for stir-frying or reheating. Cool to the touch and flame-free.

http://www.Japanesegifts.com

Shabu shabu pans, donabé casserole dishes, Japanese soup bowls and other dishes and cooking equipment.

Katagiri & Company, Inc.
224 and 226 East 59th Street
New York, New York 10022
Telephone 212-755-3566
Fax 212-838-5453
http://www.katagiri.com
Matcha (Japanese powdered green tea), Japanese food supplies, cooking equipment, dishes, books, Sanuki udon, Saikyo sweet white miso

Kitchen Etc.
Catalog Services (Department TM)
32 Industrial Drive
Exeter, New Hampshire 03833
Telephone 800-232-4070
Swiss Zyliss salad spinner: item #115529, pull cord to spin greens; clear bowl. Top rated by *Cook's Illustrated* magazine.

Lodge Manufacturing Company
South Pittsburgh, Tennessee 37380
Telephone 423-837-7181
Fax 423-837-8279
Fine cast-iron cookware made in the hills of southeastern Tennessee since 1896. Over 140 different cast-iron products, a must for fried green tomatoes and other southern foods!

The Oriental Pantry
423 Great Road
Acton, Massachusetts 01720
Telephone 800-828-0368
http://www.orientalpantry.com
Joyce Chen products, Asian food supplies, Iwatani tabletop burners

Professional Cutlery Direct
42 Branford Road
North Branford, Connecticut 06471

Telephone 800-859-6994
http://www.cutlery.com
Soehnle Cyber Electronic Scale: item #9553-04, high accuracy, greater weighing capacity, superior display visibility. Top rated by *Cook's Illustrated* magazine.

Quickspice.com
International Food Source
Telephone 800-553-5008
Fax 323-464-7713
http://www.quickspice.com
Rice cookers, Chinese and Thai hot pots, Japanese hokonabé for shabu shabu, portable tabletop stoves with carrying case by Joy Cook, brass wire cooking spoons, sushimaki sudaré (rolling mat), Japanese Mandolin Style Vegetable Slicer by Benriner, premium matcha (Japanese green tea powder) from Kobe, "spider skimmers", cooking chopsticks, Asian food supplies, tableware

Robert's European Imports
102 Fifth Avenue
New Glarus, Wisconsin 53574
Telephone 800-968-2517 or 608-527-2517
Fax 608-527-2107
roberts@shopswiss.com
Earthenware Swiss fondue pots and burners, fondue forks, plates, Swiss cowbells, many other items from Switzerland

Sur la Table
Catalog Division
1765 Sixth Avenue South
Seattle, Washington 98134-1608
Telephone 800-243-0852
http://www.surlatable.com
Fine equipment for domestic and professional kitchens, 18/10 gauge stainless steel fondue pot from Switzerland, fondue plates, condiment sets,

electric râclette cookers, 18/10 gauge stainless steel chafing dish

Trudeau

10440 Woodward Avenue

Woodridge, Illinois 60517-4934

Telephone 888-887-8332 or 630-739-4000

Numerous fondue sets including: 32-piece Lazy Susan Set that includes a stoneware fondue pot and a metal fondue pot; The Epicurian: 22-piece enamel-on-steel fondue set with wooden Lazy Susan base; The Millennium: 10 piece stainless-steel fondue set; The Standard: brushed stainless-steel 10 piece set; copper fondue pots, stoneware cheese fondue sets with convertible burners; small stoneware casserole sets for chocolate; stoneware fondue plates, condiment sets, forks, fondue fuels and extra alcohol burners. Available at fine cookware stores; Target; and Bed, Bath and Beyond.

Vista Cucina

1001 Gervais Street

Columbia, South Carolina 29201

Telephone 803-779-9288

Contact: Susan Duncan

Traditional Swiss fondue pots, enameled cast-iron fondue pots with meat splatter guard, fondue paraphernalia, fuels, quality cookware

Williams-Sonoma

Telephone 800-541-2233

Catalog

http://www.williamsonoma.com

Copper and stainless steel fondue pots with ceramic liners, quality cookware, gourmet food products, cookbooks, "Koshi-Hikari" short-grain rice direct from Japan

The Wok Shop

718 Grant Avenue

San Francisco, California 94108

Telephone 888-780-7171

Catalog/online catalog

http://www.wokshop.com

Located in the heart of San Francisco's famous Chinatown, a family-owned and operated business specializing in hard-to-find Asian cooking tools. The unique stock of merchandise includes: woks, Chinese, Korean and Thai hot pots, Ying Yang pots, Shabu Shabu pots, Chinese steam pot. The Wok Shop carries portable canister stoves, a variety of cleavers, sushi tubs, wire mesh skimmers (spoons), Oriental chinaware, Oriental vegetable seeds, Benriner slicer, fancy vegetable cutters, elegant chopsticks, Japanese lacquer soup bowls and many other items referred to throughout this book.

Quality Kitchen

To order: 800-959-9390

http://www.qualitykit.com

Swiss earthenware fondue pots, chafing dishes, Swiss-designed eight person râclette cooker topped with grill or hot stone, six person râclette cooker with grill or hot stone. The broiler melts individual pans of cheese while meats and sausages sizzle on top. Nonstick finish for easy cleanup. Professional râclette machines.

SPECIALTY CHEESE STORES

These fine specialty cheese stores carry hundreds of artisinal, domestic and imported cheeses, including all that are mentioned in this book.

The British Shoppe
45 Wall Street
Madison, Connecticut 06443
Telephone 800-842-6674
http://www.thebritishshoppe.com
From Neal's Yard Dairy: Colston Basset Stilton, Montgomery's cheddar, Keen's cheddar plus many more British cheeses, fine teas, preserves, accompaniments and traditional British fare.

The Cheese Store
419 N. Beverly Drive
Beverly Hills, California 90210
Telephone 800-547-1515 or 310-278-2855
http://www.cheesestorebh.com
This store carries 300 to 400 varieties of cheese.

Dean & DeLuca
560 Broadway
New York, New York 10012
Telephone 800-221-7714 or 212-431-1691
Catalog
http://www.dean-deluca.com
Fine cheeses and gourmet products from around the world.

Formaggio Kitchen
244 Huron Avenue
Cambridge, Massachusetts 02138
Telephone 888-212-3224 or 617-354-4750
From 300 to 500 cheeses; many are limited production artisanal cheeses from Europe and the United States. A special ripening room duplicates the optimum conditions of European caves.

Homestead Market
W6303 Hefty Road
Monticello, Wisconsin 53570
www.homesteadmarket.com
Telephone 888-234-1906 or 680-527-4242
Fax 608-527-4136
Attention: Gale

Many Homestead Market cheeses are produced in the family-run Deepeler Cheese Factory. Fine cheeses include Baby Swiss, brick and cheddar cheese. Vintage cheddars are aged up to five years. The unique, creamy Baby Swiss was originally developed by an Iowa university professor as a research project. French Brie, Swiss sapsago, Trudeau fondue pots and gel fuel pastes are also available.

House of Wisconsin Cheese
107 State Street
Madison, Wisconsin 53703
Telephone 800-955-0238 or 608-255-5204
Around fifty varieties of Wisconsin cheese including Swiss, Colby, cheddar, Brick and Edam

Ideal Cheese Shop
942 First Avenue
New York, New York 10022
Monday through Saturday 8:30 A.M. to 6 P.M.
Telephone 800-382-0109 or 212-688-7579
Catalog
http://www.idealcheese.com
Over one-hundred cheeses; a popular and very helpful source for obtaining hard-to-find imported cheeses.

Murray's
257 Bleecker Street
New York, New York 10014
Telephone 212-243-3289
http://www.murrayscheese.com
Well-known New York shop that stocks over three hundred cheeses; excellent prices.

Rothkäse USA, Ltd.
657 Second Street
Monroe, Wisconsin 53566
Telephone 800-257-3355
Price sheet available
http://Rothkäse.com

Dozens of mail-order cheeses, including hard-to-find Gruyère, râclette and Italian fontina produced the traditional European way in copper vats. A fondue cheese blend, called The Melting Pot, consists of medium-aged Swiss, Italina fontina and Gruyère (recipe included). Also Wisconsin sausges, butterkäse and horseradish-flavored Danish havarti, a new product.

Whole Foods Markets

35 stores that carry many cheeses including British Farmhouse cheeses.
Telephone 512-328-7541 (call to locate the store nearest you)

Zingerman's Delicatessen

422 Detroit Street
Ann Arbor, Michigan 48104
Telephone 888-636-8162 or 313-663-3354
http://www.zingerman's.com
Excellent descriptive catalog. A culinary Disneyland; quality gourmet products and a superb cheese selection.

FINE CHEESE PRODUCERS

This comprehensive list of cheese producers is by no means exhaustive.

Bel Gioioso Auricchio Inc.

5810 Highway NN
Denmark, Wisconsin 54208
Telephone 414-863-2123
Fax 414-863-8791
Excellent mascarpone; outstanding aged Provolone, Gorgonzola, award-winning Parmesan; available in many supermarkets.

Clemson Blue Cheese

c/o Aramark
P.O. Drawer 429
Clemson University
Attention: Chad Welborn, Manager
Clemson, South Carolina 29633
Telephone 800-599-0181
FAX 864-656-4590
http://www.Welborn-Chad@aramark.com

Crowley Cheese

Healdville Road
Healdville, Vermont 05758
Telephone 800-683-2606 802-259-2340
Fax 802-259-2347
http://sales@crowleycheese-vermont.com
Handmade premium Vermont cheese; mild, medium, sharp and extra-sharp. Available in 8-ounce bars, 2½-pound and 5-pound wheels or blocks. Crowley is the "American original" that elevated Vermont cheese to fame.

Capriole, Inc.

Box 117
Greenville, Indiana 47124
Telephone 800-448-4628 or 812/923-9408
Excellent soft fresh goat cheese
Banon Chèvre, one ounce ash-covered and aged Wasbash Cannonballs, fig-shaped, paprika-dusted Crocodile Tears, four pound tortas

Egg Farm Dairy

2 John Walsh Blvd.
Peekskill, New York 10566
Telephone 800-273-2637
Fax 914-734-9287
Wild-ripened cheddar with a mellow, complex taste; aged with wild flora instead of penicillium mold. Slow aging with a mellow complex taste.

Aged Portuguese cheese; some of the finest cultured sweet butter and natural ice creams in America.

Gethsemani Farms, Inc.
3642 Monks Road
Trappist, Kentucky 40051-9102
Telephone 502-549-3117
Fax 502-549-8281
Catalog
Excellent semi-soft cow's milk cheese from the Havarti family; mild or aged. The Trappists have operated this Kentucky farm since 1848 and support themselves through the manufacture of cheese, fruitcakes and Kentucky-bourbon fudge. For years, this has been the official White House cheese, served at state dinners.

Grafton Village Cheese Company, Inc.
P.O. Box 87
Townshend Road
Grafton, Vermont 05146
Telephone 802-843-2221
Handcrafted cheeses made from the milk of Jersey cows; high in butterfat and aged more than two years. Grafton Classic Reserve cheddar is a white cheese made from raw milk, using a one-hundred-year-old recipe. Aged more than two years.

Guggisberg Cheese
5060 S.R. 557
Millersburg, Ohio 44654
Telephone 800-262-2505
For information: 330-893-2500
"Home of the Original Baby Swiss," made by Alfred and Margaret Guggisberg who brought their cheese-making skills from Switzerland. Made with sweet, fresh milk from Amish dairies. Baby Swiss, Old-fashioned Swiss, Amish Butter Cheese, Black Wax cheddar, French Emmentaler, Râclette, Appenzeller and Gruyère.

Harman's Cheese and Country Store
Route 117
Sugar Hill, New Hampshire 03585
Check or money orders only
Telephone 603-823-8000
Catalog
Rich, crumbly two-year-old cheddar; sharp but not bitter. The cheddar is folded into Sandeman Oporto (port) then laced with Courvoisier Napoleon brandy to make a cocktail spread. Best-quality maple syrup, Atlantic blue crab claws, dried soldier beans, local honey, kipper fillets, and New England common crackers. Ask for Maxine.

Hawthorne Valley Farm
Rt. 2, Box 225 A
Ghent, New York 12075
Check or money orders only
Telephone 518-672-7500
Fax 518-672-4887
Catalog
Minimum Order Required. Handmade Swiss-style Alpine cheese; top-quality dense loaf sourdough rye that rivals Swiss or German farm bread.

Herkimer Family Treasure House
R.D. 2, Box 361
Ilion, New York 13357
Telephone 315-895-7832
Fax 315-895-4664
Catalog
Some of America's finest cheddars, including excellent New York cheddars.

Laura Chenel's Chèvre Inc.
4310 Freemont Drive
Sonoma, California 95476
Telephone 707-996-4477
Catalog

Introduced fresh goat cheese to America in the mid-seventies. Supplied cheese for Alice Water's Chez Panise in Berkeley. Eight varieties including Taupiniere, a ripe, creamy goat cheese that is wonderful for breakfast or dessert; aged Crottin has a creamy interior and crusty rind.

Leelanau Cheese
10844 E. Revold Road
Suttons Bay, Michigan 49682
Telephone 231-271-2600
John and Anne Hoyt, cheesemakers/owners learned the art of cheesemaking and worked as cheesemakers in Switzerland.
The Hoyts make and sell Swiss and French-style cheeses; fine râclette cheese is the premier cheese in their line. Cellar-cured three months; turned and brushed daily. French-style fromage blanc.

Maytag Dairy Farms
Box 806
Newton, Iowa 50208
Telephone 800-247-2458 or 800-258-2437
Maytag Blue Cheese, cheddar and Edam

Minerva Cheese Factory
Radloff Ave. (off Rt. 30)
P.O. Box 60
Minerva, Ohio 44657
Telephone 216-868-4196
Fax 216-868-7947
Catalog
Handmade cheeses fresher than fresh; made the old-fashioned way using German techniques brought from the old country. Mellow cheddar, fine Colby, Pepper Jack and goat's milk cheddar. Light cheeses with reduced fats and salts. The outstanding, nutty Buckeye Swiss is named for the state's motto, "The Buckeye State."

Mousehouse Cheesehaus
P.O. Box 527
Windsor, Wisconsin 53598
Telephone 800-526-6873 or 608-846-4455
Fax 608-846-3922
Catalog
Fine cheeses made in Wisconsin. Outstanding cheddars aged in-house. Five-year old cheddar is crumbly and aged to perfection. Three-year-old cheddar has a nutty taste. Another specialty, Mousehouse Jack is soft and buttery. Wisconsin's best all-beef pepperoni and German-style sausages. Wisconsin-made Parmesan, Romano and quality Asiago.

The Mozzarella Company
2944 Elm Street
Dallas, Texas 75226
Telephone 800-798-2954 or 214-741-4072
Twenty-five specialty cheeses; many award-winning cheeses. Scamorza, (low-moisture mozzarella), mascarpone, fromage blanc, ricotta, Queso Blanco with chiles and epazote, Montasio, goat's milk Caciotta, mozarella and the first buffalo-milk mozzarella made in America.

Peluso Cheese, Inc.
429 H. Street
Los Baños, California 93635
Telephone 209-826-3744
Fax 209-826-6782
Teleme cheese, six-pound minimum. Cheese rounds dusted with rice flour will continue to age in the refrigerator; vacuum packed teleme does not age further. Can be melted for fondue or sauce. Queso Crema and Oaxaca string cheese are also available.

Rogue River Valley Creamery

311 N. Front Street
Central Point, Oregon 97502
Telephone 503-664-2233
Catalog
Fine blue cheese made with the original Roquefort seed acquired by the family from France in the fifties. Excellent raw-milk cheddar, Jack and Mozzarella. This family owns the California Vella Cheese Company which produces Dry Jack.

Sadie Kendall Cheese

P.O. Box 686
Atascadero, California 93423
Telephone 805-466-7252
Brochure
Some of the finest unsalted, crème fraîche in America. Mild and nutty with a light fresh taste, good for dipping fresh fruit or to use in sauces.

Shelburne Farms

Shelburne, Vermont 05482
Telephone 802-985-8686
Fax 802-985-8123
Catalog
Located on the shores of Lake Champlain. Buildings designed by New York architect Robert Robertson to resemble English country houses. Frederick Law Olmsted, who designed Central Park, did the grounds. Listed on the National Register of Historic Places. The complex includes an inn, restaurant, tours, children's farmyard. Brown Swiss cows produce rich, crumbly first-quality cheddars aged six-months to two-years. Black-waxed raw milk cheddar comes in medium, sharp, and extra sharp. Extraordinary smoked cheddar. Other Vermont products: cob-smoked Vermont hams, maple syrup, honey mustard, and various jams and preserves.

Specialty Cheese Company

Telephone 800-367-1711
Mexican and Caribbean cheeses. Rich brand cheese and cream products that originated from the Middle East to the Indian subcontinent. If a product is not available in your local store, they will arrange to ship it to you. No order is too small. Many products are available at Kroger Grocery Stores.

Split Creek Farm

3806 Centerville Road
Anderson, South Carolina 29625
Telephone 864-287-3921
Literature available
Grade A goat dairy; Plain or Garden Herb Fromage Blanc (regular or unsalted); Outstanding Fromage Blanc with raspberry, kahlua, peach or blueberry Schnapps. Creamy goat-cheese logs (plain or rolled in herbs); goat cheese feta packed in oil with sun-dried tomatoes, garlic and spices. Award-winning goat's milk fudge; available in quarter pound pieces or bulk.

The Squire Tarbox Inn

Box 620
Wiscasset, Maine 04578
Telephone 207-882-7693
Soft fresh goat cheeses, award-winning, aged goat's milk, Caerphilly.

Vella Cheese Company of California, Inc.

315 Second Street East
P.O. Box 191
Sonoma, California, 95476
Telephone 800-848-005 or 707-938-3232
Monterey Jack, Dry Jack, raw-milk cheddar, Asiago

MISCELLANEOUS PRODUCTS

Albert Uster Imports, Inc.

9211 Gaither Road

Gaithersburg, Maryland 20877

Telephone 800-231-8154 or 301-258-7350

Catalog

Swiss girolle: a device with a skewer that is inserted into the top center of a round of Tête De Moine cheese or chocolate. A vertical blade is attached to the skewer, which is turned by a handle to shave off the top layer into a delicate large, ruffle. Fassbind Liqueur Concentrates (Kirsch, Pear William, Amaretto, Rum, Framboise, Triple Sec), Amaretto and Grand Marnier extract, professional pastry products, chocolate ruffle molds (to be shaved with the girolle).

Broken Arrow Ranch

P.O Box 530

Ingram, Texas, 78025

Telephone 800-962-4263

Call for brochure

South Texas antelope and Black Buck antelope; Axis vension and Sika venison; wild boar and game sausage. The meat is free-range with no gamey taste due to controlled harvesting. Antelope and vension come frozen; unused portions can be refozen because of the meat's low fat content. Boneless antelope loin (minimum one to four pounds depending on the size of the animal. Boneless vension leg fillets range from three and four pounds. Boneless loins of the tiny axis deer range from two to two and one half pounds.

The Cook's Garden

P.O. Box 535

Londonderry, Vermont, 05148

A variety of seeds for the vegetable garden including puntarelle, chicory, arugula and radicchio

D'Artagnan

280 Wilson Avenue

Newark, New Jersey 07015

Telephone 800-327-8246

Catalog

Dried mushrooms: many varieties including porcini and Japanese matsutaké; game sausages, duck prosciutto, free range meats and game.

Farm 2 Market

Roscoe, New York

Telephone 800-477-2967

Kobé beef

Gold Mine Natural Foods Company

7805 Arjons Drive

San Diego, California, 92126

Telephone 800-475-3663

Catalog

http://www.Goldminenaturalfood.com

Chinese Forbidden Rice; Indian Kalijira rice; Bhutanese red rice; Japanese organic food products, fine salts, ginger graters, suribachi and surikogi (Japanese grinding bowl and pestle)

Hollowick, Inc.

P. O. Box 305

Manlius, New York 13104

Telephone 315-682-2163

Easy Heat® Adjustable Wick Liquid Chafing Fuel (4 sizes): Size EZ 2-1-3; Small canister for room service, coffee service, home chafing dishes. Standard heat: 2 hours burn; high heat: 1 hour burn; low heat: 3 hours burn

Kalustyans

Telephone 212-685-3451

http://www.kalustyans.com

Asian ingredients; sesame oil

La Cuisine

323 Cameron Street

Alexandria, Virginia 22314

Telephone 800-521-1176

Call for a price list

"The cook's resource." Quality cookware; Fine vanilla and vanilla beans; two-ounce bottles of French steam-distilled flavor essences: Poire William, Framboise, violet, coconut, peppermint, key lime, rum, cherry, Cointreau, blueberry, mango and more; German flavor pastes: peach, Mandarine, lemon, orange, pear, Amarene cherry, vanilla; essential flavor oils: lemon, lime, orange, tangerine, grapefruit

Lotus Foods

921 Richmond Street

El Cerrito, California 94530

Telephone 510-525-3137

Fax 510-525-4226

http://www.worldofrice.com

Bhutanese red rice. Forbidden China black rice, Kalijira (baby basmati), Kaipen (pressed freshwater green algae in 13-inch by 19-inch sheets), white rice flour, Bhutanese Red Rice Flour, Forbidden Black Rice Flour, Carnaroli Rice from Argentina and Cal Riso, a Mediterranean rice grown in California.

Loriva Oils

Telephone 800-945-6748

Top-quality walnut oil, macadamia oil, hazelnut oil, available in supermarkets nationwide.

Mrs. Hanes Moravian Cookies

Moravian Sugar Crisp Company, Inc.

4643 Friedberg Church Road

Clemmons, North Carolina 27012-6882

Telephone 888-764-1402

Fax 888-764-4072

The most delicious Moravian cookies on the planet, in flavors of chocolate, vanilla, black walnut, ginger, butterscotch and lemon.

The Old Mill

P. O. Box 146

Pigeon Forge, Tennessee 37868

Telephone 615-453-4628

Built in 1830, the mill is located on the Little Pigeon River in Pigeon Forge. High-quality stone-ground white corn meal, stone-ground grits, corn flour, buckwheat flour, biscuit and pancake mixes are still produced by water power; over 28 products.

Oso Sweet Onions

Telephone 888-878-7454

Mail Order: 888-878-7454

http://www.sweetonionsource.com

Sweet onions from Chili (in season January to March)

Pacific Farms

P.O. Box 51505

Florence, Oregon 97405

Telephone 800-927-2248

http://www.freshwasabi.com

Fresh wasabi grown under conditions that mimic Japanese riverbanks. Wasabi heat is not long-lasting on the palate like chili peppers; it mellows with a delicious aftertaste. Use creamy, fresh-grated wasabi in sauces, on grilled fish and steak, in soybean dips, in mashed potatoes, marinades and vinaigrettes. Fresh wasabi salad dressings available. Half-pound bag of pure wasabi, fresh-grated, no additives, vacuum-sealed, shipped fresh via UPS two-Day Air. Refrigerated shelf life of sixty days unopened. Use within 30 days after opening or freeze. Live wasabi plants, wasabi grater, gift certificates.

Penzey's Spices

P.O. Box 933

Muskego, Wisconsin 53150

Telephone 414-679-7207

Catalog

Highest quality, freshly ground spices

http://www.penzeys.com

RiceSelect™

Telephone: 800-993-RICE

Fax 281-393-3532

Texmati, Royal Blend, Jasmati and Kasmati rice

Servass Laboratories

Indiana

Telephone 800-433-5818

Bar Keeper's Friend (cleaner for stainless steel)

Available at Walmart, Bed, Bath and Beyond, Kroger Grocery Stores, Ace Hardware, Meijers

Shepard's Garden Seeds

30 Irene Street, Torrington, Ct. 06790

Telephone 860-482 3638

Catalog

Seeds for Spring in Province Mesclun Collection, Misticanza Italian Salad Mix; specialty vegetables, herbs, flowers

Summerfield Farm

10044 James Monroe Highway

Culpepper, Virginia 22701

Telephone 800-898-3276

Call for a price sheet.

Free-roam fallow deer, veal, spring lamb and game birds, duck, cold and cold smoked salmon, rabbit, game sausages, and vintage aged dry beef. Meat cleaned and denuded (trimmed with silver-skin removed). Kobé beef available by advance order.

Sunnyside Farms LLC

P.O. Box 478

Washington, Virginia 22747

Telephone 540-675-2627

Fax 540-675-1135

The largest herd of Wagyu (wah-gyou) beef on the East Coats can be found at Sunnyside Farm in the foothills of the Blue Ridge Mountains near Washington, DC. The famous Japanese Kobé beef come from Wagyu. Virginia Wagyu are raised with no growth hormones, steroids, stimulants or antibiotics. They are not fed beer and bathed in saké but enjoy a diet of organic hay, barley, corn and soybean meal. They are bathed and groomed frequently to promote good hygiene. They are moved, weighed and inspected on the "buddy system." Working with the cattle in pairs seems to relieve undue stress. Virginia Wagyu beef should be available for sale in the fall of 2001

Sunrise Mart

4 Stuyvesant Street, Second Floor

New York, New York 10003

Telephone 212-598-3040

Matcha (powdered green tea), Japanese food products, cooking equipment

Takashimaya: The Tea Box

693 Fifth Avenue

New York, New York 10022

Telephone 800-753-203 or 212-350-0100

Matcha (powdered green tea), French herbal teas, fine Japanese tea, tea accessories, kitchen utensils, Japanese tea sweets

Uwajimaya

519 6th Avenue South

Seattle, Washington 98104

Telephone 800-889-1928

Fax 206-624-6915

http://www.uwajimaya.com

Huge supermarket of Japanese foods, cooking equipment, housewares, books and much more.

Vitasoy USA, Incorporated

Telephone 800-328-8638

Thin Azumaya egg roll wrappers and quality, fresh Asian egg noodles; available in many grocery stores.

The White Lily Foods Company

P.O. Box 871
Knoxville, Tennessee 37901
Telephone 423-521-7725
http://www.whitelily.com

Established in 1883 in downtown Knoxville, White Lily still produces the high-quality, low-protein southern flour that is in demand by fine cooks throughout the country. Called "the staple of the south." Excellent for biscuits, cakes, quick breads, cookies and muffins. Self-rising flour and bread flour are also available.

When You Know	Symbol	Comparison to Metric Measure Multiply By	To Find	Symbol
teaspoons	tsp	5.0	milliliter	ml
tablespoons	tbsp	15.0f	milliliters	ml
fluid ounces	fl. oz.	30.0	milliliters	ml
cups	c	0.24	liters	l
pints	pt.	0.47	liters	l
quarts	qt.	0.95	liters	l
ounces	oz.	28.0	grams	g
pounds	lb.	0.45	kilograms	kg
Fahrenheit	F	$5/9$ (after subtracting 32)	Celsius	C

Fahrenheit to Celsium	
F	C
200–205	95
229–225	105
245–250	120
275	135
300–305	150
325–330	165
345–350	175
370–375	190
400–405	205
425–430	220
445–450	230
470–475	245
500	260

Liquid Measure to Liters		
1/4 cup	=	0.06 liters
1/2 cup	=	0.12 liters
3/4 cup	=	0.18 liters
1 cup	=	0.24 liters
1-1/4 cups	=	0.30 liters
1-1/2 cups	=	0.36 liters
2 cups	=	0.48 liters
2-1/2 cups	=	0.60 liters
3 cups	=	0.72 liters
3-1/2 cups	=	0.84 liters
4 cups	=	0.96 liters
4-1/2 cups	=	1.08 liters
5 cups	=	1.20 liters
5-1/2 cups	=	1.32 liters

Liquid Measure to Milliliters		
1/4 teaspoon	=	1.25 milliliters
1/2 teaspoon	=	2.50 milliliters
3/4 teaspoon	=	3.75 milliliters
1 teaspoon	=	5.00 milliliters
1-1/4 teaspoons	=	6.25 milliliters
1-1/2 teaspoons	=	7.50 milliliters
1-3/4 teaspoons	=	8.75 milliliters
2 teaspoons	=	10.0 milliliters
1 tablespoon	=	15.0 milliliters
2 tablespoons	=	30.0 milliliters

Susan Fuller Slack is a cookbook and magazine food writer with over twenty years experience relating to food. She is the author of numerous cookbooks, including the popular *Japanese Cooking for the American Table*.

As a young military wife in the early 1970s, Susan and her husband relaxed by inviting friends over for a carefree evening of fun, which often included a dip into the fondue pot. Years of travel and living in Asia broadened her fondue base to include many varieties of the Asian hot pot. The demands and sophistication of entertaining increased greatly throughout her husband's career but fondues and hot pots remained a favorite style of tabletop cooking for casual parties that would dazzle guests.

Today, Susan makes her home in Columbia, South Carolina, where she often appears on television and creates culinary programs for children. She is a food consultant, teaches cooking classes and gives culinary lectures. Susan is a Certified Culinary Professional with the International Association of Culinary Professionals.